Communism in American Unions

McGRAW-HILL LABOR MANAGEMENT SERIES

Goldberg · AFL-CIO: Labor United
Saposs · Communism in American Unions
Taylor and Pierson · New Concepts in Wage Determination

Communism in American Unions

DAVID J. SAPOSS

McGRAW-HILL BOOK COMPANY, INC.
New York   Toronto   London   1959

To B. T. S.

Introduction

Recent events seem to have reduced the domestic Communist movement to near impotence. Undiscouraged, and prompted by its international mentors, it is resuming its covert activities. The immediate tactic emphasized is described as colonization. It consists in surreptitiously planting trusted adherents in unions and industrial establishments, thereby laying the ground for future expansion as opportunity presents. In the body of the study it is revealed that this strategy proved successful in the past.

Thus in spite of continual reverses, serious in nature and major in scope, the Communists persist in clandestinely boring from within the labor movement in this country. Theirs is the only ultraideological opposition movement of consequence that has repeatedly regained strength following vital defeats. Similar movements, such as the Industrial Workers of the World (IWW), experienced a meteoric rise and then receded rapidly to relatively innocuous and obscure fringe activity. But the Communists possess a prop which other vanishing oppositions lacked: a viable international operations base and ample material support from the forceful movement sustained by Soviet Russia. Because of this prop, the Communist movement has been able to demonstrate a capacity for survival and the maintenance of extensive activities unequaled by any other ultraideological opposition group in the labor movement. It is of more than historical interest to understand how they have operated thus far and to study the ways in which they have been resisted, checked, defeated, and then staged comebacks.

Communism's greatest success was achieved by operating under cover when the country was prosperous and the labor movement was growing to unprecedented proportions. To contend that the decline of Communism is attributable chiefly to our extraordinary prosperity is erroneous. It is not substantiated by the facts. From 1935 to 1950, the covert branch of the Communist movement particularly was phenomenally successful in the trade unions and in other social institutions, including the government. It can hardly be said that this was not a prosperous period. Historically, radical and pseudoradical movements in the United States have grown in strength as the labor movement has increased in importance, which always occurs during prosperous periods. The highest peak reached by the IWW, for example, came with the resumption of business activity following the "panic" of 1907 and continued until the First World War. The unusual growth of socialism in the unions covered approximately the same period. On the other hand, when the main labor movement was in the doldrums, from about 1921 through the Depression of 1929 and succeeding years, radical oppositions were also insignificant.

While Communist success or failure is not attributable primarily to depressions and poverty, social instability proved to be fertile soil for Communist activities in the United States. These activities began to make considerable headway in the labor movement when the psychological, as well as the material, effects of the Depression were still fresh in the minds of most people; the period of their phenomenal progress began after the Depression of 1929–1933 when conditions were beginning to improve and hence favorable to the resumption of intensive union-organizing activity. Badly in need of personnel with organizing ability and leadership, non-Communist labor officials accepted the cooperation of Communists and fellow travelers. Thus the covert Communist movement within the trade-union fold blossomed into a powerful force during the prosperous era of the late thirties and the belligerent early forties; its reverses and near collapse also occurred during full employment in the late forties and in the early fifties.

Deteriorating economic conditions therefore contributed less to the Communist rise and fall than did other factors. Nevertheless, it was during the so-called unprecedented depression of 1929–1933 that the zealots were bred who later become the leaders. It was primarily the aftereffects of the Depression, attended by eagerness for corrective social reforms, and the international crisis—which made Soviet Russia our ally—that gave the Communists the opportunity to nurture skillfully an intellectual climate favorable to the promotion of their activities.

[Those sophisticated in Communist policies and tactics warned against them from the outset. At first, such warnings were ignored, derided, and, through covert Communist manipulations, even discredited.] Meanwhile, the Communists became more firmly entrenched, heightening the difficulty of combating them or disentangling from their control the organizations they infiltrated. Responsible leaders hesitated to take disciplinary action against them for fear of weakening the labor movement. Employers, too, preferred to continue operating as they were rather than to stir up and encourage controversy by participating in any counteraction of Communist incursion and domination. Like employers, government administrative agencies in general shrank from taking measures within their purview to help check Communist penetration of unions. Eventually, definitive counteraction was stimulated by public exposures, reaching scandalous proportions, chiefly through congressional and state committee investigations.

Changes in the international situation, with its cold-war involvements and the hot war in Korea, also contributed materially to the creation of an intellectual climate that took cognizance of the Communist threat. Fostered by articulate and determined union leaders and members, demands for a house cleaning within the unions mounted, so that even the timid and cautious were stimulated to act.

A widespread erroneous impression pervades, even among the reasonably well informed, that the Communists confined their activities chiefly within the CIO. Actually they turned on the AFL with avidity equal to that directed against the CIO. In the AFL, they were able to penetrate only its affiliates; here their greatest headway was achieved on the lower levels. In the CIO, they were more successful, penetrating even to its central, national headquarters.

Usually, where Communists capture an organization, non-Communists retreat, leaving it in Communist hands. But in the American trade-union movement, the Communists were defeated more often than they were victorious. By resourceful leadership—often belatedly but furiously aroused and not infrequently supported, or even led, by dissenting Communist and fellow-traveler trade-union leaders—the Communists have generally been dislodged. None of the unions thus embroiled suffered permanently, except those few which remained under Communist domination. Indeed, the unions from which the Communists were eliminated usually emerged with added prestige, not only surviving intact but strengthening themselves in the course of time. On the other hand, non-Communist unions that pursued energetic organizing campaigns against Communist-controlled unions have caused their disintegration. The few still under Communist domination either remain stationary, holding strategic areas to which they have retreated, or are hard pressed and losing out in varying degrees.

Some may question the space allotted to treatment of the Communist-Hollywood affair. The abundant and incontrovertible documentary data present an excellent case study of Communist studious and sinister planning and procedure for infiltrating American unions. Similarly, the profuse and precise source material makes it possible to delineate meticulously and authoritatively how they dominate and use the unions controlled by them to further their cause. And it is also possible to relate in detail how Communist domination was combated and well-nigh entirely eliminated.

No magic formula for detecting, combating, and controlling Communist penetration and domination of unions exists, but this text, after analyzing the methods used by the Communists to influence and dominate labor organizations, describes various procedures used effectively, for the most part, to oppose and dislodge them.

I am indebted to the Philip Murray Memorial Foundation for unrestricted financial aid through Harvard University, which made it possible to get this book under way.

I also acknowledge my appreciation to Miss Margaret F. Brickett and her staff in the United States Department of Labor Library. Their eager response in locating and making source material readily available expedited the completion of this book.

Thanks are also due to the numerous trade-union officers and staff who generously aided in supplying data and in clearing up obscure points and incidents. Their assistance enriched the contents of this book. Because most of these people prefer to remain anonymous, I reluctantly refrain from mentioning names other than those referred to in the text.

Various persons in government service have also given freely of their time for consultation and in locating source material. They, too, generally prefer not to be mentioned by name. To them I am also indebted.

Above all, I can express only feeble gratitude for my wife's patience and sympathetic understanding during the throes of bringing this book into being. Dedicating it to her is but infinitesimal recognition.

Of course, I alone am responsible for the final presentation.

David J. Saposs

Contents

PART IV
Combating Communist Domination

PART I

The Communist Movement's
Inheritance from
Early Radicalism

1

Early Radical Trade-union Policies and Tactics

Throughout the history of the world's labor movements, radicals have aimed either to capture or to supplant the functioning trade-union movements that did not conform to their ideology. In the United States, as in most industrially advanced countries, Socialists strove to transform unions in accordance with their philosophy. The anarchists and their progeny, the syndicalists, undertook almost simultaneously to achieve the same objective.[1] A bitter difference of opinion developed among the radicals as to what procedure would bring the best results. Within the Socialist movement, those labeled "opportunists" by their opponents favored "boring-from-within"—working and agitating within the movement to win over its leaders and members to the radicals' ideological view. The more extreme, dubbed "impossibilists" by their rivals, insisted on "dual unionism" —the establishment of an opposing movement to supplant or destroy the existing movement. At the beginning of their activity, the anarchists worked both sides of the street, as did the Socialists. Their offspring the syndicalists—later represented by the Industrial Workers of the World, more popularly referred to as the IWW—scorned boring-from-within and vigorously embarked upon dual unionism. The anarchists and the Socialists began to ply their trades in the 1880s and were sustained mostly by non-English-speaking immigrant workers who had migrated from Germany and other Western European countries. When the Knights of Labor were the dominant trade-union movement, they were the chief target. As they faded away and the American Federation of Labor (AFL) replaced them, the radicals concentrated on either conquering the new union or supplanting it, as their tactics dictated.

Naturally, both sides used other issues, such as better wages and working conditions, honest conducting of union affairs, and so on, but the

[1] John R. Commons and Associates, *History of Labour in the United States*, The Macmillan Company, New York, 1935–1936, vol. I, pp. 616–620; vol. II, pp. 227–234 and 269–300.

main issue was whether the movement should be content with working within the present system on day-to-day issues or aspire to overthrow it for a socialist society. Another bone of contention was the structure of the union, particularly when the AFL became the dominant movement. Radicals of all shades favored industrial unionism, while the AFL was oriented toward a form of craft unionism. The borers-from-within were motivated by the optimistic thought that through exhortation they could transform the movement according to their views. The dual unionists considered such prospects futile; consequently, they turned toward founding a competing movement.

By the 1890s, the two ideas were crystallized, and their proponents staunchly and vitriolically expounded their different viewpoints, especially in quarrels among themselves. The Socialist movement, split over the issue of boring-from-within and dual unionism, had encountered defeat both in the AFL and in the Knights of Labor. These failures precipitated their taking stock as to the most effective policies and tactics to pursue toward the unions. In 1895, the impulsive Daniel DeLeon, secretary of the Socialist Labor party, launched the Socialist Trade and Labor Alliance, ostensibly to organize the unorganized but actually to supersede the two existing national trade-union centers. This action precipitated a heated controversy within the movement that resulted in the formation in 1901 of the rival Socialist party by those who favored boring-from-within. Concurrently with the disagreement over the manner of advancing the Socialist cause in the trade-union movement, the difference in emphasis on objectives deepened: should the movement stress the immediate improvement in working and living conditions—shorter hours, social insurance, and other social-reform measures—to be achieved through trade-union action and legislation by political action, or should it press for the ultimate overthrow of capitalism and the introduction of socialism? Indeed, proponents of the latter course argued, if conditions were improved, the workers would lose interest in revolutionary objectives. Such policy differences became known as "immediate demands" versus "ultimate demands." The moderates, or "borers-from-within," favored the former, as befitted their temperament and technique in appealing to the rank-and-file and trade-union leaders. The extremists, who impatiently desired to usher in the "social revolution," petulantly cried for emphasis on "ultimate demands."

The Socialist dual unionists made little headway in either the industrial or the political field as compared with their rival, the Socialist party. On the other hand, the moderates proved relatively effective in both fields. The then existing Socialist unions accepted the leadership of the borers-from-within, who emphasized "immediate demands." Similarly, Socialist-oriented trade-union leaders and members, on the whole, supported the moderates. Thus, by the outbreak of World War I, some of the largest and most influential unions in the AFL supported their cause. Among these were the Brewery and Bakery Workers, Shingle Weavers, Hat and Cap Makers, Ladies' Garment Workers, Fur Workers, Journeymen Tailors, Metal Miners, and International Association of Machinists. In addition, the Socialists were a factor in other leading unions. Even Gompers' union, the Cigar Makers, elected the secretary of the Socialist party as one of its delegates to AFL conventions. Furthermore, one of the most prominent Socialists was regularly chosen by the International Typographical Union as one of its representatives to federation conventions; over half the delegates from the United Mine Workers consisted of prominent Socialists. And the Socialists usually succeeded in mustering about a third of the votes.

The semisyndicalists, as reflected in the IWW, had more success, temporarily, than their Socialist dual-union rival, the Socialist Trade and Labor Alliance, with its close link to the Socialist Labor party. Both groups concurred in featuring industrial unionism and emphasizing "ultimate demands" in order to achieve the social revolution as quickly as possible. But they differed basically on how to achieve their objective. The SLP regarded political action as the most desirable policy, whereas the IWW contended that direct action through the general strike was imperative. The IWW, founded in 1905 as a united front of all radicals desiring to build a socialist trade-union movement that would supplant the one which accepted the capitalist system, was soon taken over by the anarcho-syndicalist-minded. Under this leadership, the IWW became one of the most colorful and boisterous trade-union movements in the history of the country. It led some of the most bitterly contested and violent strikes. In many regions, such as the harvest fields of the Midwest and the forest and lumber areas of the Northwest and South, it terrorized communities by its militancy. Public authorities reacted in kind, which resulted frequently in pitched battles, skirmishes, and guerilla warfare with bloodshed and even death.

Although the IWW set out to supplant the already functioning trade-union movement—namely, the AFL—it achieved its greatest success among the unorganized workers neglected by the existing unions. Most of these were illiterate Southern whites and non-English-speaking immigrants, recently arrived from South and East Europe. Contrary to popular opinion, the IWW did little by way of systematically organizing these workers who, a field study by the author revealed, were ignorant of IWW philosophy and understood little of its basic aims and ideals. They had, however, serious grievances, and in their spontaneous, or unorganized, strikes, the IWW proffered them dynamic and sympathetic leadership through persons who were, of course, articulate and well versed in the tenets of the organization. In some areas—among the harvest hands in the Pacific Northwest, and among the Finnish population in the Mesabi iron range—the workers were better oriented ideologically. Their local leaders—immigrants who had been in contact in Europe with labor organizations subscribing to socialist doctrines—were familiar with revolutionary philosophies and served as intermediaries between the national IWW leaders and the local rank and file. The IWW made its greatest headway in industrial centers where unions had failed or were functioning ineffectually. They spent no effort in conducting methodical organizing campaigns, confining their energies chiefly to spreading propaganda and "spotting" locals or propaganda centers. This procedure naturally advertised the IWW among the unorganized, familiarizing them with at least the outward functions of the organization even if they remained in ignorance of its basic beliefs. Thus when conditions forced them into a spontaneous strike, they turned to the organization they knew, readily accepting the leadership of the only group that had shown sufficient interest in their welfare to evoke their confidence. Upon terminating the strike, successfully or unsuccessfully, IWW leaders and organizers withdrew to other "class-war" battlefields (free-speech fights or strikes) or to the agitational trail. From the standpoint of trade-union action, the chief accomplishment of the IWW lay in providing expert leadership for spontaneous strikes by unorganized workers and in fund-raising for relief and litigation. But it also led toward the achievement of a cardinal syndicalist objective: the drilling of a large segment of workers in preparation for the final blow in abolishing the wage system through the general strike.

Because its aim was to prepare workers for the revolution, the IWW deliberately discouraged such conventional trade-union procedures as creating stable unions with large memberships, substantial treasuries, and paid officials. It also scorned engaging in such orderly collective-bargaining procedures as written trade agreements, grievance machinery, and mediation of differences in implementing terms agreed upon as a result of strikes and negotiations. All these frills, they maintained, tended to make the workers conservative and thus not good revolutionary material for the direct action that would abolish the "system."

On the other hand, local leaders and active members, supported by the rank and file, wanted the IWW to help them follow up on settlements with management by establishing effective unions that would function continuously to safeguard and promote their interests. Because of its disinterest in assisting workers to build and maintain strong unions, the IWW lost its appeal to the unorganized before the First World War. Prosecution of its leaders during and following the war was probably no more than the final stroke which broke its hold completely.

Philosophically, the IWW lost its appeal to the more articulate as the immigrant workers became Americanized, a process hastened by the war.

6

Furthermore, English-speaking workers of the South, Northwest, and other areas where IWW leadership was accepted had become more clearly oriented in Americanism during the war and had lost their interest in the type of revolutionary activity advocated by the IWW.

The moderate Socialists also found themselves in a dilemma. Their following, mostly immigrant, was becoming Americanized, too, and began to regard socialist philosophy as inapplicable to its aspirations under the conditions and practices of our society. The war tended to accentuate this feeling inasmuch as the Socialist party enunciated an antiwar policy. The Socialists were, therefore, forced into an ambiguous position during the war that branded them in the popular mind as anti-American.

Here, too, the factor that contributed most tellingly to the decline of the Socialist movement was that its chief following, the immigrant workers and their trade union and other leaders, had also become Americanized and had begun to feel that changed conditions did not warrant a Socialist movement. The offspring of the immigrants, unhindered by a language barrier, attending American schools, reading the American press and American literature, were even more responsive to the American environment. As if by osmosis, they absorbed the thinking and spirit of the average American worker. Thus practically all the Socialist-controlled unions and the Socialist trade union leaders in other unions, stimulated by the new spirit, abandoned socialism for social reform.

Most of the IWW and Socialist remnants were then reassembled by the new revolutionary star shining so brightly in the reflected glory of the Russian Bolshevik Revolution. The Communists now took over as the chief radical element operating within the American labor movement.[2]

Amorphous elements composed mostly of those nonrevolutionary individuals who left the Socialist party and described themselves as "Progressives" also carried on scattered activity. They believed AFL leadership was too stodgy and undertook to reform this trade-union center. According to their view, it needed to bestir itself, primarily in order to organize the unorganized in the mass-production industries, preferably into industrial unions. While no longer subscribing to the socialist philosophy of abolishing capitalism, these Progressives continued to propagate most of the party's social-reform policies. Thus they favored various types of social legislation that would contribute to improving social and economic

[2] The above is a résumé of the author's *Left Wing Unionism*, International Publishers Co., Inc., New York, 1926; the book contains a comprehensive analysis of the various types and shades of boring-from-within and of dual unionism as well as a description of the different participating organizations and movements, including their philosophies, policies, and tactics. See also the author's "Rebirth of the American Labor Movement" in papers presented at the New York City session of the Industrial Relations Research Association, Dec. 28–30, 1955, pp. 16–30; and Joel Seidman, *The Needle Trades*, Rinehart & Company, Inc., New York, 1942, pp. 224–231.

7

conditions. In common with the Socialists, they favored supplementing trade-union action with independent political action, opposing the AFL's limited nonpartisan political policy. The large majority of former Socialist trade-union leaders and the Socialist unions themselves inclined toward the views of this element.

In the twenties, when the Communist movement was not thoroughly understood, most of these Progressives, other liberals, and the bulk of the remaining Socialists participated in united-front movements with the Communists. They quickly became disillusioned, as succeeding accounts will show. In later periods, too, there were elements calling themselves "progressives," "liberals," and "socialists" who also collaborated with the Communists.

2

Early Communist
Trade Union Activity

As the Russians established machinery and procedures for directing the Communist movement outside their borders, the external activities of the movement began to coalesce in this country. Friction and factional intrigue within the party then were as intense as they have continued to be to the present time.[1]

In the early days of their trade union activities, the Communists vacillated between boring-from-within and dual-unionism tactics; sometimes they practiced both techniques simultaneously, although stressing one as more important than the other. Surrounded by widespread public interest in and sympathy for the Russian revolution, the Communists decided boring-from-within was the course to follow in the beginning period. Besides, the united-front idea was popular among the radicals and progressives, and some of those who became key Communist leaders, such as William Z. Foster, had participated in worthwhile boring-from-within ventures. But instead of operating as the Socialists and Progressives did—through clearly labeled organizations the identity of which was unmistakable—the Communists introduced what became their characteristic procedure: boring-from-within activities in secretly controlled, so-called "united-front organizations." These agencies consisted of disguised members of the Communist party and dedicated associates who became known as "fellow travelers" and were used in undercover operations. In this earliest period, their covert activities were much cruder than the refined and subtle processes they used later.

The first formal organization dominated by the Communists was the Trade Union Educational League (TUEL). It was founded in 1920 under the leadership of William Z. Foster, not yet known as a Communist, who had an enviable reputation among progressives and radicals as an organizing genius because of his accomplishments in the Chicago meat-packing in-

[1] For a vivid description, see Benjamin Gitlow, *I Confess*, E. P. Dutton & Co., Inc., New York, 1940, pp. 339–421.

9

dustry and his position as the pivotal figure in the great steel-organizing campaign and strike of 1918–1919.[2] TUEL was ostensibly a united-front movement of progressives, radicals, and other dissenters in the labor movement. Designed to work within the labor movement and transform it, TUEL was to function in both political and trade-union territory. Its particular target in the latter was the dominant trade-union center, the AFL.

This immediate postwar period was one of great labor unrest and witnessed many unsuccessful strikes. Employers, forced by the emergency of war to recognize unions and grant concessions, now undertook to return to prewar conditions and practices. They launched open-shop campaigns, introduced company unions and labor spies, welfare work, and armed guards. Organized labor was on the defensive. To the progressives and radicals, the most effective procedure for counteracting this employer offensive was through industrial unionism via amalgamation. TUEL adopted this issue as one of its cardinal aims.

As a new movement, the Communists were not tightly coordinated and often seemed to be working at cross purposes. Many of the influential leaders, for example, were staunch champions of dual unionism, an attitude that hampered the work of Foster and TUEL. But this problem was settled by the Communist International meeting in July, 1921, that decreed boring-from-within was to be the Communist trade-union policy.[3] A saving clause provided that where boring-from-within was not effective, it was permissible to organize dual unions. Later that year, Foster went to Russia and announced upon his return TUEL's affiliation with the newly founded Communist Red International of labor unions.[4]

In accordance with Communist totalitarian philosophy, TUEL functioned as a highly centralized national organization. Two types of subsidiary units operated on the lower levels. One consisted of fourteen industrial sections designed to cover the entire industrial spectrum. The second was made up of the local Trade Union Educational Leagues. These were mixed-membership bodies in particular localities.[5] Its official organ, the *Labor Herald*, was attractive and readable. It boasted of a paid staff

[2] The author became intimately acquainted with Foster while serving as an investigator for the Interchurch World Movement Steel Strike Inquiry of 1919; see the report of that inquiry, *The Steel Strike, 1919–1920*, Harcourt, Brace and Company, Inc., New York, 1920. From 1920 to 1922, while residing in Chicago and plying the trade of economic consultant to labor organizations, the author got to know the main founders and managers of TUEL, including Foster and Earl Browder, all of whom were soon recognized as Communists.

[3] Lewis L. Lorwin, *Labor and Internationalism*, The Macmillan Company, New York, 1929, pp. 229–231.

[4] For a description of this organization, see *American Labor Year Book*, Rand School of Social Science, New York, 1923–1924, pp. 278–286; Benjamin Gitlow, *The Whole of Their Lives*, Charles Scribner's Sons, New York, 1948, pp. 32 and 69.

[5] David J. Saposs, *Left Wing Unionism*, International Publishers Co., Inc., New York, 1926, p. 51.

of some proportions, and although its members did not pay dues, it seemed to be well financed.[6] When it was revealed in its true colors as being Communist-dominated, however, many non-Communists disaffiliated.

But the stage where the Communists would insist upon having their way, in spite of united-front principles, had not yet been reached. To most progressives and radicals, the Communists were just another radical group interested in promoting certain policies acceptable to all participants, and since the Communists were becoming the aggressive left-wing opposition within the unions, their leadership was accepted. As they became the dominant radical articulate force in the American labor movement, they began astutely to advertise themselves as inheritors of the old radicalism which they professed to improve upon.

In 1928 Communist trade-union policy, on orders from the Comintern, was changed to dual unionism. To carry out this new tactic, TUEL was transformed into the Trade Union Unity League, or TUUL, whose activities will be discussed in the following chapter.

[6] American Labor Year Book, *op. cit.*, pp. 86–92.

PART II

Communist Penetration
of the American
Federation of Labor

3

Open Communist Activities

When the Communists disbanded TUUL in 1935, it was natural they should direct their boring-from-within activities toward the AFL. It was the only substantial trade-union center, and nearly all viable international trade unions were affiliated with it. While the Communists admired the element that formed the Committee for Industrial Organizations (CIO), they did not foresee its extraordinary future prospects.[1] Even in 1937, when this committee was expelled from the AFL and began functioning as its rival, assuming the name of "Congress of Industrial Organizations," the Communists still regarded the AFL as the most fertile area for their boring-from-within activities. Not foreseeing the CIO's meteoric rise, the Communists at first ignored it; very soon, however, it proved to be fertile soil and the Communists successfully exploited it.

Writing as late as 1937, William Z. Foster said, "Since the liquidation of the TUUL, and with the Communist trade-union forces almost entirely included within the AF of L the main emphasis of the Communist party trade-union policy is again upon the revolutionizing of that body by systematic work within its ranks."[2]

From the inception of the Communist movement, the AFL was on its guard. As early as 1923, its convention refused to seat William F. Dunne, an outstanding Communist leader, as a delegate from the Butte Montana Central Labor Union. The action itself, subsequent discussion of it, and Dunne's defense attracted nationwide attention. The Communists reprinted Dunne's speech in pamphlet form, giving it wide circulation.[3]

[1] See above, pp. 123–124.
[2] *From Bryan to Stalin,* International Publishers Co., Inc., New York, 1937, p. 275; Benjamin Gitlow, *I Confess,* E. P. Dutton & Co., Inc., New York, 1940, pp. 335–336; and Benjamin Gitlow, *The Whole of Their Lives,* Charles Scribner's Sons, New York, 1948, pp. 32 and 69.
[3] AFL Convention Proceedings, 1923, pp. 256–259; E. B. Mittleman, "Basis for American Federation of Labor Opposition to Amalgamation and Politics at Portland," *Journal of Political Economy,* University of Chicago Press, Chicago, February, 1924. For a description of AFL nomenclature and structure, see *Directory of National and International Labor Unions in the United States,* U.S. Bureau of Labor Statistics Bulletin 1185, 1955, pp. 4ff.

Thereafter, the AFL issued warnings periodically. In 1939 the AFL repeated its warning in a resolution adopted at its convention: "*Resolved,* That we instruct the various affiliated national and international unions to refrain from taking into membership any known member of the Communist Party, or any sympathizer." [4]

Nevertheless, the Communists had considerable success in penetrating AFL unions, although it was not as large or as spectacular as their success in the CIO. They failed to make even an infinitesimal dent in the national AFL headquarters, but they became a power and even a considerable bother in some of the affiliates. In contrast to their success in the CIO, there is only one instance where the Communists came into complete control of an established AFL international union. This occurred in the early stages of boring-from-within when the Communists, in liquidating TUUL, attempted to fuse its affiliates with AFL unions.[5] Through an amalgamation of the fur workers' unit of the TUUL Needle Trades Industrial Union, they captured the International Fur Workers Union in 1935. William Green, as president of the AFL, threatened expulsion, but the union withdrew on its own accord in order to join the CIO.[6] Beside the foregoing instance, Communist successes within the AFL were limited to subsidiary units of the AFL and its affiliates. The Communists made considerable headway in some of the newly organized and reorganized unions during the upsurge of union organization in the early New Deal days. This occurred particularly in the amusement trades, especially in Hollywood, and in hotel, restaurant, and other service trades. In these and a few other instances, the Communists became for a brief period the dominant factor.[7]

Communists success with the newly organized unions within the AFL and later within the CIO was aided by the general unrest and organizational ineffectiveness of the Socialists and Progressives.

In the immediate post-World War I period, through the twenties and into the thirties, there was mounting unrest. The usual postwar adjustment, several business recessions, and the intervening, unprecedented economic depression contributed to the discontent. Employers, who had to deal with unions during the war, launched antiunion campaigns, involving labor spies, violence, company unions, and welfare plans. Many unions were engaged in bitter strikes, mostly defensive in nature; and nearly all were lost.

[4] AFL Convention Proceedings, 1939, p. 505 as well as pp. 31, 226–227, 132–133, 233, 409–411; see also testimony of William Green and Matthew Woll in House Special Committee on Communist Un-American Activities, 72d Cong., 2d Sess., 1935.

[5] See above, pp. 10–11; also *Daily Worker*, Mar. 16 and 17, 1935.

[6] Jack Hardy, *The Clothing Workers*, International Publishers Co., Inc., New York, 1935, pp. 147–148; Foster, *From Bryan to Stalin*, p. 273; *New York Times*, June 20, 1935.

[7] See below, pp. 19ff.; 83ff.

While the Socialists and Progressives were effective in crystallizing a progressive sentiment in the labor movement, they were too divided organizationally to bring their followers together. They functioned through a variety of fringe groups. Some of them formed an ardent and ably led opposition within the AFL. These Socialists and Progressives charged that the AFL was outmoded, that it failed to adapt itself to new and changing conditions, and that it lacked imagination and aggressiveness. This opposition contended that the way out of AFL morbidity was industrial unionism, comprehensive social-reform legislation, and concomitant, independent political action. Organizationally, the Socialists and Progressives reached the height of their influence on the labor movement at the time of the La Follette 1924 presidential campaign. After that, they began receding, operating chiefly as fringe groups. Their allies within the trade-union movement, in order to defend themselves against the growing encroachments of the Communists, began to tend toward closer alliance with the controlling AFL leaders.

When the CIO was founded, the Socialists and Progressive thought they would find a home there, and many did. But because Communists were welcomed openly, democratic radicals found themselves overshadowed. The Communists then became the leaders of radical and progressive ideas, attaining this status by having at their disposal ably led local organizations directed by the national Communist party, and assisted by its numerous front agencies. The Communists succeeded in insinuating themselves into these organizations, ostensibly non-Communist but progressive, as the spearhead of progressive thinking in the labor movement.[8]

Welcomed into the CIO, the Communists were to a considerable extent diverted from more energetic effort in the AFL. Moreover, with top AFL leaders vigorously attacking the Communists and warning their followers against them, operation within the AFL was more difficult. Nevertheless, where Communists found little resistance—among the newly organized and reorganized—or where they had attained a bridgehead through TUUL nuclei, they took full advantage of the opportunity and worked as assiduously as they did in the CIO to further their objectives.

Profiting by their earlier experience when they were isolated, expelled, or otherwise obstructed as known Communists, they introduced two new features of boring-from-within. Their followers ceased declaring themselves publicly as Communists, labeling themselves "progressives working for demo-

---

[8] James O. Morris, "The Origins of the CIO," University Microfilms (University of Michigan thesis), Ann Arbor, Michigan, 1954; David J. Saposs, "American Labor Movement since the War," *Quarterly Journal of Economics*, Harvard University Press, Cambridge, Mass., February, 1935, pp. 236ff.; and David J. Saposs, "Rebirth of the American Labor Movement," in papers presented at the New York City session of the Industrial Relations Research Association, December 28–30, 1955, pp. 16ff.

cratic causes and a progressive labor movement." They also discarded an open, formal organization, like TUEL and TUUL, for the conduct of Communist trade-union activities. In this manner they disguised their role of covert boring-from-within. Guidance and direction were to be provided secretly by the executive committee of the Party, assisted by a labor secretary and others entrusted with specific tasks. Secret members and dedicated fellow travelers, presenting themselves as progressives but actually devout Communist sympathizers, were to operate in the open as progressives. Front organizations were established to carry on in the open.

This procedural mode was temporarily effective. But gradually these Communist tactics were detected by the more alert and sophisticated in and out of the labor movement. The Communists had to expose themselves in their advocacy of certain issues, chiefly those affecting Soviet Russia's foreign policy. When these critical international issues pressed for action, it was possible for the more alert to arouse the inert by exposing the masquerade. Thus the Communist boring-from-within movement carried within itself the seed of its destruction.

4

Covert Communist Activities:
In Hollywood

Hollywood and Los Angeles presented a most cherished prize to the Communists in their effort to penetrate not only American unions but the total cultural life of American communities. Here, concentrated in a tiny geographical area, some "30,000 individuals, representing numerous talent and craft groups, are engaged in making seventy-five per cent of the world's film." [1] What a prize for a world revolutionary movement operating in accordance with superlative propaganda procedures! The Communists addressed themselves most energetically to exploiting this challenge to the full. Temporarily they were astoundingly successful. They succeeded in penetrating every nook and cranny of Hollywood. They became an influential, if not a dominating, force in every organized activity, affecting people in all walks of life. An all-out movement was launched to capture the community. Naturally, it had exaggeratedly dramatic episodes.

As early as 1925, an article appeared in the *Daily Worker*, written by Willie Muenzenburg, "a member of the Communist International and in charge of Communist International affairs," on the importance of the motion-picture industry in presenting "tremendous cultural possibilities in a revolutionary sense." At first the Communist movement undertook to produce and distribute its own films through independent units, but this procedure proved inadequate. Howard Rushmore, film critic for the *Daily Worker* from 1936 to 1939—when he broke with the Communist Party— testified: "As they went along they saw they couldn't reach what they called the masses with such 16-millimeter films and their lack of distributive methods." [2] The Communist Party had a standing cultural commission which was a subcommittee of the Central Committee, the governing body of the Party. This commission directed, among other responsibilities, Com-

[1] Murray Ross, *Stars and Strikes*, Columbia University Press, New York, 1941, p. viii.
[2] *Hearings by the House Committee on Un-American Activities Regarding the Communist Infiltration of the Motion Picture Industry*, 80th Cong., 1st Sess., 1947, hereafter referred to as "Hollywood, 1947," Rushmore testimony, p. 172.

munist activities in Hollywood.[3] Representatives of the Communist International also participated in the maneuvers to capture, or at least to influence, the motion-picture industry.[4]

Those who studied Communist objectives and were engaged in opposing them analyzed their aims and procedures; their analyses were substantiated by former Communists who had defected after participating in the movement. The grand design was to capture the industry in the interest of the Communist cause. An outstanding motion-picture director, who started as a film cutter and became a screen writer and member of the Screen Directors Guild while belonging to a Communist nucleus, summed up the Party's objectives in the industry: "The first one was to get money. The next was to get prestige. And the third and most important was, through infiltration and eventual taking over Hollywood guilds and unions, to control the content of pictures." [5] The only way the Communists could control the content of pictures was to control studios, and the only way they could do that was to take over completely the guilds and the unions.[6] "All of this was planned as early as 1939 at a conference in Carmel. There they planned to capture the maritime and other industries and then the amusement industry." [7] The program was directed from national committee headquarters in New York through a cultural commission of the Central Committee.[8]

Organizationally, the aim was to capture the labor unions. The analytical-minded Brewer [9] described the blueprint as follows: "Had these strikes been successful, and the IATSE been defeated, we are sure that the few remaining forces of resistance would have easily succumbed to the unbelievably effective machine which the Communist movement had built in southern California in 1944. With a Communist controlled union representing all Hollywood technical labor, supporting a Screen Writer's Guild, through which only pro-Communist writers could get into the industry, we

[3] *Ibid.*, pp. 175–176; for a list of Communist functionaries sent from New York to Hollywood from time to time, see *ibid.*, p. 241.
[4] *Communist Infiltration of Hollywood Motion Picture Industry, Hearings before the House Committee on Un-American Activities*, 82d Cong., 1st Sess., 1951, hereafter referred to as "Hollywood, Part 1, 1951," p. 478.
[5] *Ibid.*, Collins testimony, p. 238.
[6] *Ibid.*, Dmytryk testimony, pp. 411, 415; see also Hollywood, 1947, Oliver Carlson's testimony, pp. 247ff.
[7] Hollywood, 1947, Brewer testimony, p. 349.
[8] *Ibid.*, Rushmore testimony, pp. 174–181; Carlson testimony, pp. 240–241. Both of these were former Communist Party members.
[9] Brewer comes from Nebraska where he was an official of an IATSE local; later he became president of the Nebraska State Federation of Labor. During the Second World War, he was employed in Washington by government agencies. Following the Browne-Bioff scandal, he was assigned to Hollywood by his International. Such assignments are customary in the trade-union movement.

believe that the screen would have been effectively captured, notwithstanding the good intentions of the producers of motion pictures.

"The plan, as we see it was for Communist forces, led by Mr. Jeff Kibre, Communist agent sent to Hollywood in 1935, and his successor, Herbert K. Sorrell, to infiltrate and control Hollywood technical labor, while other Communist forces led by Mr. John Howard Lawson, whose activities have been effectively described here, were to infiltrate and control the talent guilds and so-called cultural groups in the industry. At the appropriate time these two forces were to be joined in one over-all industrial union set-up under complete Communist domination. Our International Union, the IATSE found itself as the one real effective force standing in the way of this program.

"Having failed to control our organization in Hollywood, the Communists found it necessary to seek to destroy it. Fomenting and aggravating jurisdictional irritations existing in the trade-unions structure in the studios, the Communists in 1944, 1945, 1946, and 1947, engineered and maintained a running series of jurisdictional strikes against our unions. The real purpose of the strikes was the weakening and ultimate destruction of the IATSE, which was the recognized bulwark against Communist seizure of the studios' unions." [10]

Howard Rushmore, former *Daily Worker* film critic, explained that with control of the industry, it should be possible to dictate the content of films, both positively and negatively. Then, by either supporting or boycotting specific films as it suited their purpose, they could exert additional pressure. "The Communist Party supported fully" the film *Blockade* which gave "100 per cent endorsement of Stalin's effort to seize Spain as another foreign colony of the Kremlin, and the Communist Party through all its fronts and CIO and AF of L unions which it controlled, put on a terrific campaign for *Blockade*." [11] Moreover, "they received regular information on the kind of pictures coming out from various studios and in some cases I know that the actual script, or a copy of it, rather, was sent to the Cultural Commission of the party at 35 East Twelfth Street months before the picture went into production. . . . One movie that I remember particularly was *Our Leading Citizen*, put out by Paramount, and the script . . . was sent to V. J. Jerome, who was the head of the Communist Party Cultural Commission, and I was told by the Cultural Commission that they had looked over this script and decided that this movie was one of the most anti-Communist movies in years, and that they were going to line up a boycott of it. I reviewed the movie—that was in 1939—and we called for a boycott of the picture. The next day the party had already prepared around three columns

[10] Hollywood, 1947, Brewer testimony, pp. 356–357; see also pp. 492–493.
[11] *Ibid.*, p. 173.

21

of protests from so-called progressive labor leaders, community leaders, and people like that. The letter and telegram barrage against Paramount started immediately but the entire campaign was planned to begin on the opening day of the picture on Broadway." [12]

One of the founders of the Authors League and the Screen Writers Guild, Rupert Hughes, relates a personal instance illustrating how the Communists browbeat producers into not making or showing anti-Communist pictures: "A man came to me and wanted to do an anti-Communist film but was afraid to do one directly attacking them, for fear they would wreck the theatre, so he asked me to do a picture ridiculing Communists and said Warner Brothers would be interested in it if I could furnish a story. I went over it at luncheon where Jack Warner was present, Al Jolson, who was then a stockholder, and others. They were very enthusiastic and paid me $15,000 to write a 5,000-word plot attacking American Communists. In the meantime Hal Wallace, who was their business manager, had been on vacation and he returned. He said 'You are insane to attempt even a comic picture about American Communists because they will put stink pots in every theatre that tries to show it.' They were scared off and never did the picture. I had my $15,000 and I still have my story." [13]

A prominent screen writer, who formerly belonged to the Screen Writers Guild and the Communist Party, described what was expected of screen writers by way of furthering Communist propaganda. Members were expected to "see whether you can in your own handwriting put some of your ideas of the party ideology into your writing.... They took a lot of time in teaching you why and how to do that sort of thing. They were trying to show you that no writing is good writing unless it has political meaning. In their own way, naturally, for their own purposes.... But it must not be propaganda. It must seem the right way of writing so that you hide the propaganda behind some truth. Besides, it is very easy, I say, to point out that something is wrong. There is always something wrong. It is inevitable. But their idea was always to point out what was wrong and not to show what was right." [14]

Hollywood, as an exalted and glorified one-industry community, includes a disproportionate number of persons plying talents of the emotional, effervescent type—actors, writers, and directors. Enjoying fabulous incomes, they could be imposed upon unrestrainedly to support causes claiming humanitarian objectives. And, because of their sensitivity, their con-

[12] *Ibid.*, pp. 173–174.
[13] *Ibid.*, pp. 132–133; Hughes relates other instances.
[14] *Communist Methods of Infiltration* (*Entertainment*), *Hearing before the House Committee on Un-American Activities*, 83d Cong., 2d Sess., testimony of Nicholas Bella, p. 7258. For further instances of how the Communist Party tried to influence screen writers, see Hollywood, Part 1, 1951, p. 227; see also John F. Cronin, "Labor's Great Divide," *Plain Talk*, March, 1947.

sciences could easily be pricked by persons presumably supporting movements in behalf of the downtrodden.

Nevertheless, the round-faced, slightly flabby, horn-rim-spectacled, and astute Roy M. Brewer, the pivotal figure who alerted, organized, and successfully directed the war against the Communists, acknowledged the complicated nature of the struggle. "We do not contend, nor have we ever contended that Communism is the only issue in this controversy. . . . We have a very sincere and positive conviction that a substantial portion of the trouble that has existed in Hollywood during the past ten years arises out of the efforts and the activities of those persons who are Communists, Communist dominated or influenced by Communists." [15]

Profuse documentary data are available, revealing vividly how the plan to penetrate Hollywood was developed and directed by agents from Soviet Russia who resided as Communist representatives in the United States and acted through the American Communist Party. The data also reveal their skillful fishing in troubled waters, albeit occasionally they fumbled the bites. Also, source material discloses how non-Communists and others in the community and the country were alerted successfully to fight back. Alarmed and shocked by the danger confronting them and the nation, they aroused and organized others to counteract the Communist threat. The conflicts that followed had all the dramatic overtones of Hollywood. Referring to one phase, a labor economist, Sol. Davison, who was on the ground and watched developments closely, wrote: "The conflict has all the characteristics of a Hollywood super-colossal production—with plots, counter-plots, climaxes and anti-climaxes, and a cast of Hollywood's leading labor leaders." [16] He should have added that both sides of the controversy were also studded with world-renowned motion-picture stars and with famous screen directors and writers who were active and impassioned participants. In this study, however, only the union phase will be considered.

Usually the Communists made their greatest headway in unorganized, poorly organized, and newly organized areas and industries. Hollywood came under all these categories which often carried the concomitant of inexperienced leadership. An old labor leader from another industry, who was called because of his experience to lead the 1937 strike in the Hollywood studios, found that "there wasn't much coordination." He described it as "the damndest mess I ever saw in my life." The local leaders "did not seem to grasp the entire picture. One seemed to be going in one direction and the other in another." Upon giving them "a pretty good picture of

[15] *Jurisdictional Disputes in the Motion Picture Industry, Hearings before a Special Subcommittee of the House Committee on Education and Labor,* 80th Cong., 2d Sess., 1948, p. 1746. These volumes contain a mass of material from various important sources and shall hereafter be cited merely as "Jurisdiction, 1948."

[16] Sol. Davison, "The Motion Picture Studio Strike," *The New Leader,* June 29, 1946, p. 9.

how, if they wanted to win the strike, they would have to go about it," they "literally dumped the strike in my lap and asked me if I would not cooperate with the strike committee in an advisory capacity and point out the pitfalls to them and help them get the strike on a business basis." [17]

While there had been organization in this industry practically from its beginning, the entire business and its importance in Hollywood date from the post-World War I period. "Although motion pictures were produced in Los Angeles as early as 1907, New York remained the principal seat of manufacture until after the World War. Hollywood did not attain supremacy until the great advance of the industry in 1919–1920. With film-making scattered among several contending cities and still in a migration state, with no established practices and a shifting labor force, it was impossible for the unions to attain any considerable degree of success. During the period 1915–1917 many important studios were established in Hollywood, making it a leading production center. The industry had finally settled down, choosing its home in the heart of open shop territory." [18] As the industry was expanding in the twenties and thirties, labor-organization activity increased. Aided and stimulated in the thirties by various government agencies, such as the NRA and NLRB, unionism became firmly established. "The unionization of the film studios constitutes an important development," thus adding "a new chapter in the annals of American organized labor." [19]

For various reasons, the industry was excessively sensitive to pressure groups with a presumably humanitarian appeal, and the Communists took advantage of the fact. For instance, they played on the public's revulsion to Nazi persecutions and brutality. The large Jewish element and the considerable number of liberals and humanitarians among the producers, directors, writers, actors, and others were very susceptible to appeals vicariously related to this issue.

There were also subtle business factors that a pressure group could use to influence management. Production costs were high and a small key occupational group could readily disrupt production schedules affecting large numbers of highly paid personnel. Since the product was sold directly to the consumer, a boycott or some other form of hostility by a small but well-organized group could prove costly. Furthermore, Communist threats of boycotts and sabotage by using stink bombs or other devices proved effective in frightening the producers.[20]

Other immediate factors aiding the Communists were labor racketeering,

[17] Testimony of John R. Robinson, former president, District Council No. 4, Maritime Federation of the Pacific, Jurisdiction, 1948, pp. 2382–2384.

[18] Ross, *op. cit.*, p. 6.

[19] *Ibid.*, p. vii.

[20] Hollywood, 1947, p. 172; testimony of Howard Rushmore, pp. 173ff., see also testimony of Rupert Hughes.

jurisdictional disputes, and unemployment. Employer labor policies in the motion-picture industry followed a pattern resembling that in many other industries. In the early stages they undertook to operate open shop.[21] When they found that inevitably they had to deal with unions, they succumbed to racketeering labor leaders as a means of controlling the labor and manpower situation. "After completing his closed-shop deal with producers in 1936, George E. Browne, President of International Alliance of Theatrical Stage Employees and Motion Picture Machine Operators of the United States and Canada,[22] placed all his Hollywood locals under the dictatorial rule of his personal representatives, among whom was the notorious William Bioff. These men, according to various charges, collected hundreds of thousands of dollars in dues and special assessments without any accounting to the membership. Many studio technicians objected to being herded into an organization with an allegedly racketeering leadership and to paying exorbitant dues and assessments for the support of an organization not of their own choosing. They resented the perpetuation of an emergency situation during which no membership meetings, or elections of local officers could be held." [23] Browne justified his action as follows: " 'Realizing that our studio locals operating under local autonomy would be devoured by jurisdictional wolves of labor, and the conniving of the well oiled producer's machinery' he urged the membership to accept International control. Each local separately at a meeting acquiesced." [24]

But a greater shock came when Browne and Bioff were indicted and convicted in the Federal courts "on the charge of extorting $550,000 from four big motion picture producing organizations, under threats to foment strikes in picture theatres throughout the country." [25] In between, Bioff was extradited to Illinois for having failed to complete nearly six months of a jail sentence for pandering.[26] He was also indicted for Federal income tax evasion.[27]

As is customary in the case of labor racketeers, Bioff, while lining his pockets, also secured improvements for the members of his union. This, of course, is effective strategy for holding the membership and maintaining the base of operations without which the power to carry on racketeering would wane. That Bioff secured good conditions for the worker under

[21] Ross, *op. cit.*, p. 6.
[22] Often referred to as "IA," this organization is also popularly referred to as "IATSE."
[23] Ross, *op. cit.*, p. 196; see also IATSE Convention Proceedings, 1938, pp. 128–130, and Resolution No. 6, p. 164.
[24] IATSE Convention Proceedings, 1938, p. 59.
[25] Ross, *op. cit.*, p. 202; see also Jurisdiction, 1948, pp. 1916, 1949, 1996, 2016, 2028, 2104.
[26] Ross, *loc. cit.*
[27] For *Variety*, June 11, 1940, see Jurisdiction, 1948, p. 2011; see *ibid.*, pp. 2028–2029 for other excerpts from *Variety*.

the jurisdiction of IATSE in Hollywood is attested to on all sides. Herbert K. Sorrell, president of the Conference of Studio Unions and Bioff's arch opponent, who became the key figure in the Communists' successful penetration of AFL unions, grudgingly admitted that the members supported Bioff "because Bioff did them some good. Those who had steady jobs and those key men in the studios who received hourly raises, benefited by them and Bioff was looked upon as a man who did some good for some of the people in the motion picture industry."

Furthermore, Sol. Davison, describing the substantial wage increases secured under Bioff's leadership, adds: "Bioff did not limit his collective bargaining efforts to the benefits of himself or of the IA. He extended his efforts to all organized labor in the studios, and indeed in the Los Angeles area. In 1937, Sorrell led his painters out on strike on a question of wage increases. The strike was lost and the union left without an agreement. Then, to everyone's surprise, the studios gave Sorrell an agreement and awarded a 15 per cent increase in wages to his membership." In the August 2, 1937, issue of *Variety*, Sorrell had this to say: "It is only through the aid of Mr. Bioff and his IATSE organization that we were able to reach an agreement with the Producers. I intend to thank him personally and in behalf of each member for getting our increase." [28]

It is acknowledged that the exposure and conviction of Bioff and Browne had a serious effect on the prestige of IATSE and proved exceedingly advantageous to the Communists and other opposition groups. Roy M. Brewer, successor to Bioff as IATSE International representative in Hollywood and the one who successfully spearheaded the house cleaning in his own union, leading a titanic fight against the Communists, assessed the effect of the Browne-Bioff scandal on the trade-union situation in Hollywood: "In the wake of this scandal there appeared a vacuum, and men who had been trying to beat off the Communist movement were almost helpless. It was difficult to determine as to which of these individuals were honestly opposing the dishonest element and which were Communist. So it proved to be a boon to the Communists in discrediting all the talk that had been built up about Communist infiltration." [29]

The various strikes that occurred in the 1940s in the studios were based primarily on jurisdictional differences. Many workers were still further affected by the necessity of carrying membership cards of more than one union in order to maintain employment in spite of jurisdictional fights. Unemployment in the studios at this time was another factor which the Communists took advantage of. "During the past few years the chief

[28] Davison, *op. cit.*, p. 10.
[29] *Communist Infiltration of Hollywood Motion Picture Industry, Hearings before the House Committee on Un-American Activities*, 82d Cong., 2d Sess., 1952, hereafter referred to as "Hollywood, Part 2, 1952," p. 481.

economic problem of studio craftsmen has been the shrinkage of employment opportunities." [30]

Undoubtedly the jurisdictional disputes between IATSE and most other craft unions, and the possible threat to the guilds, were the most important issue to serve the interests of the Communists. While the racketeering scandals vitally influenced the membership and the community at large, the jurisdictional differences primarily interested union officials and leaders all the way up to the top echelons of the International. Although traditional in the American labor movement, jurisdictional controversies have a deep emotional effect on labor leadership; other differences may be considered rationally, but those of a jurisdictional nature seem to become demonical. So tense did the situation in the studios become that the AFL appointed a special committee to study and make recommendations; these were not, however, acceptable to several of the unions. The Screen Actors Guild, whose members were affected by these disputes, also tried to bring the parties together, but with as little success as other mediators had. Finally, with the controversy still at fever pitch, the House Committee on Education and Labor appointed a special subcommittee whose hearings during 1947 and 1948 filled three volumes. [31]

IATSE had ambitions, shortly after the First World War, of becoming an industrial union, which caused "serious discord within union ranks." In the spring of 1918, the International Alliance of Theatrical Stage Employees and Moving Picture Machine Operators launched a movement to form one big union of all studio crafts. [32] This attempt to encroach upon studio work which the big craft unions in the AFL considered "reserved for their own members, exasperated them. Civil War broke out between these two hostile camps.... Hollywood's first real test of a jurisdictional dispute brought great confusion into the studio labor situation." [33] While IATSE did not attain its full objective, it did become a powerful union and operated at least as a semi-industrial union. Rival crafts were naturally not content, but their compensating opportunity presented itself when IATSE, in trying to force producers to favor it on jurisdictional grounds as representing the sound-track men, found itself jockeyed into a general strike in 1933. In calling the strike, IATSE had thus withdrawn from the Studio Basic Agreement entered into between the crafts and producers in 1926. [34] The crafts that had already nibbled away some of the jurisdiction belonging

[30] Ross, *op. cit.*, p. 202.

[31] See Jurisdiction, 1948.

[32] In a new and expanding industry, it is customary for unions to attempt to take as much jurisdiction as possible.

[33] Ross, *op. cit.*, pp. 8–9; Davison, *op. cit.*, p. 10; Matthew M. Levy's testimony, Jurisdiction, 1948, p. 2428.

[34] For a description of studio labor agreements since 1926, see the testimony of Pat Casey, former chairman of the labor committee of the Motion Picture Producers Association, Jurisdiction, 1948, pp. 1559–1576 and 1586ff.

to IATSE now had the opportunity to cut into that jurisdiction drastically.

"The strike was a disastrous step for the Alliance. The combined efforts of the producers and its sister unions to break the strike proved too strong for the Alliance to combat. Although its members responded solidly to the strike call, their morale was low because they never really understood why they had been called out. When they saw their jobs slipping out of their grasp, they signed up with the competing unions. . . . The loss of the strike was a staggering blow to the Alliance. . . . In its gamble for control over all studio labor, the Alliance had brought about its total eclipse in Hollywood." [35]

IATSE now proceeded to regain its losses. At this time there was a change in union administration. "George E. Browne, a vice president of the American Federation of Labor, became president of the Alliance at the 1934 convention. Known as a man of action, he lost no time in reestablishing the prestige and power of his union in Hollywood. . . . The Alliance had secured enormous power in the theatres by getting all of its demands into the NRA film exhibition code." [36] From this vantage point it could move back into Hollywood. The test came when Browne demonstrated his power in Chicago by controlling the projection booths. This brought Hollywood producers to the realization that if they wanted to avoid darkened theatres throughout the country, they must make peace with IATSE. They granted IATSE a closed shop and ordered former IATSE members to rejoin. In one fell swoop, some twelve thousand former members rejoined IATSE. And in 1936, IATSE was readmitted as a member of the Studio Basic Agreement it had flaunted and violated in 1933. Not only had IATSE obtained the first closed shop in Hollywood, but it had once again become a dominant, if not the dominant, force.[37] Thus at the 1938 convention, Browne could boast: "Prior to this agreement the membership of our West Coast Studio locals had deteriorated to such a low point that only 158 members comprised the total membership of our locals . . . the only way our members are going to secure their rightful jurisdiction was to crash in at the opportune moment, as neither the producers nor other labor internationals would lift a hand to help our studio members, which labor organizations have divided up our jurisdiction among themselves with our members being more or less outcasts in the studios and having to take for themselves whatever was offered them. . . ." [38]

Some of the smaller groups organized the Federated Motion Picture Crafts to protect their interests. This federation included Sorrell's Painters local. They called a strike and lost it. Because Federated hoped to absorb most

[35] Ross, *op. cit.*, pp. 144–148; Davison, *op. cit.*, p. 9.
[36] See Ross, *op. cit.*, p. 192.
[37] Ross, *loc. cit.*
[38] IATSE Convention, 1938, p. 52, and also p. 60; IATSE General Bulletin, December 18, 1935, pp. 1–4, and May 13, 1935, p. 4.

of the members of IATSE, the Alliance sided with management and also took away a group of laborers from the Painters local. On the other hand, when the strike was lost, IATSE generously helped the Painters secure a contract with a 15 per cent wage increase. "This was the first contract which extended direct recognition to a studio craft local. All the members of the Studio Basic Agreement had to be represented by their International officers. After concluding his closed-shop deal with the producers in 1936, Browne placed all his Hollywood locals under the dictatorial rule of his personal representatives, among whom was the notorious William Bioff." [39] It was this bitter jurisdictional struggle between IA and the crafts which motivated the International and local leaders of these unions to support the Communist-controlled Studio Conference in an effort to dislodge the Communists.

Under such conditions, wide, deep, and sufficiently troubled waters now existed for Communist fishing. And the Communists quickly and skillfully cast their line.

[39] Ross, *op. cit.*, pp. 193–196.

5

Attempts at Dual Unionism

The work of the Communists in the trade-union field was well planned, although it was ineptly handled in the beginning. At first the Communists tried to capture the International Association of Theatrical Stage Employees while trying simultaneously to penetrate the industry through a dual union with the aid of "left-wing" CIO leaders.[1]

The early story of Communist efforts to gain control of industry is related by Jeff Kibre, its key man, in a series of reports and in correspondence, copies of which were attached by the Los Angeles police department in raiding his apartment. Kibre describes in detail the Communists' strategy and its execution.[2]

[1] Sol. Davison, "The Motion Picture Studio Strike," *New Leader*, June 29, 1946, p. 11.

[2] The Kibre documents were reproduced first in the *Los Angeles Citizen*, the official organ of the Los Angeles AFL Central Labor Union, from May 19, 1939, to June 30, 1940; they were also reproduced in the IATSE Convention Proceedings of 1940, pp. 97–149. The documents are not paged but are numbered and dated, which will explain the form of reference given them in this account. Kibre is not on record as having challenged the authenticity of these documents. On the other hand, a sworn affidavit was presented by a former Communist Party member in Los Angeles, who stated that he knew Jeff Kibre as a member of the Communist Party who was "at times, assigned to 'special' work in the studio unions, more specifically in the IATSE Local 37, and to organizing special studio units of the Communist Party of the U.S.A." (IATSE Convention Proceedings, 1940, Document No. 6). This affidavit was not challenged either. Shortly after the publication of these reports, Kibre disappeared from Los Angeles and ceased participating in studio-labor activity. He did participate, however, in the Communist-led North American Aviation strike and later became an officer in the CIO International Fishermen and Allied Workers of America, which has since been absorbed by Harry Bridges' International Longshoremen's and Warehousemen's Union. (*Hearings by the House Committee on Un-American Activities Regarding the Communist Infiltration of the Motion Picture Industry*, 80th Congress, 1st Sess., 1947, hereafter referred to as "Hollywood, 1947," p. 351; *Jurisdictional Disputes in the Motion Picture Industry, Hearings before a Special Subcommittee of the House Committee on Education and Labor*, 80th Cong., 2d Sess., 1948, hereafter cited as "Jurisdiction, 1948," p. 1703.) Kibre is listed as a delegate to four CIO conventions: Proceedings, 1946, p. 18; 1947, p. 34; 1948, p. 26 and 1949, p. 22. Sorrell, in his testimony at a congressional committee hearing, made a feeble effort to discredit the Kibre documents but presented no proof. "Now, for your information, the Los

The Communists' first intention was to bore from within IATSE; the time was ripe for such opposition activity. The public had just learned that Joseph Schenck, president of the Producers Association, had lent Bioff 100,000 dollars; the members of IATSE were dissatisfied because of assessments which were not accounted for; unemployment had caused unrest; the unceremonious defeat of the crafts in their strike and the forcing of their members to join IATSE aroused resentment.[3] A group calling itself "IATSE Progressives" was formed, with Jeff Kibre as chairman. The group decided, among other things, to present a resolution to the IATSE convention of 1938, meeting in Cleveland. This step indicated a lack of understanding of trade-union processes. Resolutions are presented by local unions, not by unofficial bodies. Be that as it may, Jeff Kibre, as chairman of the IATSE Progressives, addressed a set of resolutions to the president, George E. Browne, with the statement that they embodied "months of discussion by many members of studio locals of IATSE for introduction to the Resolutions Committee of the current convention of the Alliance."

These resolutions called for local autonomy because any other arrangement "is harmful to the interests of the general membership by hindering

---

Angeles Citizen was edited by J. W. Buzzell, a thief, who stole money and who was removed by President Green because he used money that did not come to him on his pay check . . . and we got rid of the guy who put that stuff in the paper which I do not know whether it is right or not. He would put in anything that Mr. Bioff told him to put in there. If Mr. Brewer went there to get his facts, they are mud. I doubt anything Buzzell says. It may be true or it may not be true." When challenged by a committee member: "In other words, you are telling us Jeff Kibre was not a Communist?" Sorrell replied evasively, "Oh, no. I did not say that, I said that I do not know whether Kibre is a Communist or not." (Jurisdiction, 1948, pp. 1873–1874.)

Mr. George E. Bodle, Mr. Sorrell's attorney, stated that Sorrell had little to do with Kibre and that they were poles apart in thinking. Kibre favored an industrial union for the motion-picture industry, and Sorrell "stood up for the rights of the craft workers in the industry." (Ibid., p. 1993.) An analysis of the documents reveals authoritatively that Kibre was a Communist, was recognized as such, and worked in the motion-picture industry on behalf of the Communist Party.

As for the documents' being forgeries, although they are typed, they contain notations in Kibre's handwriting. Moreover, when the documents were first reproduced, some individuals mentioned in them were unknown to the editors of the Los Angeles Citizen. Later issues announced that further information had revealed them as prominent Communists. Forgers are rarely so subtle as to resort to such designs. Recently, Kibre appeared in Washington and registered as a lobbyist for Harry Bridges' ILWU. (Congressional Record, Proceedings and Debates of the 84th Congress, 1st Session, House, Thursday, June 21, 1955, Vol. 101, No. 92, p. 6377.) At a hearing before the Senate Internal Security Committee June 21, 1956, Kibre was asked whether he had been a member of the Communist Party or had used an alias. He declined to answer, invoking the Fifth Amendment's protection of a citizen's right to refrain from giving testimony that might tend to incriminate him. (Communists on Waterfront, Subcommittee on Internal Security, Committee on the Judiciary, U.S. Senate, 84th Cong., 2d Sess., 1956, pp. 1621–1627.)

[3] Murray Ross, Stars and Strikes, Columbia University Press, New York, 1941, p. 196.

the achievement of such purposes as unity of spirit and action, the improvement of working conditions, and the loyalty and respect of the members of the organization." Local autonomy became a prime touchstone of the Communists, since it was easier for them to control local studio unions than the International. With IATSE controlling the locals through receivership, however, the Communists had very little prospect of dominating any of them. It was also a popular issue to raise with the rank and file.

The remainder of the resolutions criticized and attacked the International officials for "levying a special assessment," for "disregard of constitutional provisions relating to membership," for dominating meetings "called in response to an organized demand for local autonomy," for permitting "a progressive deterioration of working conditions," for not taking "constructive action" in coping with "a critical wave of unemployment," for sabotaging the 1937 strike of "brother AFL unions," and for not cooperating with "the unions and guilds . . . in meeting industry-wide problems." The resolutions then called for various reforms in the organization.[4]

The tenor of these resolutions is hardly that which an opposition desiring to work within an organization would introduce. In a report to national Communist Party headquarters, the assistant secretary of the Ohio state Communist Party described the resolution as "more of a sweeping indictment or brief for a law suit than a resolution which can serve any practical purpose at a convention like this." [5]

Although at first the IA leaders were undecided as to what course to follow, they did give much thought to the problem and mapped out a procedure. There was a difference of opinion among them as to whether the resolutions should be accepted, since they were not introduced by a regular local or by a delegate to the convention. They must also have had in mind making a show of this dissident group. It was agreed that one of the delegates representing Hollywood Local 37 would be from the IATSE Progressives. Irwin P. Hentschel by name, this inexperienced delegate conducted himself poorly and improperly. He was apologetic and indecisive; when he took the floor to defend the resolutions, he told instead of the personal vicissitudes he had experienced following his arrival at the convention. Evidently hazed and browbeaten by officials and delegates, he was apparently marked for slaughter. His predicament was intensified further by advice from local Communists, with whom he consulted, "not to introduce the resolution." In addition, according to the assistant secretary of the Ohio state Communist Party, Hentschel had "received a telegram from Jeff Kibre, as well as a phone call from this same person, who is the leader of the rank and file movement in Hollywood and, according to Hentschel,

---

[4] IATSE Convention Proceedings, 1938, pp. 164–168.
[5] Kibre Document No. 4, letter dated June 16, 1938. The convention lasted from June 3 to June 6.

a party member, advising him to leave the convention floor at once. We concurred in the decision." [6] In Hentschel's own words: "I have had some unpleasant occurrences here at this convention. I have been ostracized; I have been cajoled; I have been called this and that; I have been called a CIO man. And now when I am near the edge of a nervous collapse, I went to the Resolutions Committee and asked that I personally be able to withdraw the resolution by the mere fact that I was beaten."

He also complained of his inexperience. "When I was appointed a Delegate, I did not even know what a delegate was supposed to do. I was never in a union meeting in all my life. . . ." And having experienced these rebuffs, he was willing to depart from the convention, "but . . . my money is being held up . . . if I had gotten my money and gotten out of town, this unpleasant occurrence would not have happened." [7] During this part of Hentschel's speech, one delegate made the point of order that the speaker was not addressing himself to the resolution. President Browne, aware that Hentschel was making a spectacle of himself, prevailed upon the delegate to withdraw his point of order.[8] Hardly a competent representative of an effective opposition for reasons of personality, Hentschel nevertheless made a fair defense of the resolution, and the Communists made up for their error in later performances.

From the Kibre documents, it is clear that Hentschel was Kibre's lieutenant, a member of the Communist Party, and that he had consulted with local Cleveland Communist leaders while attending the IATSE 1938 convention. Following this fiasco, Hentschel vanished from the scene and did not reappear until the 1945 strike in which he led a "rank-and-file activity," according to the March 12 and April 2, 1945, issues of *Variety*.[9]

That the national Communist Party was disturbed is revealed in a letter from Roy Hudson, chief Communist functionary in charge of trade-union work, to his counterpart in California, June 21, 1938. Prompted by a letter he received from an Ohio functionary, Hudson wrote: "Considering the situation in the International (that is, IATSE), our relative strength, etc., I think that presenting such a resolution to the convention was nothing short of sheer stupidity and must certainly reflect a lack of guidance upon the part of the Party to this work, because I cannot conceive of the Party's advising such a thesis being sent to the convention. . . . It seems to me that this situation requires some immediate investigation in California." [10]

Communications from various Communist functionaries were referred to the secretary of the Los Angeles branch. He in turn referred the cor-

[6] Kibre Document No. 4 in IATSE Convention Proceedings, 1940.
[7] *Ibid.*, pp. 168–171; some International unions pay the expenses of their delegates.
[8] *Loc. cit.*
[9] Hollywood, 1947, p. 545.
[10] *Loc. cit.*

respondence to Kibre marked "for discussion by the studio Industrial Units." Kibre then reported to the "Comrade . . . State Trade Union Director" that "discussions . . . have been held as follows: first, a thorough discussion with Comrade Hentschel who was a delegate from the Studio Local 37; second, detailed discussions with leading comrades in the IATSE and other studio unions; and, lastly, the industrial trade union commission, which represents both crafts and guilds." He then, on behalf of those who participated in the "discussions," defends Hentschel, the procedure, and the contents of the resolutions as dictated by conditions unfamiliar to "the comrades of the East of IATSE in the Motion Picture Industry." [11]

A vice-president who concerned himself with motion-picture matters defended the administration at length. He proudly described in glowing terms the achievements of IATSE since the disastrous strike of 1933, claiming that members had received a 20 per cent wage increase, enjoyed improved working conditions, and were kept fully informed concerning union matters; in addition, union membership had risen from 138 in 1933 to 12,000 in 1938. He also read innumerable communications from studio unions not affiliated with IATSE, expressing gratitude for its cooperation, guidance, and valuable support. He also presented other documents and referred to talks by four International presidents at the convention in which they expressed similar views of appreciation, all reproduced in the convention proceedings. Turning his guns on the opposition, he charged that "this minority we have to deal with is a direct result of CIO activity and destructive radicalism within our ranks." [12] He proceeded to present documentary proof in substantiation of his charges. Testimony before the California legislative Committee on Capital and Labor, November 15, 1937,[13] was read to the convention.

Questioned at these hearings, Hentschel acknowledged that he had no particular loyalty to either the CIO or the AFL but that "one organization universally for the labor movement is to the benefit of all the fellows concerned." He was then asked if he had corresponded with Harry Bridges. At first, he wrestled with the question, trying to evade a direct answer, but when he was confronted with a letter he had written and the demand that he answer specifically, he admitted having addressed a letter to Harry Bridges in care of the Pacific Coast Maritime Federation, San Francisco, California, on or about June 26, 1937. In this letter Hentschel wrote: "We are appealing to you for information that will help real unionism in the Motion Picture Industry. The recent strikes having further exposed the racketeering and complete domination of our locals by our International

[11] Kibre Document No. 5, IATSE Convention Proceedings, 1940.
[12] At this time, the CIO was anathema to most AFL leaders, and they tried to foist this feeling on their followers.
[13] See IATSE Convention Proceedings, 1938, pp. 58–60.

officials, have made the rank and file more determined to find a solution of their difficulties. It is only natural that they look to industrial unionism and the CIO." He asked for information and aid, including advice on the advisability of starting a lawsuit against IATSE. Bridges replied, answering the various inquiries and suggesting that "it is entirely possible that a lawsuit against IATSE may be a good method of attack." [14]

The resolutions committee recommended "non-concurrence in the resolution" presented by the dissident group, and the recommendation was approved.

An analysis of the Kibre documents, supplemented by information from other sources, presents a vivid picture of the program and tactics of the Communists in the early stages of their penetrating Hollywood unions, particularly in the crafts. While not spectacularly successful, these early activities provided the groundwork for later action and control, primarily through the Conference of Studio Unions and Guilds, especially the Screen Writers Guild.

It was the ambition of the Communists at the outset to weld the studio unions into an industrial union by capturing their respective locals. IATSE was one of the chief targets, but the Communists also coveted the other craft guilds and unions. The "left-wing" elements dominant in the California CIO were cooperating, but the advisability of affiliating the newly created union with the CIO had not been determined. The dominating element led by Kibre favored an independent union in the interim. Although IATSE, powerfully entrenched, was the principal target, an attack was also planned on the Screen Actors Guild which was resisting enlistment in the venture.

Allowing for exaggeration in claims of accomplishment, the Kibre documents are highly instructive in revealing the type of nomenclature, program, and strategy used by the Communists to penetrate the studio unions. Kibre possessed the ability to write analytically; his reports are studiously organized, concise, and pointed. His first report, dated April 23, 1938, is divided into four parts: review of plans and objectives; accomplishments; favorable elements for further progress; conclusions.[15] In a methodical manner, Kibre describes how the Communists can take advantage of the favorable situation. The unemployment issue is the most important; in addition, there is the short work week, resulting in lower earnings and wage cuts. The other crafts hold their hostility toward IATSE for having raided them and forced their members, through the closed-shop agreement, to join the international union. This, coupled with racketeering, gangsterism, and dictatorial control, has made IATSE vulnerable. All the guilds, except the Screen Actors Guild, can be counted on because they are afraid that

[14] *Ibid.*, pp. 171–187.
[15] Kibre Document No. 1, IATSE Convention Proceedings, 1940.

IATSE will destroy them. As for the Screen Actors Guild, "where the Junior Guild is the basic trade union element, we have been successful in electing a complete new slate of officers committed to the Conference." Spearheading the new movement for the crafts is the Studio Painters Union, and for the guilds, the Screen Writers Guild.[16]

The machinery for taking over the trade-union movement was carefully blueprinted. Because of the increase in unemployment during the winter of 1937–1938, the key organization was a Studio Unemployment Conference. Simultaneously, "a broad anti-IATSE movement, representing a majority of workers in the industry, has announced support of the program. . . . By bringing these two movements together on the fundamental issue of better conditions, a solid, though not spectacular movement for a federation—as the preliminary step for industrial unionism—has developed." The purpose was "to work through all crafts and guilds instead of concentrating on IATSE." Kibre emphasized that "our work is entirely through the crafts and guilds as the best method for crystalizing sentiment for industrial unionism." He complained that another group was attempting openly to organize an industrial union on behalf of the CIO, a procedure he considered fallacious: "At no time during the present stage have we fooled ourselves into thinking we could establish a CIO union overnight." Because of the strangle hold of IATSE, "we are thus faced with the necessity of moving towards an industrial union by forcing action by the crafts upon such issues as demand overwhelming joint action and cooperation. This process envisions the formation of a federation as the decisive method of breaking the control of the Internationals, and, in turn, giving the workers a sense of their mass power within the industry. This process, we feel, will inevitably result in an industrial union. Our immediate objective, then, has been the formation of a motion picture workers Federation."

In the beginning, the Unemployment Conference represented "all crafts and guilds except the IATSE" and was sparked by the Studio Painters Union. "Pressure from the IATSE later resulted in the leadership of the Teamsters withdrawing their representatives; more subtle sabotage by the leadership of the Screen Actors Guild resulted in their withdrawal. The Conference, however, spurred the move with twelve unions." [17]

The guilds shied away from the conference at the outset because "there

[16] IATSE had placed the Screen Actors Guild under obligation "by helping the guild to secure recognition" in 1937, Ross, *op. cit.*, pp. 194–195. The leaders of the guild, however, showed great perspicacity in shunning both the racketeer and Communist elements.

[17] Sorrell, who was chairman of the Unemployment Conference and next in line to carry on the work started by Kibre, belittles the role of Kibre some ten years later in testifying in his defense: "I see, from what was read in the record, that a letter or something, that Jeff Kibre was on the CIO payroll, and he took credit for organizing it. If he did, he was getting money under false pretenses." Jurisdiction, 1948, p. 1873.

was a decided hostility toward any relationship with the trade unions." Certain elements within the guilds thought it might be necessary to hold a separate guild conference. But this became unnecessary. As a consequence of enlightenment among guild members, "this movement finally came to a head with the Screen Writers' Guild sponsoring a conference of all crafts and guilds outside of IATSE to establish the freedom of all groups to select and maintain their bargaining agency. This conference . . . resulted in the endorsement of the Unemployment Conference and its program of bettering working conditions as the best means of fighting the IATSE leadership." This conference and its activities will "give the rank and file the clarity and confidence to demand the next step, a common bargaining agency and the machinery to make it effective."

In addition to its work in the open, the conference carried on covert activities. "We have utilized it [the conference] for our rank and file work in the Screen Actors Guild and the IATSE." Besides, "influential groups have been established in every major union and guild. These groups are coordinated by a regular underground apparatus. It is through these groups, based in the present organizations, committed to the objective of an industrial union for the 35,000 workers in the industry, that the present field representative is working. . . . Correct handling of possibilities, issues, etc., may lead to the formation of a Federation in the immediate future. This will undoubtedly take the form of an independent organization—since it will involve a break with the present Internationals. This will serve as the transitional stage looking towards an Industrial Union affiliated with the CIO." [18]

On February 9, 1938, Kibre wrote to Bob Reed, a fellow Communist, active in Actors Equity, and a Communist organizer who had made several trips to Hollywood and followed developments there very closely, to ask for a list of Communists in the East. Kibre opened his letter with: "Well, one thing about reds—they seldom write except on business." In this letter he describes himself as follows: "I'm still the undercover field rep. for the CIO in Hollywood." He then describes the work leading to "that long awaited showdown in the industry between the IATSE and real unity" which is "fast on the way." He also boasts of the way they "maneuvered State Assembly Comm. into an investigation of the outfit. Put the situation on the front page and blew it wide open, but was prevented from driving down the stretch and taking control when the Assembly Comm., because of weak-kneed progressives and powerful pressure, welched on us." [19]

[18] Kibre Document No. 1, IATSE Convention Proceedings, 1940.
[19] The Communists and their allies took advantage of every situation. Ross describes the fiasco of the State Assembly's investigation as follows: "The real revolt did not start, however, until the news leaked out that the president of the producers' association, Joseph Schenck, had made a loan of $100,000 to William Bioff shortly after the collapse of the FMPC (Federation of Motion Picture Crafts) in the 1937

Kibre then comes to the real reason for writing: "One strategic move remains to be set in motion: the emergence of a progressive movement in key locals of the IATSE motion picture operators unions. Threat of using the operator locals as an economic lever to enforce their policies in Hollywood has been voiced by IATSE officials. Although threat would undoubtedly be impossible of realization, it carries weight with the workers here. I have been trying to establish contact with our people (of whom I hear there are many) in various of the locals, New York, Chicago, Detroit and Cleveland. . . . Emergence of progressive movements would constitute a terrific blow in the rear for the IATSE officials, and at the same time serve a sharp impetus for fight against IATSE here. . . . I wish you would discuss the matter of IATSE action with Jack Stachel [a top national Communist official]. . . . I have taken it up with Paul Kline [L.A.C.P. secretary], but he feels personal appeal by you to V. J. [Victor Jerome] would help rather than communication thru official channels."

The omnipotent Mr. Kibre labored assiduously to enlist support and maintain contact with all who could supply aid and interest. On November 8, 1938, he wrote a long letter, as was his wont, to Lou Goldblatt, secretary of the ILWU and intimate colleague of Harry Bridges, addressing him as "My dear Lou" and informing him at length and in rather optimistic terms of developments "which might bear discussion at the Convention [CIO convention held in Pittsburgh the week of November 18] in order to clarify our general perspective." He particularly emphasized the prospect of transforming IATSE into "a thoroughly legitimate organization, then bring it into cooperation with other organizations, and finally either through the IATSE as the base, or COMPAC [Conference of Motion Picture Arts and Crafts] establish a Federation as the immediate form of industrial organization in the industry. . . . This perspective envisions the CIO as the outcome of the organization which is built . . . rather than utilizing the CIO as the direct means of organizing the workers." He also discusses the possibility of an open CIO drive, should the situation change.

Kibre could be eloquent in his indefatigable manner. In his report of October 7, 1937—with "copy sent to Harry Bridges" noted on it in his own handwriting—he states in his opening paragraph: "Throughout the country Hollywood is a magic word. It represents something apart from everyday, humdrum life; it is a world of glamour, of shadows that dance

strike. Led by 'IATSE Progressives,' the rebels got the State Assembly Interim Committee on Capital and Labor to make an official inquiry into labor racketeering on the Alliance. The investigators presented the Committee with a report giving the Alliance a clean bill of health. Several of the Committeemen challenged the veracity of the report and the committee adjourned abruptly. It held several open hearings, however, which gave the insurgents a brief opportunity to air their grievances. Shortly afterward, the Alliance lifted its two per cent assessment and for the first time in two years permitted membership meetings of the four locals." *Op. cit.*, pp. 196–197.

across the screen, of rose-colored romance. So unreal is the picture of Hollywood that comes to the average person's mind, that few understand what makes the wheels go around; that within this world of fantasy are thousands of workers of all kinds, who sweat, and who fight the same bitter struggles as other thousands of workers to secure a decent livelihood." [20] He describes the bad working conditions and the low salaries "all of the employer's own choosing, and a general attitude of company unionism prevails." Then he raises the question, "Why should the CIO trouble with Hollywood?" He gives his own answer to this rhetorical question: "Because the workers need industrial organization and because the motion picture industry is an industry of 'public persuasion' that moulds public opinion. . . ."

The insurgent group in the Alliance also resorted to court action and even complained to the NLRB, charging "producer domination of the Alliance and demanding restitution of all dues paid to the International since 1936." When all these maneuvers proved fruitless, the insurgents withdrew from the Alliance and in July, 1939, founded a new rump organization, the United Studio Technicians Guild. "The new guild admitted receiving CIO funds. In one exposé, the Los Angeles Central Labor Council also linked it with Communist influence." [21] Confident of their strength, the members of the new group insisted upon an NLRB election. IATSE resisted at first, threatening to strike, then reversed its position and participated in the election. On the whole, the campaign was energetic, with IATSE scoring an overwhelmingly decisive victory of landslide proportions. The vote, taken in September, 1939, stood 4,460 to 1,967.[22]

The Communists believed the workers would abandon IATSE if permitted to record their choice through NLRB elections,[23] but IATSE was too strongly established through the closed shop and through its ability to tie up production and distribution by strikes for the Communists to make much headway in diverting its following.

Since the Communists gained little in resorting to NLRB elections and since IATSE seemed impregnable to boring-from-within, the opposition had to search for other means of gaining control.

[20] Kibre Document, No. 7, IATSE Convention Proceedings, 1940.
[21] Ross, *op. cit.*, pp. 197–198; Jurisdiction, 1948, pp. 394–395.
[22] Ross, *op. cit.*, p. 201; Davison, *op. cit.*, p. 11; Murray Ross, "C.I.O. Loses Hollywood," *Nation*, Oct. 7, 1939; President Browne's report, IATSE Convention Proceedings, 1940, p. 60.
[23] Kibre Document No. 1, IATSE Convention Proceedings, 1940; see also Documents Nos. 2 and 3.

6

Change of Communist Policy and Leadership

The Communists and their allies were no exception to the saying that schemes of mice and men go "aft a-gley." They failed in their dual-union efforts, and they failed in their attempt at ultimate affiliation with the CIO as an industrial organization. Their efforts to destroy, or at least to discommode, IATSE through legislative investigation, court action, and NLRB elections not only misfired but boomeranged. And publication of the Kibre documents added to their misfortune. Their defeats did not, however, end in a complete debacle—the Communists are too resourceful, too dedicated to their cause to accept defeat. Besides, there was still the heated, unsettled jurisdictional dispute between the crafts and IATSE; they still had a strong and sympathetic following among the talent guilds, led by the Screen Actors Guild and strongly reinforced by the Screen Directors Guild. Lastly, the Bioff-Browne racketeering scandal was overripe for exploitation.

But the situation called for new strategy, new plans, new leadership. Kibre's industrial-union idea, calling for either an independent union or open ties to the CIO, was scrapped. And Kibre himself was spirited away when his being called a Communist and a dual-unionist enemy of the AFL destroyed his usefulness. The new program, designed to follow along the lines of established Communist trade-union policy in operating covertly within the existing AFL union, demanded a new type of organization and new leaders. Herbert K. Sorrell was tapped to take over. Known publicly as a devoted AFL trade unionist who had made a reputation as a leader in the 1937 studio strike, he was not tainted by being known as either a Communist or a dual unionist. On the other hand, Communist leaders knew him as one of their own.

And so a new organization, christened "Conference of Studio Unions," came into being with Sorrell as president. Designed ostensibly to coordinate the crafts threatened by IATSE, the new organization's guiding principles were to be openly "Democracy and Autonomy." For propaganda purposes, this was an appealing slogan, throwing into relief the two evils charged against IATSE: by establishing receiverships, IATSE had presumably denied the democratic conduct of IATSE locals by their members; by collecting assessments decided upon by the International, IATSE had negated local-union autonomy.[1] These slogans, however, were in line with Communist strategy throughout the country. Where Communists did not control the International, it was their policy to advocate democracy and local autonomy so they could more easily dominate and influence the subordinate units.

The Conference of Studio Unions came into existence formally on October 2, 1941. From an account published in *Variety* October 3, 1941, and introduced at the Jurisdiction hearings with the approval of Sorrell, we learn that "the Conference of Studio Unions was launched yesterday when the conference constitution was unanimously approved at a specially called membership meeting of Motion Picture Painters Local 644. . . . The painters after approving the conference and its constitution yesterday appointed Herbert Sorrell business representative of Local 644, Carl Head and William Ball to represent them as delegates to the conference." The account then describes the constitution and objectives: "The purpose of the conference shall be 'To unite the motion-picture unions for the protection of the autonomy and democracy of each' and 'to advance through joint consultation and action the economic welfare of the motion-picture unions and their members.' Any craft affiliated with the American Federation of Labor will be eligible to join the conference. Each conference member is to be represented by three accredited delegates, one of which shall be the business agent. . . . All action, unless otherwise specified in this constitution, shall be by a majority vote of the delegates present at any conference meeting." [2] Sorrell boasted of the democratic character of CSU. It was "a conference of democratic unions bound together to maintain the democracy and autonomy within the union." [3] This emphasis automatically favored most IATSE locals, namely, those whose autonomy had not been taken away by the International. On the other hand, it ran the risk of dissatisfying those who did not have autonomy. "In other words, some IATSE locals would be eligible and some would not. . . ." Mr. Sorrell also gloried in the provision that of the three delegates "it is

[1] IATSE President Browne explained why restored autonomy in 1938 had to be revoked when "radical elements in local 37 began jockeying for position so that they could control the destinies of the organization." He then cites various practices detrimental to IATSE instituted by this opposition. He also explained that his procedure was in accordance with IATSE regulations and traditional union practice in that he assigned a committee to investigate and acted on its recommendations. (IATSE Convention Proceedings, 1940, pp. 62–63.)
[2] *Jurisdictional Disputes in the Motion Picture Industry, Hearings before a Special Subcommittee of the House Committee on Education and Labor*, 80th Cong., 2d Sess., 1948, p. 2027; this source will be cited hereafter as "Jurisdiction, 1948."
[3] *Ibid.*, p. 1877.

clearly stated that the elected business representative and two elected ...
delegates shall constitute the required delegation. ... In other words, we
did not trust just the business agent to carry back and forth the word from
the meeting of locals to the union meeting." [4] Of course, unless business representatives were eligible, Sorrell himself could not have been a
delegate.

Roy M. Brewer complained that the CSU was a unique organization in
that it had no official standing in the AFL, that is, it was really an informal
body without a charter.[5] Sorrell rapidly demolished this argument by
showing that "Bioff set up a Conference of AFL Studio Unions. And he
was joined by most of the unions." [6] Indeed, it is not uncommon for local
unions, affiliated with various internationals but operating in the same industry, to create such informal bodies for joint collective bargaining and
other mutual union purposes. Such bodies are functioning in hotel and
other industries. Precedent for this dates far back into the history of the
AFL. For example, locals of German and Jewish workers founded central labor unions known as "United German Trades" and "United Hebrew
Trades." [7] In the building and metal trades, such central local bodies have
official standing as chartered entities in the respective department affiliated
with the AFL. Outstanding informal organizations on a national scale
are the Railway Labor Executives Association and Government Employees
General Council.[8]

Basically, CSU consisted of craft and trade locals whose members were
employed in the motion-picture industry. These included—in addition to
the Painters—Machinists, Electricians, Building Service Employees, Plumbers, Carpenters. In addition, "there was a sort of unofficial association
with respect to the molders and sheet metal workers, who were employed
in the studios in small numbers." These locals were affiliated with their
respective internationals belonging to the AFL.[9]

A number of guilds—among them the Screen Cartoonist Guild, Screen
Story Analyst Guild, Screen Publicists Guild, and Screen Office Employees
Guild—were also part of the CSU. These were affiliated with the Painters
International and sponsored by Sorrell, just as the Screen Set Designers were,
although the work they were performing was not necessarily related to that
of the Painters. These guilds should be distinguished from the "talent
guilds" which included the Actors, Writers, and Directors Guilds.

[4] *Ibid.*, p. 1955.
[5] *Communist Infiltration of Hollywood Motion Picture Industry, Hearings before
the House Committee on Un-American Activities*, 82d Cong., 1st Sess., 1951, hereafter referred to as "Hollywood, Part 1, 1951," p. 481.
[6] Jurisdiction, 1948, p. 1995; see also p. 1869.
[7] David Saposs, "Effect of Recent Economic Trends on Jewish Labor," American
Conference of Jewish Social Work, 1934, p. 18.
[8] See *Directory of National and International Labor Unions in the United States*,
U.S. Bureau of Labor Statistics Bulletin 1185, 1955, pp. 5–6 and 17–20.
[9] Jurisdiction, 1948, p. 1959.

It should also be remembered that some of these CSU affiliates dissociated themselves at different times, while others joined at a later period. Thus the Screen Office Employees Guild disaffiliated in April, 1946, and joined the International Office Employees Union, AFL. On the other hand, the Carpenters Local No. 946 did not join up until early in 1946. There was also a group of local unions, whose members were employed by the studios, that did not affiliate, such as the teamsters, laborers, and musicians.[10] On the whole, though, the membership was quite stable and consistent.

The jurisdiction claimed by IATSE very clearly overlapped that covered by the unions in the CSU. IATSE had in its fold "most of the mechanical crafts that had to do with the production of motion pictures. That is . . . the cameramen, the property craftsmen . . . the grips, the costumers, the make-up artists, and most of all the skilled crafts that worked with the shooting companies on a motion picture set, as well as some of the men who prepared the sets and built the properties for the studios."[11] It will thus be seen that there was room for jurisdictional claims and controversy.

Exact figures on membership in the rival groups are not available, but IATSE claimed a membership of about fifteen or sixteen thousand. Since total employment in the industry was estimated at thirty thousand,[12] and there were a number of unaffiliated unions and talent guilds as well as some nonunion workers, it seems likely that membership in CSU was somewhere around ten thousand. This setup, of course, gave IATSE a membership advantage. But CSU had able leadership, an adventurous, even reckless, attitude, a large number of dedicated followers, support from a great variety of front organizations, liberals, and groups shocked by the racketeering taint attached to IATSE, as well as the support of the Carpenters and Painters Internationals. Because of jurisdictional considerations, CSU was in a favorable position to challenge IATSE effectively.

Discussing in retrospect the domination and manipulation of CSU by the Communists, Roy M. Brewer, the key figure in the fight against them, recognizes that the situation was confused. Although the struggle seemed an ordinary jurisdictional dispute among AFL unions, there was in addition the shocking Browne-Bioff racketeering scandal. "In the wake of this scandal there appeared a vacuum, and men who had been trying to beat off the Communist movement [1939] were almost helpless. It was difficult to determine as to which of these individuals were honestly opposing the

[10] Jurisdiction, 1948, pp. 1701–1702 and 1788; *Hearings by the House Committee on Un-American Activities Regarding the Communist Infiltration of the Motion Picture Industry*, 80th Cong., 1st Sess., 1947, hereafter referred to as "Hollywood, 1947," pp. 344, 353. *Communist Infiltration of Hollywood Motion Picture Industry, Hearings before the House Committee on Un-American Activities*, 82d Cong., 2d Sess., 1952, hereafter referred to as "Hollywood, Part 2, 1952," pp. 486–487.
[11] *Ibid.*, p. 475.
[12] *Ibid.*, pp. 475, 485.

dishonest element and which were Communist. So it proved to be a boon to the Communists in discrediting all the talk that had been built up about Communist influence." [13]

Although in the heat of the conflict the situation was confused, from the record it is clear that CSU, judged by its pronouncements, actions, and alignments, was at least Communist-oriented. Indubitably, its guiding genius, Herbert K. Sorrell, at one time carried a Communist card and consciously furthered the Communist cause. Furthermore, the policies and tactics of CSU were directed chiefly toward promoting Communist objectives and only incidentally toward bettering the interests of the affiliated local unions and their members.

Since its origin, the CSU has consistently followed the Communist Party line. Although composed overwhelmingly of AFL local unions, the conference has invariably supported the Communist Party position against that of the federation. Thus it condemned the AFL for not affiliating with the WFTU.[14] It also supported a secession group from the Screen Actors Guild, although this union is an AFL affiliate.[15] At the time the AFL was fighting Harry Bridges and the CIO, the conference adopted resolutions supporting Bridges and the CIO.[16] Lists of actions taken at CSU meetings—recorded in the minutes and in its official paper, the *CSU News* —reveal decisions consistently like those made by the Communist Party. Thus, a resolution endorsing the second front was approved August 12, 1942. CSU also endorsed Communist-front organizations, cooperated with and assisted them in many ways; for example, on July 12, 1944, it voted support for the International Labor Defense. It also appointed a committee to work with the League of American Writers. And it gave a mailing list of members of the Conference of Studio Unions to the People's Educational Center, sending brochures of Writers Mobilization to all members.[17]

On the other side, the Communist Party, its official organ on the Pacific Coast, and many of the Communist-front organizations continuously supported the CSU, according to official records. The *People's World*, official Pacific Coast publication of the Communist Party, staunchly supported (with one exception which will be discussed later [18]) CSU, roundly de-

[13] *Ibid.*, pp. 481, 487.
[14] The World Federation of Trade Unions, founded in 1945, included Russian unions; the AFL objected to this and refused to join with the British Trade Union Congress, CIO, and other trade-union centers of the West. These later left the WFTU because it was Communist-dominated. With its headquarters in Prague, Czechoslovakia, the WFTU directs the world Communist trade-union movement.
[15] Sol. Davison, "The Motion Picture Strike," *New Leader*, June 29, 1946, p. 11.
[16] Hollywood, Part 2, 1952, p. 485.
[17] Hollywood, 1947, pp. 543ff.; Hollywood, Part 2, 1952, pp. 485ff.; Jurisdiction, 1948, pp. 1621ff. and 1829ff.
[18] See below, pp. 57–58.

nouncing and criticizing IATSE.[19] The *Motion Picture Daily* of March 17, 1947, contains "an item stating that Louis Weinstock, admitted member of the National Executive Council of the Communist Party, had raised $10,000 in support of the strike of the Conference of Studio Unions." The American Youth for Democracy organization participated publicly in recruiting pickets, and the Western Council of Progressive Business Men also supported CSU.[20]

Abroad, the line-up followed a similar pattern. CSU publications boasted that the organization was receiving support from foreign countries. This support generally came from Communist or pro-Communist sources. Vincente Lombardo Toledo, internationally known pro-Communist leader, pledged the support of the World Federation of Trade Unions and the Latin American Federation of Labor at a CSU mass meeting in Hollywood. Communist trade-union leaders from other Latin American countries and from Egypt also appeared at these meetings.[21] Richard A. Walsh, who succeeded Browne as International IATSE president, reported he found, as a result of personal investigations, that Communists and their sympathizers abroad supported CSU, whereas the non-Communist groups did not; a similar situation existed in Mexico City and Hawaii. He concluded, therefore, that this line-up was an "international affair."[22] The noted motion-picture animator, Walt Disney, related that when he became involved in a strike with CSU, "the first people to smear me and put me on the unfair list were all of the Communist front organizations. I can't remember them all, they change so often. . . . They smeared me, nobody came near to find out what the true facts were. And I even went through the same smear in South America, through some Commie periodicals in South America, and generally throughout the world. All of the Commie groups began smear campaigns against me and my pictures."[23]

In the Hollywood area, division on ideological grounds was rather distinct. Unions from the same international lined up on opposite sides. Brewer describes how these intraunion loyalties were strained: "Presumably we were in a jurisdictional dispute with the painters. . . . One of the trade union principles is that if a man is a member of an international union he should support his union in a jurisdictional dispute. I went down to the Central Labor Council and began to examine into the affiliations of the

[19] Jurisdiction, 1948, pp. 1832–1833.
[20] Hollywood, 1947, p. 544; for a description of Communist-front organizations and their Communist character, see Jurisdiction, 1948, pp. 1549–1551; and Hollywood, 1947, pp. 239, 45–46; see also U.S. Congress, House Committee on Un-American Activities, *Guide to Subversive Organizations and Publications*, 1957.
[21] Hollywood, Part 2, 1952, pp. 517–518.
[22] Jurisdiction, 1948, pp. 16881–16883; see also Hollywood, 1947, pp. 543–545.
[23] *Ibid.*, p. 283.

men in the council. I found that the president . . . was a painter, so I naturally assumed he would support Mr. Sorrell, who was also a painter. On the Executive Board of the Council was . . . [the] business agent of local 683 [IATSE]. I naturally supposed he would support me. But I found on the first vote the painter was on our side and our business agent was on the other side, the side of the Conference of Studio Unions." [24] Indeed, the first secretary of the CSU was president of IATSE Local 683; the officers of this local played an important role in organizing CSU. Another IATSE local captured by the Communists was that of the film technicians. Local 363 was placed under receivership because it supported the CSU strike in 1946, which was contrary to IATSE policy. Brewer also complained that the IATSE Costumers' local was Communist-dominated, but his union was helpless because it lacked the proof required by the California courts.[25] A similar division occurred within the CIO unions in the Los Angeles area. "During the 1945 strike the Los Angeles C.I.O. Industrial Council and the Los Angeles Branch of the Newspaper Guild supported the CSU position. On the other hand, the International Representative of the UAW flatly refused to support the strike and was joined by the right wing leadership of the Steel and Rubber Workers." [26]

Pugilistic-looking, barrel-chested Herbert K. Sorrell, distinguished by his red cauliflower ears and broken nose, carried the burden of making the basic defense for his record and the CSU's. Luck was on his side. Twice he was helped by anti-Communists: once in making his reputation as a local leader and the other time in retaining his hold in a going local union which resulted in his blossoming as the pivotal leader of a powerful movement. Both events were related to the 1937 studio strike. The key anti-Communist who directed that strike on behalf of the crafts was aghast at the inexperienced leadership; he was particularly appalled by the inept handling of the picket lines. At only one studio was there orderly and effectively conducted picketing—the captain in charge was Herbert K. Sorrell. This person recommended to the strike committee that Sorrell— up to this time merely a local union "activist" with no official status and not on the strike committee—be put in charge of all picketing. This opportunity was Sorrell's introduction to responsible leadership. He "appointed his own lieutenants for each studio and instructed them on how to conduct the picket lines, and so forth. It did not take him long to get things well organized." [27] Shortly afterward he became the business agent of his local union.

After losing this strike, prospects for the crafts were dim, especially those for the Painters Union. But Sorrell received another assist, this time

[24] Hollywood, Part 2, 1952, p. 504.
[25] Ibid., pp. 485, 498, 526, 528; Hollywood, 1947, p. 398; Jurisdiction, 1948, p. 1788; IATSE Convention Proceedings, 1948, pp. 206–222, 344.
[26] Davison, op. cit., p. 11.
[27] Robinson testimony in Jurisdiction, 1948, pp. 2384–2385.

from the man he had attacked most violently. Willie Bioff, for reasons of his own, induced, or pressured, the producers to recognize the Painters Union and to give its members a substantial wage increase after the lost strike. Through such recognition, Sorrell was able to affiliate his local union with the basic agreement, whereas before this, locals were represented only through their internationals. Thus, through accident, Sorrell was given the opportunity to become the key person in one of the historic battles between Communists and anti-Communists in the American trade-union movement.

Because Sorrell played the dominant role, he was naturally the target for attacks. In general, the charges were similar to those made against the CSU, namely, the promotion primarily of Communist interests under the guise of militant trade-union activity on behalf of the membership. Sheafs of documents were produced to prove Sorrell's consistently Communist connections and his support of Communist activities. Evidence gathered from individuals intimately associated with him was used to supplement documentary data.

A long and formidable list of fellow-traveler and front associations and activities was compiled and documented; beginning with the year 1937, Sorrell was linked with more than twenty Communist-front movements. Indeed, he proved to be a joiner par excellence, according to the mass of undisputed evidence. A partial list included the Motion Picture Democratic Committee, labor's Non-Partisan League, the Studio Unemployment Conference, the People's Educational Center, the William Schneiderman Committee, the Civil Rights Congress of Northern California, the National Federation of Constitutional Liberties of Southern California, the United American Spanish Aid Committee, the National Conference for Protection of the Foreign Born, American Youth for Democracy, the Workers Alliance, the Los Angeles Students Peace Strike in 1940, the American-Soviet Friendship Society, the Yanks Are Not Coming, and others. He supported the Ellis Patterson slate for delegates to the Democratic National Convention in 1940, during the Stalin-Hitler pact, with slogans such as: "Peace not war. No men—no arms—no loans to foreign powers. . . . We must keep ourselves out of war." He was for the immediate release of Earl Browder and for the drive to raise funds for *People's World*, official publication of the Pacific Coast Communist Party. He supported LaRue McCormic, known Communist, for state senator and Leo Gallagher, on the Communist ticket, for Congressman. He was provisional chairman of the Committee in Defense of Harry Bridges and championed the World Federation of Trade Unions.[28]

[28] Jurisdiction, 1948, pp. 1703–1709, 1619–1621; Hollywood, 1947, pp. 542–543; Hollywood, Part 2, 1952, pp. 497–498; for a more comprehensive list, see California Legislature, Senate Fact-finding Committee on Un-American Activities in California, *Report*, 1947, pp. 169–170, 172–177; for a description of the character of Communist-front organizations, see Jurisdiction, 1948, pp. 1549–1551; Hollywood, 1947, pp.

When a question was raised concerning the names of well-known non-Communists that appeared on some of the lists of front organizations with which Sorrell was associated, Judge Matthew M. Levy, attorney for IATSE and prominent socialist, evaluated the charges as follows: "There is no doubt that those who have studied the Communist situation know that there are important people, nice people, innocent people who are brought in in these conferences, I do not dispute it. I do not say that every person who is a sponsor . . . is a Communist. You have got to take, in order to determine whether a person is a Communist or a fellow traveler, recognition of the fact of how difficult it is in this underground situation to get direct, live evidence in support of Communist affiliation. You take a man's career through a period of years, and when you find that he has through thick and thin, during the storm and has sometime participated in most every important Communist front involved in situations such as these, I say that you have a right to say that kind of person is a person who is utilizing the legitimate organized labor movement for ulterior purposes. . . . Innocent people are from time to time dragged into these situations . . . dragged into these Communist fronts and the reason why you find that many innocent, decent people, even simple people withdraw after a while is because it is recognized after a while that they are Communist fronts.

"But the old standbys always remain, and those old standbys, in all of the Communist fronts are participated in by admitted Communists and by Herbert K. Sorrell." [29] And he clinched his argument: "There is no evidence, to the knowledge of the IATSE, that Mr. Sorrell has resigned or repudiated a single one of his pro-Communist connections. . . . I do not think we can say that modesty is one of Mr. Sorrell's outstanding virtues; and, therefore, his failure to speak up in repudiation of a long pro-Communist past cannot be charged to modesty." [30]

Sorrell was present when Judge Levy made this charge, but he did not contradict it then or when he testified; he contented himself instead with explaining away his association with these movements.[31]

The discerning Roy Brewer elaborated further on the point: "Those of us who are within the trade-union movement in Hollywood, who have had to meet the smear campaign of the Communists for the past several years, and who have had to meet their onslaught and their tactics day in and day out, no longer naïvely consider that non-membership in the Communist Party or the signing of non-Communist affidavits is a guarantee that those

239, 45–46; and California Legislature, Senate Fact-Finding Committee on Un-American Activities in California, *Report*, 1948, "Communist Front Organizations"; for the fellow-traveler record of a considerable number of leaders of locals affiliated with CSU, see Hollywood, Part 2, 1952, pp. 497–498.
[29] Jurisdiction, 1948, pp. 1707–1708.
[30] *Ibid.*, p. 1617.
[31] See below, p. 55–59.

48

who make such declarations and sign such affidavits, have necessarily severed their organizational or ideological bonds with Communism. We must be convinced of their non-Communism by open and out-right condemnation and repudiation of their Communist principles, Communist tactics, Communist organizations, and Communist associates. If, and when Mr. Sorrell and his associates follow this line of action, none shall be happier than we, but until this is done we remain skeptics. Formal disassociation from the Communist movement is an old Communist trick, advised by both Lenin and Stalin to their followers when the going gets hot." [32]

Both documentary evidence and personal testimony were introduced to prove that Sorrell had been a member of the Communist Party. It is not clear from the data whether he joined in 1937 or 1938, but his accusers claim that "he remained in the Party, an active and disciplined party member until 1940. . . . It is my opinion that at that point he made a deal with them that he would be relieved of some of the party tasks, but in return he would carry out their program. . . ." [33]

Documentary evidence of Sorrell's Communist Party membership consisted of a membership card in the name of Herbert Stewart. This is his mother's maiden name. On one of the cards the surname was spelled "Stewart" and on another, "Stuart." Sorrell played on this discrepancy in his defense; he also denied their authenticity.[34] The membership data was unearthed by the Los Angeles police department. Its "undercover men withdrew them from the files at the headquarters of the Communist Party in Los Angeles." [35] Two handwriting experts, one of whom testified in the notorious Lindbergh-Hauptmann case, testified that the handwriting on the cards was that of Herbert K. Sorrell.[36] The Federal Bureau of Investigation of the Department of Justice was also enlisted to examine the cards and its experts also concluded that the signatures of Herb Stewart and Herbert K. Sorrell were written by the same person.[37]

Two witnesses testified in connection with the membership cards. One was the acting captain of the Los Angeles police department in charge of subversive activities, who identified the cards.[38] The other was a person who, as president of District Council No. 4 of the Maritime Federation of the Pacific and as a participant in other union activities on the Pacific

---

[32] Jurisdiction, 1948, p. 1618.

[33] Hollywood, Part 2, 1952, pp. 497–498 (Brewer testimony). The latter statement of course is conjecture, but some former Communists have testified that such arrangements can be made.

[34] See below, p. 60.

[35] Jurisdiction, 1948, pp. 2400–2408.

[36] *Ibid.*, pp. 1607–1608 and 1612; see also p. 1544. Hollywood, 1947, pp. 345–346 and 525, Exhibit 38.

[37] Jurisdiction, 1948, p. 2280; see also *Report*, 1947, of the California Legislature, Senate Fact-Finding Committee on Un-American Activities in California, pp. 171–172.

[38] Jurisdiction, 1948, pp. 2400–2401.

Coast, had considerable experience with Communists and with Communist activities. Invited by the strike committee to act as consultant in 1937, he testified that during that strike he had occasion to associate frequently with Sorrell, having recommended that the latter be put in charge as picket captain. During this association, Sorrell discussed communism with him, defending the philosophy and even showing him his Party card. On the witness stand ten years later, he hesitatingly identified the Party card shown him but was positive Sorrell had told him he was a member.[39]

At crucial moments, Sorrell skillfully avoided confrontation by witnesses having specific and damaging information, for example, when the California legislative committee heard the handwriting experts' testimony following their examination of the signatures on the Communist Party cards.[40] Another instance occurred when Sorrell was given the opportunity to confront Robinson during his appearance before the congressional committee. Sorrell was still in Washington when he was told about a telegram from Robinson, stating: "Can identify Sorrell's Communist membership card as shown to me by him during 1937 studio strike in attempt to convert me. Can furnish detailed information covering this testimony as published, as I was very active in conducting strike." [41]

While Robinson was testifying, one of the subcommittee members suggested: "It is just my thought that since Mr. Robinson is here and Mr. Bodle and Mr. Sorrell saw fit to leave while the hearing was still in progress, that it might be well to inform Mr. Bodle that Mr. Robinson is here and if Mr. Sorrell wishes to return he can come here to check with Mr. Robinson, whom he had already said he did not know." [42] The chairman of the committee stated for the record that he had informed Sorrell accordingly

[39] *Ibid.*, pp. 2375, 2387, and 2397–2398. By now it is common knowledge that important persons were permitted to be secret members. It is also well known that at a later date important persons were not recorded as members. "It is conceded by Respondent and the evidence establishes that some portion of its membership was and is concealed. Party members active as labor leaders, mass organization leaders, members of professions, and others have concealed their party membership from the general public or from organizations in which they worked or in which they were members." U.S. Subversive Activities Control Board, *Herbert Brownell, Jr., Attorney General of the United States, Petitioner vs. Communist Party of the United States of America, Respondent; Report,* 1953 (83d Cong., 1st Sess., Senate Document No. 41), p. 105.

[40] *Report,* 1947, of the Committee on Un-American Activities in California, pp. 171–172; for Sorrell's explanation of how that happened, see Hollywood, 1947, p. 346.

[41] Jurisdiction, 1948, p. 2375. George E. Bodle was Sorrell's attorney and intimate. The California Un-American Activities Committee reported: "George E. Bodle first testified that he did not know whether he had ever received a Communist Party membership card. . . . The other statement was made in an affidavit (1954) which contains a positive statement that he had never been a member of the Communist Party or Communist Political Association. Obviously the Committee can make no present determination other than to present the facts"; 1955, pp. 448–452.

[42] Jurisdiction, 1948, p. 2419.

through committee counsel.[43] After telling members of the subcommittee he "couldn't remember" Robinson, Sorrell departed for Los Angeles before Robinson testified.[44] During the latter's testimony, the chairman directed counsel to communicate with Mr. Sorrell through his attorney; counsel reported that "subject to your direction, I called Mr. Bodle. I took with me to the office the representative of the painters international. I told him of the presence of Mr. Robinson and that you were willing to retain Mr. Robinson here if Mr. Bodle and Mr. Sorrell desired to or would come back and face him. . . . Now, I have not heard from Mr. Bodle. Mr. Gallagher told Mr. Bodle to call Mr. Lindelof and talk with him and that he was to call me back afterwards. I have not heard from him as yet, so I do not know what the Chair will feel disposed to do until we get an answer." [45]

The chairman answered this report: "The Chair has taken the position right along if Mr. Sorrell or his counsel, or delegated counsel from Washington, D.C. wanted to come over to disagree with any of its testimony, I think they would have made an appearance." [46] Sorrell acted in a similar way when IATSE published information pertaining to his Communist membership. He instituted a libel suit against Brewer "and the International president of IATSE." [47] But "the libel suit has never been pressed." [48]

At the height of his power, Sorrell was given a national, or perhaps an international, forum for expounding his position, both the offensive and the defensive sides of it. The Special Subcommittee of the Committee on Education and Labor in the House of Representatives was conducting hearings on jurisdictional disputes in the motion-picture industry, the testimony ultimately filling one lean and two fat volumes. Sorrell testified twice; the second time the testimony dealt with his alleged Communist activities, associations, and general social attitudes. He was given a free hand to develop his case with the assistance of his attorney, George E. Bodle. Occasionally, committee members and counsel interrupted with questions. Sorrell began presenting his case March 3, 1948, and finished March 10. He thus held forth for nearly nine days. The sessions filled 295 printed pages, with 54 lines to the page and 10 words to each line; his testimony for those days therefore totaled about 159,300 words. His presentation was masterful and was skillfully supported by his attorney. His aim, of

[43] *Ibid.*, p. 2445.
[44] *Ibid.*, p. 2391.
[45] *Ibid.*, p. 2441.
[46] *Ibid.*, p. 2442.
[47] Hollywood, 1947, p. 345.
[48] *Ibid.*, p. 398. Sorrell attributed this failure to the bungling of his lawyers; see below, p. 60.

course, was to disarm the committee, the audience, and the public at large. His recital was full of nuances, subtle or crude as the occasion required. An actor every moment, he revealed himself as a fluent speaker with a colorful, homespun vocabulary and a bluff, tough manner, reasonably controlled. Reservedly boastful of fighting his way through life without a college education, and again ostensibly frank, he acknowledged he had occasionally strayed from the straight and narrow, acting unlawfully in conducting mass picket lines, in resorting to rough stuff in organizing, in destroying property and beating up people, and in fighting management and such rival unions as IATSE.[49] He scoffed at threats: "Now, understand, I have been picked on. Personally I have been attacked more times than I want to smear the record up with here, not four or five times, as you have seen in the paper, but many times. I feel, and some people call me a fatalist, I don't think I am in danger from body [anybody?]. I believe in God Almighty. I think that He takes care of His people. I don't die until my time comes, and I will die then, and probably die of pneumonia. Certainly if it is my time to die, they will cut it off.

"And I have no fear of anybody. I have no fear of physical pain, because I have had physical pain to the extent that I know that you only have to endure so much and nature takes care of you—you pass out. And I don't care what it is, you don't have to fear any physical pain. I don't fear the hereafter, and I don't fear no thugs, and I don't fear anybody or anything, and I will take mine as it comes." [50]

He pictured himself as the tough, hard-boiled, humble, trade-union leader in the lower echelons. He scorned labor leaders who imitate big business by occupying sumptuous offices, employing secretaries, using buzzers, etc. Then, by insinuation, he boasted he had resisted temptation and graft and was always open and aboveboard. He shot poisoned barbs at his opponents and poured fiery scorn on them, making various insinuations that indirectly discredited his opponents. He characterized Bioff as "a bum" and "panderer" and Brewer as "a carpetbagger."

As for himself, he was, he said, an innocent, commonplace liberal and humanitarian, converted from a well-to-do conservative. "Up until 1931 or 1932 I was a Republican. I would have voted for Hoover when he ran in 1928, but I happened to be a little bit filthy rich and I had hit the stock market, and my wife and I were on a tour. We toured all over the United States, Canada and Mexico. We just had a grand time. And I did not get a chance to vote. As I say, I changed then, and I voted for Roosevelt. I voted for Roosevelt every time he ran. . . . However, let me make it clear that I did not think they should go to war, but I did think

[49] Jurisdiction, 1948, pp. 1837–1860.
[50] Ibid., p. 1919.

they should arm and keep armed and be prepared if attacked." [51]   By way of emphasizing his lowbrow status, he jocularly referred to the Independent Citizens Committee of the Arts and Sciences and Professions as "one of those high mental names that is over my head." [52]

Having set the proper scene for himself, Sorrell proceeded to discuss specific issues.   In his expansive and loquacious manner, he followed the tactical approach of censuring his "detractors."   According to Sorrell, the horrendous controversy that had the Hollywood motion-picture industry in turmoil was merely a jurisdictional dispute between IATSE and the Carpenters' and Painters' unions.   IATSE aimed to supplant these and other unions by controlling the situation on an industrial-union basis contrary to AFL philosophy.   The Painters, Carpenters, and other crafts were engaged in a life-and-death struggle to preserve and maintain their jurisdictions.[53]   "When there is a strike, or a clear cut jurisdictional issue, it is never the CSU encroaching on the IATSE.   It is the CSU trying to protect themselves from being pushed out of the picture." [54]   Moreover, in this contest the International officials, and particularly those of the Painters International, supported CSU and Sorrell.[55]

His ace in the hole was the Bioff-Browne racketeering scandal.   And Sorrell made the most of it.   He devoted much time to enlarging on the indictment of Bioff for pandering, a charge for which Bioff was convicted but never served sentence.   Then Sorrell related the facts of Bioff's indictment for income-tax evasion, for failure to declare the $100,000 which he received from a motion-picture producer.   This was followed by a recital of the indictment and conviction of Browne and Bioff for extorting money from motion-picture producers.   For good measure, Sorrell quoted a resolution adopted by the IATSE 1940 Convention defending Bioff.   To this he added the information that after Bioff had been exposed and indicted, IATSE Hollywood locals were "browbeaten and had to go along with this racketeer."   And he gleefully recalled that one of Bioff's chief supporters was "J. W. Buzzell, a thief, who stole money and who was removed by President Green because he used money that did not come to him on his pay check."   Then Sorrell threw in this barb: "It will be noted . . . that all A.F. of L. unions supported IATSE except my union and myself.   That was deliberate . . . I tell you this because I want you to know who was lined up against us." [56]

Sorrell's attorney summarized with his client's approval: "The Communist issue was first raised by Browne and Bioff in order to divert attention

[51] Ibid., p. 1877.
[52] Ibid., p. 1882.
[53] Ibid., pp. 1992–1994.
[54] Ibid., p. 1998.
[55] Ibid., pp. 1993–1994, 2030–2032.
[56] Ibid., pp. 1870–1873.

from their racketeering efforts or activities in the motion picture industry. It has been used for the purposes of diverting attention from the real causes of the trouble in the motion picture industry ever since. . . . This fight was a fight for clear unionism. . . . It was a fight to rid the industry of racketeers and gangsters." [57]

From these charges Sorrell made a deft transition to smearing the successors of Browne and Bioff. "You see, Bioff led to put the force on to elect Browne. And they worked together. When you speak of Bioff, you speak of Browne. I mean Browne and Bioff are linked together. When they back out of the picture, you will speak of Walsh and Brewer, or Walsh first and then Brewer. They were together and one is responsible more or less to the other." [58] He charged that after Walsh took over the presidency, few changes occurred in the executive board of the International. Walsh was then accused of receiving sums of money from an assessment fund, which he then deposited in his bank and upon which he paid income tax. When asked for corroborative evidence, Sorrell replied: "Well, I would not like to divulge my information source right now, because it was given to me and I want to go back for more." [59]

Nor were producers neglected or exonerated in this conspiracy charge. In Sorrell's catalogue, this group was another bête noire. "Let me tell you something . . . there is a conspiracy between Richard Walsh, Roy Brewer, and some of the major motion picture producers who have lots of money. . . ." [60] He charged that the producers favored IATSE in hiring, that men were replaced by others carrying IATSE cards. Sorrell charged that there was a conspiracy between IATSE and the producers to "drive the craft unions out of the industry." [61]

But the independent producers were exonerated. "We feel the conspiracy that exists is not only against the Conference of Studio Unions but also takes advantage of the independent producers. We have very good relations with the independent producers. We have given no favors but we do not feel that they are part of the conspiracy." [62]

Sorrell complained by way of proving his point: "We have not had any kind of contract with the producers since 1942, except the interim agreement which we obtained by going on strike in 1946. . . . The producers continuously held us out. They dealt with IATSE, signed contracts with IATSE but did not sign contracts with CSU, and kept us off balance all

[57] *Ibid.*, pp. 1998, 2120.
[58] *Ibid.*, pp. 1999, 2022.
[59] *Ibid.*, p. 2072. From all the sources available, it appears that the records of Walsh and Brewer are unassailable in so far as racketeering and misappropriation of funds are concerned.
[60] *Ibid.*, p. 2063.
[61] *Ibid.*, pp. 77–81, 2074–2076, and 2105.
[62] *Ibid.*, p. 2101.

the time by claiming somebody was asking for jurisdiction. . . . The producers used them [IATSE] to hold us up and keep us from signing new agreements to keep us in turmoil and try to destroy the Conference of Studio Unions." [63]

In defending himself against the charge that he was pro-Communist and had been a member of the Communist Party, Sorrell again assumed an offensive attitude. He did not challenge the accuracy of the long list of pro-Communist resolutions adopted by the CSU, nor did he question the list of Communist-front organizations supported by the CSU. Furthermore, he did not take exception to the documentary data linking him with Communist-front organizations either as a key official or as a participant. He did not disown either the pro-Communist pronouncements bearing his name, among others, or the statements made by him that appeared in print. He nonchalantly explained them away on principle or as a means of expediency which might be used by any devoted official of CSU or by any conscientious, liberal-minded citizen. For each count he had a ready, and seemingly plausible, answer, albeit not always convincing to the critically minded. He did, however, deny outright that he was a Communist: "I would like to answer each and every charge made against me and explain to you so you can judge, and believe me, I want you to know whether I am a Communist or not, in your opinion." [64]

As chairman and sponsor of the Studio Unemployment Conference of 1938, Sorrell belittled the role played by Kibre. The conference consisted of nearly all the AFL craft locals, although boycotted by IATSE. He discredited the Kibre documents because they were made public by I. W. Buzzell, who is "no better than Bioff; he is just a cheap chiseler." Similarly, he disclaimed any knowledge of Irving Hentschel's having played any role in "the so-called rank-and-file movement . . . that comes as a bolt of the heavens." [65]

Sorrell justified accepting help from the CIO and others in the 1937 strike because "we got absolutely nothing out of anyone except our own International people from the AF of L. Because of Buzzell and Bioff we could not get any help from the AF of L unions." And "as you must know, it takes money to run a strike. We went where we could get it. There were some CIO unions who donated very freely. Harry Bridges' CIO longshoremen in San Francisco donated $500 a week for that strike. . . . Some of the liberal actors, writers, directors, and sympathetic people who may or may not be Communists and who may or may not be accused of being Communists helped us substantially with contributions." [66]

[63] *Ibid.*, pp. 2048–2050; see also pp. 2064 and 2067.
[64] *Ibid.*, p. 1872.
[65] *Ibid.*, pp. 1872–1875.
[66] *Ibid.*, p. 1861.

Sorrell supported causes on empirical grounds, because friends asked him, or to pay off debts for assistance given, and for reasons of principle. "I encouraged my local unions to join Labor's Non-Partisan League because in that way I could help to pay off some of the debts that we owed some of the CIO unions." He denied, however, that the league was Communist-dominated. Sorrell disaffiliated from labor's Non-Partisan League in 1941 when John L. Lewis broke with the CIO and took over the league and it in turn was taken over by Republicans.[67]

Sorrell justified aiding Harry Bridges for similar reasons: "Harry Bridges gave me help when I needed it, and the least I could do was to get on Harry Bridges' committee, which meant no work, to keep him from being deported." [68] For the same reason he supported the National Federation of Constitutional Liberties of Southern California. "I think I endorsed that. I usually endorse things like that because people who helped me when I needed help are the people who endorse things of that kind." [69]

Sorrell joined a number of alleged front organizations because some friend or associate asked him to join. "I endorsed the Jewish Relief. I was prevailed upon to sponsor that organization by . . . Abe Isserman . . . a friend of mine, and he has done some things for me, and I think the organization is all right, or I would not have endorsed it." [70]

Through an associate Sorrell became acquainted with the Congress of American-Soviet Friendship. "I was in New York . . . in 1942 . . . Louis Weinstock is the secretary of District Council No. 9 of Painters in New York. Naturally, a painter goes to a painters union. I think that maybe even lawyers go to see other lawyers, I don't know about that; but I know that painters go to see other painters and they do not go looking up paint jobs to see them, they go to the office. I went to the office of Louis Weinstock and he said: 'Oh, this is fine, Herb. I will take you over to a meeting of the Congress of American-Soviet Friendship.'" Sorrell demurred, saying he was not a Communist, but went anyway.[71] He acknowledged, however, that he believes in a part of the program but not in other parts.[72]

There were other organizations Sorrell supported entirely on principle, among them the Schneiderman-Darcy defense committees, because he did

[67] *Ibid.*, pp. 1865, 1937.
[68] *Ibid.*, p. 1893.
[69] *Ibid.*, p. 1884.
[70] *Ibid.*, p. 1884–1885.
[71] *Ibid.*, p. 1926. Weinstock was a member of the general council of the Communist Party; see above, p. 45; Gitlow describes him as "the Communist whip in the AF of L Painters Union" in *The Whole of Their Lives*, Charles Scribner's Sons, New York, 1948, p. 136. See also Philip Zausner, *Unvarnished: the Autobiography of a Union Leader*, Brotherhood Publishers, New York, 1941; and U.S. Subversive Activities Control Board, *Herbert Brownell, Jr., Attorney General of the United States, Petitioner, v. United May Day Committee, Respondent*, Docket No. 111–53, 1956.
[72] Jurisdiction, 1948, p. 1901.

not believe "you should kick people around because they are members of a minority group." [73] The same considerations motivated him when he signed "a petition to release Earl Browder from jail. . . . Now let me tell you why I did it. This I am told, that Earl Browder falsified in some way his signature on a passport, and I was told that the most anybody ever served was 6 months for that offense, and I was told that Earl Browder because he was of a minority group, got either 4 or 5 years. . . . If you are going to penalize the guy because he is a Communist . . . but if you are going to put him in jail, give him the same treatment whether he is a rich man, poor, beggar, Republican, Democrat, or Communist." Then he flung out: "I signed it, and not only did I sign it, but I wrote to President Roosevelt, and believe it or not, President Roosevelt pardoned him. I do not know who is the biggest Communist, me or the man I admired most." [74]

Sorrell's adeptness at equivocation is aptly illustrated by his explanation for sponsoring and participating in a testimonial dinner for the publicly known Communist, Leo Gallagher. "Now let me tell you why I did that. I know Leo Gallagher, Leo Gallagher is a little Irishman, and he ran on the Communist ticket one time, so they tell me, and Leo Gallagher will defend Communists, but he will also defend anybody that is behind the 8-ball. I know Leo Gallagher as a little guy who goes to mass every Sunday. I know Leo Gallagher is a guy who has been over to Russia, who knows all about these things. I admire Leo Gallagher for the things he has done, and not just defending the Communists, because that is only one of the very many nice things that Leo Gallagher has done." [75]

To clinch his defense, Sorrell presented evidence of his differing with Communist policy, criticizing desultorily Soviet Russia and communism in the course of his recital. He read at length criticism of himself from the *People's World*: He was "a militant labor leader once," but now he was playing around with anti-Communists, advocating antilabor legislation, supporting a lockout when it would have been better to return to work in order to "preserve democratic unions in the studios, and now he aims to expel a union member because of Communist membership." [76] Sorrell stressed especially that the *People's World* criticized him for calling the studio strike when the war was still on in 1945, contrary to the no-strike pledge, which the Communists regarded as especially sacred. But close scrutiny of the editorial reveals a friendly attitude toward Sorrell, an uncommon trait when a Communist paper attacks a labor leader with whom it differs. "This responsibility is particularly heavy because the Conference of Studio Unions, and its leader, Herbert Sorrell, have established a record of progressive and

---

[73] *Ibid.*, pp. 1886–1887.
[74] *Ibid.*, p. 1890.
[75] *Ibid.*, p. 1892.
[76] *Ibid.*, pp. 1964, 1975, 2026.

patriotic unionism. They have been staunch supporters within the AF of L and the Community of the Roosevelt administration, and the war effort. . . . This is more disturbing when John L. Lewis and other mis-leaders of labor are trying to stampede the unions into abandonment of their strike pledge." [77] And several months later, while the war was still on, an editorial appeared in the May 1, 1945, issue of the *People's World* entitled "A Good Guy Headed Wrong." Its attitude was critical but friendly. "One of Hollywood's most accomplished actors has never had a screen credit. His name has never been on the screen," etc., etc. Then the last paragraph chides him gently: "Herb Sorrell has always been what everybody calls a good guy but when he puts himself and thousands of workers and their families in the position of breaking the no-strike pledge and hindering and hampering the war effort, he's got a tough job of still carrying on with his time-tried role of the honest crusader for democracy, clean unionism and the common man."

But Sorrell's opponents called attention to "a couple of important factors" in this connection. As has happened so often when the Communists were confronted with a development in which the attitude of the Party was unknown to them, they remained silent until the truth of the Hollywood studio strike was revealed to them from the fountainhead. Brewer pointed out that "Sorrell announced the strike in Hollywood on March 9th" to be called March 11, 1945. "Now, if the *People's World* had been so violently opposed to the strike, it is logical to assume that the minute that announcement was made there would have been a protest against it. There was not a word in the *People's World* on Monday, March 12, although all the papers in America, particularly were headlining the fact that on March 12 a major strike had occurred in the Hollywood motion-picture studios. There wasn't one word of recognition that such a strike existed, in the *People's World*, until Thursday, March 15." [78]

As soon as the war came to an end, the *People's World* and the pro-Communists took up the cudgels in their customary, vigorous manner in support of the strike. In a headline August 21, 1945, the *People's World* proclaimed, "CIO lends hand in film strike—unionists join picket lines; urge others to follow." It also declared that the "tempo of the film strike has accelerated here following Los Angeles' CIO vote Friday to boycott theatres exhibiting struck films." [79] And "increasingly as the strike has strengthened, IATSE has resorted to red-baiting tactics common to those used against democratic trade unions by union-wrecking forces. . . ."

The September 21, 1945, issue of the *People's World* devotes a full page,

[77] *Ibid.*, p. 1963.
[78] *Ibid.*, pp. 2425–2426.
[79] The Los Angeles Industrial Union Council was at this time under Communist control.

including photographs of pickets, to the "Truth about the Hollywood Film Strike—Studio Workers Fight for Basic Union Rights." The first paragraph declares, "Though the Hollywood film strike has been called many things, fundamentally it is a struggle of workers to preserve democratic trade unions in the motion picture industry." It then indicates "how you can help." This issue also runs a two-column editorial in bold type that, among other things, proclaims: "The Hollywood strike must be supported. The Hollywood strike must be won."

To prove he is not pro-Communist, Sorrell went out of his way to criticize the Communists, almost lightheartedly. "Communists as I have seen them, are usually—we call them intellectuals. They have a lot of theory, but no guts to go ahead with anything. . . . But if I had my way, no Communist would be an officer or an organizer or a business agent of the union, because he would spend all his time organizing Communists instead of spending it organizing the workers." He even accused them of "trying to destroy the Conference of Studio Unions." [80]

Soviet Russia also came in for gentle and casual criticism. "Now you understand I don't think I would live very long in Russia. Over here you raise a lot of hell if I don't think the way you do; you have that right and I will defend that right. But over there I understand they take you out and shoot you, so I am sure I would disagree with somebody and I am sure they wouldn't do like they did in Hollywood, drag you out in the desert and leave you out there; they'd actually shoot you." [81]

Sorrell also criticized the Czechoslovakian development. "It is a rather sickening thing, that Czechoslovakian situation. I think this is one of the worst things that could happen. . . . However, I think it is too bad and I thought it was too bad when Hitler took it over. I think it is too bad when Russia takes over." [82]

In his customary manner, Sorrell qualified his criticism of the Communists. He introduced a Communist pamphlet discussing labor conditions in the studios. "Now in this program it gives everybody the devil. Everybody has done wrong. They give the IATSE a black eye; they give us a black eye because they say we are the 'irresponsible leadership.' . . . Everything the Communists do isn't bad, because they had to do a lot of good things on their way in order to attract attention. This is one of the good things that I think will hit our studio workers." [83]

There is no record of Sorrell's seriously criticizing communism or Soviet Russia or condemning any of their actions except when he was defending himself at the congressional hearings against charges of being a Communist.

[80] Jurisdiction, 1948, pp. 1917–1918.
[81] Ibid., p. 2128.
[83] Ibid., p. 2070.
[88] Ibid., pp. 2067–2069.

Sorrell bolstered his defense by emphasizing that he had supported liberal movements, too: "I forgot to mention that prior to this time, one of the organizations I joined was called the Utopian Society. I do not know whether that is considered a red organization or not. It never amounted to anything. They really did not know where they were going. I joined it to find out what it was, and it fizzled out.

"Also, I joined the Epic Movement. That was a movement to elect Upton Sinclair as governor. Downey who is now senator from California, ran for Lieutenant Governor ... Culbert Olson ran for the State Senate, and we elected a number of these people.

"Now that might be considered a regular organization, because Upton Sinclair—that was during the depression, and he advocated production for use for the surplus of the people that couldn't make a living. It made very good sense to me, and I worked very hard on that in that campaign." [84] As compared with the list of Communist and pro-Communist organizations supported by Sorrell, these two so-called "liberal groups" were indeed few in number.

Notwithstanding the testimony of the two handwriting experts and the testimony of other persons, Sorrell flatly denied he was ever a member of the Communist Party. The card itself he declared "a fake." He claimed he was never confronted with the original. When he was questioned closely, he admitted that the signature on the cards looked like his. "I would say it looks pretty much like I wrote it. If you would say this was my handwriting, I would say that the 'Herb Stewart' looks like my handwriting...." [85] And when he was asked if he had made any effort to check with the handwriting experts, he replied that he had never gotten around to it.[86] He was not shown these cards when he appeared before the California legislative committee in 1941, and in 1946 he was involved in strike litigation and was therefore unable to appear before the state committee investigating the matter. Perhaps his attorney advised him wrongly. "I did a lot of things on advice of attorneys that did not always work out. Maybe I did not have the right attorney." [87]

He gave a similar reason to explain why he had not pressed the libel suit against Walsh and Brewer and IATSE when they circulated information concerning the Communist membership cards. He had broken with the attorneys who were handling the case; they withdrew the bond "without prejudice and without consulting" Sorrell. As a result, he was not able to go through with the lawsuit.[88]

A committee member challenged Sorrell as to why he did not dissociate

[84] *Ibid.*, p. 1866.
[85] *Ibid.*, p. 1953.
[86] *Ibid.*, pp. 1901–1903.
[87] *Ibid.*, pp. 1953–1954.
[88] *Ibid.*, pp. 1933–1935.

himself from the various Communist and pro-Communist organizations and activities. "Don't you think that would be the time, even though they might seemingly be adopting your program ... for you to keep yourself separate from them, rather than having your name linked with them in any way ...?" As usual, Sorrell had a ready answer: "Look, I always work to get a thing done, I work with them. And when they depart from my way of thinking, I break with them.... Now some of these things that I think are all right, you might take as a Communist front, and I still do not think they do harm." [89]

Sorrell also offered some generalizations on the difficulty of detecting whether organizations are fronts. His criterion is, "Do they come out with stuff that is good.... I belong to a lot of things I thought were good that have been called Communist-front organizations, and maybe they were, I don't know. They were good. The things I belonged to were good.... Of course, it depends who does the interpreting too, because some of these things that are called Communist-front organizations to me are just good organizations doing good." [90]

[89] *Ibid.*, pp. 1881, 1885.
[90] *Ibid.*, pp. 2069, 2070.

7

Role of the Talent Guilds

Organizationally the Communist movement in the Hollywood trade-union field was two-pronged. Although the CSU, consisting of unions of the crafts, was the main base of operations where trade unions were concerned, the "talent," or "prestige," guilds were not overlooked. But the Communists did not succeed in establishing hegemony in this sector as they had among the craft unions. In so far as placing their people in strategic positions in the Screen Actors Guild and the Screen Directors Guild (two of the three talent guilds) was concerned, they had little success. Indeed, the Screen Actors Guild took a clear-cut position on the Communist issue,[1] although some of its prominent members individually supported the Communist side.[2] Partly because the officers of the Screen Actors Guild made their peace jurisdictionally with IATSE as early as 1937, but chiefly because its leaders became alerted very early to Communist manipulations, this guild at all times resisted Communist domination, although it tried at times to play a neutral part in order to keep production going. As the struggle became more tense and the Communist threat more obvious, the Screen Actors Guild joined vigorously in the house cleaning. Here, too, the motives were undoubtedly mixed. The actors were as eager to protect the good name of the industry for economic reasons as they were to check communism for patriotic considerations. Robert Montgomery, a member of the Actors Guild since 1933 and holder of various high offices, including the presidency, when asked if he had "ever, at any time, noted any Communist influence within the guild," stated: "We have had in the Screen Actors Guild, as have other labor unions, a very militant, a very small minority, well organized, well disciplined. Those people have been active since as far back as 1933." By way of illustrating the extent

---

[1] See pp. 35–36 below for a discussion of this phase.
[2] See the testimony of Edward G. Robinson, *Hearing before the House Committee on Un-American Activities*, 81st Cong., 2d Sess., 1951; Larry Parks's testimony in *Communist Infiltration of Hollywood Motion Picture Industry, Hearings before the House Committee on Un-American Activities*, 82d Cong., 1st Sess., 1951, pp. 78–111; hereafter this report will be referred to as "Hollywood, Part 1, 1951."

of Communist strength, Montgomery related an instance in 1946 when he introduced a resolution containing an article "which came out flatfootedly against any real Communist or Fascist influence in the ranks of labor or in the motion-picture industry [and which] seemed to cause—again from a small minority—a tremendous opposition. Whether that opposition was Communist or not, I am not qualified to state. I only know that they behaved exactly as left-wing groups in various labor unions have behaved in the past and do behave at present." [3] This group which Montgomery referred to was overwhelmingly defeated.

George L. Murphy, a member of the Actors Guild for more than ten years who had held important top offices, including several terms as president, presented another concrete illustration. During the 1946 strike conducted by the CSU, the Screen Actors Guild tried to get the parties involved to submit the dispute over jurisdiction to a vote under NLRB auspices. The producers agreed, but the union leaders refused. Because the guild was under pressure to take sides, a membership meeting was called during which each side presented its case. Then a vote was taken by secret ballot, with 97.3 per cent voting not to join the strike. "Based on that figure, I would say we could safely put the figure of active Communists at below one per cent in the Screen Actors Guild, because, I assume, as is generally the case with those people, all of their people voted and some of ours may not have." [4]

Of some 500 members in the Directors Guild, only 7 were members of the Communist Party. They were outstanding directors and caucused but did not exercise undue influence in the organization.[5]

The situation was different in the third of these three talent guilds, the Screen Writers Guild. While this guild was not as completely under Communist control as the CSU, it nevertheless supported the crafts effectively. Besides, as a whole and through its members as individuals, this guild played a large role in the Hollywood community in furthering the Communist cause. An astute but not unbiased observer, Roy M. Brewer, describes its influence: "During this period, Mr. Lawson's unit had developed their fondest expectations. In 1945, the atmosphere was almost perfect from their standpoint. At that time, the Communist group in the Screen Writers Guild and the fronts which they controlled completely dominated the intellectual thought of the community. Anybody who dared to express himself openly as opposed to Communism found himself ostracized socially and otherwise." Mr. Brewer then proceeded to give

[3] *Hearings by the House Committee on Un-American Activities Regarding the Communist Infiltration of the Motion Picture Industry*, 80th Cong., 1st Sess., 1947, hereafter referred to as "Hollywood, 1947," pp. 264–265.
[4] *Ibid.*, pp. 208–209.
[5] See testimony of Edward Dmytryk, Hollywood, Part 2, 1952, pp. 413–414, and that of Frank Wright Tuttle, p. 629.

illustrations.[6]   This characterization is supported by others, some of whom
had been active in inner circles but had defected.   Edward Dmytryk, a
former active Communist member and a famous screen director, testified
that the Screen Writers Guild "largely led the fight in Hollywood on
various Communist-front activities." [7]

When the Screen Writers Guild was organized in 1933, the Communist
screen writers, many of them world-famous names like Donald Ogden
Stewart, Dalton Trumbo, and Ring Lardner, Jr., managed to elect a number of their group to the board of directors.   By 1937, they had seven
members out of fifteen.   At this time, there was strong sentiment against
them, and the opposition organized to dislodge them from control.   But
the Communists very cleverly preached unity.   A motion was made and
carried to retain the entire existing board of directors.   From then on, the
Communists dominated this guild, including control of the official paper.[8]
They resorted to the usual techniques of the Communists in dominating
labor organizations.   One prominent writer, who belonged to the opposition, complained: "The meetings I have attended have been conducted so
that the Communists have downed anyone who attempts to raise a non-
Communist voice. . . ." [9]   Another participant described how meetings were
prolonged: "They call a meeting, they start arguments, it gets to be around
twelve o'clock and they are still going, the people go home and then they
pass what they want." [10]

The dominating figure in directing Communist activities in Hollywood
was a member of the Screen Writers Guild, John Howard Lawson.   He
was one of the "Hollywood Ten," convicted for contempt of Congress.[11]
Various former Communist Party members testified that he was a member
of the Party.   His record in support of Communist causes and fronts is
much longer than that of Sorrell.   As presented to the congressional committee, it takes up more than six pages in small type.[12]   Lawson did not
take issue with the record.   During the notorious hearings on Hollywood
in 1947, he followed a course of conduct now familiar as the one usually
followed by Communists appearing at trials and hearings.   He insisted
upon reading denunciatory statements, presenting arguments instead of an-

[6] Hollywood, Part 2, 1952, pp. 488–491; John Howard Lawson was a key figure,
as will be shown in succeeding pages. See also Report, 1947, of the California
Legislature, Senate Fact-Finding Committee on Un-American Activities in California, pp. 260–262, where George Campbell testified that, as a Communist, he
was a member of a cell directed by John Howard Lawson from 1937–1940.

[7] See testimony of Morrie Ryskind, Hollywood, 1947, p. 182; testimony of Richard
J. Collins, Hollywood, Part 1, 1951, p. 228; testimony of Edward Dmytryk, ibid.,
pp. 413 and 415.

[8] Hollywood, 1947, p. 125, testimony of John Charles Moffitt.

[9] Ibid., p. 62, testimony of Samuel Grosvenor Wood.

[10] Ibid., pp. 184–187; Hollywood, Part 2, 1952, p. 413.

[11] See below, pp. 75–76.

[12] Hollywood, 1947, pp. 296–304, and also pp. 174–177 and 110–112.

64

swering questions, denouncing procedures as illegal, fascist, reactionary, designed to destroy unions, interfering with freedom of speech and thought, redbaiting, etc. From the beginning, he was obstreperous and argumentative in response to questions; he declared the committee illegal, claiming that its procedure was designed to break unions, to persecute innocent people, to deny freedom of press and speech. Mr. Lawson: "You have spent one week vilifying me before the American public. . . . And you refuse to allow me to make a statement on my right as an American citizen. . . . The rights of American citizens are important in this room here, and I intend to stand up for those rights. . . . The raising of any question here in regard to membership, political beliefs, or affiliations is absolutely beyond the powers of the committee." [13] These were Lawson's responses to questions from committee counsel and members; they reflected an attitude on the part of pro-Communist witnesses that was planned and studied in advance, as some witnesses admitted at later hearings.[14] Ten of the witnesses at this hearing were cited for contempt and convicted, with the United States Supreme Court sustaining the convictions on appeal. Their case became notorious as that of the "Hollywood Ten." After serving their jail sentence, several of them recanted and then testified before the committee in an orderly manner.

Former Communists who were active with Lawson in Hollywood agreed that he was the pivotal figure in the Communist apparatus. One testified that "he was considered to be the last word." [15] Another described him as the "high lama" of the Communist Party in Hollywood.[16] A third was more explicit. He described John Howard Lawson as "the leader of the party. The intellectual leader of the party. A dictator, and absolutely the last word, against whom you couldn't say a word. You were slapped down. He was, no doubt, a man of great knowledge, no doubt a tremendous actor. I felt he was absolutely heartless." [17] Instances were cited to show how he injected himself into situations on behalf of the Communist Party, and some witnesses told with considerable relish how skillfully he adapted himself during sudden reversals of Party policy.

The president of the Screen Writers Guild, Emmett Lavery, was not accused of being a Communist; rather, he was charged with being consciously a fellow traveler. Morrie Ryskind, who was one of the early

[13] Hollywood, 1947, pp. 290–296; for other instances of a witness' defying a committee, see *ibid.*, testimony of Dalton Trumbo, pp. 329–334; see also pp. 112 and 125. Trumbo was the first editor of the *Screen Writer*. See also testimony of Ring Lardner, Jr., *ibid.*, pp. 479–482; for latter's Communist record, see pp. 483ff.
[14] Hollywood, Part 2, 1952, Dmytryk testimony, pp. 426–428.
[15] Hollywood, Part 3, 1952, p. 630.
[16] Hollywood, Part 2, 1952, p. 417.
[17] Testimony of Nicholas Bella, *Communist Methods of Infiltration (Entertainment)*, *Hearings before the House Committee on Un-American Activities*, 83d Cong., 2d Sess., 1954, p. 7254.

opponents of Communist control in the Screen Writers Guild, said: "I would say that today, under the leadership of Mr. Emmett Lavery, the guild is completely controlled by the Communists. I think this is proven by the publication, the *Screen Writer*, which is edited by Mr. Gordon Kahn." [18]

Rupert Hughes, who had bitter word battles with the Communists, insisted: "Lavery is a good Catholic, he says, but I say a man whose views are Communist, whose friends are Communists, and whose work is Communistic, is a Communist." [19]

Lavery appeared in his own defense. Literate and polished, rounding out his phrases correctly, he was as evasive as Sorrell but less loquacious. He resented accusations of communism, particularly the charge that he was "a Communist masquerading as a Catholic." He then expounded his philosophy: "Let me say, frankly, that I take my social essays from the Gospels of the Apostles and not from Karl Marx. In particular, I take my social essays from the encyclicals of Leo XIII. The Catholic Church has a broad affirmative social program which is rather far reaching, very progressive and very democratic. I believe in it. To make it more concrete, my approach to the field of social action is identical with that of people such as Archbishop Lucey of San Antonio. Bishop Haas, of Wisconsin [*sic*]; Bishop Sheil, of Chicago. . . ." He disagreed that communism was a present danger, defended various Communist-front organizations, quibbled about the Anti-Nazi League and its successor, American Peace Mobilization. Naturally, he defended the Screen Writers Guild as a conservative organization and terminated his testimony by reiterating that, by setting an example, by leading a better life, he would accomplish more than by fighting communism. When asked, "As you watch the aggressive imperialistic policy of Soviet Russia by diplomatic moves backed up by military threats in its encirclement of all the border countries in Europe and see that paralysis creeping over Europe, how would you combat that?" Lavery's answer was emphatic and concise: "I still think . . . the answer is to live a better life at home and live a better life abroad." [20]

[18] Hollywood, 1947, p. 187; see also p. 125.
[19] *Ibid.*, p. 129; for further citations on Lavery's social outlook, see also pp. 123–124.
[20] Hollywood, 1947, pp. 419–459; see also *Report*, 1947, of the Committee on Un-American Activities in California, pp. 281–288—he conducted himself in a similar manner before this committee.

8

Role of Stagehands Union

IATSE, leading the fight against the Communists, naturally bore the brunt of the opposition's attack and carried most of the responsibility. It is a matter of speculation, of course, whether IATSE would have conducted the vigorous battle on principle alone if its jurisdiction—indeed, its very existence—had not been so effectively challenged in Hollywood by CSU. The perspicacious Brewer acknowledged this motivation: "And recognizing that the purpose of closing the studios down was to destroy our union, it naturally became paramount to our interests that they not succeed in their endeavors." [1]

Although there was a feeling that the Communists were capitalizing on the situation, no concerted effort to fight them was made until May, 1945, when Brewer was put in charge of IATSE interests in Hollywood. President Browne attacked the Communists at the IATSE convention in 1940,[2] but he failed to follow up his verbal attacks with action. IATSE was also slow in cleansing itself of racketeers and gangsters. It proceeded in a forthright manner only when stimulated by the scandal of Browne and Bioff, with its attendant, unfavorable publicity, and by the persistence of CSU and its allies in capitalizing on this black record. Indeed, when Brewer arrived in Hollywood in 1945, his assignment was merely "to attempt to resolve the jurisdictional dispute between his union and the Painters." [3] Not until the strike of 1945 did Brewer become convinced of the Communist angle; then his next step was to convince other interested parties of the threatening situation. President Walsh, Brewer's superior, slowly accepted his diagnosis, but it took Brewer longer to convince top American Federation of Labor leaders. There was also difficulty in getting others to recognize the problem. "During the course of the strike (1945), it had been almost impossible for us to convince people of the Communist nature of this situa-

---

[1] *Hearings by the House Committee on Un-American Activities Regarding the Communist Infiltration of the Motion Picture Industry*, 80th Cong., 1st Sess., 1947, hereafter referred to as "Hollywood, 1947," p. 354.
[2] IATSE Convention Proceedings, 1940, p. 78.
[3] Hollywood, 1947, p. 347.

tion. Everyone thought we were only trying to justify our position, and we were not able to convince even Eric Johnston [president of the Motion Picture Association of America] that the real trouble was this Communist influence. . . . The AF of L realized that Sorrell had been an unruly individual, but they were not convinced that Communist infiltration was as serious as we pointed out to them. . . ." [4]

There was also general confusion with reference to Communist intrigue, characteristic of the rest of the country, that was obscured further by the shocking scandal of Browne and Bioff. As Brewer describes the situation: "I think it is very important to recognize that in this conflict in Hollywood, as is almost always the case in a conflict in which the Communists are involved, you never get a chance to fight it out on a pure Communist and anti-Communist issue. If you did, it would be relatively simple. The real danger of Communists is that they come in and exploit a disagreement, as they are doing throughout the nation and throughout the world, and create a situation which causes a violent conflict; and while they may not be the ones who fight all of the war, they are certainly the ones who direct it and who benefit from the victory." [5]

Concerning the aftermath of the Browne-Bioff affair, Brewer said: "In the wake of this scandal, there appeared a vacuum and men who had been trying to beat off the Communist movement [1939] were almost helpless. It was difficult to determine as to which of these individuals were honestly opposing the dishonest element and which were Communist. So it proved to be a boon to the Communists in discrediting all the talk that had been built up about Communist infiltration." [6]

When the indefatigable Brewer became convinced of the Communists' role in the Hollywood union situation, he proceeded systematically to develop an intensive opposition. His fight against the Communists, possibly because of his socialist background, was conducted on an enlightened and ethical basis. He conscientiously differentiated between liberals, democratic socialists, and totalitarians.

In this anti-Communist struggle, IATSE was assisted by other union groups whose local leaders were familiar with the situation through proximity. The position of the Screen Actors Guild has already been referred to. Some of the local crafts not especially involved in jurisdictional differences, such as the Teamsters, who had members employed in the studios, supported IATSE. So did the AFL Los Angeles Central Labor Union and the California State Federation of Labor.

[4] *Communist Infiltration of Hollywood Motion Picture Industry, Hearings before the House Committee on Un-American Activities*, 82d Cong., 2d Sess., 1952, pp. 512–513; hereafter this report will be referred to as "Hollywood, Part 2, 1952."
[5] *Ibid.*, p. 496.
[6] *Ibid.*, p. 481.

Efforts were also made to organize nonparticipants in the community to aid in the anti-Communist fight. One of these groups was the Motion Picture Alliance for the Preservation of American Ideals, founded in 1944, which consisted of persons in the industry and in the community but had no particular connection with labor. At one time this group boasted 1,100 members, many of them prominent leaders in their respective organizations.[7] But the going was rough. One of the founders and leaders complained: "I think we were very conscious of it, had been for some time, but like everyone else, we probably hadn't done anything, because it is quite an effort and you get quite smeared, and a lot of people would like to duck that. It is fun to play bridge, for instance, rather than to check on something like that." [8]

On the other hand, because of the confusion caused by racketeering and the jurisdictional issues, many articulate disinterested groups sided with CSU. The Catholic archdiocese, sustained by the archbishop and his official organ, vigorously supported Sorrell and the CSU. Two priests assigned by the archbishop published a report blaming the producers and declaring: "The strike cannot be beclouded with cries of Communism and radicalism. . . . The strike is not Communist inspired nor Communist dominated." This report was published in the official paper of the archdiocese, March 24, 1947.[9] A prominent Jesuit priest, a member of the faculty of Loyola College, Los Angeles, wrote several favorable articles between 1945 and 1947 which appeared in the well-known Catholic weekly, *Commonweal*. He also testified before the congressional committee. In the June 20, 1947, issue of *Commonweal*, he wrote eloquently of Sorrell's possessing "certain qualities which, to me, are a reflection of genuine holiness." Father Durme also testified in 1948 that "I am completely convinced in my mind Mr. Sorrell is not a Communist." The holy father also positively denounced the Communist Party card attributed to Sorrell as a forgery. On the other hand, he denounced Brewer as a self-seeker.[10]

The press was divided. *Variety*, the accepted trade paper, definitely took up the cudgels for Sorrell and CSU. Beginning in 1939, *Variety* carried on a virtual crusade against Bioff and IATSE. In its cryptic, journalistic style, it also whooped it up for CSU and Sorrell as late as 1947: "Sorrell is the type of representative of which all labor can be proud. He makes a deal. His men live up to it. He is from the ranks of his craft." Sorrell

---

[7] Testimony of Mrs. Lela E. Rogers, Hollywood, 1947, p. 230; see p. 56 for statement of principles.

[8] Testimony of Samuel Grovenor Wood, Hollywood, 1947, p. 58.

[9] *Jurisdictional Disputes in the Motion Picture Industry, Hearings before a Special Subcommittee of the House Committee on Education and Labor*, 80th Cong., 2d Sess., 1948, p. 1971. This source will hereafter be cited as "Jurisdiction, 1948."

[10] *Ibid.*, pp. 1964–1970.

later accused the editors of *Variety* of yielding to pressure for business reasons and turning against him.[11]

Most high officials of the international unions involved were concerned primarily with safeguarding or extending their jurisdiction and were indifferent to the Communist charge. They either ignored it or dismissed it as unimportant, although they were thoroughly familiar with Communist tactics and objectives and had, in other situations, generally acted against them. In supporting CSU, these international officials disregarded the warning of their own California Federation of Labor and that of the Los Angeles Central Labor Union.[12] They also seemed unconcerned by the warning issued by the chairman of the three-member special committee of the AFL executive council appointed to study the Hollywood jurisdictional problem. Felix H. Knight, president of the Brotherhood of Railway Carmen, vice-president of the AFL, and chairman of the executive council committee, reported in 1948: "There is a very bitter feeling in that industry in Hollywood and there are numerous other interests working there, some of them working with these people, but for the ultimate result of their taking over and then we would have other organizations representing these people in Hollywood." [13]

Two Internationals in particular had large stakes jurisdictionally, the Carpenters and the Painters. Others, such as the Electrical Workers, Machinists, Plumbers, and Building Service Employees, were also affected but on a smaller scale. In a joint meeting in Chicago, the International presidents of these unions notified the producers that they were supporting CSU in its 1945 strike.[14]

The International presidents of the Carpenters and Painters staunchly, even stubbornly, supported Sorrell and CSU. The late William L. Hutcheson, taciturn and willful president of the Carpenters and vice-president of the AFL, boasted: "No Communist can obtain or retain membership in the Brotherhood if it becomes known that he is a Communist. . . .[15] We would not take on as a cooperative to assist us to gain our ends, any known Communist. . . .[16] I have told Mr. Sorrell to his face that if he were a Communist, I did not want to have anything to do with him. . . ." [17]

When asked, "In other words, you do not have any personal knowledge of any affiliation of any kind that Mr. Sorrell or any of his co-workers . . . have associated with the Communists?" Mr. Hutcheson replied, "I have none other but rumors." When pressed further, "But for instance, when

[11] *Ibid.*, pp. 2001–2018; 2028–2038, and 2060.
[12] Sol. Davison, "The Motion Picture Strike," *New Leader*, June 29, 1946, p. 11.
[13] Jurisdiction, 1948, p. 1538.
[14] *People's World*, July 23, 1945, p. 4.
[15] Jurisdiction, 1948, p. 1380; see also pp. 1414–1415.
[16] *Ibid.*, p. 1577.
[17] *Ibid.*, p. 1558.

you see one charge after the other saying a man is a member of this group . . . ," he replied, "If I were to believe everything that I have heard and read in the papers about myself, I would be ashamed to even look in the mirror." [18] As the members of the committee delved further into the question, Hutcheson became facetious and argumentative and began to quibble.[19]

Was Hutcheson forthright in his position? He avoided visiting Hollywood to make a personal investigation,[20] but there is evidence to indicate he was well informed. Ronald Regan, then president of the Screen Actors Guild, told of a conversation Hutcheson had in 1946 with a committee of the guild: "He asked the Screen Actors Guild to submit terms to Mr. Walsh, for Walsh to give in the settling of this strike, and he told us to tell Walsh that if he would give in on these terms, he, in turn, would run this Sorrell and the other Commies out—I am quoting him. . . ." [21] The late Edward Arnold, then an Actors Guild officer, substantiated the holding of a conference with Mr. Hutcheson.[22]

Joseph Combrano, who described himself as "general representative" of William L. Hutcheson, president of the United Brotherhood of Carpenters and Joiners,[23] was fully aware of the Communist threat in Hollywood. In testifying before the three-man committee of the American Federation of Labor, he referred first to the early efforts at Communist infiltration when "we were all pretty well disturbed over the situation, and while the Carpenters themselves had some jurisdictional disputes, they were all set aside to clean up this disturbance. . . ." And, referring to the current situation: "We will fool around here until somebody else comes in to take over, which will happen just as sure as you are living, because such a moment is here already and implanted in those studios." [24]

It is hardly conceivable that Hutcheson was not kept fully informed by his personal assistant. Moreover, he had experienced encounters with the Communists. In the twenties, they were a problem in his International. He fought them vigorously and successfully. As vice-president of the AFL and delegate to its conventions, he was familiar with the Communist issue in the unions.[25]

Amiable and dynamic Lawrence P. Lindelof, president of the International Brotherhood of Painters, Decorators and Paperhangers of America,

[18] *Ibid.*, p. 1559.
[19] *Ibid.*, pp. 1410–1414.
[20] *Ibid.*, pp. 1703–1704.
[21] Hollywood, 1947, p. 216.
[22] IATSE Convention Proceedings, 1948, pp. 231–232.
[23] Jurisdiction, 1948, p. 530.
[24] *Ibid.*, p. 1703.
[25] Maxwell C. Raddock, *Portrait of an American Labor Leader, William L. Hutcheson,* American Institute of Social Science, New York, 1955, Chap. 11, "The Fifth Column," pp. 159–166.

Sorrell's parent union, assumed an attitude similar to that of Hutcheson. He proclaimed: "We have in our constitution the same clause as is contained in the constitution of the Brotherhood of Carpenters and Joiners, and while I heard the indictments against our representative, or the local representative of Hollywood, Herb Sorrell, I have always adopted the policy that I want to hear both sides of the story ... before I commit myself." Then he added that he had known Sorrell about ten or eleven years. "I cannot say that Herb Sorrell is a Communist. He may be a radical, he may have some very progressive ideas, but I could not accuse Herb Sorrell of being a Communist." Lindelof also proudly asserted that, during the last six months, his organization expelled twelve Communists.[26] His testimony is incredible in light of his experience with Communists. Besides, he had presided over his International's convention at which Sorrell defended the WFTU against attacks made by Robert Watt, AFL International representative, explaining that the AFL had rejected an invitation to join in forming this new International.[27] In addition, Lindelof, like Hutcheson, was familiar with the AFL's special committee report.

Local non-Communist labor leaders, who supported CSU and Sorrell, were more frank in explaining their position than most international officials. A seasoned anti-Communist, George A. Mulkey, veteran of violent encounters with the Communists in the Pacific Northwest and elsewhere while serving the International Brotherhood of Electrical Workers, was "convinced" of the Communist nature of CSU, explaining as follows: "I was convinced of it personally before the 1945 strike occurred, but my theory was somewhat disproved, because the Communists did not support the action of the Conference of Studio Unions in 1945." [28] Mulkey also explained the position of the local business agent of the Electrical Workers, who kept his union in CSU although he, too, was cognizant of its Communist control. Discussing the matter with the business agent, Mulkey was told: "You know how it is, we have to more or less go along over there. I didn't like it any better than you did." [29]

Another local leader with unpleasant memories of fighting Communists, having been victimized by them, nevertheless did nothing to expose Communist control of CSU even though he was convinced of their influence. To the question, "Did you report to anyone his [Sorrell's] connection with the Communist Party?" Robinson answered, "Oh, no, no. We had a strike to win. We had a strike to win and those things. ... It was no time to start any arguments about whether a man was a Communist or anything else at that time. ..." [30] And when asked why he did not remove

[26] Jurisdiction, 1948, pp. 1600–1602; see also p. 1931.
[27] Ibid., p. 1619.
[28] Ibid., testimony of George A. Mulkey, pp. 1655–1656.
[29] Ibid., pp. 1670–1671.
[30] Ibid., p. 2393.

Sorrell as picket captain when he found out about his Communist connections, since he had appointed him, he replied: "But once I set him up there, I couldn't very well take him out, because he had proven such a good job handling the pickets, that I would have looked rather ridiculous. However, I knew I had to do something to keep the Communists actively down." [31]

This attitude of non-Communist leaders is characteristic of how men act in responsible positions. They almost invariably hesitate to resort to drastic action that would precipitate controversy. Often they hope, even when it is merely wishful thinking, that the matter will adjust itself without erupting into bitter conflict or unpleasantness. Only a cataclysm and persistent pressure with actual or threatened scandal will move them to drastic action. Furthermore, while IATSE acted expeditiously and determinedly in self-defense against the Communists, its leaders were loath to act in similar fashion against Browne and Bioff when the latter were exposed as racketeers. When allegations against Bioff received wide publicity on the Pacific Coast and elsewhere, the International vice-president operating in that territory defended him: "Representative Bioff, who was on the Coast directing the studio locals, was one of those against whom this attack was directed. No man ever had to undergo such an attack of mudslinging and malicious propaganda predicated on sheer black malice. Anything that could be said and anything that could be done to ruin the man, his wife and family was attempted. How he stood up, I do not know...." [32] Following this sentimental defense, a motion was unanimously adopted that "this convention go on record as endorsing and approving the action of President Browne's personal Representative Bioff and Vice President Halmden in their handling of the Studio Locals under International supervision, and that this convention extend to its officers a rising vote of confidence." [33]

As the attacks on Bioff intensified because of a grand-jury investigation demanded by the California Legislature, Bioff sent in his resignation. Simultaneously, a special committee, authorized by the IATSE 1938 Convention, studied the Hollywood situation. In its report, the committee ignored the accusations against Bioff, reporting merely on the status of studio locals. The president called a special meeting of the general executive board in September, 1938, that expressed confidence in Bioff, urging him to withdraw his resignation.[34] Later, Bioff was "induced" by the IATSE Hollywood locals and other AFL studio unions to represent them in collective-bargaining negotiations; he consented to do so and obtained favorable conditions, receiving ample praise for his accomplishments.[35]

[31] *Ibid.*, p. 2412.
[32] IATSE Convention Proceedings, 1938, p. 186.
[33] *Ibid.*, p. 187.
[34] IATSE Convention Proceedings, 1940, pp. 60–62.
[35] *Ibid.*, pp. 61, 65, 67.

At the IATSE general executive board meeting in February, 1940, Bioff was defended and praised by the AFL representative sent by President Green to help in Los Angeles, the secretary-treasurer of the Los Angeles Central Labor Union, and by "International Representative Dave Beck of the International Brotherhood of Teamsters, Chauffeurs, Stablemen and Helpers of America." [36] Only in November, 1941, after Browne and Bioff had been indicted, did they both resign. Walsh was selected by the general executive board to fill the unexpired term.[37]

At the 1942 convention, the new president offered the following excuse for delay in action: "Inasmuch as our former President served the International in a wholly satisfactory manner in various official capacities for many years, it must be assumed that he had become the victim of circumstances beyond his control. If he was cognizant of the acts being perpetrated by his appointees, possibly he was left with the alternative of remaining silent or paying the supreme penalty. The difficulty of having to make a choice between the two, with the latter a price beyond recall, should be readily apparent and is a distinct throwback to the adage of self-preservation. Taking the human side, I am certain it is a decision that would be relished by none. . . . As the legal prosecution had started outside our ranks, it was left entirely in the hands of the courts to establish the innocence or guilt of the accused. The Organization, however, remained completely loyal to the last. Every aid and assistance was extended to preclude the possibility of anyone working in behalf of the Alliance being unjustly prosecuted and punished for promoting its advancement." [38]

This demonstration of *esprit de corps* is characteristic in all organizations and intimate human relations. Friends and colleagues are defended to the bitter end. The fact, however, that Browne, International president and dominant figure in the organization, was personally involved gave him the opportunity to direct IATSE not only in shielding the culprits but in not bringing Bioff's misdemeanors to the attention of the members.

Because the racketeering scandal could not be played down, IATSE finally took definite action to clean house, which was completed in 1948 by barring Browne and Bioff "forever from membership" in IATSE. President Walsh also acknowledged that "through betrayal by a few former leaders, the Alliance had been brought to its lowest level. . . ." [39]

[36] *Ibid.*, p. 206.
[37] IATSE General Bulletin, July 1, 1942, pp. 9–10.
[38] IATSE Convention Proceedings, 1942, pp. 67–68.
[39] IATSE Convention Proceedings, 1948, pp. 87–88; Jurisdiction, 1948, pp. 1957 and 2435–2437; following their expulsion, Browne and Bioff ceased being active in the labor movement. Some seven years later, Bioff, who was living quietly in Arizona, was assassinated in "a gangster-type explosion at his Phoenix home." (*New York Times*, November 5, 1953.)

The attitude of the motion-picture producers was not different from that of the International labor officials. For a time, the producers thought it advantageous to play the contending sides against each other. Partly under duress, they worked with Bioff, believing they could control labor relations through him. Next they leaned toward CSU, thinking they could weaken the union's hold on the industry.[40] On the other hand, the producers feared such violent boycotts from the Communists as picketing, planting stink bombs in local theaters, and other similar acts. Above all, as the Communist issue received wider and wider currency, they feared a generally unfavorable reaction. Dmytryk thought the producers were pleased at first with the obstreperous behavior on the part of the "Hollywood Ten" in defying the congressional committee, especially since some believed the hearings were designed to hurt the industry.[41] The chairman complained that his committee had been subjected to pressure not to investigate Hollywood and not to call certain people to testify. He charged that the committee failed to receive necessary cooperation from Eric Johnston, president of the Motion Picture Association of America. He also averred that counsel for the association, Paul V. McNutt, had issued statements "critical of the Committee." [42]

In Mr. Johnston's testimony, it developed that the producers, on advice of counsel, rejected that part of a statement he had presented to them in which they would agree "not to employ proven Communists in Hollywood jobs where they would be in a position to influence the screen." [43] They reversed themselves promptly after public reaction to the conduct of the "Hollywood Ten" manifested itself.[44]

As former chairman of the labor committee of the Motion Picture Producers Association, in which capacity he served for more than twenty years —until July 1, 1947—Mr. Pat Casey denied there was any Communist influence in the studios. He was asked, "Is there anything in this jurisdictional dispute that has been Communist inspired?" He gave an unequivocal answer: "I don't think so. My God, I have heard Communist, Communist. It gets down to when you do not agree with somebody, you are a Communist." [45]

The producers assumed a liberal and philosophical position, which was aptly voiced by Dore Schary, executive in charge of production at RKO-Keith's: "Up until the time it is proved that a Communist is a man dedi-

[40] Davison, *op. cit.*, p. 11.
[41] Hollywood, Part 2, 1952, pp. 248–249.
[42] Hollywood, 1947, p. 310.
[43] *Ibid.*, p. 312.
[44] See John Cogley, *Report on Blacklisting*, Fund for the Republic, New York, 1956, vol. I, *Movies*.
[45] Jurisdiction, 1948, pp. 1570–1571; for IATSE criticism of this attitude, see p. 1726.

cated to the overthrow of government by force or violence, or by illegal methods, I cannot make any determination of his employment on any other basis except whether he is qualified best to do the job I want him to do." He then insisted that communism is not a great danger in the United States, and that Communists were defeated when they tried to dominate guilds and unions.[46] He was asked whether "a new situation has arisen in America today that is not completely covered by law" and whether it is not desirable "that the American people, while maintaining an attitude of tolerance, should also maintain an alert attitude to prevent further inroads of this menace to its welfare?" Mr. Schary answered optimistically, "Certainly I believe that America and the American people should be alerted and very vigilant about their prerogatives. My point is that they are." [47] Following the 1951 hearings and the consequent critical interest of the public, the producers have acted expeditiously and eagerly against those accused of being Communists or pro-Communists.[48]

[46] Hollywood, 1947, pp. 470, 472, 476.
[47] *Ibid.*, p. 477.
[48] See below, p. 80.

9

Lessons from the Rout
of Hollywood Communists

With the loss of the 1946 strike and with the AFL's adjustment of jurisdictional differences,[1] the bells tolled for the CSU and Sorrell. This time there was no non-Communist to come unwittingly to his rescue. Chance was indifferent to his fate. And the skids were well greased. Sorrell was expelled from the Los Angeles Central Labor Union because of membership in the Communist Party and because he betrayed the interests of the American Federation of Labor by supporting the Screen Players Union, an independent, against the Screen Extras Guild, an AFL affiliate. The SPU was defeated by the SEG in an NLRB election.[2] In another NLRB election, Sorrell's Painters Local 644, Motion Picture Painters and Scenic Artists, was defeated by IATSE as the bargaining representative of the Painters.[3] With the settlement of jurisdictional differences, the other craft locals gradually disaffiliated from the CSU.[4]

Other decisive blows followed in quick succession. Sorrell was tried by his International and was found guilty of having participated in Communist activities. He was barred from office for five years.[5] Then the International revoked the charter of Local 644, and Sorrell thereby lost his job as the local's business agent. This development resulted in Sorrell's suing the International for breach of contract. Seeking to recover wages for a two-year period under the terms of a three-year contract with Local 644, Sorrell lost his lawsuit in the Los Angeles Supreme Court. His attor-

---

[1] For a description of the adjustment of the jurisdictional disputes, see IATSE Convention Proceedings, 1948, pp. 83–86 and pp. 206–222.

[2] Sol. Davison, "The Motion Picture Strike," *New Leader*, June 29, 1946.

[3] *Communist Infiltration of Hollywood Motion Picture Industry, Hearings before the House Committee on Un-American Activities*, 82d Cong., 2d Sess., 1952, hereafter referred to as "Hollywood, Part 2, 1952," p. 497.

[4] *Jurisdictional Disputes in the Motion Picture Industry, Hearings before a Special Subcommittee of the House Committee on Education and Labor*, 80th Cong., 2d Sess., 1948, later referred to as "Jurisdiction, 1948," Mulkey testimony, pp. 1628, 1648, and 1654.

[5] Hollywood, Part 2, 1952, pp. 497, 527.

ney was undecided whether he would appeal.[6] According to the latest reports, Sorrell is now leading a quiet life as a painter-contractor.

Aroused by the exposé and the public's unfavorable reaction, the talent guilds also acted. The Screen Directors Guild instituted a loyalty oath for its members;[7] members of the Screen Writers Guild, shocked by the revelation, revolted. "The 1947 elections were held in the heat of the former hearing, the hearings in 1947 of this committee, and there was a great deal of feeling on both sides at that time, and the progressive slate was defeated. And since that time, it is probably true that no Communists have been on the board of the Screen Writers Guild."[8]

This chapter in the history of Hollywood is now but a fading nightmare. Jane K. McGuiness, a motion-picture executive at Metro-Goldwyn-Mayer and a founder of the Motion-Picture Alliance for the Preservation of American Ideals, declared that "had Sorrell and his group won the strike . . . they would have had a tight hold on many of the important guilds and craft unions within the industry."[9]

The reflective and analytical Brewer summed up the situation: "The trend of the time has aided our cause. Important persons in the industry, who a few years ago greeted our story as too fantastic to believe, are now looking at it with recognition and concern. But we know from experience that the Communists will not give up—the prize is too great. We hope, therefore, that with the help of the committee, the Communist menace in the motion-picture industry may be successfully destroyed, to the end that Hollywood labor may be spared in the future the strife and turmoil of the immediate past."[10]

Participants in this horrendous struggle against Communist infiltration and domination have made observations and arrived at conclusions that merit consideration.

It was generally agreed that the Communists could not influence the content of a script—"it was possible of accomplishment only in terms of the whole tendency of the country." Thus, "a great many things that seem in retrospect to be left wing were really part and parcel of the times. . . ." Communists do not try to put in pure propaganda but angle it "in the framework of the period."[11]

Many joined the Communist Party through front organizations. These fronts featured issues that attracted the liberal- and progressive-minded but were yet in the interest of the Communist cause. Recruits then began to

[6] *The New York Times*, July 23, 1955.
[7] Hollywood, Part 3, 1952, p. 645.
[8] Hollywood, Part 1, 1951, testimony of Richard J. Collins, pp. 227–228.
[9] *Hearings by the House Committee on Un-American Activities Regarding the Communist Infiltration of the Motion Picture Industry*, 80th Cong., 1st Sess., 1947, hereafter referred to as "Hollywood, 1947," p. 147.
[10] *Ibid.*, p. 357.
[11] Hollywood, Part 1, 1951, Collins testimony, pp. 234–239.

look upon the Communist Party as the spark plug that fired the action for worthy, humanitarian objectives; with a little urging, they joined the Party.[12] Later, some problem would arise—a sudden reversal in policy or an act that went against a person's conscience—and the breakaway would begin. Usually it was a slow one for there develops "a certain mental incest" which makes one hesitate.[13] Thus one former member, a prominent screen director, broke with the Party over ideals, but, despite his complete disillusionment prior to the 1947 hearings, he believed he must go through with the Party program to sabotage the hearings if he was not to be accused of cowardice. After serving his jail term as one of the "Hollywood Ten," he decided he must complete the break.[14]

One former Party member explained how individuals who have reached the pinnacle of success and are financially affluent are attracted by communism. Remembering his struggle for success and working side by side with persons earning a mite compared with his fat salary, he hears of misery and injustice in the world, and his conscience is stirred. He would like to square his right to live in luxury with those who have less. The Party offers him this chance. "The Party has a very good explanation for everything that troubles a man. . . . So when a man accepts this thing he thinks he is following the truth." [15]

There was also the feeling that "the Communist Party is conspiratorial, subversive and even in certain cases treasonable." [16] Another did not think that "the Communists in America would be of any consequence at all if they were in the open. We could lick them on any ground, in any battle, if we knew them for what they really are. But it is the deception that makes them dangerous." [17]

The head of the Screen Writers Guild, Emmett G. Lavery, warned: "I think if we make political martyrs out of them we make it easy for the Communists. . . .[18] My only concern with respect to this whole proceeding . . . is merely that people might go back home and think that they have been political martyrs. An election in November which is coming up in our Screen Writers Guild might be seriously affected, and not for the better, if people thought that perhaps government had interfered any more than was necessary in the normal operations of the Guild." [19] Considering that the Communist group was defeated at the election referred to, Mr. Lavery's prognostication was hardly borne out.[20]

[12] Hollywood, Part 3, 1952, pp. 627, 644–645; Part 2, 1952, pp. 418–420; see also pp. 420–423.
[13] Ibid., p. 645.
[14] Ibid., pp. 430–436.
[15] Ibid., pp. 418–423.
[16] Ibid., p. 437.
[17] Jurisdiction, 1948, p. 1793.
[18] Hollywood, 1947, p. 450.
[19] Ibid., p. 444.
[20] See above, p. 66.

The philosophical Brewer describes the outcome differently: "The Communist Party in Hollywood at a certain point developed a tremendous and powerful degree of control in the Hollywood community, not only in the labor unions but in the community itself, and in order that there might not be any misunderstanding, I want to make it clear that this extensive control does not exist in Hollywood today.

"The Hollywood strike of 1946 and the subsequent hearings of this Committee in 1947 did a great deal to awaken the people of that community to this menace, and since that time their influence has declined. There still are a lot of them around, as this Committee is proving, and we feel this Committee is doing a great service in ferreting them out, but the back of their power that they had in 1945 and 1946, so far as its influence over the community is concerned, has been broken.... The real power that they had in Hollywood was through their front organizations. The strength of the underground organization probably is as great today as it was then. It has been hurt some. But so far as the front organizations with which they dominated the thought and life of the community, they have been affected by the activities that transpired."

As for the effect of the 1947 hearings, "It shocked the community in a way that is hard to describe. As one of a small group that had been trying to make the community aware of what was going on I was cognizant of the problem we had in convincing the community of what was taking place under their noses and the community did not believe it. But when the hearings in 1947 took place and these individuals conducted themselves in the manner they did, it hit Hollywood like a broad slap in the face, and they began to take a new look, and since that time the Communist movement there has been pretty much on the defensive." [21]

Brewer was firmly of the opinion that it was necessary to shock the community out of its complacency. "The difficulty has been to understand the nature of this problem." That the shock treatment was efficacious is evident in that "the fellow who has any taint of Communism on him today is having a tough time." [22] A screen writer who was named as a Communist testified that he was told by a producer that his "money people would no longer accept me. Simultaneously [another producer] ... asked permission to take my name off the previous picture...." [23] The "Hollywood Ten" were all disemployed as a result of the publicity resulting from their conduct at the hearings and their conviction for contempt of Congress.[24]

[21] Hollywood, Part 2, 1952, pp. 476, 489, and 492.
[22] *Ibid.*, pp. 490–491.
[23] Hollywood, Part 3, 1952, Tuttle testimony, p. 645.
[24] Several recanted voluntarily, appearing at subsequent congressional hearings and describing their underground and other Communist activities. Some instituted lawsuits for unpaid wages under contracts canceled by the studios. Ring Lardner, Jr.,

It is the opinion of those who were active against Communist infiltration that counterorganization is indispensable. Adolphe Menjou declared: "The eternal vigilance of the Motion Picture Alliance for the Preservation of American Ideals, by its vigilance, has prevented an enormous amount of sly, subtle, un-American class-struggle propaganda from going into pictures." [25]

Brewer concurred in this opinion: "I feel . . . that the one potent force that stood between complete control of the industry by the Communists and their defeat at the crucial point in 1945 were the AF of L unions. We had other people who helped us, but that was the force that blocked their way and made final victory possible. . . . The community is very militant today in fighting it." [26]

Then Brewer threw out some hints on how to fight Communists and warned against "coexistence" or cooperation with them.

"There is one little device which we used which might be of help to those people reading this record in connection with fighting Communists in unions. We feel we are old hands at it. That is based on this fundamental premise, that you can never support a Communist in any activity, no matter how good that activity may be on its face because any time a Communist brings in a good program he is bringing it in for a purpose which he will ultimately use for the Communist Party. . . ." [27]

---

instituted a lawsuit for damages amounting to $25,000 against Twentieth-Century Fox Studios. After going through a number of court stages, it was settled through private negotiation, and the terms of settlement were not disclosed. The lawsuit of another screen writer is still in litigation (*New York Times*, Sept. 1, 1955); see *Annual Report of the Committee on Un-American Activities, 1951*, 82d Cong., 2d Sess., Feb., 1952, pp. 7–9; for a list of those who, "through the knowledge gained during their own past membership in the Communist Party, have been of invaluable assistance to the Committee and the American people in supplying facts relating to Communist efforts and successes in infiltrating the motion picture industry," see *Annual Report of the Committee on Un-American Activities, 1952*, 82d Cong., 2d Sess., Jan. 3, 1953, pp. 40–41; and for a list of persons who have been "identified as present or past members of the Communist Party," see *ibid.*, pp. 41–56.

[25] Hollywood, 1947, p. 94.
[26] Hollywood, Part 2, 1952, p. 531.
[27] *Ibid.*

10

Infiltration of the Hotel
and Restaurant Workers Union

An outstanding example of successful Communist penetration on the lower levels of an AFL international union is that of the Hotel and Restaurant Employees and Bartenders International Alliance. When the order had been given to dissolve TUUL and to join existing unions,[1] the Food Workers Industrial Union found conditions in the Hotel and Restaurant Employees Union especially favorable: The time was propitious. Membership was at low ebb. The union was still in the doldrums, caused not only by the 1929 Depression but also by prohibition's decimating most of its membership, originally recruited from bartenders. In the New York area, conditions were especially favorable because racketeers had infiltrated some of the straggling locals. By 1935, racketeering in this and in other unions in the New York area had become a public scandal. The members of these unions, with the aid of the International, attempted to correct the bad conditions, but in the clearing out, the International became involved in litigation. Only through the intervention of the state government, when Governor Herbert Lehman appointed Thomas E. Dewey as a special district attorney, was it possible to rid the union of racketeers.[2]

The leaders in the International were especially interested in rehabilitating local unions in the strategic New York area. They were, therefore, willing to overlook Communist orientation of the FWIU. At this time, too, the Communists were still regarded by many people as merely another radical group, despite the unfortunate and disruptive experience such unions as the needle trades, coal miners, machinists, and others had encountered from

[1] See above, pp. 15ff.
[2] Jay Rubin and Michael Obermeier, *Growth of a Union; the Life and Times of Edward Flore,* The Historical Union Association, 1943, pp. 225–242, 243–250; see also *Catering Industry Employee,* June, 1935, p. 9; and Matthew Josephson, *Union House, Union Bar: The History of the Hotel and Restaurant Employees and Bartenders Union,* AFL-CIO, Random House, Inc., New York, 1956, pp. 211–221. This official history appeared after the above chapter was completed, but it does not contain any new data on the phase discussed herein.

Communist infiltration in the 1920s. The task was also eased by the fact that HRE membership included a large group of immigrants with a Socialist background.

The *Catering Industry Employee* published discussions favorable to industrial unionism, independent political action, and theoretical analysis of Marxism and the class struggle. Thus the secretary of one of the large New York locals, who was known as a socialist, quoted Karl Marx to the effect that unions and a labor political party are "schools for workers in which they forge their class conscious character. These two schools prepare and train them to identify themselves with the class struggle which will ultimately emancipate them from slavery." [3]

The FWIU made overtures for amalgamation, not only in New York, but in other localities where its units existed. There was, however, opposition to a merger in the lower echelons of the union, although all concerned conceded that the members of the FWIU should be accorded "the right to come in as members the same as any other applicant." The general executive board "granted an appearance" to "Mr. Jay Rubin, International Secretary of the Food Workers Industrial Union, along with two other members of their National Board," devoting "quite some time . . . in going into their proposition." [4] At its May 13–18, 1935, meeting, the general executive board ruled as follows: "While the petition for amalgamation of the Food Workers Industrial Union with ours to come in as a whole was vigorously opposed by a number of our locals, all your New York and Brooklyn locals were against this proposition; it was the opinion of the Board that, in principle, we favor their application . . . and to give the application of these people through the country favorable consideration. The acceptance of the applications in question being from individuals and not as a unit." [5] This decision was endorsed by the 1936 convention. The report of the committee on officers epitomized the general sentiment: "The absorption of the Amalgamated Food Workers and the Food Workers Industrial Union in New York into local unions of our International should also be recorded as a long step in the direction of progress and toward greater unity among the workers in our industry. Your Committee recom-

[3] Officials encouraged such discussions, *Catering Industry Employee*, July, 1935, pp. 28–29; June, 1936, pp. 20–21; Sept., 1935, pp. 44 and 43; Nov., 1936, pp. 14–15; May, 1936, pp. 8–9. See also obituary of General President Ernst, a member of the liberation movement who was born in Croatia while it was under Austro-Hungarian rule; in the United States he fought for civil rights and against discrimination and in 1922 ran for Congress on the Socialist ticket, *op. cit.*, August, 1954, pp. 7–12. Max Pincus is also eulogized for service to the movement; as president of Local 302, New York City, he did yeoman work in organizing chain cafeterias. He came to the United States in 1903, a union man and a Socialist, *op. cit.*, June, 1936, pp. 44, 94.

[4] *Ibid.*, June, 1935, pp. 9, 16.

[5] Hotel and Restaurant Employees and Bartenders International Union Convention, hereinafter referred to as "Hotel Proceedings," 1936, pp. 39–40.

mends that the General Executive Board continue to encourage amalgamation. . . . The hope for our future lies in greater unity among the workers in our industry and in a better understanding among ourselves." [6]

This action was, in part at least, taken in desperation because of the disorganized state of the industry. In their eagerness to rehabilitate the union in New York City, the officials were confronted with choosing between the racketeers then in the union or the Communists who were operating in the industry and offering amalgamation. The officials acted in full knowledge of the maneuvers and tactics of the Communists in many AFL unions as well as in their own union. In 1929, several members of Local 202, Cafeteria Workers, joined in a strike conducted by a dual union. During their trial, they frankly admitted they were members of the dual union and also of the Communist Party. As a result, these members were expelled from the International. The 1936 convention discussed this general problem of ways and means of disciplining Communists within the union.[7]

The leaders were not only aware of Communist tactics but they warned their associates and members through their official journal. In the year when admittance of FWIU was being considered and discussed, warnings against Communist maneuvers appeared in print several times. Thus the July, 1935, issue featured the following notice at the top of the "President's Page": "WARNING FROM AMERICAN FEDERATION OF LABOR —WAR ON REDS—The *united front* plan of the Communists for taking over labor leadership in the United States was effectively scotched this week by American Federation of Labor President Green, when through Matthew Woll, he warned that any local unions affiliated with the American Federation of Labor that admit Communists *will not be recognized* and they may expect to have their *charters withdrawn.*" [8]

And in the September, 1935, issue, the "President's Page" contained the following:

"BE ON YOUR GUARD

"Orders from Moscow are—Sacrifice your organization and enlist in the American Federation of Labor, secure administrative positions where possible and give special thought to securing admission to the Central Labor Unions and Federation Conventions as delegates. Why? The answer is easily discerned. Destroy the American Federation of Labor and Communism will reign supreme.

"Some of the Moscow group have already made their entrance into our unions, while others have knocked at our door, and failed to secure admission. But do they stop there? No!" [9]

[6] *Ibid.*, 1936, p. 68.
[7] *Ibid.*, 1936, pp. 13 and 107–115; see also Josephson, *op. cit.*, pp. 172, 176.
[8] *Catering Industry Employee*, p. 5.
[9] *Ibid.*, p. 4.

President William Green and the AFL were, at this time, conducting a vigorous campaign against the Communists as described above.[10]   When President Green, however, addressed the HRE convention, he spoke of the CIO dissension but did not mention the Communist issue.[11]

It is significant that, while these warnings were conspicuously featured in the official publication, no mention of this danger was made in the general executive board minutes where admittance of the FWIU was considered and acted upon favorably.

Following their admittance into the New York area, the leaders of the FWIU soon came into control of the most important positions in the local joint executive board and in some of the largest locals.   And when the Hotel Trades Council [12] was founded, one of FWIU's two outstanding leaders became its president.   Similarly, the other key Communist trade-union leader was finally elected secretary of the New York State Hotel and Bartenders Alliance.   Simultaneously, membership increased, and the unions made extraordinary headway in securing recognition and collective-bargaining agreements from employers.   Recognition was usually secured after turbulent strikes which included mass picketing and considerable violence.[13]   As the Communists gained control, they began using union machinery for Communist propaganda; they siphoned off union funds to support Communist causes; and they began to discriminate and to make matters unpleasant in other ways for those who would not accept their leadership or attempted to resist or criticize their Communist activities.   Soon resentment began to manifest itself in protests.   These efforts to resist Communist encroachments and oust their perpetrators divide themselves into three stages.

The meteoric rise of union membership in the New York area plus success in obtaining union recognition and collective-bargaining arrangements with management impressed International leaders a great deal.   Heretofore, New York had been the sore spot organizationally; now it became the shining light.

General President Flore wrote in October, 1935: "New York City is not the only hunting ground in the United States . . . but we must set ourselves where our labor is most needed and New York City today is a whirl of activity, and in this whirl-pool of action, new problems and alignments are taking place which need the counsel and advice of the International Union. . . ." [14]   Impressed by the idea of a program for extending organiza-

[10] See above, pp. 15–16.

[11] Hotel Proceedings, 1936, pp. 72–77.

[12] This is a joint, informal organization of AFL local unions whose members are employed in the industry, including building service and such maintenance employees as electricians, engineers, firemen, painters, upholsterers.

[13] Rubin and Obermeier, *op. cit.*, p. 306.

[14] *Catering Industry Employee*, October, 1935, p. 5.

tion by a delegation from the New York local executive board, the general executive board voted in June, 1937, to contribute $25,000, which was equaled by the New York locals.[15]

The Communist leaders also very cleverly catered to International officials. They refrained from introducing embarrassing resolutions at International conventions. If any were introduced, they scrupulously refrained from supporting them. In political contests within the International, they supported the administration. Thus, at the 1938 San Francisco convention, when Flore was opposed for reelection by a group whose leaders were Chicagoans accused of having racketeering connections, the Communists supported the administration.[16] As a result, International officials accepted the Communists and gave them a free hand in the locals and in areas where they were strong.

There was a sort of tacit understanding. The local Communist leaders did not inject themselves into the affairs of the International, and the International gave the Communists a free hand in the conduct of their local affairs. As the Communists became more sure of themselves, they retaliated by opposing the reelection of particular International officials who were hostile to them and more alert to their maneuvers and tactics. Thus, they supported an opposition candidate to the incumbent general secretary-treasurer, Edward S. Miller, whom they regarded as an enemy.[17] In this they failed.

On the other hand, they sided with the administration in opposing and defeating for reelection John J. Kearney, vice-president of District 1, who was one of the staunchest anti-Communists but had otherwise displeased the administration.[18] Emanuel Garriga was the Communist bête noire Number 1. At an earlier convention, they ran a well-known Communist against him, but this ended in dismal failure. In the 1947 convention, they supported a non-Communist, but because Garriga had administration support, he was reelected vice-president by 1,554 to 1,279 votes.[19] In 1949, Garriga was reelected without opposition.[20] Of course, this was an old and established tactic of the Communists, not only to wreak vengeance but to eliminate those who were best aware of their tactics. Nevertheless, they scrupulously refrained from challenging the administration on policy or in otherwise manifesting hostility to it.

Another form of pandering to International officers took the form of publishing in 1943 a laudatory book signed by Jay Rubin and Michael Obermeier, who were then two key Communist trade-union leaders in the

[15] Hotel Proceedings, 1938, p. 85; Rubin and Obermeier, *op. cit.*, p. 279.
[16] *Ibid.*, pp. 279–291; Josephson, *op. cit.*, pp. 241–246.
[17] *New York Times*, May 7, 1947; Hotel Proceedings, 1947, pp. 116–118.
[18] *Ibid.*, 1947, pp. 122–129.
[19] *Ibid.*, 1947, pp. 129–134.
[20] *Ibid.*, 1949, p. 117.

hotel and restaurant industry of the New York region, on the leadership of the International president, entitled *Growth of a Union: The Life and Times of Edward Flore*. This is a rather restrained document praising Flore and his union, describing achievements in New York, and cautiously sustaining Communist ideas mixed with progressive thinking. The following quotation is an example: "Workers here and in other countries—even those which are now enemy, who look to the Allies to help free them from the ruthless enslavement in which they find themselves—dream of a future peace, unity of workers the world over, and a planned economy of plenty, of labor solidarity with workers the world over to prevent forever the waste, destruction, horror, and death of war. Flore was confident that these 'dreams' might be crystallized soon into real world-wide labor unity among the labor movements of America, Great Britain, the Soviet Union and other United Nations in time to enable labor at the peace table to exert its full influence for creating a truly democratic, people's post war world." [21]

Just as there was unfavorable sentiment against admitting the FWIU, so anti-Communist opinion continued to express itself, even within the New York locals. As the Communists grew in influence, opposition sentiment also grew. Gradually, the opposition began to pressure International officials and to voice its views. The outburst took articulate form at the 1941 convention, although in a rather subdued way and without specific charges against either individuals or local unions. The ideology and factional practices of the Communists were criticized and attacked. Three outstanding Communist trade-union leaders answered but in a guarded manner. Since the opponents were not yet ready to come to grips, drastic, specific action was not attempted. The International nevertheless found it necessary to go on record concerning this issue. Actually, International officials desired less specific declarations than those from lower-level leaders and their supporters in the membership group. The officers' report to the 1941 convention took cognizance of the pressure by declaring, "Freedom of speech is a guarantee granted to all in accordance with the constitution of the United States. Freedom of speech, however, either by the written or spoken word, does not grant a special privilege or license for destructive criticism, subversive, controversial, or contrary discussion inimical to the interests of our country and its institutions, or against the basic principles of the AFL and our International. . . .

"The printing of bulletins, pamphlets, and newspapers seeking to influence our members with philosophies and ideologies inconsistent with American traditions, and inconsistent with the aims of the Trade Union Movement, must be eliminated.

"One of the outward signs of disloyalty and sabotage in a local union, its officers and members, is the ganging up or grouping together in private

[21] Rubin and Obermeier, *op. cit.*, p. 318 and also p. 314.

conferences in meetings and the spreading of scandal misrepresentation of union officers through the issuance and distribution of written material.

"We recommend that a law be enacted prohibiting and forbidding that practice." [22]

But General President Flore, in his opening address, went out of his way to appease the Communist element. While the war was being waged in Europe, during the Stalin-Hitler pact period, he stated:

"There is not a movement in these United States that is more loyal to the support of its government and that will do more to further the interests of the government in keeping our country at peace, and, if it is possible at all, keep it from becoming involved in this European war that is now raging." [23]

And, at the close of the convention, General Secretary-Treasurer Hugo Ernst made a passionate appeal for tolerance in a long speech that was clearly directed against the leaders of the anti-Communist elements.[24]

The attack against the Communists was led by two outstanding delegates from the East. One was from New York City, an international representative, elected vice-president from the New York district at this convention. The better informed, and later a key person in cleaning out Communist infiltration, he contented himself with making a veiled attack on "those who emphasize philosophy and are parasites." He proclaimed that this matter was "a burning issue that extended from the Atlantic to the Pacific, even though New York was more affected than any other city." [25]

The other attack against the Communists was made by the vice-president from the Boston or New England district. Using a blackboard, he gave a lengthy lecture on the philosophy of communism and the intrigues of Communists. But he made no specific charges.[26]

The Communist leaders were also restrained, realizing they were in the minority and could make headway only by concealing their true motives and identity. Their chief speaker declared that his local union "since its admission to the International Union had been a most loyal and devoted builder of the International Union." He also related how the local unions had been revived in the last "five or six years," and that their efforts had "brought from chaos, from confusion the International membership in District 2, that represents at least, if not more than 30 per cent of our total membership, with contracts of which we are proud." He then appealed to the body not to permit the sessions of the convention to become "a battleground of factionalism as it was faced with important problems." The officers and delegates were urged by him "not to be misled by any

[22] Hotel Proceedings, 1941, officers' report, p. 26.
[23] *Ibid.*, 1941, Flore's opening address, p. 4.
[24] *Ibid.*, 1941, p. 252.
[25] *Ibid.*, 1941, pp. 163–164.
[26] *Ibid.*, 1941, pp. 172–175.

rumors or slanders that may be circulated." [27]   Two others from a New York local labeled as Communist-controlled, who were recognized as outstanding leaders of the Communist faction, also spoke in laudatory terms of the New York situation.[28]

No one participating in the convention attempted to refute the claim that Communist leadership in New York had reactivated the movement and secured favorable conditions through collective bargaining and written trade agreements.   But, although International officials exerted themselves to keep the controversy within bounds, they failed in their effort to suppress resentment against the Communists.   Thus, the convention voted an amendment to the constitution which read:

"Any member who associates himself or herself with any organization or any group that expounds or promotes any doctrine or philosophy inimical and subversive to the fundamental principles and institutions of the government of the United States, the AFL and this International Union, shall after investigation by the General President, or by any person designated by him to investigate, be granted a hearing, after which the decision of the General President shall be binding, unless reversed on appeal by the General Executive Board." [29]

In addition, a resolution was adopted instructing the officers to "investigate any and all Communist activities of any and all members of our International union and, when found to have connection with the espousing of Communism, that said member or members be expelled." [30]

Other action taken by the convention revealed the strong non-Communist position of an overwhelming majority of the delegates.   No vote was recorded on a resolution opposing Lend-Lease and demanding a referendum before declaring war, during the Hitler-Stalin pact, but the committee recommendation of nonconcurrence was approved without debate.[31]

A recorded vote is available, however, in the contest for vice-president for District 2, including the New York City area, and presents a mathematical measurement of Communist strength in mustering the votes of delegates at the convention.   According to the constitution, the country is parceled out by districts with a vice-president in charge of each.   While the vice-president is selected from members of a local in the particular district, he is elected by the convention at large.   The issue was clear, since the views and affiliations of both candidates in regard to the Communist issue were known.   Both had unequivocally participated in the debate, each revealing his position unequivocally.   Both were members of the same local, the largest in the International and Communist-controlled.   The anti-Com-

[27] *Ibid.*, 1941, pp. 161–162.
[28] *Ibid.*, 1941, p. 217.
[29] *Ibid.*, 1941, p. 199.
[30] *Ibid.*, 1941, p. 111.
[31] *Ibid.*, 1941, p. 246.

munist, on a roll-call vote, was elected by 1,712 against 285 for the Communist candidate.[32] This vote reveals the strong anti-Communist feeling among the convention delegates and, since most of them were rank-and-filers, undoubtedly reflected the sentiment of the membership.

Because of the war, no conventions were held from 1941 to 1947. International officers were at first not very diligent in carrying out the mandate of the 1941 convention to investigate Communist activity and to expel the guilty ones. The 1947 convention consequently witnessed the release of pent-up resentment. Even prior to the 1947 convention, however, the pressure was so great that officials felt compelled to take some action. But, at the outset, the action was mild. For example, the general executive board at its March, 1944, meeting adopted a motion that "general officers be instructed to continue their efforts to keep the publications, issued by our local unions, within the scope and principles of the American Federation of Labor and the International Union." [33]

In 1946, the union's official publication poked fun at the Communists by printing a sarcastic comment on how dictatorship and arbitrary decisions, in accordance with the Party line, dictated from abroad, forced the expulsion of Earl Browder.[34] Another item reprinted the statement on communism adopted at the American Federation of Labor 1946 convention. The account that accompanied it stressed that the statement made a distinction between radical and liberal ideas and communism, and it further explained that the criticism was not directed at communist theory but at Communist intrigue and interference in the internal affairs of America for the purpose of preventing the development of free institutions and at the use of American institutions to spread their subversive doctrines.[35] While International officers did not openly attempt to check the Communists, they did warn them privately and pleaded with them to heed the resentment they had aroused, to curtail their Communist activities in union organizations, and otherwise to check their followers. General President Hugo Ernst, who succeeded Edward Flore upon his death in 1945, pleaded against drastic action at the 1947 convention and placed the blame upon the Communists. "We have warned these people in a friendly manner.... I warned them and told them what they should do, in order to eliminate the friction that is bound to arise from such conduct.... However ... I can say to my friends who may be affected ... that it is entirely their own fault, because they did not heed friendly advice ... when the question did not reach the critical stage that it has now.... I do not care what political belief any person has, as long as they devote their time and their energy to the betterment of

[32] *Ibid.*, 1941, pp. 181–183.
[33] *Catering Industry Employee*, April, 1944, p. 13.
[34] *Ibid.*, March, 1946, p. 21.
[35] *Ibid.*, November, 1946, pp. 29–31.

the labor movement and the unions of which they are members or officers exclusively. I have paid my compliments to the officers of Local 6 for the splendid work they have done in the hotels in New York which we tried unsuccessfully to organize a good many years ago. After these boys and girls came into our organization, we were able to organize these hotels, so that today, practically speaking, every large hotel in New York is organized ... and had these people and other people in other parts of the country refrained from using their official position for other than trade union principles, probably we would not be confronted with this issue that is before us now." [36] Warnings were of no avail. And the dissatisfaction of the non-Communists was mounting against Communist domination and intrigue and their effect upon the reputation of the International and its affiliates. A resolution introduced at the 1947 convention was entitled "Opposing Classification of International Union by Press As Being Communist Controlled." [37] One delegate complained on the floor of the 1947 convention, without being challenged: "I regret to say that for six years the International Union has not seen fit to carry out the provisions of Resolution 77 and therefore the cancer which we saw in 1941 encroaching upon the body of the International union has now become so great that we seek to take this drastic measure and write new language into the International Constitution." [38]

Hearkening to overwhelming sentiment, International officers finally took action. On February 15, 1946, the general executive board "considered the New York situation as presented before the Board by several local officials of New York in person and upon receipt of communications on the same subject, the Board feels warranted in giving serious consideration to the conditions existing in New York, affecting the interests of our International and its subordinate unions and its membership." And "by unanimous vote appointed an investigating Commission ... consisting of three General Executive Board members (General President, General Secretary-Treasurer, and the Vice President from the Florida region) ... and two members of the New York labor movement not affiliated with our International." The commission was assisted by the general counsel and an International auditor.[39]

The first meeting took place in New York City, March 20. "The Commission held sessions for about eight weeks and conducted extensive hearings.... Most of the witnesses were cooperative, some were evasive and engaged in equivocation...." [40] At its October 13 meeting, the general

[36] Hotel Proceedings, 1947, p. 196.
[37] Ibid., 1947, p. 180.
[38] Ibid., 1947, p. 192.
[39] Catering Industry Employee, April, 1946; see also Hotel Proceedings, 1947, pp. 44–45.
[40] Ibid., 1947, pp. 44–45.

executive board considered a report of the investigation commission. On the basis of the report, it decided to place an observer in the New York local joint executive board [41] in order "to see that no action ... will be harmful to the interests of the International Union." The energetic, sophisticated, and astute district vice-president was designated as observer. The general executive board also "voiced its disapproval of the many articles appearing in the 'Voice' of Local 6 and publications of other local unions on matters not directly germane to the work of the International Union and the American Federation of Labor." [42]

In its report, the investigation commission found that "the record discloses that substantial Communist sympathy and influence exists among some part of the leadership and some of the members of our New York Locals 1, 6 and 89."

The commission also found:

"1. Some leaders and members are sympathizers with the Communist cause and engage in activities that aid and assist in the Communist cause.

"2. That there is carried on continuous activity to propagandize Communism.

"3. That some persons carry on activities in the unions and under color of the union, promote and foster the Communist program and objectives.

"4. That contributions have been asked for and accepted from union members, in union halls, in support of organizations known to be promoting and aiding Communist groups.

"5. That there have been direct donations of many thousands of dollars from union treasuries to Communist front organizations, publications and functions.

"6. That some of the above mentioned local unions maintain affiliations with and pay initiation fees and dues to organizations that have no labor affiliations and which organizations are Communist fronts."

The commission also found it necessary to devise "appropriate action ... for eliminating all Communist ties and influences in accord with the International Constitution and the will of the membership." It therefore recommended that the International "impose upon those locals ... the duty of cleaning their own houses. ... If not complied with within a reasonable time ... that formal hearings be instituted and appropriate discipline be imposed."

This action should be a "warning and recommendation ... equally applicable to the situation wherever it may exist. ...

"The Commission points out that this is not a witch hunt" and that its

[41] This is a form of organization established by unions that were founded originally by German Socialists in order to coordinate the work of the local unions in a metropolitan area. This organizational form is also known as "joint board," particularly in the Needle Trades, and is even more commonly known as "district council."

[42] Catering Industry Employee, November, 1946, pp. 9, 15.

recommendations are "in accord with constitutional declaration and principles against subversives." [43]

The order to clean house was disregarded by the locals referred to. Nor did the observer of the New York local joint board report any results. In the meantime, the 1947 convention assembled.

[43] Hotel Proceedings, 1947, pp. 44–45.

11

Revolt at the 1947 Convention

The 1947 convention was emotionally surcharged, full of drama and controversy. Many of the delegates, reflecting the feelings of the more articulate membership, came to the convention imbued with a passionate determination to protect the good name of the organization by laying the basis for driving the arrogant and domineering "subversives" out of the union. Their feelings are mirrored best in the action that occurred when the convention adopted the majority report barring Communists from holding union office. The convention proceedings record: "At this point a number of delegates carrying American flags stood before the rostrum while the delegates joined in singing 'God Bless America.' " [1]

On the other hand, the Communists and their sympathizers stood their ground, coming prepared to defend their position not as Communists but as faithful, successful, and progressive trade unionists. Their tactic was to defend liberal unionism and to point with pride at their record in achieving it. They were nettled, nevertheless, by the treatment they received and the reaction of the great majority of delegates. Their chief spokesman defiantly complained: "I know the spirit of this convention, and if you leave it to the judgment of those who can boo loudest, definitely discussion and debate will be cut off.... I am not going to be ruled off this floor by a mob." [2]

That the convention was unruly is attested to by the obviously disturbed appeal made by the scholarly, usually urbane, and superlatively liberal general president: "Let's have a little order let's not get hysterical. That's just the trouble with you fellows." [3]

International officials pursued a course typical of those motivated by their

---

[1] Hotel and Restaurant Employees and Bartenders International Union Convention, hereafter referred to as "Hotel Proceedings," 1947, p. 188. This reaction was not an isolated occurrence. This study reveals that the bitter resentment against Communist domination and exploitation of unions was general.

[2] *Ibid.*, 1947, p. 195.

[3] *Ibid.*, 1947, p. 194.

immediate objective: as custodians of the organization, maintaining it intact and at the same time reducing friction to a minimum. This seems to be the general reaction of responsible union leaders. Realizing that emotionally aroused delegates could not be restrained in their determination to take action against Communist influence within the organization, the officers made every effort to keep the delegates from taking drastic action.

Speaking for the administration, the general president appealed for discretion and calm consideration, warning of the danger of going to extremes. To reinforce his appeal, he quoted an adage credited to Benjamin Franklin: "They who give up essential liberty to obtain temporary safety neither deserve liberty nor safety." Then he added in his own words: "I plead with you to let good sense rule your decisions and not hysteria nor hatred. . . ." [4]

But the majority of the delegates knew what they wanted. They and the members themselves had considered the problem for nearly a decade and were in no mood to pay heed to officials who permitted the situation to go from bad to worse. They therefore threw the book at the Communists by itemizing, stipulating, and denouncing communism for what it was. Actually, the policy statement adopted at the convention merely enlarged upon the findings of the investigation commission approved by the general executive board. [5]

Titling the declaration "Opposing Classification of International Union by Press as Being Communist Controlled," the statement "reiterates that" the American Federation of Labor "has consistently denounced Communism as inimical to our form of government and hostile to the principles of the AF of L." It also took umbrage because, "according to the press," their International "is listed by the State Department among those organizations either Communist controlled or Communist penetrated. And since this classification places an odium upon our entire membership, which it does not deserve," it was imperative to take corrective action.

The declaration then proceeds to indict the Communist movement as follows: "1. It is not a political party. 2. It is a conspiracy designed to overthrow the American government and other democracies by force and violence and reduce them to totalitarianism. 3. It is directed from Moscow." 4. Communists strive to arouse antilabor sentiment "for the purpose of bringing about repressive, punitive and prohibitory legislation against bona-fide labor unions, in the belief that the American people would rebel against their government because of their loss of liberties and embrace the Communist doctrine." 5. Recent exposés prove that "every Communist is a potential saboteur against American democracy and a potential espionage agent of Soviet Russia." 6. The declaration ended by emphasizing op-

[4] *Ibid.*, 1947, p. 188.
[5] See above, pp. 91–92.

position and denouncing "all other forms of totalitarianism." [6]   In order to combat Communist charges of fascism against those who opposed them, it became the custom to insert denunciation of all forms of totalitarianism in statements criticizing communism.

In the debate on the report, the fat was really in the fire.   The views of the proponents of the resolution were concisely summarized by one of their ablest spokesmen: "The AF of L represents a force which holds within its power the ability to expose the hypocrisy and ruthlessness of this foreign 'ism,' which has crept into our national life, an 'ism' built and supported by dishonor, deceit, tyranny and deliberate policy of falsehood. . . .   They have maneuvered themselves into positions where a few Communists control the destinies of hundreds who are either willing to be led or have been duped into obeying the dictates of others." [7]

Realizing that it was in the helpless minority, the pro-Communist opposition first attempted to secure an agreement that neither side would debate the issue but would merely record that its representative on the committee of resolutions voted "No."   This arrangement was agreeable to the committee but not acceptable to the convention.[8]   The opposition then participated in the debate.

Although well known as Communists, the leaders of the opposition did not meet the issue squarely.   They made no attempt to defend communism or Soviet Russia, to refute charges of sabotage and espionage, or to deny their use of union machinery, paraphernalia, and funds to further the Communist cause.   Instead, in order to divert attention from the real issue—characteristic of the Communists—they posed as liberals and progressive trade unionists.   Furthermore, in this instance, they could, and did, irrefutably boast of their accomplishments in having built strong and successful local unions.   Their chief spokesman and member of the committee maintained that the real issue is "reaction in the United States."   And that "this convention instead of directing its attention to Communism, instead of trying to purge honest liberals and progressives, instead of planning restraints on the right of freedom of expression, should devote itself to the greater dangers that face all of us—dangers that we have already recognized and about which we have not done very much."   Then he warned: "If this resolution is adopted it will be playing directly into the hands of those forces who are trying to place upon labor the shackles and the restrictions that would establish the very same conditions that the resolution and the speakers in support of it are condemning—involuntary servitude and a long period of no strikes." [9]   Another pro-Communist delegate argued: "It took

[6] Hotel Proceedings, 1947, pp. 180–181.
[7] Ibid., 1947, p. 186.
[8] Ibid., 1947, p. 182.
[9] Ibid., 1947, pp. 180, 182, 187.

many years to achieve what our local has achieved—the fourth largest in the International. But how easy it will be for the employers, for the labor haters in Washington to break down what we have built up." [10]

The opposition presented a minority report which opposed restriction of civil rights, favored recognition of the rights of minority parties, and called for action that would prevent war. This report was overwhelmingly defeated and the majority report adopted with enthusiasm and acclaim.[11]

In the course of logic, action to restrict Communists within the union was in order. Resolution 54, reported out by the committee on law, provided for a new section in the constitution that would stipulate "no member . . . shall be eligible to hold any elective or appointive position . . . if he or she is a member of or subscribes to subversive doctrines of any organization such as, the Nazi, the Fascists, the Communists, the Ku Klux Klan or Columbian groups or organizations." [12]

In justification of this amendment, it was argued: "We surely deserve the right to regulate our unions, supervise the officers and make sure that our membership is not exploited by those who believe in Communism." It was pointed out that liberties are not infringed upon since the amendment provides for orderly procedure in implementing the resolution.[13]

Countering with a minority report, the opposition attempted to eliminate the drastic features of the majority report. It provided for adoption of "the proposition that local unions, that officers should not use the name of the organization to establish certain restrictions but instead it should be referred to the General Executive Board for action." They pleaded that since the constitution already covers the subject, it would be best to leave it to the general president and the general executive board to handle.[14] The drastic and far-reaching nature of the amendment, the opposition warned, would prove detrimental to others. "This resolution, if adopted, does not only affect Communists, but it will affect everyone with an independent point of view. . . . If you have a different opinion, at the next convention . . . and someone does not like you, he will be able to put a label on you and you will not be seated as a delegate." [15] Then this delegate, one of the trio regarded as the leading Communists in this organization, again boasted ostentatiously of their success: "We from New York represent more than half the membership. . . . We are organized and we carried through the fight against racketeering in New York City. . . . As far as our achievements in New York City are concerned we are nearly 100 per cent organized insofar as the hotel industry is concerned. Up

[10] *Ibid.*, 1947, p. 193.
[11] *Ibid.*, 1947, p. 188.
[12] *Ibid.*, 1947, p. 189.
[13] *Ibid.*, 1947, p. 196.
[14] *Ibid.*, 1947, p. 195.
[15] *Ibid.*, 1947, p. 190.

until 1935 and 1936 our International Union represented only a small group. Since 1941 we have grown to a membership of 79,000 to 85,000. . . . In 1941 we had 31,000." [16] Two carefully composed, written statements defending the Communist side were also presented and printed in the proceedings.[17]

Exhortation from the revered general president to adopt the minority report was not heeded. "I feel that the resolution is rather drastic. I feel that too much power may be given to one individual and that he may abuse it if he is not liberal enough or broad-minded enough to take all the circumstances into consideration. . . . It seems to me the sure thing would be to refer this matter to the General Executive Board and let's establish a Commission to investigate. . . . I fear we might do our organization more harm if we again let passion instead of reason rule our behavior." [18]

Just as the Communist-dominated locals failed to heed the 1946 recommendation of the general executive board to clean house, so they defied the policy declaration and the constitutional amendments enacted by an overwhelming vote of the convention. Their defiance was manifested by placing more of their followers in important union positions, taking reprisals against those who sided with the non-Communists by removing them from office, and by hindering locals that supported the administration. International officers were thereby compelled to take positive action in accordance with the convention mandate and the amended constitution.

Cleaning out Communists, racketeers, or any other undesirable element from a national trade-union center differs materially from expurgating them from within an international union. In the former case, in accordance with the principle of trade autonomy, expulsion is the only procedure. In the case of the latter, the international can, in accordance with constitutional provisions, step in and clean house by reorganizing subordinate units. The course becomes usually an arduous administrative undertaking. This is what the Hotel, Restaurant and Bartenders International proceeded to do after long procrastination and attempts to cope with the problem by pleading with the local Communist leaders to mend their ways and to do their own house cleaning.[19] Complying with the pleadings of International officials meant the Communists would have to eliminate themselves, or at least discontinue what to them was their most important mission, namely, promotion of the Communist cause.

Confronted with this obstinate situation, the general executive board finally took action: "Evidence was submitted which indicated that the

[16] *Ibid.*, 1947, pp. 191–195.
[17] *Ibid.*, 1947, pp. 210–212.
[18] *Ibid.*, 1947, pp. 196–197.
[19] The constitutions of national trade-union centers give their officers the same authority in relation to directly affiliated locals and to state and city units acting directly on behalf of the national center.

Local Joint Executive Board of New York City, was not functioning in the best interests of all affiliated locals. It was moved, seconded, and carried unanimously that the General President be directed to place the Local Joint Executive Board in trusteeship and to institute a program which would insure proper functioning of the Local Joint Executive Board." [20]

Naturally, the Communist opposition fought back. Following the pattern of the Communists in similar cases, they sought refuge in the courts. Thus, "when the General President arrived in New York to carry out his program ... he was served with a restraining order. . . ."

The local non-Communist supporters of the International's administration did not remain inactive. Immediately upon application by the New York local joint executive board for an injunction against the International's instituting a trusteeship, Local 15, a large non-Communist local affiliated with the local joint executive board, protested that the president of the latter acted "without authority and without a vote" in applying for the injunction. Local 15 called attention to section 156 of the constitution which states that a subordinate unit must exhaust all remedies within the organization before resorting to the courts. This is a common provision in international union constitutions. The judge had no alternative but to dissolve the temporary restraining order, and a trustee was appointed.[21]

The pro-Communists had no choice but to submit. They were, however, still in control, and fortune favored them again. The general officers did not relish the prospect of a bitter controversy that would entail expulsions and replacing pro-Communist officers by appointment rather than by elections. Indeed, they still had hopes of adjusting the differences amicably. They therefore restored autonomy to the joint local executive board on December 19, 1948, with a vague compromise the chief feature of which consisted of the selection of a forceful anti-Communist as president of the local joint executive board and a staunch Communist as secretary. The three locals accused of being Communist-dominated and which, with their combined membership, controlled the local joint executive board were not affected.[22]

At best, the compromise proved an uneasy truce. The Communists were still in power. They mustered their forces and resumed the fight to hold their position. The local non-Communists were not satisfied either. They, too, fought back. Several misrepresentations particularly incensed them. Two officers of Local 6 were quoted in the *Amsterdam News*, a Negro

[20] *Catering Industry Employee*, May, 1947, p. 47; minutes of the general executive board, officers' report in Hotel Proceedings, 1947, p. 18; *New York Times*, May 7, 1947.

[21] *Catering Industry Employee*, June, 1947, p. 35.

[22] Hotel Proceedings, 1949, p. 18; *New York Times*, June 18, 1947, and Nov. 27, 1947; *Catering Industry Employee*, May, 1948, p. 8; Matthew Josephson, *Union House, Union Bar*, Random House, Inc., New York, 1956, p. 324.

daily, to the effect that the constitutional amendments enacted at the International convention in 1947 "would lead to eliminating Negroes from the union." The staunchly anti-Communist president of Local 16 in New York City wrote a heated denial. He accused the vice-president of Local 6 of having "falsely and maliciously interpreted" the amendments.[23] This was indeed a sore point since the Hotel and Restaurant Employees had a considerable Negro membership, having taken in Negroes ever since its inception. Besides, Negroes were a growing employee group in union jurisdiction. Furthermore, in 1936, the International convention had "removed all vestiges of the 'color line,'" forbidding segregated locals.[24] On the other hand, the Communists had pinpointed Negroes as their most promising recruits.

Another provocative contention which involved officials of the International aroused bitter resentment. Harry Reich, pro-Communist president of Local 89 and general manager of the New York local joint executive board, claimed that its officers agreed to withdraw the petition for a permanent injunction against the International officers on condition that "there would be no trusteeship in the Joint Executive Board." Since a trusteeship was invoked, this charge meant accusing the International officers of bad faith. The general president interpreted it as such and printed the written agreement "to show that this charge was unfounded." [25]

An attack was also made from within on Local 6, the Communist stronghold. In this case, the specific target was the president, Michael Obermeier, who was being harassed from other sources. A Committee for Trade Union Democracy, consisting of non-Communist members of Local 6, was organized to defeat him. The charge was that the leaders kept "Communist functionaries on the local union payroll, and had failed to secure adequate wages for the members." [26]

Union attacks also came from other sources. Michael J. Obermeier was defeated, 75 to 56, as secretary-treasurer of the New York State Culinary Alliance and Bartender's League of the International Union. The secretary of Local 302 in New York, a firm supporter of the International administration, declared: "For the first time in seven years the secretaryship has been wrested from those elements that always wave the flag and actually represent the interests of some other nation." [27] On September 17, 1948, the New York Central Trades and Labor Council unseated two delegates for following the Communist Party line. One of these represented Local 6.[28]

[23] *Catering Industry Employee*, June, 1947, p. 4.
[24] Josephson, *op. cit.*, pp. 226–227; see also pp. 17, 18, 36, and 142.
[25] *Catering Industry Employee*, May, 1948, pp. 4–6.
[26] *New York Times*, Oct. 16, 1947.
[27] *Ibid.*, Aug. 19, 1947.
[28] *Ibid.*, Sept. 17, 1948.

Government action through the Immigration and Naturalization Service also contributed to the embarrassment of the Communist group: it initiated deportation proceedings against Obermeier as an "alien Communist." [29] At the deportation hearings, Obermeier admitted he was a member of the Communist Party from 1930 to 1939 and a member of TUUL between 1933 and 1935.[30] Obermeier was therefore charged with and convicted for perjury because he had denied in applying for citizenship that he was ever a member of the Communist Party. In July, 1950, he resigned as president of Local 6, following his conviction. After losing his appeal in the United States Supreme Court, he began in April, 1951, to serve his two-year sentence.[31] Upon completion of his prison term, he was deported.[32]

Even though the controversy went on locally, following the raising of the trusteeship, International officials put themselves out in their effort to steer a neutral course. Thus, trying to be fair and liberal-minded, the International's administration merely attacked Communist activity in general. In the February issue of their official publication, a critical editorial appears entitled "Communist Saboteurs on Capitol Hill." It chides the "Communist Dominated UE and the Civil Rights Congress for their boisterous, unmannerly and uncouth behavior in lobbying tactics." [33] An editorial in a succeeding issue gloats over the rupture in relations between the CIO and the "Communist-dominated WFTU" and concludes with an indictment: "Wherever Communists have attained some degree of influence in American unions they have insisted upon running the whole show. . . . The arrogance of Communists, their domineering way, has brought on a wave of resentment against them which has swept them out of a number of larger unions in this country and their influence is rapidly drifting down to zero." [34] And in another issue was featured the full text of the statement made by Jackie Robinson, "the star second baseman of the Brooklyn Dodgers," before the House Committee on Un-American Activities. It carried the obvious title, "Jackie Robinson Goes to Bat." [35]

[29] *Ibid.*, Oct. 8, 1947.
[30] *Ibid.*, Nov. 2, 1947.
[31] *Catering Industry Employee*, August, 1950, p. 3; *New York Times*, Apr. 11, 1951.
[32] See above, pp. 86–87.
[33] *Catering Industry Employee*, February, 1949, p. 40.
[34] *Ibid.*, March, 1949, p. 7.
[35] *Ibid.*, September, 1949, pp. 3–4; see also articles in similar vein in previous issues: "Ouster of Reds by Garment Union Upheld by Court," June, 1947, p. 22; "How Reds Fight to Control Unions," describing fake rumors, spread by Communist opposition in the U.A.W., that Walter Reuther is contemplating running as vice-presidential candidate with Robert A. Taft and is taking up with Gerald L. K. Smith, the "notorious anti-labor demogogue, and with other Fascist elements," November, 1947, p. 21; an editorial, "The Way of Communist Termiting in Unions," July,

In so far as internal affairs of the union were concerned, the general officers made every effort not to appear to take sides in the controversy between the non-Communists and the Communists, although the latter abused, denounced, and defied them. In the officers' report signed by General President Ernst and General Secretary-Treasurer Miller, there appears an explanation of their duties: "We have explained to various gatherings of our local union officials, that the General Office under the present Administration does not attempt to tell the local unions how to run their affairs. The General Office is a service department—always at your beck and call for help or advice, to try to pull your local out of difficulties and place it on the road to progress." [36]

General President Ernst, eager to have things run smoothly and to pour oil on troubled waters, ran an article on the "President's Page" discussing: "Hysteria and Democracy: A Plea for Sanity." [37] Both he and the general secretary-treasurer participated in functions conducted by the three locals charged with violating the constitution. As an example, the official organ ran an account headed, "General President Ernst Addresses Local 6 Convention." The article is accompanied by a photograph showing the general president shaking hands with Michael J. Obermeier on the platform. The general president is credited with the following remarks: "Presently attempts are being made to secure the deportation of Brother Obermeier on the grounds that he is not a citizen and holds political views allegedly contrary to American institutions and traditions. We do not share Brother Obermeier's political views, which is our privilege, but we also extend to him the right to adhere to these views so long as the resultant action on his part does not violate the rights of others. In the light of these considerations we condemn the efforts to deport him as a violation of civil liberties. . . ." This issue also contains an editorial by John Bookjans, managing editor, pleading that "minority rights must be respected," even while recognizing that Russia is not a democracy.[38]

The general president also presided at the installation of Local 89 officers.

1948, p. 3; "Rejoices in Defeat of Communists at U.A.W. Convention in 1947" attacks Communists' unscrupulous tactics in trying to defeat Reuther, January, 1948, p. 25; in another issue are two items telling of the founding of the Inter-American Federation of Labor, open only to "free trade unions," and an account of Green's assailing Wallace's third party, February, 1948, p. 3; another issue runs an editorial, "The Communists Are in Retreat." "In their effort to capture the Labor Movement, the Communists have met with repeated reverses of late both in AF of L and CIO," September, 1947, pp. 2–3; "Communist Party in CIO Slumping Heavily" describes the attack by Murray on Communists at Portland convention and tells of the reorganization of the CIO's Greater New York Council by the revoking of its charter, December, 1948, p. 9.

[36] Hotel Proceedings, 1949, p. 35.

[37] Catering Industry Employee, July, 1949, p. 2.

[38] Ibid., January, 1948, p. 20.

The president of this local, Harry Reich, had accused the general officers of breaking their promise by establishing a trusteeship for the local joint executive board after it failed to press the restrain-order in the courts.[39]

Retaining control of three large locals, and through them dominating the local joint executive board, the pro-Communists, following the lifting of the trusteeship, proceeded to strengthen their position. Undoubtedly encouraged by the neutral attitude of the International officials, they seemed to act on the assumption that the stronger they were in the New York area, the less they had to fear from the opposition in New York and throughout the country. They acted in order to eliminate non-Communists from local official positions and to replace them by their own adherents. Powerful Local 6, Communist-dominated, suspended three business agents for circulating a petition asking the International for a separate charter.[40] General President Ernst ordered the agents restored, but at the succeeding election they were defeated.[41] Indeed in this election, the membership overwhelmingly returned to office those who supported the local administration against International Union charges. "Not a single candidate of the opposition ticket was elected.... Several opposition candidates holding jobs as business agents were defeated ... with the candidates for the main offices on the administration ticket rolling up approximately 13,000 ... the opposition's highest vote was 1,755." These results were interpreted by the administration of Local 6 as indicating "how strongly the overwhelming majority of ... [the] workers reject the attempt of would-be disrupters of their union to split up Local 6.... It also showed their decisive repudiation of efforts to foil them through raising false issues." [42]

Emboldened by their success, the pro-Communists elected Michael J. Obermeier, president of Local 6, as their general manager, the controlling executive office. The Shop Delegates Council approved the selection by acclamation. The Communists also turned their guns on the International vice-president of the district, Miguel Garriga, who had successfully directed the fight against them in this region. Although he had been elected by the convention, the Communists accused him of disruptive tactics against Local 6 and demanded that the International Union remove him.[43]

Able not only to maintain but to strengthen their hold, the pro-Communists came to the 1949 convention full of confidence. Taking advantage of a decision to revise the constitution at this convention, they

[39] *Ibid.*, May, 1949, p. 31.
[40] *New York Times*, May 21, 1947; *Daily Worker*, May 21, 1947.
[41] *Catering Industry Employee*, May, 1948, pp. 32–33; *New York Times*, Nov. 5, 1948.
[42] *Catering Industry Employee*, March, 1948, pp. 32–33.
[43] *Ibid.*

were prepared to secure deletion of the anti-Communist and antitotalitarian provisions adopted at previous conventions. Delegate Jay Rubin—one of three outstanding Communist leaders, a key figure in Local 6, and president of the New York City AFL Hotel Trades Council—and another delegate from Local 6 opposed retention of that section barring Communists and other subversives from membership and from holding office.[44]

They not only failed in this attempt, but the clause was strengthened, indicating that the delegates, most of whom were from the rank and file, were more determined than ever to clean house. The clause provided that "no person shall be eligible for, or continue to hold office in the International Union or any of its subordinate affiliates, or serve as a convention delegate, if such person associates himself with Communist, Fascist or similar organizations, or the Ku Klux Klan or the Columbians...." Similarly, it clearly authorized the president to act and stipulated what procedures he was to follow.[45]

Notwithstanding the efforts of International officials, the festering sore could not be healed. Indeed, it reached a stage requiring surgical treatment. Attempts of top leaders to reconcile the conflicting groups through compromise and their appeals and warnings to the Communists to curb their activities proved futile. The efforts of the leaders and the persistence of the anti-Communists did, however, serve the purpose of alerting the non-Communists, some fellow travelers, and even some formerly staunch Communists. Thus the power and influence of the Communists, including their chances for further inroads into the union, were effectively checked and even reduced. Conversely, the Communists entrenched themselves even more solidly in certain sectors from which they could not be displaced without drastic action on the part of the International. Local efforts of non-Communist leaders and members proved inadequate.

While International headquarters was still uncertain of the desirability of drastic action, and this was especially true of General President Ernst, it was evident such action could no longer be postponed. "Hugo Ernst was always a 'loyal organization man,'" wrote the author of the union's official history. "If the majority had spoken, even though he disagreed, he must obey their wishes." [46]

Besides, conditions for house cleaning were favorable. "While these gradual steps [by International headquarters] were being taken, serious dissension broke out late in 1949 within the leftist-controlled Hotel and Club Employees Local 6, with its President, Martin Cody, and business agent, Charles Collins, heading the left wing faction, and Secretary Gertrude Lane and Jay Rubin, who was the President of the New York Hotel

[44] Hotel Proceedings, 1949, pp. 170–171.
[45] Ibid.; Josephson, op. cit., pp. 324–325.
[46] Josephson, op. cit., p. 325.

Trades Council, now heading the opposition." [47]   These two, as a husband-and-wife team, were undoubtedly the ablest of the Communist leaders.

In taking action at this time, it was decided to concentrate on the real source of power instead of attacking the over-all local joint executive board that exercised only authority delegated to it.   Since Local 6, with its approximately 30,000 members, was the spearhead of Communist strength and inspiration and now had a strong opposition functioning within it, the International's administration picked this unit for attention.   Thus, as J. W. Brown, general counsel for the International, reported: "During the summer of 1940, the Officers of the International who had been watching the situation in Local 6 for several years, received a volume of complaints concerning the friction and dissension within Local 6 and the Communist activities of certain officers. . . .   An investigation was ordered in September 1950." [48]   A trusteeship was established, in accordance with the constitution, over Hotel and Club Local 6, New York.   In appointing International Representative Bert Ross as trustee, General President Ernst explained to the local officers and members that "he invoked his powers to order the trusteeship only with the greatest reluctance and after extensive investigation had resolved that only by such a step can the present menace of Communism be eradicated from Local 6."   He charged that "grievances had been neglected, and that the true functioning of the local had been disregarded."   Ross was given orders to cleanse the local of "Communist elements." [49]

The trustee took over September 29, 1950, and "at the first meeting of the local Administrative Board, all 15 members voted to concur in President Ernst's decision." [50]   The *Daily Worker*, however, "came out with a page one blast" against the International's action.[51]   In whirlwind fashion, Ross called meetings of the various local boards and committees and announced his proposal to oust subversives. He declared all offices vacant and then reappointed all but the president to serve subject to investigation of their qualifications, and compliance with the International constitution." [52]   Following investigation, he dismissed on October 6 the "former Moscow correspondent for the *Daily Worker* . . . as editor of the 'Voice.' " After this action, "the paper counteracted Communist propaganda" pertaining to the receivership.   The trustee also dismissed the general organizer,

[47] *Loc. cit.*
[48] *Catering Industry Employee*, February, 1951, p. 17.
[49] *Ibid.*, October, 1950, p. 7; *New York Times*, Sept. 21, 1950.
[50] *Catering Industry Employee*, October, 1950, p. 7.
[51] *Ibid.*, July, 1951, p. 23.
[52] *Ibid.* As a result of its large membership, it was decided to divide Local 6 into sublocals, each with the usual governmental machinery but accountable to the parent local.   Local 6, acting as the coordinating body, functioned through its elected officers and met at stated periods in "convention," a common practice with locals having large, unwieldy membership groups.

four vice-presidents, and eight business agents, the assistant to the secretary-treasurer, the office manager, labor chief, welfare director, switchboard operator, several secretaries, and a number of minor employees, declaring their "Communist connections were clear." [53]

These suspended officers immediately instituted legal proceedings, including injunctive action. "The court closely examined all of the applicable provisions of the International Constitution and upheld each of the provisions, ruling that the trials were fair and in accordance with due process." The hearings lasted five weeks and were featured by "the glaring and obvious lack of substantial evidence the plaintiffs could bring to bear." The Communists tried to turn the trial into "the familiar Communist propaganda circus. . . . Finally the thirteen walked out, refusing to appear before the investigating committee. . . ." The officers were found guilty and were suspended for three years. "Autonomy was restored to Local 6 after nine months of Trusteeship." [54] Shortly after autonomy was granted at a local convention, "the administration ticket scored a one-sided triumph in the largest 'turn-out vote' in Local 6 history. . . . On June 13, 1951, the Trusteeship Ticket, administration ticket, swept everyone of the 157 offices." [55]

Success in eliminating the Communists from Local 6 resulted in their replacement in other New York locals through the normal election process.[56] The New York area of the Hotel and Restaurant Employees Union was now out from under Communist domination.

This, then, broke the Communist stronghold in the International. There were, however, other scattered areas where Communists held important local positions. In the official organ's April, 1951, issue there appears an item to the effect that "in the March 9th election of officers for Local 302 . . . with real regret it must be reported that the opposition concentrated its work among our new members. . . . Many of these are Spanish speaking . . . and . . . the opposition also had the aid of the Communists." [57] At hearings before the House Un-American Activities Committee, it developed that two union officials of the Troy local had until recently been Communist Party members.[58] In 1953 the Appeals Division of New York State upheld a lower-court decision on the expulsion of a business agent of the Albany Local 4711 because of associating "with Communist organizations and supporting Communist doctrines." [59]

[53] *Ibid.*, Feb., 1951, p. 16.
[54] *Loc. cit.*, and July, 1951, p. 23; *New York Times*, Feb. 3, 1951.
[55] *Catering Industry Employee*, July, 1951, p. 24.
[56] Josephson, *op. cit.*, p. 328.
[57] *Catering Industry Employee*, April, 1951, p. 23.
[58] *New York Times*, July 15, 1953.
[59] *Ibid.*, Dec. 24, 1953; see also *Investigation of Communist Activities in Albany, New York, Hearings before the House Committee on Un-American Activities*, 83d

The Communists also insinuated themselves into the Hotel and Restaurant Employees locals in Washington. A business agent, James McNamara, worked with them, and they, in alliance with Communists from other parts of the country, promoted his election as district vice-president at the 1938 convention. He served in this capacity until 1941. McNamara testified under oath he was not "ideologically" a Communist, but that he had worked with them because he needed their help in organizing hotel workers in Washington. He admitted, however, he had made contributions which might have been dues and had participated in meetings that apparently were Communist caucuses. He also testified that he did not stop the use of his name by Communist-front organizations.[60]

The administration of the International, despite its harrowing experience with Communists and largely because of the influence of General President Hugo Ernst, separated itself from those who demanded stringent government action against the Communists. An editorial in the official organ in 1951 voiced disagreement with the government in prosecuting the eleven Communists under the Smith Act: "Perhaps there are Communists that are a real danger to our governmental system, but these Communists are more or less anonymous.... Jailing leaders is not the answer to halting Communist ideas.... Eternal vigilance through education is the remedy." [61] On the other hand, the International convention did indicate its disassociation from communism and its activities. The following clause appeared in a resolution adopted unanimously at the 1953 convention: "Whereas, the Negro Labor Committee of the United States of America, composed of workers, Negro and white, who have successfully fought off attempts by the Communists to use them, is one of the major groups that has coordinated the democratic efforts to banish discrimination and segregation from our land"; the convention endorsed the committee's work and donated $500.[62] General President Ernst also took occasion to dissociate himself from the *March of Labor*," a Communist publication which, in publishing a garbled account of his talk on unity, conveyed the impression that he agreed with its views.[63]

In contrast to several previous conventions, that of 1953 was a calm one. The Communist issue having been disposed of, only routine business was conducted.

Cong., 2d Sess., 1954, Part 4, pp. 4378–4380; Part 3, pp. 4308–4310; Part 6, pp. 448–449.

[60] See *Communist Methods of Infiltration (Government-Labor)*, *Hearings Before the House Committee on Un-American Activities*, 83d Cong., 2d Sess., 1954, pp. 3025–3041.

[61] *Catering Industry Employee*, August, 1951, p. 4.

[62] Hotel Proceedings, 1953, p. 174.

[63] *Catering Industry Employee*, May, 1953, p. 4; for a description of this publication, see *Report on the March of Labor*, U.S. Congress, House Committee on Un-American Activities, 1954.

12

Effect of the Expulsion
upon the Union

Motivated by a decent respect for the opinions of mankind, the Hotel and Restaurant Employees Union felt it necessary to explain and justify their resorting to drastic action in ousting the Communists. An editorial in their official publication, captioned "Communist on the Way Out," addressed itself to this task. Since, during the struggle with the Communists in HRE, conflict was occurring on a much grander scale in the CIO, this editorial begins by congratulating the CIO for expelling the Communist-dominated unions. It then ridicules the "whining of the *Daily Worker*" and, following this introduction, proceeds to explain that it was not difficult for the Communists to penetrate unions because "during the hectic organizing activities to take advantage of the Wagner Act unions were too preoccupied to be on the alert. Later, Russia became our war ally and it was regarded as good patriotism to work with the Communists and to overlook their foibles. It was when friction developed with Russia, and the Communists began to resort to character assassination and unscrupulous tactics to control unions that it became necessary to expel them." [1]

It is difficult to evaluate the factors which weighed most heavily in bringing about the expulsions. Undoubtedly, the cumulative effect of all factors motivated the officers and members to react against the Communists in the manner they did. Patriotism certainly was important. Communist opposition to the Marshall Plan and to NATO aroused the members. One delegate summarized the reaction: "I resent very much ... these types of people here.... I have seen them in action from coast to coast.... They are against the Marshall Plan ... because it has helped these people that they want to get their hands on...." [2]

Treason and espionage also concerned the members. The official pub-

[1] *Catering Industry Employee*, July, 1950, pp. 7–8.
[2] Hotel and Restaurant Employees and Bartenders International Union Convention, hereafter referred to as "Hotel Proceedings," 1949, p. 163; see also pp. 146–147, an address by President William Green in which he describes Communist opposition to the Marshall Plan.

lication quoted with approval: "Communists should not be driven underground in the opinion of William Henry Chamberlin . . . in a recent issue of the *New Leader* . . . he says:

"No American, except for a few unrepresentative rabid reactionaries, would wish to persecute anyone for holding unconventional ideas. But Americans, except philosophical anarchists, would admit that overt breaches of laws against treason, espionage, betrayal of confidential information, perjury and passport frauds should be punished." [3]

Deception and simulation were other factors that angered the members. One delegate declared, "I know you for what you are, not for what you tell me you could be." [4]

Harassment was an additional irritant: "They will hound you to desperation. They will set no end of traps for you to place you in a false light before the members." Much of the pressure to take action against the Communists came from "delegates who in their own local unions had been going through harrowing experiences with Communists."

General President Ernst, in a speech to a Dutch trade-union delegation, succinctly summarized the general attitude: "We learned from bitter experience that Communists in unions are undesirable, partly because their totalitarian ideologies sharply conflict with American democratic traditions, and partly because of their desperate efforts to make unions subservient to Communist party dictation. Communists resort to tricks and ruses that cause endless friction and discontent—to state it mildly. Their policy is to rule or ruin.

"In some unions, Communists succeeded in so firmly entrenching themselves as to call for extraordinary methods to dislodge them. . . .

"But in a number of locals in our International, Communists have made themselves conspicuously obnoxious by conducting Communist propaganda through union channels and by milking union treasuries for the support of Communist front organizations. This made it necessary at the last convention of our International, held in April, 1947, to adopt an amendment to the constitution barring Communists from holding office." [5]

The experience of HRE with the Communists reveals certain conditions and practices that have occurred in the trade-union movement whenever the Communist problem arose. Unstable conditions—unemployment, low wages, poor working conditions, racketeering, weak union organization, union jurisdictional rivalry, and similar unsettled conditions—gave the Communists, where they had nuclei operating in the area, the opportunity to inject themselves. Usually, they took effective advantage of the situation. Only where experienced and ideologically sophisticated leaders were present to

[3] *Catering Industry Employee*, May, 1947, p. 26.
[4] Hotel Proceedings, 1949, p. 163.
[5] *Catering Industry Employee*, June, 1948, p. 6.

counteract them were they prevented from taking over. Generally, top officials, concerned primarily with organizing the workers and lacking necessary personnel, accepted and tolerated the Communists. Invariably, oriented anti-Communists protested. They were usually supported by the alert members. Ambitious and jealous leaders, or aspirants to leadership, finding the Communists in their way, also associated themselves with the opposition. Anti-Communist agitation, with its specific exposures of Communist designs and abuses, and the growing opposition which resulted from this, aroused the indifferent non-Communists, local as well as high-level leaders, and even some "devoted" fellow travelers and Communist members. But these elements generally lacked the strength to combat Communist control successfully alone.

Not until International officials, or the over-all national leaders of the trade-union center, yielding to insistent pressure, joined with the local dissidents was it possible to eliminate Communist domination. It required the combination of high and local officials and alert members to arouse the rank and file—who heretofore had submitted to Communist control—to support necessary action. As described by the International general council, which played a leading role in the Communist purge, this was the experience of HRE: "All of the governing bodies of Local 6 agreed unanimously with the action of the International, and the rank and file cooperated wholeheartedly. . . . The loyal officers of Local 6 cooperated closely with the office of the General Council. Due to this wholehearted cooperation, suitable evidence was obtained concerning the membership and Communist activities of the officers of the local. . . ." [6] Similarly, the official publication reported favorable response from the membership throughout the country: "Great satisfaction has been expressed by members of Local 6 and other locals throughout the United States at the victory which the International Union won in having its constitution and the ouster of Communist elements sustained by the Supreme Court of New York in the Local 6 Trusteeship." [7]

In practically all these efforts to dislodge Communist control of unions, the defection of Communist and fellow-traveler officials usually threw the balance in favor of those who were engaged in the house cleaning. Indeed in nearly all instances, it was the union officials who discarded Communist affiliation and chose to function primarily in their capacity as union leaders that made it possible to wrest control of the union from the Communists, whether local or international. Where the leaders in control remained in the Communist fold, it was practically impossible to reform the union. In such cases, expulsion or other peremptory action was the only course. Thus, while Local 6 was "long considered one of the strongholds of the left

[6] *Catering Industry Employee*, February, 1951, p. 163.
[7] *Catering Industry Employee*, March, 1951.

wing in the AF of L," yet "in recent months, its leaders had moved to the right in a political and economic conflict with Communist policy. However, it is known that a number of leftists still have been active in union affairs." [8]

Among those who had abandoned their Communist connections were the two outstanding local union leaders who had contributed most to the building of the union in New York City. They were Jay Rubin, then and at present president of the New York Hotel Trades Council and mastermind of Local 6, and his wife, Gertrude Lane, secretary-treasurer of Local 6. Both of them were pivotal leaders within the Communist group, possessed extraordinary executive ability, and were forceful personalities, an essential leadership attribute. In an obituary of Gertrude Lane Rubin, the International vice-president of District 2, who, as International representative designate was trustee during the cleansing period, affirmed: "One of the most severe tests of her career came in 1949 when, with the local union seriously split by bitter internal factional struggles, she and her associates agreed to cooperate with the International Union during a period of trusteeship to last until democracy could be restored." He further added that "without her help, he would not have been able to accomplish his mission in the short space of a year." [9]

These Communists and union leaders explained that, having contributed so much of their lives to the building of the union organization, they chose to preserve it. In a pamphlet issued by this group, the following paragraph appears: "Some locals were said to have leftists and Communists among their leadership in the early days of the hotel organization. The best of these leaders discovered what AFL President William Green has seen: A trade unionist will come to realize there can be only one boss—the union and its members. These rejected disruptive orders, and for the good of the union helped clean house." [10]

Whole unions, whether international, regional, or local, escaped from Communist domination only if some of the key leaders discarded their Communist connections. These leaders chose to remain trade unionists first, rather than Communists or fellow travelers. They had worked industriously to build the union; it had become part of them—their creation. In this effort they had carved a career for themselves. Most of them were irked by having to submit to orders from a remote source given by persons not familiar with either the industry or the union. Moreover, this distant direction was not guided by the problems and needs of the members but by

[8] *New York Times*, Sept. 21, 1950.
[9] *Catering Industry Employee*, December, 1953, pp. 16–18; Matthew Josephson, *Union House, Union Bar*, Random House, Inc., New York, 1956, pp. 325–329.
[10] A *Union of Unions*, issued by the New York Hotel Trades Council, 1952, p. 20, quoted in Josephson, *op. cit.*, p. 325.

the interests of Soviet Russia. Thus aroused and, finding it necessary to decide, they put the interest of their union and their future as trade-union leaders above their allegiance to the Communist Party line.

Fears of top union officials that vigorous action against entrenched Communists would endanger the affected units proved unfounded. Indeed, experience and later developments revealed that the Communists could not be eliminated except by forthright action. Certainly the locals were not destroyed, or even materially weakened. Instead of losing, they gained in membership and in effectiveness in fulfilling their trade-union function of protecting and promoting the interests of their adherents. Furthermore, concern that such expulsions would reflect unfavorably upon the International and thereby also affect the strength of the entire labor movement has not been substantiated by experience.[11] The pattern is the same, within both the AFL and the CIO.

Similarly, the dire predictions of Communists and fellow travelers, eloquently supported by numerous liberals, that checking or eliminating them would result in irreparable damage to the particular organizations in which they operated and to the movement at large, by impairing their efficiency and their democratic nature, have not eventuated. Such contentions overlook the basic democratic and patriotic intuitiveness of the American rank and file and of run-of-the-mill union leaders. It reveals an unwarranted lack of confidence in the innate honesty and decency of the average union member who is thoroughly indoctrinated and dedicated to human rights and democracy.

There may, perhaps, be valid disagreement on the timing. Officers in the lower echelons and the alert rank and file pressed for early and quick action. The administration of the International aimed at delaying action and hoped to correct the situation by reasoning with the Communist leaders. The fact remains, nevertheless, that without pressure from members who threatened to revolt and thereby disregard orderly procedure, top leaders might not have acted even when the time was ripe.

At any rate, the cleansed units remained intact, possibly because of the skillful guidance of the chief leaders. Besides, these unions, locally and nationally—like most unions in the United States—have flourished. Furthermore, the democratic nature of the locals and of the International was not impaired.

It is true the New York locals were in the doldrums until the middle thirties. But so were the locals in the rest of the country. Moreover, this was characteristic of the entire labor movement, with minor exceptions. It is also true that the New York locals, dominated by the Communists, made extraordinary progress under their tutelage. And so did other locals

[11] See General President Ernst's report as delegate to the AFL convention, *Catering Industry Employee*, December, 1935, p. 11.

throughout the country. They all prospered in proportion to the size of the industry in their area and under their jurisdiction. In 1941, the International boasted that it was the fourth largest in the AFL. This was cited as "evidence of our growing membership." [12] In 1949, the committee-on-officers report gleefully proclaimed, "Our International is now the third largest within the AFL." [13]

It is true the Communist element played an important role in cleaning out the racketeers in the New York area. But so did other groups. All of them cooperated with public authorities without whose participation the house cleaning might not have been achieved.[14] And when the racketeers and ex-bootleggers attempted to capture the International in 1938, the membership and the convention delegates defeated them, thus assuring honest, able leadership and preserving the democratic nature of the International.[15]

Following reorganization, the International could boastfully report in an article entitled "All Locals Gain in '51" that "early last month, the New York Local Joint Executive Board, following one of the most fruitful years in history, elected officers for the current term." It also reported that "every local union affiliated with the New York LJEB made substantial advances during 1951, in some cases marking up gains of historic importance not only to hotel and restaurant workers in New York City, but to workers in our industry throughout the country since developments here are bound to affect conditions elsewhere in the industry.... The gains take on added significance in the light of the inflationary trends affecting workers' wages, as well as in the light of certain signs that conditions in our industry are not too healthy."

The article then particularizes by describing the gains made by most of the individual New York locals. "The three waiters unions—Locals 1, 16 and 219—now in process of the highly complicated task of merging, won two major victories: the five-day week and a pension plan.

"Local 15, Manhattan's Bartenders Union, after a long struggle, achieved its goal of the five-day, 40-hour week, as well....

"Local 89, our cooks union, and Local 60, the Delicatessen Countermen's Union, won not only their employer-paid pension programs, but general wage increases as well.

"Local 302, first of New York City's culinary unions to put in force an industry-wide pension plan among cafeterias here, scored another substantial social advance in 1951 by negotiating an agreement under which cafeteria employers are underwriting the cost for erection of a union medical

[12] Hotel Proceedings, 1941, p. 23.
[13] Ibid., 1949, p. 82.
[14] Jay Rubin and Michael Obermeier, Growth of a Union: The Life and Times of Edward Flore, The Historical Union Association, 1943, pp. 225–250, 279.
[15] Ibid., pp. 279–291; Josephson, op. cit., pp. 241–257.

clinic to carry on a program of preventive medicine to help keep cafeteria workers well.

"The giant Local 6, composed of housekeeping, culinary and bar employees in Manhattan's hotels and clubs, succeeded in cutting through the red tape binding wage controls and won approval of the Wage Stabilization Board to a general wage increase and a number of fringe benefits.

"Throughout this year of real progress, the New York Joint Board has had the closest support from the International Union. . . .

"The Board looks ahead into 1952 with a real sense of challenge to organize the unorganized. . . ." [16]

The International continued joyously to enlarge on the success of the New York union situation following the purge. After reporting that the New York LJEB reelected the entire administration ticket, the official journal contained the following comment: "Local labor observers have interpreted the sweeping endorsement of the board's incumbent officers as a sign of real harmony and effective work by the board in recent months toward working out inter-union problems along democratic, trade-union lines.

"In previous years, many here felt that political factions and political alignments interfered with the orderly handling of the problems which are bound to arise in the area where jurisdictions are severely complicated." [17]

And, in the October issue, it ran the following report:

"Local 6 Pays Tribute to Ross on Success of Trusteeship, at the Statler Hotel, September 27.

"The testimonial dinner followed a two-day convention of the Local.

"It was for his work in cleaning out the Communist elements in Local 6 and ending the factional strife that had rent the Union that the dinner was tended.

"Ross [was] gratified that revised by-laws contained the same anti-subversive clause that is in the International Constitution." [18]

Further expressions of self-congratulation and gratification were made at the 1953 convention. In the nominating speech presenting the name of Bert Ross for vice-president representing District 2, "which embraces the largest membership in our International . . ." [19] his essential qualifications for the post were enumerated. It was particularly stressed that "he has already installed harmony and unity through his close cooperation and valuable counsel. He has promoted union principles throughout the nation's metropolitan district. . . ." [20]

In his closing remarks at the convention, General President Ernst hap-

[16] *Catering Industry Employee*, February, 1952, pp. 26–27.
[17] *Ibid.*, March, 1951, p. 27.
[18] *Ibid.*, October, 1951, pp. 22–26.
[19] *Catering Industry Employee*, October, 1951, pp. 25–26.
[20] Hotel Proceedings, 1953, p. 219.

pily announced that "the New York LJEB deserves credit for having initiated and carried through the question of unity, and I want to thank them for their thoughtful consideration of this matter and assistance." [21]

During this period, there were other instances of Communist penetration in many subsidiaries of AFL internationals. While in no other instances was the temporary success of the Communists on the extensive scale that it was in Hollywood or in the HRE, the subversive element generally proved troublesome and often required effective attention. Vestiges of this element still remain well concealed in some unions, but, for the present, they are not a threat.

[21] *Ibid.*, 1953, p. 266.

PART **III**

Communist Infiltration
of the CIO

13

The Situation within the CIO

Physically and intellectually conditions during this period were more favorable for Communist infiltration of the newly created CIO than of the well-established AFL. As earlier chapters have shown, where conditions in AFL affiliates were favorable, the Communists were successful in their infiltration attempts, but they failed to pierce the armor of the national AFL center as they did in the CIO. In AFL affiliates, Communists made most headway where leadership and membership were liberally or radically oriented, where the union, operating in either organized or unorganized areas, was often weak, and where racketeers and other socially unsavory elements tainted the old leadership, already poisoned by incompetence and apathy. In addition, there were usually bitter jurisdictional claims and conflicts that favored Communist penetration.

In the case of the CIO, however, there were other important factors favoring the Communists' objectives. The motivating spirit of the CIO differed from that of the tradition-bound AFL. Believing that mass-production industries could be organized only through industrial unions and revivalistic organizing campaigns and resenting bitterly the AFL's insistence on the craft unions, the CIO stood enthusiastically for fundamental social reform and adventure. To these people, the staid AFL business-union outlook was an antiquated hindrance to progress. Such an ebullient attitude as the CIO's was stepped up even more by the advent of the New Deal which encouraged especially elements with a liberal or radical background. Moreover, the need to resort to an emotional, even evangelical, approach in order to arouse the unorganized and previously cowed masses and to organize them into viable unions in itself generated an all-pervasive feeling of brotherhood and tolerance. Even the superlatively practical and ordinarily placid leaders, smarting from the AFL's peremptory rejection and taunting and sensing they would regain status by pioneering in an unprecedented social adventure, fell prey to the new emotionalism. Visions of a new order aborning transformed them into evangelistic social reformers and dreamers of new things to come.

Superimposed on the vision of creating a new labor movement, and perhaps a new social order, was the pressing need for experienced and competent personnel to master the gigantic and quite tangible task of organizing mass-production and related industries. Workers were clamoring to be organized—some even besieged CIO headquarters. The field was wide open. There was scarcely time to train personnel—and anyway, here at hand were reasonably qualified individuals who were eager to offer their services.

This was not the time, it seemed, for ideological niceties. Lewis not only overlooked past escapades of the Communists, he embraced many of his former non-Communist enemies whom he had previously forced out of the United Mine Workers. Among them were John Brophy, Powers Hapgood, and Adolph Germer.[1]

Among the Communists there were many who fitted the CIO's need for experienced personnel; they did not wait to be called—they offered their services. With the others, they were gladly received.

Confident, strong-minded, the CIO leaders probably felt they could later take care of those Communists and fellow travelers whom they could not bend into conformity with CIO standards of loyalty. Perhaps they were fortified by their earlier successes in ousting Communists. Perhaps time and new incentives had rubbed away the bruises incurred in earlier conflicts. In any case, when they were criticized, the non-Communist high command, motivated by a new mood, protected the Communists. Hard-pressed for personnel, they not only accepted the Communists but permitted them to recruit others, thereby increasing the Communists' power and influence. When the leaders awakened to the threat, by then hanging over them, it was impossible to do anything except continue in their course, unless they risked shaking the organization to its foundations, perhaps even destroying it, by resorting to drastic action. They were loath for practical reasons to take this risk unless overpowering circumstances forced them to it. And those circumstances were slow in materializing.[2]

---

[1] J. Raymond Walsh, CIO, *Industrial Unionism in Action*, W. W. Norton & Company, Inc., New York, 1937, p. 162; for background of persons mentioned, see *Who's Who in Labor*, The Dryden Press, Inc., New York, 1946, pp. 40, 149; *American Labor's Who's Who*, Hanford Press, New York, 1925, p. 84.

[2] The above analysis is based on *Official Reports on the Expulsion of Communist Dominated Organizations from the CIO*, Publication No. 254, Congress of Industrial Organizations, Washington, September, 1954; see also Max M. Kampelman, *The Communist Party vs. the C.I.O.: A Study in Power Politics*, F. A. Praeger, New York, 1957, especially part 2, pp. 7–163; Benjamin Stolberg, *The Story of the CIO*, The Viking Press, Inc., New York, 1938, pp. 273–276. From intermittent conversations with Brophy, Carey, and others who prefer to remain anonymous but were either the author's intimate friends or long-standing acquaintances, the author obtained information pertaining to the above analysis. In addition thereto, the author, as a government employee in the field of labor since 1936, was in a favorable position to observe the work of the CIO, both at national headquarters and throughout the country.

The Communists' movements alone would not have entrenched them so solidly within the CIO; the attitude of the organization's key leaders aided them, both directly and indirectly. The tone of tolerance, even of invitation, was set by John L. Lewis, pivotal personality who spearheaded the founding of the CIO and ruled it as an absolute monarch by unanimous consent of the members. Philip Murray, Van A. Bittner, Sidney Hillman, John P. Brophy, and others reacted similarly. Lesser lights followed their lead. Perhaps early in the beginning, these leaders were not completely aware of who were Communists and who were not. As one leader put it: "We were not as careful in selecting personnel then as we are now." [3] But it soon became common talk, and many important persons in and out of the CIO called attention to the disastrous policy of entrusting Communists and fellow travelers with responsible positions. Even Lewis criticized the office workers at the second convention and warned CIO regional directors not to hire Communists as their secretaries in CIO affairs. In the second and third (1939 and 1940) conventions, Lewis took public notice of the charges and denounced those who made them; he went even further and condemned Communist meddling. Still the top leaders and their subordinates persisted in placing Communists and fellow travelers in important jobs. Thus, Harry Lundberg warned Lewis, Brophy, and others as early as 1937 that Bridges was a Communist and that the Pacific Coast Maritime Federation was Communist-dominated, but Bridges was, nevertheless, appointed West Coast director by Lewis.[4]

Without being in a position to probe the minds of these leaders, it is difficult to understand clearly what prompted them to place Communists so readily and even enthusiastically in important positions. Lewis, Hillman, and Brophy had bitter and harrowing experiences with the Communists during TUEL and TUUL days. At that time, they readily declared the Communists dual unionists, expelled them, and amended their constitutions, barring them from their unions.[5] Yet, in spite of their bitter battles with Communists in their own unions, they accepted them in building the CIO. Then, as criticism began to mount against Communist influence in the CIO, the leaders took the defensive in playing down the importance of the Communists instead of actually checking their power.[6]

From the very beginning, as this study has indicated, there was opposition to Communist influence and even successful efforts to prevent them

[3] Brophy interview, March, 1955, and subsequent conversations.
[4] Brophy interview; Philip Taft, "Strife in the Maritime Industry," *Political Science Quarterly*, June, 1936, p. 228; and conversations with Lundberg.
[5] David M. Schneider, *The Workers' (Communist) Party and American Trade Unions*, Johns Hopkins Press, Baltimore, 1928, chaps. 2–6; Philip Taft, "Communism in American Trade Unions," *Proceedings, Industrial Relations Research Association*, Dec. 28–30, 1953, p. 23; Albert Epstein and Nathaniel Goldfinger, "Communist Tactics in American Unions," *Labor and Nation*, Fall, 1950.
[6] See William J. Smith, "Attention Van Bittner of the CIO," *Plain Talk*, December, 1946, pp. 21–22.

from becoming established in certain areas and in certain unions. A few key officials at CIO headquarters made heroic efforts to check further Communist infiltration and the exercise of Communist influence. Among these was James B. Carey, secretary-treasurer, who had first welcomed them and worked with them in the UE (United Electrical Workers) but who had been defeated for International president in 1941 because he would not drop his opposition to the Stalin-Hitler pact and to other internal Communist practices.[7] Thereafter, he and a few others exerted themselves with minor success in counteracting Communist influence.

Some CIO affiliates were more successful. In industries where CIO unions had previous histories of stable and effective unionism, and the leaders and members had fought the Communists successfully, the latter were prevented from establishing themselves again. The Amalgamated Clothing Workers and the United Mine Workers stand out as examples. Also, in those newly organized unions guided and headed by experienced leaders, the Communists were prevented from getting a substantial foothold. Organizing work in the textile industry, although nominally headed by Sidney Hillman, was under Emil Rieve, a hardheaded and sophisticated former Socialist who was then head of the Full Fashioned Hosiery Workers Union. He carefully assembled an experienced staff, most of whom were alert to Communist aims and practices. Although Communists had already been active in the textile industry, Rieve and his staff prevented their getting too serious a hold. With Philip Murray and his superbly competent, experienced, and anti-Communist lieutenants in charge of the steel organizing campaign, the Communists were able to penetrate only in certain localities and on lower levels. When Communists were spotted, or became too dangerous a threat, they were discharged. Maurice Travis' case illustrates the point: an able and astute Communist, he was expelled from the Steelworkers Union as "a Communist disrupter" in 1941.[8] Through such cautious organizing efforts, some of the newly founded unions escaped serious difficulty with the Communists.

Similarly, the Communists found it difficult to establish a beachhead in many industries not seriously penetrated before this by radicals. Certain factors militated against the infiltrators' success: They were barred from many industries where company unions functioned. Company-union leaders were carefully selected. In addition, most organizations used a highly selective hiring policy—recruiting workers through local clergymen, specific fraternal orders, and veterans' groups. In areas or establishments where leadership was provided by Catholic workers, especially by those trained in Catholic labor schools, the Communists also found it difficult to infiltrate effectively.

[7] See above, pp. 147–148, 151–152.
[8] *Official Reports on the Expulsion of Communist Dominated Organizations from the CIO, op. cit.,* p. 17.

Such practices were relied upon extensively in gas-and-electric utilities, telephone, oil, and chemical industries. In oil and chemical industries, most of the collective bargaining is still conducted by "independent" unions, the lineal descendents of the former company unions. This situation still exists to some extent in the telephone industry. There are, however, exceptions. The Communists captured the General Electric Company union in Schenectady, which had a considerable Socialist history.[9]

In the early stages of CIO assertiveness, the Communists were skeptical and even hostile toward its efforts, just as they were toward the NRA and the New Deal.[10] Still fresh to their memories were the rebuffs, bruises, and eventual dismal defeats of the recent skirmishes and battles with the prominent CIO leaders during the boring-from-within days. They could hardly have forgotten their encounters and defeats with Lewis,[11] Hillman,[12] and Dubinsky.[13]

In a way, the Communists looked upon the CIO as a rival that was capitalizing on some of its issues, particularly that of industrial unionism.

[9] Walsh, *op. cit.*, pp. 65–66, 70, 72, 109, 127, and 143; Jack Barbash, *Unions and Telephones*, Harper & Brothers, New York, 1952, pp. 8ff., 12ff., 21ff., 51ff., and 100; Stolberg, *op. cit.*, pp. 213, 223; Kampelman, *op. cit.*, pp. 96ff.; *Characteristics of Company Unions*, U.S. Bureau of Labor Statistics Bulletin 634, 1935, chaps. 7 and 8. A careful perusal of H. S. Roberts, *The Rubber Workers*, Harper & Brothers, New York, 1944, reveals no mention of either TUUL, TUEL, or Communist activities in the rubber industry. Neither are these names listed in the book's index. The Rubber Workers not only escaped practically all factionalism, they organized under their own rank-and-file leadership which stemmed chiefly from the company's union leaders. In the early fifties, the Communists became influential in the Rubber Workers' national hierarchy. The executive board even removed the president; he was later reinstated at a special convention and the Communists were shortly dislodged. See J. M. Thurber, "Our History, 1935–1955," *United Rubber Worker*, Akron, Ohio, September, 1955, and Stolberg, *op. cit.*, pp. 213–217. Similarly, Barbash mentions Communists only once, to the effect that some telephone workers feared the CIO because of its Communist taint, p. 102. In chap. 11, pp. 212ff., Barbash lists outstanding leaders of the Communications Workers of America, all of whom were graduates of company unions, first going independent, later affiliating with the CWA, which subsequently joined the CIO. From 1917 through 1940, the author made various field studies for foundations and government agencies. Among other subjects, he investigated company unions, and the above description is, therefore, reinforced by his own findings. Concerning Schenectady and the General Electric Company, see *Investigation of Communist Activities in the Albany, N.Y. Area, Hearings before the House Committee on Un-American Activities*, 83d Cong., 1st Sess., 1953, part 3, pp. 4304, 4319, 4320, 4334, 4337, 4338, 4339; part 4, pp. 436–471, 4370, 4380, 4381, 4382, 4383; part 5, pp. 4398–4399, 4403, 4404, 4410–4418; part 6, 4440, 4441, 4443, 4448–4449, 4453, 4457–4459, 4461; and *Fifth Interim Report*, Massachusetts Special Commission on Communism, Subversive Activities and Related Matters within the Commonwealth, Boston, Wright & Potter Printing Company (legislative printers), 1955.

[10] See above, pp. 123–124; see also Kampelman, *op. cit.*, pp. 15–17.

[11] See House Special Committee to Investigate Communist Activities, 71st Cong., 2d Sess., 1936, vol. II.

[12] Matthew Josephson, *Sidney Hillman*, Doubleday & Company, Inc., New York, 1952, pp. 274–280.

[13] Joel Seidman, *The Needle Trades*, Rinehart & Company, Inc., New York, 1942, pp. 153–184.

They soon realized, however, that the CIO offered them unprecedented prospects. Once this idea became clear, they set out with their usual energy to implement their objective. They proceeded to inject themselves either openly or covertly into the TUUL units that remained following the dissolution of its national structure, making the most, too, of Communist Party members and followers in most of the industries and trades where the CIO was operating. Testimony of former Communists reveals that this was not done accidentally or haphazardly; it was planned and directed by top Party leaders and carried out through the labor secretary and other emissaries. As conditions dictated, caucuses, or "nuclei," were formed by industry or by area. Usually operating secretly, these units conducted the work of penetration. Indeed, plans for control of such important industries as the automobile industry were made by the Comintern, the highest sources of Communist authority.[14]

As the CIO developed, the Communists, aided by their conferees in the national offices and by the entire Communist movement as well as by their disciples, labored assiduously to capture more and more of its units. With the open machinery of TUEL and TUUL discarded, they decided to create secret machinery, since previous experience had shown that open and aboveboard boring-from-within and dual unionism were both ineffective. Communist trade-union activities must not be openly and organically linked to the Communist movement.

Foster, in taking stock, evaluated the situation as follows: "In the earlier stages of its work, the TUUL developed a number of sectarian weaknesses which injured its general efficiency. The first was a tendency ... to develop its union programs upon a too advanced revolutionary basis and to identify the organization too closely with the Communist Party. This, of course, had the effect of checking the growth of the organization by making difficult its contacts with the conservative workers and by narrowing down the TUUL united front with the left Progressives...."[15]

Thus it was decided to operate in disguise, without openly revealing their true identity or objectives. The few who were known Communists did not deny their affiliation with the Party, but they did deny the existence of any organized activity directed from within or from outside the union to which they belonged. To the sophisticated—mostly former or current radicals of various denominations—the disguise was transparent. As the Communists became active and as the policies they advocated and the tactics they pursued became evident, even the less sophisticated began to detect the existence of a Communist conspiracy. Even so, this attempt at

[14] Benjamin Gitlow, *The Whole of Their Lives*, Charles Scribner's Sons, New York, 1948, pp. 319ff.; see also above, pp. 135ff.
[15] William Z. Foster, *From Bryan to Stalin*, International Publishers Co., Inc., New York, 1937, p. 278.

covert tactics brought better results than either open boring-from-within or dual unionism.

Top CIO leaders who were well aware of the situation had one ready answer to non-Communist complaints. They advised the complainers to organize and oust the Communists, but they offered no assistance except in rare cases. Those in the lower echelons were dissatisfied with this complacent attitude of their leaders. As one of them put it, it was like treating mature and responsible people as if they were Boy Scouts whose function was to do good deeds and to train for overcoming minor obstacles in outdoor living.[16] This early opposition to the Communists, like that of later years, was relatively ineffective. And the Communists came out into the open and revealed themselves only in order to carry out support of Soviet Russia's international policies and aims; then they were spotted throughout the CIO as an organized, conspiratorial, disguised movement. It was only when international developments reached a point that affected Russia's fortunes in vying with Western democracies that the top leaders were forced to act. Their move then was the action-inducing catalyst that resulted in the ousting of the Communists from their strong entrenchment in the unions. So widespread was their influence, however, that only such an overwhelming eruption could bring about their expulsion.

Following their policy of proceeding in disguise, the Communists' next step was to create secret machinery of a rather simple nature. As usual, the basic policies were determined by the Comintern through the Red International of Labor Unions,[17] and were directed by the national committee of the Communist Party. The routine work was entrusted to a labor secretary who was aided in vital matters by members of the national committee. In addition, important individuals were assigned to and stationed in certain areas to direct the work of particular unions or regions. The work of the members within an individual union was coordinated by a caucus. "There is ample affirmative evidence of a credible character that policies of Communist-dominated unions were in fact controlled by secret Communist Party caucuses." One witness at a congressional hearing, a former member of the Communist Party, testified under oath as follows: "We have often had some of the top leaders of the Communist Party attend

[16] Conversation with Bill Seligman, then business agent of the Shoeworkers' local in Los Angeles, in the Fall of 1947.
[17] Statement by Philip Taft in *Communist Domination of Unions and National Security, Hearings before a Subcommittee of the Senate Committee on Labor and Public Welfare*, 82d Cong., 2d Sess., 1952, pp. 169–177; Subversive Activities Control Board, *Herbert Brownell, Jr., Attorney General of the United States, Petitioner, vs. Communist Party of the United States of America, Respondent; Report*, 1953, pp. 64–67; Benjamin Gitlow, *I Confess*, E. P. Dutton & Co., Inc., New York, 1940, pp. 335–336, 477–478; *Investigation of Communist Activities in the Pacific Northwest Area, Hearings before the House Committee on Un-American Activities*, 83d Cong., 2d Sess., 1954, part 2, pp. 6105–6109, Barbara Hartle's testimony.

our meetings. Even when they did not attend meetings, why, whoever had the job as educational director for that particular club would have a mimeographed copy of an order or plan or whatever it might be . . . and they would bring this to the club and then report from that directive they received from the Communist Party headquarters." [18]

"The CIO reports furnish additional direct evidence of collaboration between Party functionaries and union leaders in the determination of union policy." In the CIO trial of the International Longshoremen's and Warehousemen's Union, "both [Michael Quill and Hedley M. Stone, secretary-treasurer of NMU] testified that Harry Bridges had, over a period of years, participated in numerous secret meetings between Communist Party functionaries and officers of Communist-controlled unions in the CIO at which the party functionaries instructed the union officers as to the party line and as to the positions that they were to take in the CIO and in their unions. Needless to say, these meetings were concealed from the CIO and the rank-and-file membership of the unions. Such meetings took place from the inception of the CIO, to Stone's knowledge, until 1945, and, to Quill's, 1948, these being the dates of their respective breaks with the party. Such meetings took place contemporaneously with every CIO convention and were often held at the time of the CIO Executive Board meetings. The party functionaries in these meetings included Eugene Dennis, William Z. Foster, John Williamson, Roy Hudson, Robert Thompson, Jack Stachel, and William Schneiderman," [19] all high Communist Party officers.

Kenneth Eckert, an active member of the Communist Party from 1930 to 1948, first an employee and later an executive board member of Mine, Mill from 1942 to 1948 (except for a period of Army service in 1944–1945), testified in the case of Maurice E. Travis with reference to Communist domination of the International Union of Mine, Mill and Smelter Workers. His testimony, summarized by the trial examiner, is as follows: "From about 1945 to 1948, Eckert and Travis served together on the Steering Committee of the Communist Party within Mine-Mill, the functions of that committee being to receive instructions from the Party and to carry out within the union the policies and procedures which the Party dictated. To insure compliance the National Committee of the Communist Party [the top Communist Committee in the country] designated a special liaison representative who actually sat as a member of the Steering Committee. The Committee, comprised of about five members, at times held caucuses of

[18] *Public Policy and Communist Domination of Certain Unions, Report of the Subcommittee on Labor and Labor-Management Relations to the Committee on Labor and Public Welfare*, 83d Cong., 1st Sess., 1953, Senate Document no. 26, pp. 4–5.
[19] *Official Reports on the Expulsion of Communist Dominated Organizations from the CIO, op. cit.*, pp. 111ff.; Kampelman, *op. cit.*, pp. 111–116.

Communists within the union to decide, for example, on such matters as successors to vacant offices; and it considered, for example, in March, 1948, whether affidavits of compliance should be made by Mine-Mill officers pursuant to Section 9 (h)." [20]

There was not only the matter of determining policy but of implementing it. In the case of Mine, Mill, where few Communists were to be found in the union, as soon as they had won over Reid Robinson, they began to build a machine in order to circumvent the non-Communist executive board. A kitchen cabinet was established with outsiders who were brought in as employees. These were all Communists who had worked in the Communist movement with different Communist and fellow-traveler organizations. "The record shows that there was constant undermining and badgering of opponents, careful and strategic placement of friendly organizers, and shifting, shelving, or removal of uncooperative organizers. The machine worked quietly, sometimes unnoticeably, but effectively. . . . Secret caucuses with Communist Party functionaries, an unseen Steering Committee, secret caucuses within the organization and effective communication to machine participants at the local levels—all of these combined to give the Communists more and more effective control." [21]

This form of colonization and machine manipulation was a common practice where the Communists were not in complete control or were in the process of gaining control. Evidence is available of similar procedures used by the Communists in the National Maritime Union, United Farm Equipment and Metal Workers Union, Transport Workers Union of America, and others. [22]

An effective means of control was through the United Office and Professional Workers of America. Members of this union were carefully selected for their Communist orientation and placed in office positions of other CIO unions. Through them the Communist Party and its officials were able to check on the operations of the union and its officials. For example, there was considerable controversy concerning an agreement the union had with the National Maritime Union. The anti-Communists opposed it, but the agreement was signed. [23] Other CIO unions also hired their clerical help through the United Office and Professional Workers Union. As early as 1938, the situation had become one of public con-

[20] Trial Examiner Report in the case of Maurice E. Travis, Secretary-Treasurer, International Union of Mine, Mill and Smelter Workers and Compliance Status of International Union of Mine, Mill and Smelter Workers, NLRB, June 7, 1954, mimeographed, p. 5.

[21] Vernon H. Jensen, *Nonferrous Metals Industry Unionism, 1932–1954*, Cornell Studies in Industrial and Labor Relations, vol. 5, Cornell University Press, Ithaca, N.Y., 1954, p. 300; see also pp. 46–47, 51, 56.

[22] Kampelman, *op. cit.*, pp. 66–67, 59–60, 118.

[23] *We Accuse: A Factual History of the Seamen's Labor Movement*, Post Office Box Address, 1st printing March 26, 1940, pp. 90–93.

troversy within the CIO. At the convention, John L. Lewis blasted certain office workers and warned regional directors not to hire Communists as their secretaries. In a statement issued by Lewis at the CIO Executive Committee meeting following the close of the convention in Detroit, it was clear that Lewis' warning was prompted by information that office workers who were members of the CIO Office Workers' Union had supplied confidential facts on union business to Communist officials.[24]

As for immediate tactics for use in the unions, the Communists made themselves adept to the occasion. In the Mine, Mill Union, where there was a small Communist following, they resorted to covert and conciliatory tactics, avoiding open conflict with non-Communist elements. "When the Communists occasionally voiced opposition to conservative policies of unionism, they were always careful not to challenge the concept of collective bargaining. As a matter of fact, they usually created the impression of being militant bargainers and staunch defenders of the workers' interests." [25] Communist leaders could further Communist propaganda subtly "because the programs of the CIO and the Communist Party overlapped on some issues. The Communists cunningly made part of their program conform to the program of bona fide liberal and progressive organizations, particularly labor unions, in order to create the appearance of acceptability for their entire program." [26]

On the other hand, where they met with effective resistance, as in the automobile union in the late thirties, their tactics were belligerent and disruptive. At first, the Communists tried to win over Homer Martin, the president of the UAW, as they had won over Reid Robinson of Mine, Mill. "They promised to build him up into a figure second in prestige and prominence only to John L. Lewis, if he would follow the advice and leadership of G. K. Gebert, the Communist leader. . . . Finally, the negotiations broke down as Martin refused to make the deal and particularly rebelled at the Communist demand that they name the central office staff of the union." [27] Following this failure, war was declared on Martin, and the Communists resorted to every conceivable tactic to embarrass and destroy him and his associates. They vilified and slandered non-Communist leaders. They instigated unauthorized strikes and quickies. They misrepresented the union's policies and charged its officials with betraying the interests of the members.[28]

In routine organizational matters, the tactics of the Communists differed. When they were trying to gain control of a union, or already

[24] *New York Times,* July 12, 1938.
[25] Jensen, *op. cit.,* pp. 296ff.
[26] *Ibid.,* pp. 56–61.
[27] Kampelman, *op. cit.,* p. 63; see Edward Levinson, *Labor on the March,* Harper & Brothers, New York, 1938, pp. 266ff.
[28] Stolberg, *op. cit.,* pp. 172ff.; Kampelman, *op. cit.,* p. 63.

dominated it, as with Mine, Mill, they adhered strictly to the Communist theory of centralism. But in unions in which they encountered opposition, as with the auto workers, they vehemently demanded extreme decentralization. "Martin wants control over the national affairs, and a large measure of national control over the local units. Mortimer fights for local autonomy and greater independence of the officers ... Mortimer ... wants the furthest possible extension of democracy within and without the locals."[29]

[29] Walsh, *op. cit.*, pp. 274–275.

14

Penetration of Affiliates

The Communists worked their way simultaneously into the parent body of the CIO and its affiliates. Thus they not only became powerful in the national office but exercised influence in such subordinate units as the state, county, and city industrial union councils, local industrial unions, and others. In some of these CIO subdivisions, they were merely strong minorities; in others, they were the controlling faction; in still others, they dominated the unit completely.

Communist infiltration of national CIO headquarters was simplicity itself. When the CIO was getting underway, some Communist-sympathizing intimates of John L. Lewis brought Lee Pressman to his attention, urging Lewis to retain him as counsel. He was hired, although John Brophy, next in command, felt that the limited funds available could have been put to better use. Pressman—youthful, personable, vivacious, brilliant, and quick-witted—immediately won Lewis' confidence. He became not only the head of the legal department but, as John Brophy describes it, the "prime minister." He directed general and administrative affairs at headquarters, and Lewis made few moves without consulting him; routine matters could not receive Lewis' endorsement unless they had first been cleared with Pressman. The latter admitted having been a Communist Party member for a short period; [1] that he worked very closely with the Communists is certain. For instance, a former Communist, Eugene V. Dennett, active in Seattle and Washington state trade-union activities, testified that when he attended the 1938 CIO convention, he was told by Roy Hudson, an outstanding Party official working out of national Communist Party headquarters, chiefly in the trade-union field, to consult with Lee Pressman whenever he was uncertain. [2]

[1] See his testimony before the House Committee on Un-American Activities, 81st Cong., 2d Sess., part 2, 1950; see also *Cumulative Index to Published Hearings and Reports of the Subcommittee to Investigate the Administration of the Internal Security Laws of the Senate Committee on Judiciary, 1951–1955*, 1957, for additional citations.

[2] *Investigation of Communist Activities in the Seattle, Washington, Area, Hearings*

By pure chance, Len DeCaux was selected as publicity director and editor of the *CIO News*, official publication. He was working for the Federated Press, which later proved to be a Communist-controlled news service. Brophy had contact with him in that capacity, but he remembered him as a student at Brookwood Labor College when he was a director of the college. Because the CIO was hard-pressed for a publicity director with a labor and progressive background, Brophy recommended DeCaux to Lewis. The latter raised the point that DeCaux had served on the *Illinois Miner*, an anti-Lewis weekly; Brophy replied that he thought DeCaux would prove reliable; if not, he could be dropped.[3]

Other department heads, such as the director of the research and education department, were either under strong Communist influence or were tolerant toward Communists and their activities.

Thus, Communists and fellow travelers were scattered throughout headquarters. "Planted" by the national center, they received sustenance and support in the subdivisions and affiliates. Usually the officers of these growing units would turn to the national center for guidance on policy and for assistance in selecting technical staff personnel. Legal and legislative advice, for example, came from the legal department, and when affiliated units sought legal talent, they generally turned to the legal department for recommendations. A similar procedure was followed in regard to organization, publicity, research, education, and other personnel needs. In this way, the Communists, through their followers in key positions at national headquarters, were in an admirable position both to direct policy and to place its adherents in strategic posts throughout the entire CIO.

With Communists and fellow travelers in control or in pivotal, influential positions in either international unions or other subdivisions, the Party was exceedingly well placed. Thus, Harry Bridges, in addition to being president of the ILWU, was in charge of the CIO California area. Michael Quill, besides being president of the Transport Workers Union of America, headed up the equally important New York metropolitan Industrial Union Council.

Communist followers were equally successful in other areas—Chicago and Illinois, Milwaukee and Wisconsin—and were thereby powerfully ensconced throughout the hinterland as well as at national headquarters.[4]

before the House Committee on Un-American Activities, part 2, 84th Cong., 1st Sess., 1955, pp. 430–431; for Hudson's record, see *Cumulative Index, op. cit.*
[3] For the record of DeCaux and the Federated Press, see *Report on the March of Labor*, U.S. Congress, House Committee on Un-American Activities, 1954, pp. 11–13; see also *Cumulative Index, op. cit.*
[4] The above analysis is based on *Official Reports on the Expulsion of Communist Dominated Organizations from the CIO*, Publication No. 254, Congress of Industrial Organizations, Washington, September, 1954; Max M. Kampelman, *The Communist Party vs. the C.I.O.*, F. A. Praeger, New York, 1957, especially pp. 7–163; Benjamin Stolberg, *The Story of the CIO*, The Viking Press, Inc., New York, 1938,

The Communists' procedures in establishing themselves in many international unions varied, depending upon specific situations. In these efforts, the Communists in most instances met with more vigorous opposition at the outset than they had encountered in the CIO proper.

Maritime is an example of an industry in which former TUUL nuclei, aided by other Communist Party members and followers, took control of the newly organized CIO unions. Since the 1920s, union organization on shore and on ships had been, with some exceptions, weak. The IWW, particularly, and other radical groups carried on agitation but had little success in establishing substantial organization. They did succeed in indoctrinating many of the rank and file and local leaders or militants who had a vague sympathy toward radicalism and a distrust of AFL leaders. With the advent and implementation of the National Industrial Recovery Act, union activity was stimulated. At first, action showed itself primarily in the International Longshoremen's Association and in the International Seamen's Union. But dissatisfaction with the leadership of both unions continued to mount, and finally crystallized under the aegis of radically minded individuals influenced by two opposing ideologies. One group was motivated by IWW teachings, and the other was Communist-oriented. Leadership rivalries also affected the disagreements that ensued. The Communist-oriented element exercised minor influence while functioning through the Marine Workers' Industrial Union, a TUUL unit transformed in 1933 from the defunct TUEL Marine Workers' Industrial League.[5] With the change of Communist trade-union policy to boring-from-within, their adherents became influential. For a time they worked harmoniously with the other radical elements, since they all had common grievances against the established leaders and their policies. But differences developed, and, except for certain sectors, the Communist-oriented groups became dominant.

Harry R. Bridges, the shrewd and dynamic Australian, and his able coterie captured the longshore organization on the Pacific Coast. Following fruitless negotiations with the leaders of the AFL Longshoremen's Union, Bridges pulled out his group. It assumed the name of "International Longshoremen's and Warehousemen's Union" and became a CIO affiliate. But the old ILA, led by Joseph P. Ryan, maintained its hold on the Atlantic and Gulf Coasts.

An unauthorized strike on a vessel berthed on the Pacific Coast in 1936 brought Joseph Curran to the front as a fearless and progressive leader. Various other events occurred which brought Curran into the leadership

pp. 273–276. From intermittent conversations with CIO leaders, who are either intimate friends or long-standing acquaintances of the author, the latter obtained information not available in documents.

[5] William Z. Foster, *From Bryan to Stalin*, International Publishers Co., Inc., New York, 1937, p. 240.

of the Atlantic and Gulf Coast seamen, including his participation in a sympathetic strike with the Pacific Coast seamen. The unsympathetic attitude of the leaders of the AFL Seamen's Union gave the dissident elements an opportunity to discredit them. The upshot was the formation of the National Maritime Union, with Curran as its president and Communist Party members or followers as most of its other key officers. It, too, joined the CIO and became a leading union in it. In an NLRB election, it won the right to represent the seamen on the Atlantic and Gulf Coasts. But on the Pacific Coast, Harry Lundberg, sophisticated in the ways of Communist procedures, and not relishing being subordinated to Harry Bridges, kept his Sailors' Union of the Pacific in an independent status. Another unlicensed seamen's personnel union, the Pacific Coast Marine Firemen and Oilers, also resisted Communist invasion and remained independent. The National Union of Marine Cooks and Stewards, however, and the American Communications Association were Communist-controlled. The two other important unions of licensed personnel were neutral, although at times some of their officials were pressured or cajoled into siding with the Communist-dominated unions. While not, therefore, in complete control of the maritime industry, the Communists were firmly established in significant sectors, in both the East and the West.[6]

A somewhat different procedure, but with similar objectives and even greater success, was pursued by the Communists in gaining control of the International Union of Mine, Mill and Smelter Workers. As the pivotal union in the nonferrous metal industry, it was a coveted prize. This union and this industry possessed a long and rich radical and belligerent heritage. An attitude of tolerance toward radical doctrines and a suspicion of "redbaiting" permeated the rank and file and gave the Communists an excellent opportunity to follow their aims. The MM, as it is commonly designated, did not grow substantially during the late thirties or early New Deal period. It was weak and, therefore, unimportant; only a few locals were sturdy and well established. The MM was one union that did not profit from the NRA. But by 1939 it developed new energy. Con-

[6] The foregoing account is based on the following sources: "Strife in the Maritime Industry," *Political Science Quarterly*, June, 1939, pp. 216–236; the same author's "New Unionism in the United States," *American Economic Review*, June, 1939, pp. 313–324; Foster, *op. cit.*, pp. 238–240, 256, 260–263; Stolberg, *op. cit.*, pp. 188–205; *We Accuse: A Factual History of the Seamen's Labor Movement*, Post Office Box Address, first printing March 26, 1940, pp. 12, 14, 25–33, 73; J. C. Record, "The Rise and Fall of a Maritime Union," *Industrial and Labor Relations Review*, October, 1956, pp. 81–92; Robinson testimony in *Jurisdictional Disputes in the Motion Picture Industry, Hearings before a Special Subcommittee of the House Committee on Education and Labor*, 80th Cong., 2d Sess., 1948, pp. 2379–2382, and 2412. For more detailed accounts of organizations and persons, see *Cumulative Index, op. cit.*, and *Digest of the Public Record of Communism in the United States*, Fund for the Republic, New York, 1955, hereafter referred to as "*Digest of the Public Record.*"

centrating wisely on important areas and firms, MM gained 20 per cent in membership during the ensuing year. In the meantime, some Communists worked their way into strategic places, as was evident by the adoption of such resolutions as the one designating the *Peoples Press*, a pro-Communist publication, as MM's official organ. The non-Communists, however, were in control, headed by Reid Robinson who later became the pivotal figure in the Communist domination of the organization. At this time, the Communists were critical of Reid Robinson who continued to battle them through 1937 into 1938. Then, slowly, he came under their control. They catered to him, flattered him, and made it worth his while to join them. Because his executive board and many other officers were not in sympathy with his change in allegiance, Robinson surrounded himself with a kitchen cabinet of outsiders, selected by the Communist hierarchy. These persons were brought in mainly from the East. The key individual was Ben Riskin, a well-known Communist.

This practice marked a significant example of Communist colonization as an established policy: skilled and tried Communists were put in positions in unions even though they had not worked in the industry or participated previously in the activities involved.

Robinson's prestige was heightened by national CIO headquarters. On the motion of an important pro-Communist, James J. Matles, director of organization, United Electrical, Radio and Machine Workers, he was elected in 1940 as a CIO vice-president. On the other hand, efforts by the non-Communists to defeat Robinson as MM president in 1940 failed. With the guidance and assistance of his kitchen cabinet, he was able to control the union. Labor historian Vernon E. Jensen [7] summarized the manner in which the Communists gained control of the MM: "The record shows that there was constant undermining and badgering of opponents, careful and strategic placement of friendly organizers, and shifting, shelving, or removal of uncooperative organizers. The machine worked quietly, sometimes unnoticeably, but effectively. Secret caucuses with Communist Party functionaries, an unseen steering committee, secret caucuses within the organization, and effective communication to machine participants, at the local levels—all of these combined to give the Communists more and more effective control."

In the postwar period, the Communists gained control of the executive board by one vote. They then proceeded through ballot stuffing and other such devices to clinch their control completely. They were in command so solidly that when Robinson became politically discredited and a hindrance to their operation within the union, they deposed him with no difficulty,

[7] Vernon H. Jensen, *Nonferrous Metals Industry Unionism, 1932–1954*, Cornell Studies in Industrial and Labor Relations, vol. 5, Cornell University Press, Ithaca, N.Y., 1954, pp. 46–47, 51–56, 300.

although, of course, he was assured employment and income. Communist power in MM was further illustrated by the replacement of Robinson by a Communist, Maurice E. Travis. When he, too, proved awkward, he was transferred to the position of secretary-treasurer, and John Clark, fairly active in the union, was put in his place.[8] Clark has functioned since then as Mine, Mill president. When he appeared at congressional hearings in 1952, he joined Travis in invoking the Fifth Amendment.[9]

A similar procedure was followed by the Communists in penetrating the United Automobile Workers Union. The first unsuccessful efforts at organizing the automobile industry were made following World War I. The United Automobile, Aircraft and Vehicle Workers Union, formerly the International Union of Carriage and Wagon Workers, a semi-industrial union, made some headway in the industry. It became involved in jurisdictional disputes with other metal-trades unions and in 1918 was expelled from the AFL.[10] It continued to struggle but made no headway. In 1929, TUUL forces won the leadership of the Detroit local, and it was then expanded into the Auto Workers Union (TUUL). This union, like most TUUL unions, carried on agitational activities, participated in strikes and mingled with the unemployed. During NRA days when the AFL chartered Federal locals, the Auto Workers Union, in accordance with the changed Communist policy, disbanded itself and ordered its followers to join AFL unions.[11] Thus, the Communists came into the union with experienced leaders and tried militants. They banded themselves into small units and developed some sort of following, but their path was strewn with even more obstacles than in the Mine, Mill and Smelter Workers Union and in the maritime industry. Although unionism in the automobile industry

[8] The above account is based primarily on the scholarly analysis given by Vernon Jensen in his book, *Nonferrous Metals Industry Unionism*, mentioned in the preceding footnote. See also Kampelman, *op. cit.*, chap. 22, pp. 135ff.; *Official Reports on the Expulsion of Communist Dominated Organizations from the CIO*, *op. cit.*, hereafter referred to as "Official Reports"; for additional data see under "Organization" and "Persons" in the *Cumulative Index*, *op. cit.*, and in *Digest of the Public Record*, *op. cit.*

[9] See his testimony in *Communist Domination of Union Officials in Vital Defense Industry—International Union of Mine, Mill and Smelter Workers, Hearings before the Subcommittee to Investigate the Administration of the Internal Security Act and Other Internal Security Laws of the Committee on the Judiciary*, United States Senate, 82d Cong., 2d Sess., 1952. For further reference to Clark's activities, see *Cumulative Index to Publications of the Committee on Un-American Activities, 1938–1954*, U.S. Congress, House Committee on Un-American Activities, 1939–1941–, Jan. 20, 1955; and *Cumulative Index to Published Hearings and Reports of the Subcommittee to Investigate the Administration of the Internal Security Act and Other Internal Security Laws of the Senate Committee on Judiciary, 1951–1955*, January, 1957.

[10] *Handbook of American Trade-unions*, U.S. Bureau of Labor Statistics, 1926, pp. 43–44.

[11] Foster, *op. cit.*, pp. 238–239, 257; *Handbook of American Trade-Unions, op. cit.*, p. 173.

lacked the consistent history of nonferrous metal mining or of the maritime industry, the Communists in the automobile industry encountered the most effective and knowledgeable opposition. While the rank and file of this industry swelled with "hillbillies" from the Ozarks, "poor whites" from farther south, and Negroes fresh from the plantations, a considerable number of workers were recruited from industries in which unions had functioned effectively for long periods. Most of the skilled and semiskilled were in this category. Thus, the United Mine Workers members who abandoned the sick coal industry in the twenties flocked in droves to the automobile centers. On top of that, every radical fringe group colonized experienced and ideologically sophisticated followers. There were the Stalinists, Lovestonites, Trotzkyites, Musteites, Proletarians, and Socialists.[12] A fair number of the leaders in all factions were college men—Homer Martin, R. J. Thomas, Walter Reuther, and many others. Practically all the outsiders who played an important role behind the scenes, such as Jay Lovestone and A. J. Muste, were college men.

Some of the radicals who were colonized by their parent groups held important and strategic positions in the union. Under the Homer Martin regime (he was elected president in 1936), the Lovestonites rode high. His confidential assistant, director of research, and others belonged to this sect. Nevertheless, the Communists, although not in control, played an influential and—to further their objectives—a strongly disruptive role. By instigating unauthorized strikes among the newly organized workers, in disregard of trade-agreement provisions, they kept the union in turmoil during the Homer Martin regime. In addition, they conducted a vituperative, polemical campaign at a time when education in the simple principles of trade unionism should have been of prime concern to those who sincerely desired a substantial organization. The 1937 recession provided more than sufficient opportunity for their purpose.

Knowing that disruptive tactics had to be supplemented by positive policies if they were to embarrass the Martin administration and become a force in the affairs of the union, the Communists initiated their usual united-front movement. Their aim was to coalesce the various opposition units into a unified group. The Reuther brothers, who later became outstanding leaders in this union, joined but remained only long enough to learn the group was Communist-dominated, then withdrew. In internal factional fighting, the Communists succeeded in electing some of their own people to international positions, including Wyndham Mortimer, who became their mainstay, as vice-president. Through deals with ambitious

[12] George D. Blackwood, *The United Automobile Workers of America, 1935–51,* University of Chicago Library, Department of Photographic Reproduction, 1951, chap. 16, pp. 323ff., discusses the different ideological groups.

136

non-Communist international officials, among them R. J. Thomas, Richard Frankenstein, and George Addes, they succeeded in extending their influence even further in the union.[13]

Martin fought back, expelling Mortimer, Frankenstein, and Addes. Through the intervention of top CIO officials, however, including Lewis and Hillman, a truce was declared at the 1937 convention of the Auto Workers union and a compromise was arrived at which reinstated the expelled officers.[14]

As often happens in bitter factional struggles, the compromise did not really kill the controversy. Issues in which serious differences could be magnified were ever present. One of these was the renewal of the General Motors contract in 1938. Because of the recession and prevailing unemployment, it was renewed on the old terms by the Martin administration. The Communists and their allies made an issue of this, criticizing the arrangement. Again the struggle became overheated, threatening the union. Once more the national CIO headquarters intervened, led by Lewis. "Although it became more and more obvious to close observers," writes Blackwood, "that the split was based on personal and ideological foibles of the leaders of the international and did not extend far down into the ranks of the union, the fission seemed to be irreparable." Lewis, nevertheless, urged a compromise.[15]

In the meantime, as Gitlow, who was a key Communist Party commissar in the trade-union field, related, the Communists came into control of pivotal locals in the auto industry in 1939, 1940, and 1941. They also became entrenched in such strategic locals as those of the tool-and-die makers and aluminum and parts plant workers. They resorted to sabotaging through strikes, disorganizing production, and damaging material. In most plants, they controlled the shop stewards.[16] At the same time, Martin was losing out with the executive board of his union, which helped to continue the controversy. It now became clear to the CIO leaders that the conflicts among the different factions were jeopardizing the future of the union. Philip Murray and Sidney Hillman thereupon issued a letter on February 8, 1939, urging the union to discontinue its destructive wrangles. The outcome was the elimination of Martin and his replacement by R. J. Thomas. As the "most important forces in the successful fight against

---

[13] Benjamin Gitlow, *The Whole of Their Lives,* Charles Scribner's Sons, New York, 1948, p. 316; E. V. Dennett testimony, *Investigation of Communist Activities in the Seattle, Washington, Area, Hearings before the House Committee on Un-American Activities,* part 2, 84th Cong., 1st Sess., 1955, p. 435; Blackwood, *op. cit.,* pp. 84–85, 101.

[14] Blackwood, *op. cit.,* pp. 88–93, 102.

[15] Blackwood, *op. cit.,* p. 107.

[16] Gitlow, *op. cit.,* pp. 310–323.

Martin," the Communists succeeded in retaining their allies, including Mortimer and Addes, in their international offices. Thomas gradually came under their influence.[17]

"In his search for troops," said the *Wage Earner*, a Detroit labor paper of anti-Communist persuasion but of consistent accuracy in these matters, "Thomas accepted mercenaries of doubtful loyalty. Communists and Communist followers began to appear in key staff positions. The UAW's educational department became infiltrated. Soon Thomas himself began to talk the language of the Party line. The same man who, four years ago, angrily rejected Communist support at the Buffalo Convention, now declared he could not help it if the Communists liked him. . . . Thus, gradually, R. J. Thomas was knitted into the 'left wing' of which Addes had been the leader." [18]

Neither the struggle of personalities nor the opposition to Communist power in the UAW was allayed by the new developments. It required one more extraordinary struggle before bitter factionalism and Communist influence were reduced to an insignificant, albeit still troublesome, force. This phase is discussed in the next chapter.

[17] Blackwood, *op. cit.*, pp. 108, 117–121.
[18] Quoted by Jack Barbash in *Labor Unions in Action*, Harper & Brothers, New York, 1948, pp. 213–214.

15

Early Opposition
to Communist Activities

From the very beginning of the CIO there were resistance and indignation within its organization toward Communist infiltration and domination, emanating mostly from knowledgeable and alert leaders on the lower levels. They were supported by alert rank-and-filers and militants, most of whom had a radical orientation and could, like their leaders, detect Communist-disguised activities. With some exceptions, top-level leaders welcomed the Communists' cooperation in spite of their former trying experience with them, because they were hard-pressed for trained personnel. It was thus the lower-level leaders and their aroused rank-and-file followers who carried on the struggle in this early period. In vain did they appeal to the top leaders for aid. The latter, singularly intent on building and keeping the movement intact, preferred to play the role of conciliators. Such an attitude inevitably redounded to the advantage of the Communists who were already in strong positions. There were, of course, exceptions, as in the automobile union where the Communists were defeated despite the intervention of top CIO leaders as conciliators.

Key leaders of the CIO seemed to be operating on the basis that their prime responsibility was to build the new movement with the resources at hand, disregarding ideology and such other differences as personal ambitions and rivalries. Certainly, factional and other differences did not impede the growth and development of the new movement; it could even be claimed that these conflicts contributed to the success of the CIO. Perhaps the leaders confused this stimulus with the fact that conditions were unusually favorable for organization and that a large proportion of workers wanted union organization. Simultaneously, public protest was heard against Communist influence in the CIO. The eminent philosopher and educator John Dewey was in this group that had taken a keen interest in organized labor and voiced its concern.[1]

[1] Max M. Kampelman, *The Communist Party vs. the C.I.O.: A Study in Power Politics*, F. A. Praeger, New York, 1957, p. 20; Edward Levinson, *Labor on the*

While Communist opposition asserted itself throughout the CIO, it developed more extensively in certain affiliates. Open conflict was most tense in metalliferous mining, maritime, and the automobile industries, as has already been mentioned, and so these received considerable public attention.

In the Mine, Mill and Smelter Workers Union the two groups came to grips several times, and in the 1941 convention their differences were aired vehemently. "The right wing had superiority in voting strength, but not in leadership. It felt it had won the victory, and in a sense it had. The truth is that events related to the war effort intervened and, most important, the left wing—not without additional rebuffs, however—outmaneuvered the undisciplined right wing." [2] Even though the opposition worked under a disadvantage because it lacked woefully "leadership, program and communication," [3] and the Communist faction benefited from "international events and activities related to the prosecution of the war, and . . . the merger of the die casters with Mine-Mill," [4] the opposition nevertheless persisted. Thus in 1943 discord once more came into the open at the executive board meeting.

Philip Murray addressed the meeting, "tongue-lashing" Robinson but informing the board members that "they themselves would have to set their house in order." [5] Robinson was deprived "of his closest advisers," but the executive board left him his office staff and organizers. But, aided by the war and through "careful maneuvers and strategic placing or sifting or removing organizers," the Communists continued to strengthen their hold on Mine, Mill.[6] Thus, "the opposition was licked twice because of the tight control of the union by the lefts." [7]

Similar controversies occurred in other CIO affiliates. Even before the CIO was formed, opposition to Communist operation began to crystallize in the maritime industry. As early as 1935, Harry Lundberg showed misgivings about Communist influence in that industry on the Pacific Coast. He made his views known to the chief CIO officials at national headquarters. Later, he refused to affiliate his Sailors' Union of the Pacific. Besides the ideological, there were other differences, mainly jurisdictional and personal. But had Lundberg been Communist-inclined, these differ-

March, Harper & Brothers, New York, 1938, p. 282; Benjamin Stolberg, *The Story of the CIO,* The Viking Press, Inc., New York, 1938, pp. 152ff.

[2] Vernon H. Jensen, *Nonferrous Metals Industry Unionism, 1932–1954,* Cornell Studies in Industrial and Labor Relations, vol. 5, Cornell University Press, Ithaca, N.Y., 1954, p. 78; see also chap. 7, pp. 69ff.

[3] *Ibid.,* p. 68.

[4] *Ibid.,* p. 299; also pp. 91–92, and chap. 10, pp. 108ff.

[5] *Ibid.,* p. 102.

[6] *Ibid.,* p. 299.

[7] *Ibid.,* p. 193.

ences would probably have been overcome.[8] In 1938, the West Coast Marine Firemen, Oilers, Water Tenders and Wipers Association ousted its Communist administration.[9] It followed Lundberg's course and continued to operate independently. This is the earliest instance of a thoroughly Communist-dominated union's clearing itself. The Longshoremen remained under Harry Bridges and the Marine Cooks and Stewards under Hugh Bryson; both continued within the CIO until expelled because of Communist domination.

On the Atlantic and Gulf coasts, the Communists succeeded in controlling the National Maritime Union, founded in 1937, which included unlicensed seagoing personnel. In contrast to developments on the Pacific Coast, the Longshoremen remained with the old AFL affiliate.

Joseph Curran was chosen president of the NMU. Although most of the officials associated with him were either Communists or fellow travelers, Curran, in spite of working with the Communists, was not a member of the Party.[10] Simultaneously with the founding of the NMU, a rather forceful rank-and-file movement came into existence. The leaders of this opposition, most of whom possessed a radical background of some sort, immediately recognized the Communist coloration of the NMU administration. At the founding convention they opposed the Communists in the drafting of the constitution because the latter revealed both an anarchist concept and no appreciation of the type of government needed for a modern union. In an industry where members are out on the high seas the greater part of the time, a highly decentralized union is called for, requiring officials to obtain permission at membership meetings for every act, including expenditures, no matter how small. The opposition also fought constitutional provisions permitting affiliation of various organizations as auxiliaries. It had in mind particularly the International Labor Defense, a Communist-front organization. Furthermore, the opposition opposed a provision which would have permitted the NMU to affiliate with or support a political party. The fear here, as the debate revealed, was that NMU would align itself with the Communist Party or with some other political organization supported by it.[11] The wrangling that transpired at the founding convention set the pattern for future internal strife. Of

[8] Philip Taft, "New Unionism in the United States," *American Economic Review*, June, 1939, p. 321; Taft, "Strife in the Maritime Industry," *Political Science Quarterly*, June, 1939, pp. 228ff.; based also on conversation with Brophy and Lundberg.
[9] Stolberg, *op. cit.*, p. 195.
[10] See above, pp. 171–172; 192–195.
[11] *We Accuse: A Factual History of the Seamen's Labor Movement*, Post Office Box Address, 1st printing March 26, 1940, pp. 76–82. NMU Convention Proceedings, 1937, p. 117; for ILD, see *Cumulative Index to Published Hearings and Reports of the Subcommittee to Investigate the Administration of the Internal Security Laws of the Senate Committee on Judiciary, 1951–1955*, 1957; and *Digest*

necessity, the opposition soon organized into one of the best coordinated Communist oppositions ever to function in a CIO union. Within a year, by 1938, it was operating on a nationwide basis and publishing a paper financed entirely by membership contributions. Officially, it labeled itself the *Rank and File* and aimed to "save the union from Communist domination."[12] Its publication was known as the *Rank and File Pilot* to distinguish it from the NMU official publication called merely *The Pilot*.[13] Thus, "a small group of seamen, knowing the aims and purposes of the Party boded no good for them ... fought consistently against the efforts of the Communists to capture the seamen and their union."[14] A ferocious encounter ensued, running for a number of years and resulting in vituperation and even in pitched battles.

In the election of officers in 1938, the opposition ran a full slate except against Curran. When the results were made known in August, the opposition came out the victor. They elected the secretary-treasurer and five out of the seven members of the national executive council. They also captured the Atlantic district committee and the Gulf district committee. "And they won the great majority of the minor union offices all along the Coast and the Gulf."[15] There could be no more conclusive proof to reveal the attitude of the members. In the end, however, it turned out to be a short-lived victory. Although capable of recognizing Communist domination, the rank-and-file group lacked experience as trade unionists and leaders of a large movement. In giving its official version and in discussing events at the constitutional convention, the opposition complained: "It should be recollected that the seamen delegates who opposed them were practically unschooled in the art of double-crossing and that they also lacked the benefits of the expert advice which the Communists received during the constant caucusing throughout the convention."[16] Living up to their name, the rank and file refused to accept aid from others experienced in such contests. Because of Curran's popularity, he was not opposed for reelection, and the Communists thus retained a favorable foothold in the union. They therefore reorganized their forces for a successful counterattack. With outside help, they created confusion by spreading rumors that the rank-and-file movement included spies. "The entire Party machine was rallied on a national basis to combat this new menace. Very carefully at first in meetings a spy psychosis was built up and more

---

of the Public Record of Communism in the United States, Fund for the Republic, New York, 1955.

[12] Taft, "Strife in the Maritime Industry," p. 234.

[13] Stolberg, *op. cit.*, pp. 203–205.

[14] *We Accuse, op. cit.*, Introduction.

[15] Stolberg, *op. cit.*, p. 204; *We Accuse, op. cit.*, p. 83; Philip Taft, *The Structure and Government of Labor Unions,* Harvard University Press, Cambridge, Mass., 1954, pp. 198–199.

[16] *We Accuse, op. cit.*, p. 82.

carefully nursed along. The membership was drowned with resolutions, speeches, endless propaganda." After the efforts to discredit the rank-and-file movement had been expended for some time, purges in the form of expulsions were begun. The *Rank and File Pilot* and Jerome King, newly elected secretary-treasurer, were particular targets. But first, lesser lights had to be disposed of in order to create the proper atmosphere. In 1939, trials were started, charging many of the less important leaders of crimes against the union. Expulsions were ordered and confirmed at packed meetings.[17] The major stroke came against Jerome King. At a meeting on May 12, 1939, King and a number of key officers were denounced by Curran as enemies of the union and as inefficient union officers. NMU officials were assisted in launching the attack by noted Communists and their allies, including Harry Bridges who journeyed from the Pacific Coast for this purpose. A trial committee was selected, and King was put on trial first. Fourteen charges were lodged against him, running from the accusation of conspiring to turn the union over to the AFL to mismanagement of the office and conspiring with steamship owners. King made a lengthy reply, denying and refuting the charges point by point, and larding his statement with quotations from official union documents and other sources. After a hectic trial, King was found guilty by the trial committee and expelled from the union for ninety-nine years.[18]

With other less important expulsions, the opposition was wiped out and the Communists were again in control of the NMU. They were not dislodged until the CIO launched its great expulsion wave, when Curran and other NMU officials joined in turning upon the Communists.[19]

Discord over Communist penetration of the UAW, as shown by earlier accounts, was also tense and also erupted into fierce battles. In this case, the anti-Communist leaders matched, if they did not excel, the Communist leaders in ability and experience. In the early days of the union, the Communists set themselves the task of capturing it. First, they catered to President Homer Martin, promising to promote his fortunes so that he would become preeminent as a labor leader, providing he accepted their guidance. Among the conditions demanded of Martin was Communist control of the central office staff;[20] under Joseph Curran they had succeeded in attaining this objective in the NMU. But Homer Martin pursued his own course. In retaliation, the Communists called "wildcat" strikes, broke up union meetings, circulated slanderous rumors branding Martin as ir-

[17] *We Accuse, op. cit.,* pp. 93–108, 113–117; see photostatic newspaper clippings and other matter, p. 4; for Communist Party participation see p. 112.

[18] *We Accuse, op. cit.,* chap. 20, pp. 136ff.; Kampelman, *op. cit.,* p. 65; Taft, *The Structure and Government of Labor Unions,* p. 199.

[19] See above, pp. 158–159.

[20] Kampelman, *op. cit.,* p. 63; Stolberg, *op. cit.,* p. 177; Herbert Harris, *Labor's Civil War,* Alfred A. Knopf, Inc., New York, 1940, p. 136.

responsible and a weakling. In the early period, the Communists, by organizing a unity group, secured non-Communist allies. The Reuther brothers belonged to the unity group opposing Martin before they became aware that it was Communist-dominated and withdrew. Leading CIO officials also turned against Martin. Then John L. Lewis and Philip Murray tried their hand at reconciliation, but to no avail. Martin and his associates fought back. He accused the unity group of "irresponsibility and disruption, and of having fomented a multitude of unauthorized strikes which were jeopardizing the union's contractual relations with the corporations." At a historic convention in Milwaukee in 1937, the controversy was the main topic. The Martin group won on various issues against the unity faction and it seemed that Martin would have won control of the union if Lewis had not insisted on a compromise calling for the retention of the anti-Martin union officials in their strategic posts.[21] The hopes for solidarity which sprang from the 1937 convention did not materialize.

Taking advantage of the prevailing, unfavorable economic conditions, the Communists continued their campaign against Martin. They accused him of betraying the interests of the members; they instigated more wildcat strikes and unauthorized sit-downs. Martin fought back, aided this time by Lewis and other prominent CIO leaders. Nevertheless, the Communists pressed their campaign with some success. By playing on Vice-President Richard Frankenstein's ambition, they won him to their side. Frankenstein, one of Martin's close associates, was a former college football player, striking in appearance, immaculately groomed, theatrically inclined. He succumbed to Communist promises that included the prospect of his nomination for lieutenant governor on the Democratic ticket.[22]

Communist strategy sought to find some way of removing Martin from the presidency. In June, 1938, when an International executive board meeting held in Washington adjourned and the Martin adherents left town, the unity group convened a rump meeting and lodged charges against Martin. Deeming that an emergency had arisen, Martin reconvened the entire executive board. By a majority vote, the supporters of the unity group were suspended from their official positions in the International. Among them were Frankenstein and three other vice-presidents and the secretary-treasurer, as well as the executive board members adhering to the unity group.

The suspended leaders fought back through their well-organized machinery. They called rump and illegal meetings at which they tried to force through resolutions in their defense; they also attempted to hold a special convention to take up their suspensions. But they received little favorable response from the ranks. Consequently, they turned to Lewis for inter-

[21] Stolberg, *op. cit.*, pp. 170–172; Levinson, *op. cit.*, pp. 268–271.
[22] Levinson, *op. cit.*, p. 271.

144

vention. It seemed the membership was unsympathetic to national CIO interference. Sentiment was developing against the disruptive procedures of the Communists. The Martin administration, supported by 155 local presidents representing almost three-quarters of the local membership, demanded that Lewis permit the UAW to clean house. Although Martin had an overwhelming majority in the executive board and in the local unions, Lewis came forth with a peace proposal. Martin resisted, but the Communist coalition group eagerly accepted, since it gave them the opportunity to hold at least a beachhead, if not a stronger sector, in the union. Indeed, any amicable adjustment would mean avoiding complete expulsion.[23] Disheartened and disillusioned, Martin, who was an emotional man, gave way to R. J. Thomas. The suspended officers were reinstated.

The change led to a realignment of the union's political forces. The Reuther group, with Walter Reuther, their leader, now a vice-president, definitely withdrew from the Communist-dominated unity faction. In the meantime, George F. Addes, secretary-treasurer, also severed relations with his Communist allies. With the aid of these two and their followers, and with his own skill in balancing contending forces, Thomas remained president for more than eight years. He developed the itch to become a power in his own right, however, and began to play with the Communist remnants. Soon he was mouthing their ideas and phrases and was receiving their support. Simultaneously Addes and Vice-President Richard Leonard broke with Reuther and joined Thomas. Reuther now found himself isolated in auto-union officialdom. His opponents became closely allied with the Communists, supporting the latter's causes and joining their front organizations. They also appointed Communists to key positions and gave them control of the education department. In his astute and daring manner, Reuther, who was gradually emerging as a prominent leader in charge of the General Motors division, waged battle with a view to gaining control of the union. His opponents could not dislodge him from the vice-presidency, but, having control of union machinery, publications, and treasury, they were in an advantageous position to fight him. Undaunted, Reuther carried the battle to the members. In what has become his characteristic mode of procedure, he surrounded himself with able associates and launched a vigorous campaign. In the beginning, he directed his darts against other officers of the International. In this manner, he advertised himself through the union. He then turned on Thomas, declaring himself a candidate for the presidency, as Thomas' replacement. At the 1946 convention, Reuther was elected president "by a narrow margin." Thomas succeeded in being elected vice-president. Thus, the three other International officers, and a majority of the executive board, were lined

[23] Stolberg, op. cit., 179–186; Taft, The Structure and Government of Labor Unions, p. 219.

up against Reuther.[24] "He was thus in the extremely difficult position of acting as President of a union, the control of whose governing body was vested in an anti-Reuther coalition."

Neither Reuther nor the opposition was content with the arrangement. One or the other would have to give way. Since the opposition was in control of the International, it proceeded to maneuver in order to strengthen its political fences so as to eliminate Reuther. One effective way was to augment union membership by those who would vote with them. An easy way of accomplishing this presented itself. The Communist-dominated CIO affiliate, the United Farm Equipment and Metal Workers of America, popularly referred to as "FE," should be incorporated into the auto union. As is evident by its full name, the International Union of United Automobile, Aircraft and Agricultural Implement Workers of America and FE had overlapping jurisdictions. What would be more logical than their amalgamation? The Reuther opposition seized upon this prospect.

A special CIO committee of top leaders studied this jurisdictional problem and supported the idea of the merger. Since the FE was a Communist-dominated union, this element opposed outright amalgamation that would dilute its cohesive strength. The anti-Reuther group therefore agreed to admit FE "in a semi-independent status. This would have solved the jurisdictional problem, preserved the FE leadership and autonomy, and yet added a sufficient number of anti-Reuther votes in the next UAW convention to defeat him and his group."

Aroused by this new turn of events, the Reuther group mustered its forces to oppose the adoption of the merger plan submitted to a referendum vote of the members. In contrast, the anti-Reuther group advocated outright merger. Both sides campaigned strenuously throughout the country. Notwithstanding the advantage held by the anti-Reuther group in controlling the organization, with its staff, publications, and funds, the membership referendum defeated their merger plan. This revealed Reuther's strength with the rank and file. Appreciating his advantage, he intensified his campaign for control of the organization, selecting a slate of his own for all the national offices. Since the convention elects the officers, his group launched a campaign to induce local unions to designate delegates favorable to them. The remainder of the administration being Communist-oriented, he made communism an important issue. But he did not rely on this issue alone. He presented a positive program, at the same time accusing the opposition of mismanagement, ineptness, and of having made insufficient progress. At the 1948 convention, Reuther won a sweeping victory. He was now in complete control of the union.

This is the early outstanding instance where the Communists met their match in an able and vigorous opposition and where an outright appeal

[24] Blackwood, *op. cit.*, chap. 13, pp. 253ff.

to the members on the Communist issue resulted in an unequivocal positive response. This is also the first instance where the Communists and their allies were effectively dislodged from power in an international union without help from the national center. Indeed, high officials of CIO looked askance at the Reuther-group activities. It is also a case illustrating the attempts of CIO top leaders to obtain compromises which helped to strengthen the Communists' position within the International. Had the national CIO leaders not intervened with peace settlements, the Communist faction might have been reduced to relative impotence much sooner. Even though they were established in high places in a national union, profiting from alliances with other key officials, they and their allies were eliminated without substantial assistance from the national CIO. The non-Communist leaders did not fear or hesitate to challenge the Communists and their allies, nor were they impeded by the redbaiting charge which the Communists used to good effect in other contests. The opposition came to grips with the Communist issue of meddling in union affairs in the interest of furthering Russia's foreign policies and imperialistic ambitions. In the 1947 struggle, the anti-Communist group presented this issue in a forthright manner. A most telling campaign tactic was the circulation of copies of the *Daily Worker* which clearly revealed Communist support of the Reuther opposition. The Reuther victory was even more significant because it occurred when top CIO leaders were still hopeful of peaceful coexistence, while yielding to pressure by making some effort to counteract Communist control and domination. It encouraged Communist opposition throughout the CIO to intensify its efforts to eliminate Communist influence and domination in that movement.[25]

Opposition to Communist activities manifested itself in other CIO industrial-union affiliates. For example, in the Transport Workers Union, controlled by the Communists under Michael J. Quill, from the very beginning an opposition led by Catholic adherents functioned sporadically from 1937 to 1947. Weak but vocal, it became more effective in postwar days. It demanded primarily the ousting of the Party line and strict compliance with trade-union democracy.[26]

When James B. Carey, a devout Catholic, became aroused during the Stalin-Hitler pact stages of the war by the isolationist and pro-Russian direction of his International, he took issue in a fearless and forthright manner. By this time, however, the Communists were sufficiently entrenched to withstand the opposition. Thoroughly aroused to the Communist danger, Carey continued his opposition, even when the UE changed its attitude toward the war with the collapse of the Stalin-Hitler alliance.

[25] Blackwood, *op. cit.*, pp. 271–273, 274, 297, 357–361; Stolberg, *op. cit.*, pp. 156ff.; Kampelman, *op. cit.*, pp. 58–65; and conversations with UAW leaders.
[26] Stolberg, *op. cit.*, p. 226; Kampelman, *op. cit.*, pp. 118–120.

His reward was defeat as president of the union. Nevertheless, he persisted in fighting with the aid of a devoted guard.[27] This opposition grew in strength in postwar days.

Even in those CIO units directly accountable to the national CIO, where leaders were in a better position to allay friction, opposition to Communist control and domination manifested itself in this prewar period. Without encouragement from the national leaders, however, the opposition was by necessity limited in nature. As early as 1938, four powerful local unions in Los Angeles decided to withdraw from the CIO industrial union council. They were locals from the International Ladies' Garment Workers, the United Auto Workers, the United Rubber Workers, and the United Shoe Workers—representing 20,000 members. Their complaint was against Bridges and his Communist cohorts. Complaints were usually against Communist control through frauds and votes of paper locals, against the use of Communist tactics to the detriment of CIO unions not Communist-controlled, against appointing Communists to union positions regardless of qualifications, and against subordinating the interests of the CIO and trade unionism to communism.[28]

Similarly, resentment against Communist influence began to show itself publicly on the national CIO level. Because the Communists took an isolationist position, they were now able to conceal their real objective of furthering Russia's foreign policy. While they hailed Lewis for his personal vendetta with Roosevelt, they boldly attacked the President as a warmonger and Fascist ally. With equal vehemence they also attacked those CIO leaders who supported Roosevelt's foreign policy. Hillman, whom they later praised and glorified, was singled out especially for castigation because of his close relationship with the President; he was charged with "subordinating the labor movement to the Wall Street war program." Hillman retaliated by supporting a resolution at the 1940 CIO convention prohibiting Communists, Nazis, and Fascists from holding union office.[29] George Baldanzi, executive vice-president of the Textile Workers Union, also attacked the "isolationist," pro-Communist influence of DeCaux and Pressman. Lewis defended them.[30]

But just as opposition to communism began to crystallize, the war situation changed and with it, Communist war policies. The struggle between the Communists and the anti-Communists dimmed in the CIO as it did in the country at large. It was now a united war effort to defeat Hitler Germany and the Fascist axis.

[27] Kampelman, *op. cit.*, pp. 97–99.
[28] Stolberg, *op. cit.*, p. 154.
[29] Kampelman, *op. cit.*, pp. 22–24; CIO Convention Proceedings, 1940, pp. 122–125.
[30] Kampelman, *op. cit.*, pp. 22–27.

Had the principal CIO leaders in this prewar period taken a firm anti-Communist position and firmly supported the opposition, it undoubtedly would have been possible to dislodge the Communists' hold and reduce it to an ineffective minority. What the Communist opposition badly needed was moral support and, where the leaders were inexperienced, skillful guidance. Both could have been provided but were not. Evidently the top leadership, dedicated to creating a strong national movement vis-à-vis the AFL and staunch employer opposition, was more interested in allaying conflict. They made every effort to keep the discord under control, hoping for ultimate reconciliation. How these leaders could expect such a happy solution is difficult to comprehend in the light of their previous and recent experience with Communist infiltration. Possibly they merely hoped to postpone the inevitable until the CIO was more firmly established, which, of course, occurred, whether by design or accident, in the postwar period.

Evidence warrants the conclusion that the Communists could have been dislodged from control even of those unions in which they later became so strongly established that the only solution was to expel them. In the Mine, Mill and Smelter Workers Union, the opposition won out at conventions but failed to control the presidency and, consequently, the paid staff. In this manner, the Communist-led group outmaneuvered the inept opposition, even though the latter had the support of the membership. "Yet too much blame should not be heaped upon other individuals in Mine, Mill, whose lapses of judgment, failure to comprehend, or inadequate power or finesse in their limited realms were far less decisive, even though not less significant, than the lack of vigorous supporting leadership from those at the head of the CIO. The CIO is an avowed protector of the democratic tradition and practices of unionism. It gave verbal support on the side during the early leadership struggles within Mine, Mill, but when concrete help was actually needed and could have been decisive, the dependent compatriots were left to fight almost alone because the leaders of the CIO themselves were also mixed up in struggles for power and therefore could not lend aid. When even a little open support from CIO officials might have been decisive in assisting their right wing friends among the leaders within Mine, Mill to carry their case to the rank and file, these leaders found themselves unassisted and outmaneuvered. When the struggle came to a head-on conflict in 1946, the help was not enough, and the issues were subsequently left clouded and confused. It was soon too late to break left-wing control." [31]

A nearly analagous situation existed in the maritime industry. Lundberg, an experienced leader, kept the Communists from winning control. The Firemen and Oilers opposition also aroused the rank and file to vote the

[31] Jensen, op. cit., pp. 306–307.

149

Communists out of office. This opposition was astute enough to keep the Communists from regaining control.[32] But the opposition in the National Maritime Union, even though it won in a rank-and-file election, was cheated of the fruits of victory because, as in Mine, Mill, the president, Joseph Curran, remained in office and with the control of the appeals board was able to circumvent the will of the membership. Had Curran sided with the opposition, as he did in 1948, the Communists would have been eliminated from control of this important union. His bitterest opponents and critics acknowledged that "had Curran wished to line up with the seamen against the Party, the Communists would have been beaten. Though the majority of the seamen are not Communists or in sympathy with them, they have faith in Curran. Thus the Communist Party is able to mislead them through Curran whom the seamen have been carefully trained to believe in." [33]

In the automobile industry, the story was somewhat different. Astute leadership within the union combated the Communists effectively, but intervention by the national CIO leaders brought on compromises. This occurred three times. The Communists were ousted following the war only because Walter Reuther and his associates would not compromise, insisting on a decisive contest. The leaders, like Lewis, Hillman, and Murray, successfully kept the Communists out of their own unions but welcomed them in unorganized areas and industries. Indeed, not only directly but indirectly they shielded them by bringing about compromises at critical times when the Communists were on the verge of defeat. It was only where the non-Communist leaders within particular unions or on organizing committees were sufficiently alert that the Communists were kept out, were ousted, or were opposed in other ways by an aroused rank and file. Usually, the opposition leaders were current or former non-Communist radicals who were conversant with Communist ideological objectives, policy, and tactics. At a future period, the leaders, too, became aroused and took charge of the anti-Communist expulsion movement, leading it to victory.

[32] Stolberg, *op. cit.*, p. 152.
[33] *We Accuse, op. cit.*, p. 170.

16

The Communists'
Postwar Position

There was a lull in the conflict with the Communists following the attack upon Soviet Russia by Nazi Germany. With Russia as our ally, the opposition was too patriotic to press its objections to Communist influence, although it did not permit itself to be blinded to ultimate Communist objectives. The new situation not only gave the Communists a breathing spell, especially in those unions where the opposition was ably led and well-supported by the membership, but it also enabled the Communists and their allies to strengthen their hold and extend their power in all directions so that ultimately drastic surgery was required to sever them from the main body of the CIO. Indeed, they secured such a foothold in some unions that expulsion was the only solution.

War-bred unity, however, was only surface deep. The inevitable struggle for power was merely postponed. At times, discord could not be checked, and it broke out into the open, even during the war. "Occasional discord did take place, particularly from those CIO leaders who were now convinced that, even though the exigencies of war might call for international unity on the war front, democratic principles and democratic trade unionism were incompatible with the true totalitarian nature of the Soviet Union and its fumbling, but eager satellite in the United States, the Communist Party." [1]

James B. Carey, the alert, energetic, and determined president of the UE, who was at first intrigued by the Communists, then later—during the Stalin-Hitler pact—recognized their deception, was one who dared take issue with them during the war. At the UE 1942 convention, he attacked the Communist-sponsored resolution calling for a second front. Carey also joined with others in fighting the UE Communist-oriented leaders on

[1] Max M. Kampelman, *The Communist Party vs. the C.I.O.: A Study in Power Politics*, F. A. Praeger, New York, 1957, p. 32.

151

the Erlich-Alter execution case.[2] His reward was defeat as president.[3]
Nevertheless, as secretary-treasurer of the CIO, he continued to oppose
Communists publicly and administratively. In their eagerness to promote
the war effort, the Communists at times overextended themselves, thus
providing militant anti-Communists with ammunition with which to attack
them. In his great enthusiasm, Harry Bridges even suggested a nonstrike
agreement that would continue beyond the war. The Communists actually
opposed legitimate strikes, which convinced the articulate opposition more
than ever that they were placing the interests of the Soviet Union above that
of the American workers. A notable instance was their opposition to
the Montgomery Ward strike of 1944, conducted by the Retail and Wholesale Employees of America. This union was under non-Communist leadership and, in a sense, a rival of Harry Bridges' Longshoremen's and Warehousemen's Union, which also organized some of Montgomery Ward's
operations. The motives, therefore, were mixed, but the public declaration was worded so as to feature opposition to strikes during the war. John
Brophy, representing the national office, upon investigation justified the
strike.[4] On the other hand, most of the leading CIO leaders, such as Sidney Hillman, developed a working alliance with the Communists.

At the time of the first postwar CIO convention, in 1946, the Communist
issue again came into prominent focus. Unity could not be maintained
between the determined and fundamentally contradictory elements. At the
same time, tension was developing between the United States and the Soviet
Union over foreign policy, to which the alert anti-Communists sensitively
responded. Late in 1945, evidence of the split became apparent in differences over the handling of the China conflict. The national CIO office
was indecisive, whereas the strong anti-Communist element sided with the
nationalists. Another serious difference arose when the Wisconsin state
CIO industrial union council and the Milwaukee council, dominated by
the Communists, opposed the reelection of Senator Robert La Follette, Jr.
In this instance, the national office took a firm position against its own
subsidiaries. In other situations, Philip Murray oscillated. He praised
Communist leadership on some occasions and condemned Communist meddling at other times. He still tried to balance off both sides.[5]

Perturbed and chagrined by criticism of his failing to take action, Murray yielded at the 1946 convention to the pressure of non-Communist
members of the executive board. He was still anxious, however, not to take
drastic action since his primary aim was to preserve unity. He therefore
encouraged a resolution which would receive the unanimous approval of

[2] Two Jewish Socialist leaders in Poland, prominent also in the international
socialist and labor movements, who were victims of the usual Communist purge.
[3] Kampelman, *op. cit.*, pp. 32ff.
[4] Kampelman, *op. cit.*, p. 39.
[5] Kampelman, *op. cit.*, pp. 41 and 102.

convention delegates and participated in the deliberations of a special committee, evenly balanced with six members, whom he appointed. This committee reported to the executive board, which also gave unanimous approval to the resolution. In presenting the resolution to the convention, Murray, in a lengthy and somewhat confused talk, denounced Communist domination. Simultaneously, he accused those making the charges of malicious slandering and declared that the CIO was a trade-union organization that "would not tolerate interference from not only the Communist Party ... but other political parties." He rather unclearly declared, furthermore, that the resolution was not "a repressive measure. ... The matter of legislation concerning subjects of this description is one that becomes the exclusive property of each of the international unions affiliated with the national CIO movement ... but it does provide definitely certain charts and certain courses, that when this subject matter is disposed of, should be and in fact must be adhered to within the councils of the national CIO and all of its affiliates." [6]

As is to be expected of a compromise resolution, it was rather general in terms and somewhat platitudinous. It protested that the CIO was "an American institution, dedicated to the attainment of its well-defined social and economic objectives within the framework of American political democracy"; its basic purpose was to organize American workers into trade unions; it "records with pride its achievements in protecting and enhancing the interests of its members. ... The CIO as an American institution has no interests apart from the interests of our people and our country. ..." Then the resolution ends on a minor note of Communist criticism: "In pursuit of the principles set forth herein and adopted by the CIO Executive Board, we ... resent and reject efforts of the Communist Party or other political parties and their adherents to interfere in the affairs of the CIO. This serves notice that it will not tolerate such interference." [7]

Although Murray suggested there was no need for discussion and urged a unanimous vote, two die-hard delegates from the Communist group stood up when the no's were called for. Before adjournment, Murray announced that the two dissenting delegates had reconsidered and had withdrawn their opposition. It would seem they were induced by their Communist comrades to reverse themselves in order not to irritate Murray further.[8] Later events revealed that the compromise resolution did not satisfy anyone; neither did it succeed in reducing the ardor of the Communist opposition.

[6] CIO Proceedings, 8th Constitutional Convention, November, 1946, pp. 111–113; see also Kampelman, op. cit., pp. 44–45; Vernon H. Jensen, Nonferrous Metals Industry Unionism, 1932–1954, Cornell Studies in Industrial and Labor Relations, vol. 5, Cornell University Press, Ithaca, N.Y., 1954, pp. 173ff.
[7] CIO Convention Proceedings, 1946, p. 114.
[8] Kampelman, op. cit., p. 47; the author was an observer at this convention.

Where its constitution permitted, the CIO did take decisive action. Because of the constitutional provision concerning trade autonomy, the national CIO office is not permitted to inject itself into or interfere with the internal affairs of its affiliated industrial unions. It can recommend, but it cannot order. The contrary is true with reference to its immediate branches, which in a state or municipal area carry out the general functions of the CIO on a basis parallel to that of the national CIO office. These are known as "industrial union councils," state, city, and county, and as special organizing committees.[9] The executive board amended the rules, limiting the action of the state and local industrial union councils and organizing committees to policies determined by the national CIO.

Since a great number of local and state industrial union councils were under Communist control, this action was a severe blow. Max M. Kampelman presents a list in his scholarly study that shows these councils were, in most important cities and states of the Midwest, Communist-dominated.[10] On the basis of common knowledge and personal observation, it is certain that the Communists exercised similar power throughout the country.[11] In accordance with the new rules, orders were issued by the national office forbidding support of Communist-controlled organizations and causes. As a follow-up, activities of these units were checked.[12]

Ostensibly chastising the Communists, the general resolution not only did not please anybody, but it was so vague it lent itself to various interpretations. Philip Murray and his associates still hoped and strove for unity.[13] "Murray feared that a split—within the CIO would significantly weaken the organization, encourage the AFL toward raiding, and lead toward eventual destruction. Murray, who continued to feel the need to prove himself in the eyes of history, certainly had not inherited the Lewis mantle to preside over the liquidation of the CIO empire." [14] Finding themselves on the defensive, the Communists began to place more emphasis on unity, the banner under which they had thus far made extraordinary gains. But because of Philip Murray's action at the 1946 convention and his many public pronouncements, the anti-Communists felt that he was approaching closer to their side. They were thus encouraged to intensify their attacks on the Communists not only with a view to resisting their encroachments but to dislodging them. In this manner, the anti-Communist forces gained in cohesion, determination, and strength. By 1947, the conflict took on considerable momentum. They were en-

[9] Jack Barbash, *Labor Unions in Action*, Harper & Brothers, New York, 1948; Kampelman, *op. cit.*, p. 51; and CIO Convention Proceedings, 1946, p. 231 and p. 58 for a listing of the number and a description of their activities.

[10] Kampelman, *op. cit.*, p. 51; *Labor Fact Book*, 1947, International Publishers Co., Inc., New York, p. 116.

[11] Earl Browder, *Political Affairs*, July, 1943, pp. 928 and 1117.

[12] Kampelman, *op. cit.*, pp. 52–53.

[13] Jensen, *op. cit.*, p. 189.

[14] Kampelman, *op. cit.*, p. 39.

couraged by the overwhelming victory of Walter Reuther and his group in sweeping the pro-Communists out of office. In this year also, Joseph Curran, president of the National Maritime Union, defected and threw down the gauntlet of battle to his former Communist associates. Oppositions began to assert themselves in other national industrial unions, such as Mine, Mill and UE.[15] Outstanding developments occurred in the state and local industrial union councils which began to follow the lead of the national convention hard upon the heels of its adjournment and to improve upon its action by unequivocal pronouncements. The Massachusetts state council at its convention adopted a constitutional amendment barring Communists from holding office. Within the same time, the New Jersey state council declared itself more outspokenly to the effect that "Communism is alien to the philosophy and desires of the American people." It also expressed resentment at Communist efforts to interfere in the affairs of the CIO. The Communists were ousted from control of the Wisconsin and Milwaukee industrial union councils. Similar successes were achieved in the Chicago and Illinois councils and elsewhere.

Following up its original action, the national office proceeded to impose stricter control over state and local councils. It ordered them not to send delegates or grant gifts to any organizations except those listed by the national office. Included in the approved list were the American Legion, the Army and Navy Union, and Veterans of Foreign Wars. Excluded were the well-known Communist-dominated organizations, including the Civil Rights Congress and the National Lawyers Guild.[16]

Minority oppositions also began to assert themselves in the affiliated industrial unions. Once more the national CIO, through its executive board, had to inject itself into a tremendous struggle in Mine, Mill. A special committee of three executive board members, although finding that "the basic factor in the dissension was Communist infiltration of the Union," nevertheless recommended a compromise which maintained Communist control.[17] Feeling its power, the Communist-controlled executive board of MM took issue with even this mild recommendation, challenging the right of CIO intervention. It did later make some changes in accordance with the special committee recommendations.[18]

James B. Carey and his associates also took new courage and by 1947 reactivated an effective opposition within UE. A few locals ousted their officers who were regarded as pro-Communists. But the UE retained its hold, particularly in the large plants of General Electric, Westinghouse, and other important electrical manufacturing firms.[19] The opposition also formed a UE Members for Democratic Action and issued a paper called the

[15] Jensen, *op. cit.*, p. 189; Kampelman, *op. cit.*, p. 110.
[16] Kampelman, *op. cit.*, pp. 54–57.
[17] Jensen, *op. cit.*, pp. 183–194.
[18] Kampelman, *op. cit.*, p. 57.
[19] *Ibid.*, p. 102.

Real UE. It continued its activity notwithstanding that it was ordered by the UE executive board to disband as a dual organization. This action was approved by the national convention. But Carey and his associates persisted. Their activity did not succeed in defeating the Communists, but it acted as an effective irritant, simultaneously preparing the ground for taking over many locals when the UE was expelled by the CIO.[20]

Another instance in which the opposition organized in a special unit to counteract Communist domination was the formation in New York of a CIO Committee for Democratic Trade Unionism. Representing important unions, thirty-four leaders took the initiative in this undertaking. The immediate stimulus was Communist opposition to the senatorial and gubernatorial Democratic candidates, men with long-standing labor records.[21]

In short, by the end of 1947, anti-Communist activity had gathered momentum. Communists were removed from office and from many state, county, and city councils, and they were encountering persistent opposition within the industrial unions. Even the national office began to initiate measures to cope with Communist domination. Indeed, the national office was definitely a house divided against itself. Legal, press, and public relations departments harbored the Communists. Led by James B. Carey, secretary-treasurer, most of the other departments were anti-Communist. Office atmosphere was charged with suspicion and intrigue. Len DeCaux's resignation in the summer of 1947 was an additional manifestation of the effectiveness of the opposition.

While the exchange of letters between DeCaux and Murray placed the severance of relations on personal grounds, it was publicly regarded and proclaimed as a victory for the non-Communist opposition.[22] In testimony under oath before the House Un-American Activities Committee, DeCaux, "on grounds of self-incrimination," refused to "confirm that he was asked to resign from his CIO employment by Philip Murray because of alleged Communist Party affiliation." [23]

Now it required some extraordinary occurrence to precipitate definitive action on the part of the national CIO. Such an occurrence followed quickly.

[20] *Ibid.*, pp. 103–111; also UE Convention Proceedings, 1947, pp. 129–170; and Franklin G. Anderson, "Union Workers at the Switch," *Plain Talk*, April, 1947, pp. 19ff. Anderson wrote as a member of UE Democratic Action.

[21] *Ibid.*, p. 39.

[22] Kampelman, *op. cit.*, p. 85; Joseph M. Brown, "Labor Out of the Red, 1947 Balance Sheet," *Plain Talk*, February, 1948, pp. 10–12.

[23] *Report on the March of Labor*, U.S. Congress, House Committee on Un-American Activities, 1954, pp. 11ff.

17

The 1948 and 1949 Conventions

As fundamental issues clashed with the dynamics of Soviet Russia's totalitarian and imperialistic ambitions, it was inevitable that the CIO, basically an American institution, should take drastic action to rid itself of the Communists within its fold. And it was natural that the CIO should remain loyal to American and democratic traditions when vital domestic and international issues became irreconcilable with those of Soviet Russia. This change in attitude toward the Communists coincided with the change in our national policy and in that of the Western European nations. The immediate issues that precipitated action were: (1) our decision to embark on foreign economic and military aid programs that became known as the "Truman Doctrine" and the "Marshall Plan," and (2) Communist sponsorship of the Wallace presidential candidacy on the Progressive Party slate with a pro-Soviet platform. In the charges which led to the expulsion trials and decisions, discussed in following sections, other reasons are given. But they are only incidental to the basic differences referred to heretofore.

Events at the 1947 convention must have convinced Philip Murray and his associates that ultimately drastic action could not be avoided. Just as the anti-Communists pressed for decisive action, so the pro-Communists assumed a bold and open position on important issues contrary to general CIO policy. Even before the 1947 convention opened, the anti-Communists began to assert themselves, evidently encouraged by Murray and other leaders. In fact, Murray began to express himself publicly. When Andrei Y. Vishinsky, then Soviet spokesman at the United Nations, attacked the United States' "warmongering"—in accordance with the Soviet's new policy—Murray disagreed publicly.[1]

Lee Pressman, as secretary of the preconvention resolutions committee, secured the approval of Van A. Bittner, its chairman, for a compromise on the foreign-policy resolution, omitting specific mention of the Marshall

[1] Max M. Kampelman, *The Communist Party vs. the C.I.O.*, F. A. Praeger, New York, 1957, p. 88; *New York Times*, Oct. 9, 10, 1947.

Plan. Emil Rieve and James B. Carey disputed the omission and succeeded in inserting a clear-cut endorsement of the plan. To emphasize the difference more pronouncedly, Secretary of State Marshall availed himself of an opportunity to address the convention in support of his program.[2] A verbal anti-Communist barrage ensued during the debate on the resolution. In addition to defending the ideas and programs endorsed by the resolutions, charges against previous Communist inconsistencies and transgressions in criticizing American foreign policy were repeated. Even Murray entered the controversy in behalf of the anti-Communists. The Communists stood their ground, but the resolution was overwhelmingly approved.[3]

As a result of these occurrences at the 1947 convention, the sluice gates holding anti-Communist resentment in check were now thrown wide open. The onrush followed. Both national industrial unions and industrial union councils redoubled their anti-Communist activities. To cite a few cases: The New York chapter of the Newspaper Guild, a consistent follower of the Communists, elected to office for the first time a completely anti-Communist slate. The New York State industrial union council also cleaned house. A similar change occurred within the Minnesota industrial union council, previously dominated by the Communists.[4] Through the leadership of the presidents of two important, Communist-controlled unions, action against the Communists was initiated. Michael Quill broke with the Communists, denouncing them as "crackpots" and setting to work to eliminate them from control of the Transport Workers Union. Joseph Curran and his associates, estimating that approximately 107 out of the 150 elected officials in the NMU were Communists, successfully took over control now as anti-Communists. This was also the period when Reuther defeated the pro-Communists in the UAW.[5]

The national CIO also participated in the house cleaning, both among its subsidiary units and within the national headquarters. Several industrial-union council charters were revoked and new ones established to replace them. Other councils were reorganized. But the incident which revealed dramatically that the CIO was determined to pursue its course in eliminating Communist influence was the resignation of Lee Pressman as its general counsel. The exchange of letters between Murray and him, formalizing the severance, was couched in the same friendly tone as that between DeCaux and Murray. Nevertheless, having been the pivotal figure in the conduct of CIO affairs at national headquarters, Pressman's

[2] CIO Convention Proceedings, 1947, pp. 258–263.
[3] Ibid., p. 276.
[4] Kampelman, op. cit., pp. 91–96.
[5] Ibid., pp. 120–121; Joseph M. Brown, "Labor Out of the Red: 1947 Balance Sheet," Plain Talk, February, 1948, pp. 10–12.

withdrawal was hailed as a greater Communist defeat than the DeCaux resignation.[6]

Success attended attempts through 1948 to eliminate Communist influence within the CIO. The 1948 convention served as a forum for full and open discussion of the issues dividing the Communists from the non-Communists. Contrary to his efforts at previous conventions, Murray made no attempt to discourage discussion. Indeed, he was sharply outspoken in his criticism of the Communists. Other prominent leaders, such as Walter Reuther and Emil Rieve, followed a similar course. All took the Communists severely to task for not adhering to CIO policy and decisions. Accused of being disloyal to the CIO, they were also charged with overlooking the shortcomings of Soviet Russia. The convention obviously was in a fighting mood, further evidenced by the heckling of those delegates who sided with the Communists. More discussions of a controversial nature occurred at this convention than at previous ones. The debates were of high caliber, although the Communists speakers were jeered and occasionally challenged from the convention floor. The atmosphere was tense and charged with feeling as the two sides came to grips on basic issues for the first time at a CIO convention. Murray maintained order splendidly. The enthusiasm shown by the delegates in attacking the Communists had been stimulated by current events. The convention was in a jubilant mood because of the reelection of President Truman who had been supported by the CIO and opposed by the Communist-dominated unions. They were also elated by the dismal showing of Henry Wallace who, in their eyes, was the Communist candidate. Murray, by joining in, must have added to the zest of the delegates' attack; some members undoubtedly were encouraged by Murray's outspoken criticism to participate themselves.

The Communists had the choice of submitting or fighting back. They chose the latter but with seeming halfheartedness, perhaps knowing they were already defeated. They acknowledged they were in the minority, and some of their delegates appealed for tolerance, although without yielding defense of their position. Unity was a theme they stressed, although it was well recognized on all sides by now as a Communist camouflage. The Communists still showed deference to Murray; they evidently hoped to forestall more of the drastic action they had been experiencing since 1946. This air of humility contradicted their behavior outside the convention. The Communist press in particular assumed a belligerent and highly critical position, even denouncing Murray. The *People's World*, published in San Francisco and thus reaching convention delegates in Portland on November 24, 1948, described the proceedings of the convention as a lynching bee.

[6] *Ibid.*, pp. 115–116.

The *Daily Worker* was no less denunciatory. The official organ of the United Office and Professional Workers ran an article before the convention entitled "The Murray We Knew." [7]

Debate centered around six issues, all of which were interrelated in that they affected Communist programs and power within the CIO. Two of these were organizational in nature. One was the recommendation of the committee on the constitution that a new section be added to Article 8 providing for a "non-recurring special per capita tax of 3¢ per member per month" to be used for the "Southern Organizing Drive" and "for the general organization and other purposes of the CIO." The only opposition came from delegates of well-known Communist-dominated unions. They gave various reasons for opposing it, such as the heavy financial responsibilities of the individual unions. One of the Communist delegates tried to embarrass CIO leaders by suggesting that a public accounting of CIO finances be made.[8] It would seem that the hidden motive for opposing the per capita increase was the feeling that, with Communist influence in the national office diminishing, Communist effectiveness in the affiliated units would be hurt by further strengthening of the national organization. The amendment was carried.

Some criticism was directed toward their ineptness as trade unionists. These attacks centered mostly around criticism of the smaller Communist-dominated unions. Non-Communist strategy was evidently to expose the Communists for using up their energy and finances in Communist activity and for neglecting essential organizing work.[9]

Murray introduced the question in his opening remarks at the convention: He deplored the fact that at this time, when the CIO was at the height of its prestige, "we have mighty industries in the United States in the field of government services, public workers, white collar workers, and workers employed in the retail and other fields, where ample opportunity is provided to organizations such as ours to organize the unorganized." While he did not want it regarded as "seeking the enactment of vindictive and repressive legislation," nor as "a question of Communism," nevertheless the CIO "was created to organize the unorganized, not to issue charters to small cliques. . . . Something of a constructive nature designed to bring more people into these organizations must be worked out by this convention." [10] All the instances cited by Murray concerned jurisdictions covered by Communist-dominated unions.

The resolutions committee, now with a secretary of non-Communist sympathies, responded to Murray's criticism with dispatch. Curran, who had

[7] See the *Daily Worker* from November 22 to 28, 1948; also CIO Convention Proceedings, 1948, pp. 300 and 340.
[8] *Ibid.*, 1948, pp. 403–411.
[9] *Loc. cit.*
[10] *Ibid.*, 1948, pp. 17–20.

disassociated himself from his former Communist collaborators, had replaced Pressman.

A special resolution bearing on the recommendations made by President Murray on the first day of the convention was presented. It repeated Murray's statement that "the primary objective of our organization is to effectively organize men and women into labor unions for their mutual aid and protection." Since a few of the affiliates had not fulfilled this objective, the resolution provided that "this convention empower the National Executive Board of the CIO to investigate the situation ... and to take such appropriate action ... as may be ... necessary." [11]

The Communists were really alarmed; evidently they suspected a plan to dispose of these unions. At first, they opposed the resolution by the indirect argument that these unions did not receive needed help and that the industrial unions claiming jurisdiction over white-collar workers were not successful in garnering these workers into their respective unions. Their real fear was revealed by an inquiry of one leading Communist delegate: "Does this resolution give to the Executive Board the right to revoke or suspend the charter of an affiliated union, or does it give authority to the Board to set up administrations over affiliated unions"? [12] Murray answered that only investigatory power with instructions to recommend action was intended. He did not conceal the irritation of the non-Communists. "Every single, solitary resolution recommended to this convention that portends developments, constructive developments of the movement, is opposed by these representatives representing these weak organizations. You have had manifestation of it on the floor of this convention. You see it every day. I am not going to protect cliques, small cliques of men whose interests are promoted and propagated by the *Daily Worker* and the Communist Party, from small organizations, from little membership in big industries, where people are yearning for the opportunity to become members of unions." [13] On a rising vote, Emil Rieve, the presiding officer, announced, "The resolution has been carried, as it looks to the Chair, by far more than two-thirds of the vote." [14]

Questions which focused more clearly the differences over basic issues were among other subjects heatedly debated. They were interrelated with Communist political strategy and international policy. Armament, the Marshall Plan, the conduct of the WFTU, and the Wallace presidential candidacy were the disputative issues.

Differences over political action appeared on the surface as a quarrel over domestic affairs. The Communist-dominated unions within the CIO tried

[11] *Ibid.*, 1948, p. 336.
[12] *Ibid.*, 1948, p. 341.
[13] *Ibid.*, 1948, pp. 343–344.
[14] *Ibid.*, 1948, p. 344.

to justify their support of Henry Wallace's candidacy on the ticket of the newly created Progressive Party on just such grounds, but CIO leaders and the non-Communists refused to regard it in that light. Thus, within the CIO and at its 1948 convention, the controversy over support of Wallace revolved around the Communist issue. The Communists tried to justify their position on purely technical grounds which, in themselves, were valid. The resolution on political action, as well as the report of PAC Director Jack Kroll, charged that the formation of the Progressive Party was designed to "divide our movement." This act of the Communists linked them as allies of the National Association of Manufacturers: "Two years from now— or four years from now—the Communists and the NAM may again be campaigning together. They may again be seeking to confuse and divide us in order that they may conquer us." [15]

In fighting back, the Communists once again used the appeal of unity. One delegate declared, "It seems to me first that the major task before this Convention is to guarantee that the American people, whether they voted for Truman or Wallace, shall be united at this time, and that the CIO can unite them in fighting for peace, for the repeal of the Taft-Hartley Act, for the reenactment of the Wagner Act, for price roll-back control, for civil rights for all the people, for housing, and for other progressive legislation." [16] This approach very cleverly insinuated that "the results of the November, 1948 election" were not "as great a victory for the American people," as the CIO leaders claimed.[17] In support of this contention, they featured such sore spots as civil rights and Taft-Hartley. They also appealed for tolerance and respect of basic human rights, which is contrary to "interference with the democratic expression of unions and of the CIO; full freedom of political expression and differences must be preserved...." [18] The Communists also boasted of the "record of consistent and enthusiastic loyalty to Murray and the CIO and all forms of activity of the CIO, regardless of our political differences." [19] Finally, they fell back on the technicality that nonpartisanship means the right to support the Progressive Party or any other party.[20]

But the CIO leaders and their non-Communist associate delegates refused to permit diversion of the discussion to technicalities and generalities. They called a spade a spade and labeled the opponents Communists and fellow travelers. Philip Murray declared: "I do know that the third-party movement was not conceived by Henry Wallace. I certainly know that the third-party movement in the United States of America during the year

[15] *Ibid.*, 1948, pp. 264 and 278.
[16] *Ibid.*, 1948, p. 279.
[17] *Ibid.*, 1948, p. 264.
[18] *Ibid.*, 1948, pp. 280–281.
[19] *Ibid.*, 1948, p. 288.
[20] *Ibid.*, 1948, p. 287.

1948 was not conceived within the councils of the American labor movement.... The Third-Party comporting itself, as it did, to the wishes of the Kremlin, organized a movement to drive Truman out of the White House." [21]   And Van A. Bittner, chairman of the resolutions committee, inquired: "If the Communists wanted to run Henry Wallace for President why in the name of God did they not have the courage to run him on the Communist ticket?" [22]   On a rising vote, the secretary-treasurer reported 537 delegates in favor of the resolution and 49 against.[23]

The heated debate over the three issues vividly illustrated the differences on specific foreign-policy matters.   Action on all these, as on the others, pinpointed the irreconcilable differences and the conviction of the non-Communists that their adversaries were champions of the interests of a foreign and aggrandizing power.   Opposition to the Marshall Plan and adequate armament also raised the relationship of the CIO to the WFTU in the international trade-union field.   The WFTU, dominated by Communists who controlled the executive and administrative machinery, took the same position toward international policies of the Western democracies, and particularly of the United States, as did their Communist colleagues in the United States.   The same discord that showed itself in the CIO arose within the WFTU.   Officials representing CIO in WFTU reported on their frustrating experiences, which were similar to those at home: "Last November, soon after our 1947 convention, the WFTU Executive Bureau met in Paris in a diplomatic atmosphere from which allied wartime unity was vanishing.   Sharp disagreement among the affiliated unions was at once apparent on the question of the European Recovery Program.... The quarrel was accentuated by press accounts of the diverse points of view of WFTU President Deaken and WFTU General Secretary Louis Saillant....   The WFTU Executive Bureau next met in Rome ... in May 1948, and was immediately followed by a meeting of the larger Executive Committee.   At these meetings, which lasted twelve days, there was prolonged discussion of one item on the agenda: the functioning and administration of the WFTU Secretariat.   The CIO and representatives from the other democratic trade union movements subjected the activities of the General Secretary and his staff to searching criticism both as to the policy and efficiency.   An agreement was reached in an effort to preserve the WFTU and restore its original all-inclusive nature and to keep it from becoming the instrument of any one group....   The course of the WFTU, however, continued stormy and was further adversely affected by the diplomatic crisis over Germany and Berlin.   In September, 1948, the Executive Bureau met again for its regular meeting....   The deteriorating inter-

[21] Ibid., 1948, p. 301.
[22] Ibid., 1948, p. 292.
[23] Ibid., 1948, p. 303.

national situation, and the cleavage between East and West rendered these meetings nearly valueless. . . . There is no doubt that the structure of the WFTU is, at present, subjected to considerable strain and there is little expectation that the strain will be relieved unless the diplomatic situation improves." [24]

On the basis of this report, a resolution was introduced commending the CIO delegates and authorizing the CIO officers and executive board "in consultation with the British TUC and other free trade union centers, to take whatever action in relation to the WFTU and the international labor movement as will best accomplish CIO policies and objectives." [25] The Communists read the handwriting on the wall but attempted to erase it by following the international policy of avoiding a break. One of the prominent Communist delegates appealed for unity: "I feel very strongly that this resolution actually, because of the differences which we have on the Marshall Plan and ERP, is paving the way for the withdrawal from WFTU, and if that is true, I say it is most unfortunate. I say I cannot agree with it. I say ways and means must be found because of the importance of world solidarity among the working class to build WFTU." [26] The resolution carried.

Appeals of unity by the Communists fell on deaf ears this time. Such a disguise for giving the Communists their own way, either by supporting their position or by refraining from attacking the policies of the Soviet Union, had become too well known. The denouement of this drama occurred during the discussion of armaments and the Marshall Plan. That the Communists regard these subjects as crucial is evidenced by their submission of a minority report. It lacked the vitriolic tone the Communists used for ERP discussions outside the convention. The chief objection they now expressed was that "the report accepts without criticism a continuing high level of expenditures for armaments, peacetime conscription and for the Truman Doctrine and Marshall Plan to preserve such fascist regimes as in Greece and China and Turkey and rebuild the Nazis in Western Germany. . . ." It also contended that "a plan administered by the representatives of Wall Street to further a cold war against the Soviet Union holds no hope for the foreign lands or for America." [27]

Retorts, in addition to containing both defense and praise of the Marshall Plan, repeated the usual charges that the Communists were disrupters and were serving a hostile foreign power. As the discussion proceeded, President Murray's resentment of the Communists grew in intensity. He showed it by such remarks as: "I am sick, I am sore, I am

[24] *Ibid.*, 1948, p. 262.
[25] *Ibid.*, 1948, pp. 157–158.
[26] *Ibid.*, 1948, p. 262.
[27] *Ibid.*, 1948, pp. 157–158.

tired of these subtle maneuverings on the part of certain people who, in plying their trade, would endeavor in a skilled way to undermine the interests of this mighty labor organization." And again: "This organization, surely to God, has not reached the stage in its life where it is ganging up, as it might be implied by Board Member Henderson, with Wall Street— Wall Street. . . ." Then came this telling rebuke: "I have witnessed in the course of the past twelve months the sorry spectacle of degraded thinking going on in the councils of the Congress of Industrial Organizations. The protagonists of the Soviet system of thinking have never stood upon a floor, either in an executive board meeting or a convention hall, and criticized a single solitary thing that Russia has done since the end of the war. No— they have contented themselves with a general condemnation of their own country." [28] On a standing vote, the record shows the motion to approve the committee report was "unanimously agreed to." [29]

No drastic action was taken against any of the Communist-dominated unions. The smaller and weaker ones were criticized for their poor organizing accomplishments as revealed by their membership figures. The Communist leaders were also castigated for their un-American and pro-Soviet attitude. But their status in the CIO remained unchanged. In his remarks upon reelection, Murray still held out the olive branch: "I should like—and again if this is at all possible, to have such of the organizations— and these are only a few of them—as may be engaging themselves in the propagation of Communist doctrines amongst their membership, to cease and desist; and to provide, through the medium of their official organs all of the pertinent information that has to do with the development of the trade union movement and the widest possible publicity concerning the policy decisions of this tenth Constitutional Convention of the CIO." [30] This wish was never fulfilled.

Following the 1948 convention, restraints were discarded. With Murray's fiery and outspoken condemnation of the Communists and his clearcut decisions against them on significant issues, the road was open for decisive action. On the other hand, the Communists, well aware now that compromise which would enable them to pursue their course was no longer possible, fought back. They had the choice of continuing according to Communist International dynamics or of capitulating. Some of the leaders who were part of the Communist apparatus followed the latter course. Among them were Joseph Curran and Michael Quill. But, in general, the leaders remained in the path which led down the precipice of schism and isolation, away from the main stream of the labor movement.

Various events indicating a complete break was inevitable occurred be-

[28] *Ibid.*, 1948, pp. 164–165.
[29] *Ibid.*, 1948, p. 178.
[30] *Ibid.*, 1948, p. 423.

fore the 1949 convention. Smarting from the unceremonious treatment their followers had been subjected to at the 1948 convention, the Communists voiced resentment and defiance. Their attack on the CIO and its leaders was intensified. Moreover, they challenged the hostile attitude toward Communists within the CIO. At stake was their control of important unions, their continued success in preventing criticism of Soviet Russia, and the channels through which they carried Communist propaganda. This new Communist attitude toward the CIO was reviewed succinctly in two official Communist publications. *Labor Fact Book*, compiled by the Labor Research Association and described as a "direct auxiliary of the Communist Party," reported that for the first time in the history of the CIO, minority views were voiced at its convention. It distinguished the Communist delegates from the others by calling them the "Progressive" opposition. In this connection, it criticized the convention for its undemocratic conduct, charging that elected delegates were ignored. It also found fault with the convention because wages, living standards, and other such matters were almost forgotten in the urge to chastise the opposition. It then reviewed the Communist position on the issues discussed, reiterating and improving the arguments at the convention.[31]   John Williamson, labor secretary of the Communist Party, criticized the 1948 convention in the same vein in *Political Affairs*, the Communist "theoretical organ." In addition, he again denied the charge that the Communist Party intervened in the internal affairs of unions.[32]

Action as well as verbal challenge resulted in the Communists' defiance of CIO actions and broadened the breach before the 1949 convention. On the domestic scene, continuing jurisdictional differences between the FE

[31] *Labor Fact Book, 1949*, International Publishers Co., Inc., New York, pp. 109–114; *Investigation of Un-American Propaganda Activities in the United States, Report of the House Special Committee on Un-American Activities*, 78th Cong., 2d Sess., 1944, p. 47; see also U.S. Congress, Senate Committee on the Judiciary, *The Communist Party of the United States of America, What It Is, How It Works; A Handbook for Americans*, 84th Cong., 2d Sess., 1956, p. 91, wherein Labor Research Association is labeled as "a Communist Front Organization"; the association is also listed by the United States Attorney General as a "Communist Front Organization"; see also *Digest of the Public Record of Communism in the United States*, Fund for the Republic, New York, 1955, p. 71; and listings in *Cumulative Index to Publications of the Committee on Un-American Activities, 1938–1954*, 1955, p. 1191.

[32] *Political Affairs*, January, 1949. The House Committee on Un-American Activities cites *Political Affairs* as an "official Communist Party monthly theoretical organ," *Report on the Communist Party of the United States as an Advocate of Overthrow of Government by Force and Violence*, 1948, pp. 5 and 36; see also Report 209 on The *Communist Party of the United States as an Agent of a Foreign Power*, April 1, 1947, p. 25; also the Senate Internal Security Subcommittee describes *Political Affairs* as "the theoretical monthly magazine of the Communist Party . . ." in *The Communist Party of the United States, op. cit.*, p. 65. See also *Report on the March of Labor*, U.S. Congress, House Committee on Un-American Activities, 1954, p. 22.

and UAW grew into a significant bone of contention between the Communist and non-Communist factions in the CIO. As early as 1945, a jurisdictional committee of the CIO had recommended amalgamation with UAW. FE leaders opposed it and were sustained by a referendum vote of their membership. Later, the Communists tried to use this union by amalgamating it with the Auto Workers in order to provide votes which would enable UAW officials, who were in alliance with the Communists, to gain complete control of the union by ousting Reuther. We have seen how he succeeded in blocking the maneuver.[33] Since there was an overlapping in jurisdiction, now that the UAW was under the leadership of Reuther and his anti-Communist associates, they pressed for a solution.

When the two organizations were unable to settle their differences, the jurisdictional committee studied the question and in July, 1948, reported that no action had been taken to carry out its recommendations. Following the 1948 CIO convention, the executive board ordered FE to carry out the recommendations on a sound organizational basis so that the interests of its members would be safeguarded. A committee was appointed to facilitate the fusion. Communist members of the CIO executive board opposed the decision, and the FE leadership declared open warfare by refusing to comply, denouncing the decision as contrary to union principles and abusing the leaders. In this attitude, it was supported by the Communists within and without the CIO. Since this had become a public issue, the jurisdictional committee reviewed the matter in the spring of 1949 and once more repeated its recommendations of amalgamation. The committee also expressed resentment at the insolent and abusive campaign conducted by FE and its supporters. It commended the UAW, on the other hand, for its cooperative spirit and decent attitude.[34] As no amicable adjustment resulted, the matter came to the 1949 convention for disposition.

Another straw in the wind was a development in the UE. James B. Carey and his associates persevered at great odds, with resourceful leadership and little assistance from the CIO, in mustering a strong opposition within UE in spite of decisive defeats at conventions. The opposition was aided by the fact that UE leaders had supported Wallace, a good talking point since most of the workers were undoubtedly pro-Truman and pro-Democratic party, as the 1948 election returns revealed. Another factor aiding the opposition was the decision of the UE leaders not to sign the non-Communist affidavits as provided by the Taft-Hartley Act. This decision proved a particularly powerful talking point. It was discussed at local union meetings. Some of the locals applied for registration with the

[33] See above, p. 146.
[34] CIO report of the committee dealing with UAW-FE dispute, April 4, 1949; Kampelman, *op. cit.*, pp. 58–62; CIO Convention Proceedings, 1949, pp. 334 and 347.

NLRB but were informed that their International must sign the affidavits first. These and general clarification of the air on the Communist allegiance of the UE leaders caused an upsurge within the union that the opposition ably capitalized upon. Powerfully ensconced, the UE leaders fought, resorting to unscrupulous manipulations in order to keep control of important locals. This was but a forewarning of what was to happen at the UE convention.

The test came during the 1949 convention in the spring of that year. Both sides seemed to be evenly divided. The opposition came close to electing its candidate for president. Indeed, it would seem that the administration remained in control by doubtful manipulations. "An analysis of the convention voting showed that convention delegates of eight locals casting 419 votes had been instructed by their membership to vote right wing, but had disregarded these instructions. Further, the convention credentials committee disqualified one instructed delegation casting 38 votes and seated a left-wing delegation in its place. This, claimed the Carey forces, would have elected their candidate for UE president, Kelley, by a vote of 1,957 to 1,878 for Fitzgerald and would have by similar margins defeated Emspock and Matles as well." [35] This experience revealed the difficulty of defeating the Communist administration of a union. It also revealed that they will not hesitate to stoop to undemocratic and unethical means to stay in power. Similar experiences were encountered with like results by the non-Communists in other unions, such as UAW and NMU.[36]

An event that foretold the future was the action of the CIO and other democratic unions in the international trade-union field. In common with other free trade unions affiliated with the WFTU, the CIO encountered similar difficulties with the administrative branch of that organization. Because of their trusting attitude, and the mistaken advice of Leon Jouhoux, prominent French trade-union leader, the leaders of the democratic unions joined with the Russians and their satellite unions in turning the administrative branch of the WFTU over to disguised Communists. As the international situation became tense and as Soviet Russia began to differ with its allies and to ignore its treaty commitments, the differences began to reflect themselves in the WFTU. Since the organization was under Communist control, the Soviet Union's position was favorably featured and the democracies were grossly misrepresented. Immediately after the Soviet Union opposed, with all its power, the projected plans for European recovery, its agents within the WFTU followed this line regardless of decisions taken by the WFTU itself. WFTU publications began to carry abusive stories about trade-union leaders—particularly the American, English and French trade-union leaders who refused to depart from the WFTU policy and follow the Moscow line. The trade-union work of the federation was ob-

[35] Kampelman, *op. cit.*, p. 111.
[36] See above, pp. 141–147.

structed and hindered at every turn by the Communists." [37]   In desperation, the democratic unions withdrew from the WFTU in January, 1949.[38]

It was now clear to the CIO leaders how impossible it was to work on an honorable basis with Communists, particularly in the same organization or movement.

"The CIO stands on the threshold of a Convention whose effects are certain to have an important and lasting impact on the affairs of our country and of our labor movement."   With this opening sentence of his report to the Congress of Industrial Organizations, Philip Murray revealed the grim determination of the leaders to come to grips with the basic problem confronting this movement.   He followed it up by particularizing: "During much of its history, the CIO has been a united organization.   Its members and the leaders of all our unions have had a unified approach toward the problems that beset us.   Unfortunately, that has not been true for some time past.   A small but noisy clique of union officials has followed a policy of harassment, of opposition and of obstructionism to the general and specific aims of our democratic labor movement."

Then he pointed out the dissidents: "I have examined at great length, the 'demands' of the small group within the CIO who adhere to the program of the Communist Party. . . .

"The Communist program for American labor is a program of destruction. . . .   More than that, the program of the 'left wing' would enslave us to the aims and aspirations of a party whose interests are not those of American labor but are directed toward establishment of a retrogressive dictatorship in our life. . . .

"The leaders of this small group of unions in the CIO have indicated increasingly, during the past year, that they are interested in the benefits of CIO affiliation without regard to the responsibilities that such affiliation clearly entails. . . .

"The policy of obstructionism, to which there has necessarily been such frequent reference, has extended from the field of legislation, international affairs and political action into the mighty struggles of many of our unions to achieve improvements in their agreements with industry."

Murray complained of the Communist attacks on him and resented their criticism of the manner in which the Steelworkers were conducting their strike.   He accused them of "unjustified meddling." [39]

Murray's indictment was powerful and couched in unequivocal terms.

---

[37] CIO Convention Proceedings, 1949, p. 178.

[38] *Ibid.*, 1949, pp. 59, 178, 215.   While in the position of economic adviser to the Director of the Labor Division, U.S. Economic Cooperation Administration, Paris, the author followed this development.   Previously, as Chief Reports and Statistics Officer, Manpower Division, U.S. Office of Military Government for Germany, the author attended as observer the founding meeting of the WFTU in Paris, in 1945, and thereafter followed its activities in his official government capacity.

[39] *Ibid.*, 1949, pp. 52–55.

The convention tone was unmistakably set. As an opening volley for the offensive, the committee on the constitution recommended "insertion of a new Section 4" to Article IV, "concerning officers and Executive Board" members, to the effect that "no individual shall be eligible to serve either as an officer or as a member of the Executive Board who is a member of the Communist Party, any fascist organization, or other totalitarian movement, or who consistently pursues policies and activities directed toward the achievement of the program or the purposes of the Communist Party, any fascist organization, or other totalitarian movement, rather than the objectives and policies set forth in the Constitution of the CIO." [40] Well-prepared, the Communists fought back furiously, using as diversion from the real issue every argument in the democratic catechism—violation of civil and minority rights, encroachments on trade autonomy, initiation of witch hunts—and repeating previous arguments of unity and the need to fight the common enemy, the employer, by concentrating on bread-and-butter issues. They took pains to quote previous statements by Philip Murray in which he condemned the above practices. One of the delegates inquired: "What has happened suddenly? Have we changed from that policy that was laid down by Philip Murray to a policy of dictating to members of the Union as to whom they should elect to represent them?" [41] Another delegate argued: "The members of my union see this issue very clearly, they think the issue is whether or not they, the tax-paying members, have the right to decide ultimately their own destinies." [42]

The non-Communists took up the cudgels with gusto and definiteness, answering arguments concisely and earnestly. The venerable trade-union leader, Emil Rieve, congenitally anti-Communist, who successfully kept Communists out of his union and joined with others to resist Communist influence within the CIO, proclaimed, "I have waited for this opportunity for a good many years.... It is here, we ought to act...." [43]

Walter Reuther, agile, mercurial, and articulate, who had tried to work with the Communists, found it impossible, and had defeated them decisively in his own union two years before, denounced them roundly: "Every time you get into this basic question as to whether or not free people, through their democratic organizations, have a right to protect themselves and their freedoms, these people raise pious, hypocritical slogans, they talk about unity, they talk about autonomy, they talk about democratic rights of the minority, they raise the civil rights issue, and they do everything they can to becloud the real issues involved in this debate.

"There is room in our movement for an honest difference of opinion.

[40] *Ibid.*, 1949, p. 240.
[41] *Ibid.*, 1949, pp. 240–242.
[42] *Ibid.*, 1949, p. 265.
[43] *Ibid.*, 1949, pp. 245–246.

Sincere opposition is a healthy thing in the labor movement. But there is a fundamental difference between honest opposition and sincere difference of opinion and the kind of obstructionism and sabotage carried on by the Communist minority.... They are not a trade union group ... they are not free men, they are not free agents working in this movement.... They are colonial agents using the trade union movement as a basis of operation in order to carry out the needs of the Soviet Foreign Office. And, when you try to understand the basic characteristics of the Communist minority opposition group, you have got to differentiate between the kind of a minority opposition group of that kind and a minority group that has a basic, honest trade union opposition in their differences with the official policies of our organization.... I say the record is clear. They have failed to carry out the kind of a program geared to the needs of American workers, and have blown hot and cold, based on the Party line.

"We don't challenge the Communist Party's right to stand up in America and have their say.... We challenge and we are going to put a stop to their right to peddle the Communist Party line with a CIO label on the wrapper...." [44]

Joseph Curran and Michael Quill, thoroughly knowledgeable through participation in Communist policies and tactics, joined in the attack. In the course of the debate, they revealed many Communist operational techniques and procedures.

The querulous and theatrical Quill, who had recently locked horns successfully with the Communists in his union, related how they insisted on dominating the union in carrying out their objectives. When he offered them a compromise, they rejected it, wanting "all or nothing."

The burly Curran, neither subtle nor unequivocal in his manner of speaking, who broke with the Party as early as 1945 and eliminated Communist influence in his union, denounced them mercilessly. "In 1944, all of a sudden within the Communist Party, a decision was made. It was the Politburo, as I understand it. It was handed down to the National Committee. The National Committee handed it down to the section organizers. The organizers handed it to their people within the trade union movement.... I do not know about the dialectical approach to these matters, but that's the way it was. And they came into our Union ... and proposed that we adopt a policy that there shall be no strikes after the war.... I revolted at that and our Union was virtually split wide open over that basic economic question; and whatever relationship I had with those forces up to that point were completely broken, and I would have cracked the skull of anybody that came near me and urged that kind of program.

"These unions took it upon themselves—and I am speaking of the leadership—to place loyalty to the Communist Party and its program above loyalty

[44] *Ibid.*, 1949, pp. 266–270.

to the CIO, and they went out and did everything in their power to wreck the CIO in the interest of the Communist Party, and so we ought to stop kidding ourselves about that." [45]

Other pivotal non-Communist leaders, including Philip Murray, spoke at length. Murray repeated the history of and his experience with the Communists, concluding with the accusation that they failed to function as trade unionists: "Who could have been more tolerant over these issues than I have been? How many years have I expended in a futile effort to resolve these differences between the leaders of these alleged left-wing unions and the leadership of the National CIO? How many days and countless hours have I expended in that futile endeavor, in my office in Pittsburgh, in my office in Washington, in my hotel room in Washington and in hotel rooms in other cities throughout the United States, attempting to prevail upon them to recognize the fact that there is a trade union line to be respected here in the United States of America, and that it must be an independent, democratic trade union line. I have failed in every single, solitary endeavor in that respect—wholly unable to resolve any of these important issues.

"I say to the delegates attending this convention that we must provide some sensible, orderly regulations for the guidance of our International Unions and our membership. We must discontinue this practice of permitting the CIO Executive Board and CIO convention to be used as sounding boards for the dissemination of Communistic propaganda within our movement." [46] The resolution carried.

Having laid the basis for its new powers by amending the constitution, the convention proceeded to try them out. Two unions were picked for this purpose. The UE had actually anticipated expulsion by making demands in the form of an ultimatum upon the CIO president, by withholding payment of the per capita tax, and by walking out of the convention instead of remaining to defend themselves. A long bill of particulars and justification for the expulsion of UE was presented by the resolutions committee. "We can no longer tolerate within the family of the CIO the Communist Party masquerading as a labor union.... The false cry of these mis-leaders of labor for unity and autonomy does not deceive us. In the name of unity, they seek domination. In the name of autonomy they seek to justify their blind and slavish willingness to act as puppets for the Soviet dictatorship and its foreign policy with all its twists and turns from the Nazi-Soviet Pact to the abuse of the veto in the U.N., the Cominform attack upon the Marshall Plan, ECA, the Atlantic Treaty and the arms aid to free nations." [47]

[45] Ibid., 1949, pp. 257–261.
[46] Ibid., 1949, pp. 274–281.
[47] Ibid., 1949, pp. 302–305.

Although the UE delegates did not appear at the convention, their side was ably defended. Their protagonists demanded a trial outside the convention. The answer, "What are we to do, subpoena the delegates? The delegates from the UE are accredited delegates to this convention. . . . They should come here now and face this question, but they haven't the guts to debate it in the open," was the retort of George Baldanzi, executive vice-president of the Textile Workers of America.[48] Allan Haywood, CIO vice-president and director of organization, accused UE and other Communist unions of hostile conduct in slandering and abusing CIO officers and others. He also charged that the UE and some of the other Communist union leaders neglected to organize workers under their jurisdiction. It was further charged that at the UE convention, held in Cleveland a few months earlier, CIO leaders were abused and condemned. A similar procedure was followed by its official publication. "They stand for Cain and Abel Unionism, gangsterism and terror; selling out labor's political freedom by hog-tying it to a single reactionary political party; dictatorship, no voice for the rank and file; the use of the Ku Klux Klan and race baiting as an organizational tactic; chartering of stool pigeons and company agents."[49]

Walter Reuther pointed out that due process was observed throughout. The UE failed to have its representatives present at an executive board meeting, ignored a meeting of the committee on constitution, and now their delegates absented themselves from the convention. They had three opportunities of which they failed to avail themselves.[50]

Murray, after again reviewing Communist undercover tactics, concluded in his talk: "I am not one of those who care to resort to the method of expelling unions. There is enough room within the CIO movement to differ about many subjects, many ideas, questions of reform within the CIO, economic, social and trade union policy—yes, plenty of room, but there is no room within the CIO for Communism." On a rising vote, the presiding officer declared: "The resolution has been adopted by more than the required two-thirds vote." [51]

Expulsion of the FE was an anticlimax. No one seemed interested in discussing the case. The resolution was read, setting forth that "the workers in this field suffered because of divided jurisdiction between the FE and the Auto Workers, that a committee was appointed to study and make recommendations, that FE refused to recognize the Committee and instead resorted to abuse and vilification; hence it is recommended that the charter be revoked and the FE stand expelled." The motion to approve carried.[52]

[48] Ibid., 1949, p. 308.
[49] Ibid., 1949, p. 315.
[50] Ibid., 1949, pp. 313–317.
[51] Ibid., 1949, pp. 320–327.
[52] Ibid., 1949, pp. 334–336, 347–348.

18

The Grand Expulsion

Plans for the grand expulsion of Communist-dominated unions from the CIO were made in advance of the 1949 convention. An amendment to the CIO constitution, adopted at the convention as section 10 of article VI by an almost unanimous vote, gave the executive board power by a "two-thirds vote, to revoke the Certificate of Affiliation or to expel or to take any other appropriate action against any national or international union or organizing committee the policies and activities of which are consistently directed toward the achievement of the program or purposes of the Communist Party, any Fascist organization or other totalitarian movement, rather than the objectives and policies set forth in the constitution of the CIO. . . ." [1]

This amendment was followed up by resolution No. 67, instructing the executive board "immediately to exercise its powers . . . and to take appropriate action to protect the CIO and to prevent the use of the good name of the CIO by those who insistently directed their policies and activities toward the achievement of the program or the purposes of the Communist Party, and Fascist organizations or other totalitarian movements." [2] With such a positive mandate, the executive board promptly proceeded to implement it. "In November, 1949, shortly after the Convention closed, President William Steinberg of the American Radio Association, a member of the CIO Executive Board, filed charges against several unions alleging as to each that its policies and activities 'are consistently directed toward the achievements of the program or the purposes of the Communist Party rather than the objectives and purposes set forth in the constitution of the CIO.' President Steinberg requested that appropriate action be taken by the Executive Board to expel the charged organizations from the CIO.

"The CIO Executive Board thereupon authorized President Murray to

[1] CIO Convention Proceedings, 1949, pp. 288–289; *CIO Constitution,* Congress of Industrial Organizations, Washington, D.C., 1952, pp. 17–18.
[2] *Ibid.,* p. 336.

appoint a committee or committees of Executive Board members to conduct hearings on the charges and report back to the Executive Board. Notice of the charges and the appointment of the Committees was sent to the unions." [3]

Although the Communists had lost out in the 1948 and 1949 conventions, in some of the industrial unions, and in many of the local and state industrial-union councils, they assiduously fought these expulsion procedures. It became evident that they would challenge every effort to expel them.

"Emil Rieve, Chairman of the committee designated to conduct hearings on the charges against the United Public Workers of America and the United Office and Professional Workers of America, scheduled hearings on the charges against those unions, toward the end of November, 1949." On December 9, these two unions filed identical suits in the United States District Court in Philadelphia. These suits sought to enjoin the committee from conducting the hearings and ultimately to enjoin any action by the CIO executive board looking toward the expulsion of the UOPWA and UPWA from the CIO.

"The allegations in the complaints, which were substantially repeated in other suits brought thereafter" included, among other technical legal points, the following: that article VI, section 10, of the CIO constitution . . . was invalid because (a) it invaded the autonomy guaranteed to CIO affiliates, (b) it was contrary to public policy as restricting the political activities of unions, and (c) the amendment could not be given a retroactive application." [4] In all, five suits were initiated by these three unions in order to enjoin the CIO from carrying out the convention mandate.

"Contemporaneously with this litigation, a somewhat similar suit was brought in a state court in California by the California State Industrial Union Council to enjoin the revocation of its charter." [5]

All "the suits brought by the Communist-line unions ended in failure; in none were they even able to secure a temporary injunction." [6]

With temporary legal impediments removed, it was possible for the committees to proceed with dispatch. Aided by the legal department, every precaution was taken to assure due process to the officials of the accused unions. Due notice was given, full opportunity to present their case and to question hostile witnesses was made possible, transcripts and exhibits of the hearings were made available.

[3] CIO Convention Proceedings, 1950, p. 144.
[4] Ibid., 1950, pp. 144–145. The Food, Tobacco, Agricultural and Allied Workers also sought judicial protection.
[5] Ibid., p. 146.
[6] Ibid., pp. 144–146. These lawsuits are summarized, including citations, in Digest of the Public Record of Communism in the United States, Fund for the Republic, New York, 1955, pp. 441–442.

Adjournments were granted to enable the accused to study the testimony and to present rebuttal witnesses. The case presented by the CIO in each instance was thoroughly prepared, specialists from the research staff prepared documentary evidence delineating the manner in which the particular leaders and unions through their official publications, convention action, and other official pronouncements followed and oscillated with the Communist Party line. These data were reinforced with documents from official Communist publications.

Headed by Stanley Ruttenberg, director of research and education, documentary analysis was presented to show the obvious parallel between the Communist programs and those of the accused unions. This evidence also showed how changes in Communist Party policy were reflected by policy changes in the accused unions. Witnesses were presented who had participated in union–Communist Party caucuses and in other activities but had now dissociated themselves from this "conspiratorial movement." Among these were such prominent union officials as Michael Quill, president of the Transport Workers, and M. Hedley Stone, treasurer of the National Maritime Union. Quill and Stone testified, "showing direct Communist control of ILWU. Both testified that Harry Bridges had, over a period of years, participated in numerous secret meetings between Communist Party functionaries and officers of Communist-controlled unions in the CIO at which the Party functionaries instructed the union officers as to the Party line and as to the positions that they were to take in the CIO and in their unions.... Such meetings took place from the inception of the CIO, and continued, to Mr. Stone's knowledge, until 1945, and to Mr. Quill's until 1948, those being the dates of their respective breaks with the party. Such meetings took place contemporaneously with every CIO convention, and were often held at the time of CIO Executive Board meetings. The Party functionaries who participated in these meetings included Eugene Dennis, William Z. Foster, John Williamson, Roy Hudson, Robert Thompson, Jack Stachel, and William Schneiderman." [7] Homer Wilson and Kenneth Eckert, both former executive board members of Mine, Mill and former Communist Party members, "testified in detail as to the manner in which the program of the Communist Party was translated into the policy of the Mine, Mill and Smelter Workers.... Both Wilson and Eckert made it perfectly clear to the committee that the fact this union followed the Communist Party line was not accidental. It was the result of complete domination of the union leadership by the Party. The Party group within the union had a systematic working apparatus for making its decisions and for transmitting those decisions into union policy. At the top there was a Party steering

[7] *Official Reports on the Expulsion of Communist Dominated Organizations from the CIO*, Publication no. 254, Congress of Industrial Organizations, Washington, D.C., September, 1954, p. 111.

committee of four members. This committee, of which Eckert and Maurice Travis, now Secretary-Treasurer of the union, were members, determined Communist policy within the union. They did this in consultation with the leaders of the Communist Party. Meetings were frequently held with Communist Party leaders such as William Z. Foster, the Chairman of the Party, Eugene Dennis, its General Secretary, John Williamson, its Labor Secretary, and Gil Green its Illinois Director. In addition there was a regular envoy of the Communist Party who was designated as liaison man between Mine, Mill and the Party.

"Both Eckert and Wilson testified in detail to the control which the Communist Party machinery exercises over the affairs of the union. Such matters as who should be the officers of the Union, or whether the 1947 report of the CIO investigating committee should be accepted, or whether the union should comply with the Taft-Hartley Act, were first decided by the Communist Party steering committee, then transmitted to the progressive caucus and finally presented to the union's executive board or its membership for approval.... Eckert and Wilson named names, place and dates...." All efforts of the investigating committee to get Mine, Mill officials so accused to answer questions were refused.[8]

The Communist Party not only directed the affairs of the unions it dominated, it also established machinery for influencing national CIO policy. Both Quill and Hedley Stone testified to the holding of Communist Party caucuses in which they and officials of other Communist-dominated unions participated over a period of years. At the caucuses the position of the Party and the course to be followed within the CIO were discussed. Communist functionaries were always present to expound the Party line and to give instructions. "One such meeting of particular importance ... took place in New York shortly after the CIO convention in Boston in October, 1947, and was attended by Dennis, Williamson, and Robert Thompson and others for the party and ... representatives of the controlled unions. Dennis announced that the Communist Party would back Wallace on a third-party ticket, and instructed the Communist-controlled unions to support him.

"This meeting was followed by similar meetings preceding the 2-day CIO executive board meeting in Washington in January, 1948. At these meetings Williamson, speaker for the Communist Party, instructed ... the ... union representatives to endeavor to have the CIO executive board support Wallace, and, if that were impossible to achieve, to at least block any CIO resolution opposing Wallace." At the executive board meeting referred to, Harry Bridges had "unsuccessfully sought to postpone the CIO's taking a position by proposing a referendum of the membership....

"M. Hedley Stone, secretary-treasurer of the National Maritime Union

[8] *Ibid.*, pp. 11 and 17–21.

and himself a Communist from around 1935–1945, testified to . . . participation in numerous such meetings between Communist Party functionaries and the Communist Party faction in CIO." He cited many instances, listing dates, names of functionaries, and subjects discussed, and described the nature of instructions given by Party representatives. Mr. Quill also supplied information about occurrences at particular meetings, including the names and affiliations of those in attendance. These meetings followed the pattern of those described earlier.[9]

In defending themselves, the Communists practiced their usual tactics of delay, not only through legal procedures but also by asking for postponements. They also asked for adjournments in order to digest the testimony presented and to present additional witnesses for rebuttal purposes. Usually they returned to the hearings without introducing other witnesses. Generally they rehashed statements presented at earlier hearings. In such instances as the MM and ILWU, an effort was made to present a strong case with written statements, documentary material, and witnesses. The latter followed the technique used by Communist witnesses appearing before government investigations: refusing to answer pertinent questions for which evasive or equivocal replies could not readily be concocted. To illustrate: "The committee also attempted to check the accuracy of the testimony of Wilson and Eckert by asking questions of the Union's representatives at the hearing. Mr. Travis was asked, for example, whether he had in fact participated in meetings attended by such leaders of the Communist Party as William Z. Foster, Eugene Dennis and John Williamson at which the policies of Mine, Mill were determined. He refused to answer the question. Mr. Travis was asked whether his position on policy matters within the Union was formulated at meetings with members of the Communist Party. He refused to answer the question. Mr. Travis was asked, finally, whether as a member of the Communist Party, he was under a duty to carry out the decisions of the party, irrespective of his own opinion as to their propriety for his union. He refused to answer." [10]

The investigating committee, in describing Travis' career, revealed how the Communist Party colonized its important members and secured their selection for key union positions: "The career of Maurice Travis affords a good example of the role of the Communist Party within the Mine, Mill and Smelter Workers Union. Travis was a steel worker. He was expelled from a local of the United Steel Workers of America as a Communist disrupter in 1941. Shortly thereafter, he was placed by the Communist Party on the Staff of Mine, Mill and Smelter Workers. After less than 2 years with the union, he was chosen by the party to be executive assistant to the president. Later he became vice president and, by virtue of Reid Robinson's resignation in 1947, president of the union. The party, how-

[9] *Ibid.*, pp. 111–113.
[10] *Ibid.*, p. 18.

ever, decided that his Communist affiliation was too well known for him to function effectively as president. Accordingly, the Communist Party steering committee determined to support for the presidency a candidate who was not known as a Communist follower but who could be relied upon to go along with party decisions. . . . And in accordance with this decision . . . Clark was elected and now serves as president, and Travis as secretary-treasurer." [11]

In some cases, only a perfunctory defense was presented. Thus, the United Office and Professional Workers made but a feeble attempt in its defense. Its officers, although present at the hearing, "chose not to present any testimony or documentary material in response to the charges. . . . The president of the UOPWA delivered a statement denouncing the trial committee of the CIO and submitted some 20 letters from rank and file committee members. . . . No other oral testimony or documentary material was offered. . . ." [12]

Some of the defendant unions pursued delaying action. The Food, Tobacco, Agricultural and Allied Workers Union was notified on November 7, 1949, of the charges, and the union was fully represented when the hearings began, as scheduled, January 6, 1950. The defense opened with a statement by its president, followed by the testimony of five witnesses representing local unions. Then the FTA officials asked for adjournment in order to have time "to prepare rebuttal testimony." When the trial hearing was reconvened twelve days later, January 19, a brief was presented "on behalf of the union." The union, however, presented no oral testimony but requested a further postponement. It was agreed by all concerned that there would be no other meeting of the committee to hear testimony, but the union might file a further statement before February 1. This additional brief was received by the committee February 2. On February 1, the union requested an additional hearing so that it could present further oral testimony. The request was granted, and the committee met for the third time on February 6. At this third hearing, the union presented a mimeographed brief virtually identical to the typewritten brief which had been submitted February 2. Although the February 6 meeting was convened at the request of FTA for the sole purpose of affording it an additional opportunity to present oral testimony, FTA offered no oral testimony whatever.

"The committee is forced to conclude that the officers of FTA acted in utter bad faith in repeatedly demanding these postponements and additional hearings which they failed to utilize." [13]

The International Fur and Leather Workers Union obtained a post-

[11] *Ibid.*, p. 17.
[12] *Ibid.*, p. 56. This was the procedure followed by the Communists in their press; see *Political Affairs*, January, 1950.
[13] *Official Reports on the Expulsion of Communist Dominated Organizations from the CIO, op. cit.*, p. 24; see also pp. 48–49, 54.

ponement until after its impending convention. At the convention it was decided, on recommendation of the officers, that the union should choose not to appear. Instead, the trial committee was notified that the union had decided to disaffiliate. The resolution stated that the delegates "reject the so-called charges of the CIO officials against our union as false, dishonest, and fraudulent.

"We reject the Kangaroo hearing set by CIO officials as a deliberate sham and hypocritical attempt to perpetuate a colossal swindle not only on the members of our union, but also upon all members of CIO and the entire labor movement. We refuse to be accomplices in such a barefaced fraud.

"Our union, built by the sweat and toil and sacrifice of our members, is dedicated to the well being of our members and to the preservation of their autonomous and democratic rights of free Americans . . . this convention goes on record to disaffiliate from CIO." [14]

This resolution reveals the attitude of the accused unions in carrying out their defense at the trials and in public generally. Indeed, the *Daily Worker* [15] revealed the nature of the defense in a series of articles immediately following the 1949 CIO convention and the expulsion of the UE and FE. The unions, in pursuing their defense, followed the line laid down in these articles; they avoided meeting the issues squarely but fought back with propaganda, vilification, and denunciation. They diligently and studiously evaded the issue of Communist Party domination, accused the CIO of redbaiting and witch-hunting, charged that the trials were illegal, accused the trial committees of bias. These countercharges the CIO trial committees resentfully denied.

In spite of the Communists' efforts to divert the trials from the main charge against them, the trial committees' findings concentrated on the basic charge, namely, "that the policies and activities of the (accused) unions are consistently directed toward the achievement of the program and purposes of the Communist Party rather than the objectives and policies set forth in the constitution of the CIO." [16] All other charges and countercharges of the defendant unions became dependent upon this basic consideration and interrelated with it.

Proof that the unions followed the Party line was in the form of documentation from official publications. The evidence was related step by step, stipulating the issues and particularizing the events, as follows:

"The program of the Communist Party in the United States can be divided into some five different periods, from the time of the formation of the CIO to the present. Each of these periods corresponds to a particular period in the international relations of the Soviet Union.

[14] *Ibid.*, p. 85.
[15] December 6, 7, 8, 9, 1949.
[16] *Official Reports on the Expulsion of Communist Dominated Organizations from the CIO, op. cit.*, p. 12.

"1. Collective Security and the popular front. The first period extending from shortly after Hitler's acquisition of power until August, 1939 was the period of collective security and the popular front.

"During this period the American Communist Party of the United States supported a policy of collective security and urged that the United States enter into such a system with the Soviet Union. . . .

"During this period the American Communist Party found that the interest of American labor lay in the elimination of fascism whenever it was found. . . .

"2. Russian German Pact. In August, 1939 the foreign policy of the Soviet Union abruptly changed. . . . The change in Soviet strategy immediately brought about a violent change in the program of the Communist Party of the United States. The American Communist Party lost interest in the evils of nazism and fascism. The threat to American labor, the party now said, was the 'imperialist war.'

"3. All out aid to Russia. On July 22, 1941, Germany, in disregard to its 10-year nonaggression pact, attacked the Soviet Union.

"A second rapid reversal in the policies of the American Communist Party took place. In essence, the party went back to its prepact position of the collective security days, but with its policies turned to the war crises in which the Soviet Union found itself. . . . But the party continued to grind its axe. The United States and Russia did not see eye to eye on military strategy. The Russians wanted the immediate opening of a second front. And so the Communist Party decided that American labor had an interest in this question of military strategy, and that it was to labor's interest to bring pressure on the military commanders for the immediate opening of a second front.

"4. Tehran. The second front issue was a symptom of the lack of confidence which the Communist Party felt, during this period, in the genuineness of American-Russian collaboration. These doubts, however, vanished when President Roosevelt met with Premier Stalin at Tehran, and an agreement was reached on the basic problems confronting the two countries. . . . The fact that the United States and the Soviet Union had reached an agreement meant to the Communist Party that all problems between labor and capital in the United States were on their way to being settled. Tehran became the watchword, the magic touchstone, which not only solved foreign problems but laid at rest all of labor's problems.

"In short, during this period the Communist Party, then called the Communist Political Association, was—as it later described itself during one of its periodic orgies of Marxist self-criticism—an opportunist tail to the capitalist class. . . ."

"5. The post-war period. With the close of the European War, differences and tensions began to develop between the Soviet Union and the United States.

"Accordingly the 'American' Communist Party again reversed its field.

"The policy of the American Communist Party in the postwar era did not exhibit any rapid and sudden shift, since the international position of the Soviet Union did not exhibit such shifts. . . . This opposition became clearer as the diplomatic conflict between the United States and the Soviet Union developed and deepened. The post-war Communist policies included the following specific items:

"1. Identification of the Chinese Communists with the 'democratic' forces in China;

"2. A claim that the United States had failed to live up to the Yalta and Potsdam agreements, and a demand that United States foreign policy be based on friendship with the Soviet Union;

"3. Opposition to the Truman Doctrine;

"4. Opposition to the Marshall Plan;

"5. Support of Henry Wallace and the Progressive Party in 1948;

"6. Opposition to the Atlantic Pact;

"7. Support of the Communist dominated World Federation of Trade Unions and opposition to the CIO and AFL sponsored International Confederation of Free Trade Unions;

"8. Denunciation of the CIO as a tool of reaction and imperialism, and

"9. Support of the UE in its fight with the CIO.

"Throughout this curious history, the Communist Party has never ceased to claim that it makes its decisions on the basis of a genuine appraisal of the interests of the American people and of American labor. This claim is, of course, false. The record shows that the basic purpose of the Communist Party is the support of the Soviet Union and that the program of the party is designed with only the interests of the Soviet Union in view.

"The Communist Party's single-minded devotion to Russia controls its position on domestic issues, as well as on matters of foreign policy. . . ." [17]

Another finding declared that at no time did these unions or any adherents to the Communist Party line offer any criticism of or take exception to Communist Party or Russian programs or policies.

"One fact of great significance. Never in the history of the ACA (American Communications Association) has any policy been adopted which in any way ran counter to the policies of the Communist Party or to the interests of the Soviet Union as those interests are reflected in the program of the Communist Party." [18]

The findings in these trials is aptly summed up as follows:

"The basic question posed by the charge against IFLWU is whether it is an honest trade union, genuinely devoted to the advancement of the Cause of American labor and American democracy, or a union whose policies and

[17] *Ibid.*, pp. 71–75.
[18] *Ibid.*, p. 76; see also on this point, pp. 20, 57, 61.

activities are determined by the Communist Party. To this question there can, in the light of evidence, be only one answer. 'The IFLWU (International Fur and Leather Workers Union) has for years followed the tortuous paths of the Communist Party. Over the years it has been interventionist, isolationist, and then isolationist again. The IFLWU's occupancy of these contradictory positions have inevitably coincided with the Communist Party's tenure of them, and can only have resulted from the IFLWU's subservience to the wishes of the Communist Party and the Soviet Union. Indeed, the IFLWU's publications are rife with Marxist and Stalinist doctrine, and Soviet propaganda.' " [19]

Just as documentary evidence was presented to prove that the accused unions were puppets of the Communist Party line, so witnesses were used who were former Communist Party members, or had otherwise participated in the inner circles that controlled and directed the programs, policies, and activities of these unions. Some of the testimony was quoted earlier.[20]

Stung by countercharges and claims of leaders of the defendant unions, the investigating committees took meticulous pains to reply in their findings.[21] And in this connection certain salient trade-union practices and constitutional provisions were also cleared up.

One of the points stressed by the Communist-dominated unions was that they functioned effectively in the labor relations area through collective bargaining. This was in answer to the CIO charges that they ignored its main aims, namely: "The objectives of the CIO are to bring about the organization of the working men and women in America, to extend the benefits of collective bargaining to them and to secure legislation protecting and extending our democratic institutions and civil rights and liberties, all to the end that the cherished traditions of our democracy be perpetuated." [22]

In answer to these claims of the Communist-dominated unions, the investigating committees stressed membership and the organizing accomplishments of some of these unions. "The slavish adherence by the FTA leadership to the program and policies of the Communist Party has resulted in a steadily declining membership ..." of from 46,700 in 1947 to 22,590 in 1949.

"Total membership potential, according to FTA figures is between 200,000 and 300,000 people.... Significantly, the sharp drop came at a

[19] *Ibid.*, p. 98, and see also pp. 103, 106; for a similar enunciation of changes by Communist-controlled unions in accordance with Communist Party-line changes, see also *Communist Domination of Union Officials in Vital Defense Industry—International Union of Mine, Mill and Smelter Workers, Hearings before the Subcommittee to Investigate the Administration of the Internal Security Act and Other Internal Security Laws of the Committee on the Judiciary,* U.S. Senate, 82d Cong., 2d Sess., 1952, pp. 2ff.

[20] See above, pp. 161, 171–172, 176–178.

[21] See above, pp. 160–161.

[22] *Official Reports on the Expulsion of Communist Dominated Organizations from the CIO, op. cit.,* p. 61.

time when much of the energy of union leaders was being dissipated in opposing CIO policies, in attacking the leadership of the CIO, and in espousing the various changes, in line of the Communist Party." [23]

Another Communist-dominated union was attacked and answered in this manner:

"So it is this union, the UOPWA (United Office and Professional Workers of America), by following the twists and turns, the zigs and zags, of the Communist Party line has prevented itself from genuinely representing the interests of the white-collar workers of America. It has failed dismally to organize those workers and most of the few that it has organized have been driven away from it as the subservience of the union to the Communist Party became more obvious. In the fiscal year of 1946–1947, this union reported to the CIO an average dues-paying membership of approximately 45,000. But as of November, 1949, this membership has dropped to the pitiable figure of approximately 12,000." [24]

The answer to the ILWU, which beyond doubt was successful, gauged by trade-union standards, was somewhat different. "The ILWU stressed at great length the economic gains it had achieved for its members. Indeed, the oral testimony given by ILWU consisted in the main of statements by members of its executive board that ILWU was a democratic union which had achieved great economic gains for the workers in its industry.

"It is unquestionably true that, during those periods when the Communist Party line had required, ILWU leadership had been militant. ILWU's present chiefs came into the leadership of ILWU at a time when militancy was the order of the day for the Communist Party, and they are still trading on the reputation for militancy built up long ago." Then follows a paragraph describing how the ILWU followed the Communist Party line by cooperating with employers, favored a National Service Act, "and urged that the no-strike pledge be continued after the war." [25]

The evidence and arguments of the CIO that the Communist-dominated union failed fully to pursue pure trade-union procedures are rather tenuous. It is at least partially true that the leadership of some of these unions, particularly those like FTA and UOPWA, had ineffective leadership and devoted considerable time and money to Communist Party activities. No other union efforts, however, were more successful in the fields covered by these jurisdictions. On the other hand, the ILWU, Fur, and UE had leadership as competent as the most successful unions. Moreover, purely from a trade-union point of view, they were as effective organizationally— as revealed by their membership—as any of the superlatively successful

[23] *Ibid.*, pp. 30–31.
[24] *Ibid.*, p. 68.
[25] *Ibid.*, p. 114.

unions, and their record in securing wages and better working conditions for their members through collective bargaining is at least as favorable as that of any of the outstanding unions. Undoubtedly, their achievements in the trade-union field enabled them to hold the loyalty of their members, the great majority of whom were not Communists.

Two other points pertaining to constitutional trade-union policies and practices were made by the trial committees. In these instances, the reasoning of the CIO was on more solid ground:

Trade autonomy: In defending themselves, the Communist-dominated unions very effectively resorted to issues and arguments that had become cardinal points in trade-union and liberal thinking. Trade autonomy is a trade-union principle accepted universally in Western countries and by democratic trade-union movements everywhere. Communist unions behind and this side of the iron curtain have not accepted this principle; their unions are subject to highly centralized control. Nevertheless, the defendant unions pled for protection under the principle of trade autonomy. The CIO answer was definite. "The FTA asserts as a defense that they are defending the autonomous rights of that union. . . . In the name of autonomy they seek to disguise their uniform and slavish adherence to the foreign policy of the Soviet Union. . . ." [26] "The CIO is a voluntary association of free trade unions dedicated by its constitution to the protection and extension of our democratic institutions, civil liberties, and human rights. Free unions are voluntary associations of freemen, held together by common loyalties and the element of decency and honesty. . . .

"The certification of affiliation of the CIO is a symbol of trust, democracy, brotherhood, and loyalty in the never-ending struggle for the working men and women for a better life. There is no place in the CIO for an organization whose leaders pervert its certificates of affiliation into an instrument that would betray the American workers into totalitarian bondage." [27]

"Moreover, there is no room in the CIO, or in any other voluntary association of independent members, for an affiliate whose policies over a period of time contravene and tend to undermine the fundamental objectives of the organization.

"Within the CIO there is the greatest freedom for difference of opinion on political and trade union matters, so long as those differences stem from an honest belief as to what constitutes a good trade union policy or the best method of promoting the objectives set forth in the CIO constitution. But there is no room for differences of opinion when those differences reflect a fundamental divergence in basic objectives such as the divergence between the CIO and the Communist Party. A voluntary association created to

[26] *Ibid.*, p. 32.
[27] *Ibid.*, p. 21.

promote certain objectives is fully entitled to exclude from its midst those who rejected such objectives and accept an entirely contrary set of values." [28]

Responsible opposition: A secondary answer to the trade-autonomy contention by the accused unions was the reply of the CIO that these unions were not performing the function of a responsible opposition. While conceding there must be room for oppositions, the CIO contended that there is no room in a voluntary organization for irresponsible oppositions.

"The issue posed by the charges against MCS (International Union of Marine Cooks and Stewards of America) is whether it is an honest trade union, genuinely devoted to the advancement of the cause of American labor and democracy, or a union whose policies and activities are determined by the philosophy and the program of the Communist Party. The issue is one of basic loyalty. The purposes of the Communist Party are wholly antithetical to the basic objectives of American industrial unionism. And the question as regards MCS is whether that union is devoted primarily to the CIO on the one hand or to the Communist Party on the other." [29] And further: "The charge against UPW (United Public Workers of America) is not that it differs from CIO policy. Under the CIO constitution, unions have a right to differ on policy matters if they honestly believe that the policies they advocate are the proper ones to achieve the objective set forth in the CIO constitution. The charge against the UPW is much more fundamental. The charge is that the leadership of this union does not adopt its policies on the basis of any honest objectives of American industrial unionism set forth in the CIO constitution, but rather, adopts policies and takes action with regard only to the achievement of the antithetical purposes of the Communist Party. The charge, in short, is disloyalty to American trade unionism. . . . The basic question posed by the charge against the UPW is whether its leadership is an honest trade union leadership, genuinely devoted to the advancement of the Cause of American labor and American democracy. . . ."

"The charge is not aimed at affiliates which honestly differ with CIO policies. . . . However, there is no room in the CIO or in any other voluntary association of independent members, for an affiliate whose policies over a period of time contravene and tend to undermine the fundamental objectives of the organization." [30]

The other countercharges made by the defendants dealt with broader political and social phases—as, for example, that the CIO also followed the Communist Party line and that the CIO was resorting to redbaiting and witch hunts. The trial committees made vehement replies that were

[28] *Ibid.*, p. 102.
[29] *Ibid.*, p. 125.
[30] *Ibid.*, pp. 12, 53; see also David J. Saposs, "Communist Tactics in the Trade Unions," *Daily Labor Report*, Bureau of National Affairs, Washington, D.C., October 1, 1954.

full of resentment at "the preposterous charge that the CIO followed the Communist Party line from 1938 to 1947. The committee states categorically that this charge is false. It is compounded of confusion and distortion. . . ." [31]

This countercharge was taken up point by point: "The ACA has submitted a 43-page 'statement' in support of its claim that ACA's policies were, until the post-war period, the same as CIO's. . . ." This assertion is "equivalent to an assertion that CIO policy paralleled Communist policy. . . . The committee has examined the material which ACA submitted to 'prove' this preposterous claim. It finds that this charge is wholly false and completely unsupported by evidence." [32] The CIO defense was that, like the Communists, it had followed the Roosevelt foreign-policy program, but that the Communists deviated from this program when doing so would favor Soviet Russia. Then this rebuttal was illustrated by specific situations:

"The CIO opposed Nazi and Fascist aggression in 1938, as [did] President Roosevelt and the entire liberal movement in the United States. The Communist Party and ACA also opposed Nazi aggression during this period.

"After the German-Russian pact was signed and war with Europe began the CIO opposed direct involvement in the war, as did President Roosevelt. The CIO continued to support Roosevelt's program of aid short of war to those fighting Hitler, and it supported the defense program. The CIO in fact proposed several plans (the Murray and Reuther plans) to increase production for aid to the Allies and for national defense, and its representatives participated in the National Defense Advisory Commission and the National Defense Mediation Board. The Communist Party and ACA, on the other hand, opposed aid to the Allies, declared that the war was being fought for nothing but profit, opposed the national defense program and asserted that the administration was trying to drag this country into the war.

"The CIO, in 1945, urged that all surplus troops be brought home. It did not, like the ACA and the Communist Party, couple this demand with criticism of American policy vis-a-vis China.

"The CIO has frequently in the past and still today does denounce those who would use the cry of 'Communist' to destroy honest American tradition. But, at the same time, it has also frequently announced its rejection of Communism and 'any movement or activity of subversive character, Trojan horses, or fifth columns' (CIO executive board resolution of June 4, 1940). Its members 'resent and reject efforts of the Communist Party . . . to interfere in the affairs of the CIO.' (Resolution adopted by the CIO convention, November 18, 1946.) ACA, on the other hand, has opposed 'redbaiting' not on the ground that false charges of Communism are dan-

[31] CIO Convention Proceedings, 1950, pp. 19ff.; contains an itemized comparison.
[32] Ibid., 1950, pp. 81ff.; see also p. 52.

gerous and should be opposed but rather on the apparent theory that all charges of Communism, true or false, should be rejected." [33]

This defense by the CIO is not conclusive. While it is not true that the CIO followed the Communist Party line, as the accused unions did, there is no doubt that at times the CIO was overly tolerant of Communist activities. As a result, the Communists succeeded in shaping CIO declarations to conform to their propaganda programs either by omission or by subtle phraseology. It is also true that the CIO, its affiliates, and subsidiaries refrained from directly criticizing the Soviet Union and Communist policies, with a few exceptions. While this attitude was clearly motivated by the desire not to stir up dissension, it nevertheless gave the Communists their opportunity to convey the impression that the CIO adhered to the Party line.

Short shrift was made of the charge of redbaiting and witch hunting. Evidently there was a feeling in CIO circles that no exhaustive defense was needed to counteract these charges but that an explanation would suffice. To a "moving denunciation of the evils of promiscuous Red-baiting" made by one of the defendants, "the committee . . . agreed that the promiscuous labeling of all progressive American trade unionisms as Communist is wrong and should ever-lastingly be opposed. But neither of these things has relevance to the charge. The fact that the cry of Communism has in the past been falsely used against the genuine American trade-unions does not make the charge against the UPW false. The boy who cried 'wolf' was wrong in doing so when there was no wolf. But that did not make the real wolf less a wolf when he appeared. The committee's function was to discover whether this union consistently pursues the program of the Communist Party. It was not aided in this function by the repeated assertion that the charge of Communism had been falsely made in the past." [34]

The trial committees, following the position taken by the non-Communist leaders in general, took strict precaution in their reports not to charge the bulk of the membership with subscribing to Communist programs and policies. The membership in general was absolved. In remaining within the union and accepting Communist leadership, the members were subject to deception.

"The committee wishes to make it clear that its findings . . . are based . . . on the policies and activities of the union which its leadership has proposed and directed. Those findings carry no implication that the individual members of the union are Communists or favorable to Communism. To the contrary, the committee is persuaded that many of the members . . . have been taken in by the evasion and the subterfuge, the devices and maneuvers, which the Communist-minded leaders of this union have used to maintain

[33] *Ibid.*, 1950, pp. 81–82.
[34] *Ibid.*, 1950, p. 51.

themselves in power, concealing all the while the fact that the union's policies and activities were not the real informed decision of the members but determined in accordance with the line of the Communist Party." [35]

Special consideration was expressed for government workers who were members of Communist-dominated unions: "The members of the UPW are, in the main, government employees. Although the persistent Communist Party line tactics of its leadership have driven out of the UPW the major portion of its American membership,[36] the committee has no doubt that there still remain within the union members who are fooled by the pseudo unionism and the false militancy of the UPW leadership. And there are undoubtedly others who have opposed that leadership but have remained within the union. But the committee wishes to make it crystal clear that its condemnation of that leadership, and of the union, does not necessarily reflect a condemnation of each individual member." [37]

By the end of spring, 1950, the horrendous task of cleansing the CIO of Communist-dominated unions was officially completed by its trial committees and executive board. There remained only the approving action of the 1950 convention, which was readily forthcoming. The resolution "Approving and Adopting Action of the Executive Board in Expelling Communist Dominated Unions from the CIO" was adopted "by the unanimous vote of the delegates accredited to this convention." [38]

This undertaking was indeed "a unique process in the Annals of . . . labor history, both in the United States and in other nations." [39] President Murray could recapitulate in his report to the 1950 convention: "We have made much headway in the course of the past twelve months. I am proud to report that despite the fact that you authorized your officers and your Executive Board, one year ago this month to kick some ugly elements, some traitors out of your movement, we accepted your mandate. The Board, through its special committees conducted hearings of the officers of many of these International Unions formerly affiliated with CIO, and through the democratic processes of trial provided these people an opportunity to present their point of view and their testimony to our committees. Your CIO Executive Board and its committees found Mine, Mill, Food-Tobacco, United Office and Professional Workers, United Public Workers, American Communications, International Fur and Leather Workers, International Longshoremen and Warehousemen's Union, the

---

[35] *Ibid.*, 1950, p. 22; see also pp. 169, 114.

[36] This union had a considerable membership of non-Americans employed by the U.S. government in the Panama Canal Zone.

[37] CIO Convention Proceedings, 1950, p. 55; for a discussion of the reaction of the rank and file when properly aroused, see pp. 217–221.

[38] CIO Convention Proceedings, 1950, pp. 477–481.

[39] *Official Reports on the Expulsion of Communist Dominated Organizations from the CIO, op. cit.*, p. 3.

Marine Cooks and Stewards, International Fishermen and Allied Workers guilty—found them guilty and operating communistically controlled unions, and we expelled them. We want no truck with them. We want nothing to do with them. We provided a way for other segments of our national population to do likewise. . . .

"In addition to the unions that I have enumerated here two other unions also left us, because they were going to be removed—the old UE and the Farm Equipment Organizations. So here we have a total of eleven national and international unions formerly affiliated with CIO who are no longer with us, and the reason they are no longer with us is because you don't want them." [40]

Murray might also have added that several unions that had been under strong Communist domination were recaptured by non-Communists. Among these were the National Maritime Union, Transport Workers, and Furniture Workers. Similarly, local and state industrial-union councils were also rid of Communist domination.[41]

It is not like the Communists to fail to follow up every step in a struggle. Thus, one of their unions, the National Union of Marine Cooks and Stewards, appealed the executive board's decision to the convention, in accordance with constitutional provisions. In this manner they put up a last-ditch fight, undoubtedly with little hope. The union notified the CIO officers that it would appeal the decision to the convention and would send representatives to argue the appeal. But the union failed to comply with the constitutional provision that an appeal must be presented within ten days prior to the convention's opening. The appeal was accepted, nevertheless, but no representatives appeared. In the appeal itself, the same arguments that had been made before the trial committee were repeated. The appeals committee considered the petition and in a lengthy report that repeated the findings of the trial committees, recommended that the appeal be denied. After a brief comment by President Murray, the report was approved "by the unanimous vote of the delegates accredited to this convention." [42]

Having disposed of the Communist controversy, the 1950 convention, unlike its predecessors, returned to its normally calm atmosphere. Indeed, in referring to the Committee-on-officers report, Murray could say: "I doubt if there is any matter in the report that is sufficiently controversial in nature to necessitate a seriatim report." [43] And, "Thanks to these procedures, there is an unprecedented degree of unanimity and understanding in the

[40] CIO Convention Proceedings, 1950, p. 21; for Communist reaction, see *Labor Fact Book, 1951*, International Publishers Co., Inc., New York, pp. 98–99.
[41] Dick Reynard, "CIO Ousts Last Red Unions," *New Leader*, Feb. 25, 1950, pp. 1–3.
[42] CIO Convention Proceedings, 1950, pp. 471–477.
[43] *Ibid.*, 1950, p. 237.

ranks of the CIO concerning our present needs, our goals and aspirations." [44]

At its 1950 convention, CIO leaders were in a jubilant mood. A tremendous load had been removed from their shoulders. They had faced the dreaded task of splitting the organization; confronted with the imperative pressure to take action, they had proceeded in a workmanlike and determined manner to rid the organization of the incubus. Perhaps some barnacles remained on the bottom of the sturdy ship, but otherwise it was only jolted, not seriously damaged. Finding themselves still a going concern of considerable magnitude, they had good cause to rejoice at their accomplishments in resisting a formidable, subversive enemy and in immediately patching up the scars.

Thus, it was not mere braggadocio that Murray put into his annual report: "The CIO, through this series of proceedings, has given the Communist movement in America the most serious setback in all its history. The Communist conspiracy to capture the labor movement has been exposed, and the influence of its perpetrators is rapidly waning.... By removing the obstructionists, we have gained effectiveness and militance." [45] And the Committee-on-officers report proclaimed: "We rejoice with our President in this setback to the totalitarians." [46]

On the other hand, it was acknowledged that "the conflict was costly in money. It has been costly in the expenditure of energy and effort. It was a conflict we could not avoid if we were to protect not only our American freedom but the basic principles of trade unionism." [47]

Conclusive financial data is not available, but the following statement by Murray indicates that large expenditures were made by CIO. "One year ago this organization decided to expend a fixed sum of money to combat Communism in the electrical manufacturing industry and to combat Communism in other industries over which our CIO organization assumed jurisdiction. Your national CIO, following the expulsion of UE and Farm Equipment was required to finance the work of the newly formed IUE. The cost incident to the prosecution of that campaign culminated in expenditures from the national organization here of approximately seven hundred and fifty to eight hundred thousand dollars. That money had to be expended to fight Stalin, to fight Moscow, to fight imperialism, to fight aggression here at home, to fight sabotage and to fight the saboteurs, to fight the dirty, filthy traitors of American trade unionism." [48]

[44] Ibid., 1950, p. 70.
[45] Loc. cit.
[46] Ibid., 1950, p. 238.
[47] Ibid., 1950, p. 94.
[48] Ibid., 1950, pp. 354–355.

19

Purging Affiliates

Anti-Communism avalanched not only in the CIO proper after the 1946 convention but also within its affiliates. The mild resolution criticizing Communist meddling was accepted by the non-Communists as the go-ahead signal. After this, the battle against the Communists gathered greater and greater momentum. Reassurance that support could be expected from national headquarters intensified anti-Communist activity. Following the resignation of DeCaux as *CIO News* editor and head of information, and the departure of Lee Pressman as general counsel and chief factotum of the CIO general office, the anti-Communist barrage developed into a full-fledged battle for final victory.

Simultaneously with the attack on the Communists within the national CIO office, leaders in many of the CIO Communist-dominated unions waged battle to recapture the unions. The extent of their success was relative to the power and influence these leaders wielded in their respective unions and to the astuteness with which they waged their ouster campaigns. In other words, wresting control of the Communist-dominated unions and keeping them within the CIO depended largely on the role of the non-Communist leaders in their respective internationals. In the case of the National Maritime Union, the turn in events which led to the recapture of the union was the defection of Joseph Curran, ably assisted by M. Hedley Stone. The latter admits he was a Communist. Curran merely acknowledges that he worked with them and was part of the "apparatus." Although he followed the Party line in all respects, he emphatically denies having been a Communist. As Curran relates the story: "Don't let anybody get the impression that I was a member of the Communist Party." [1] He was first alerted when in 1944 he began to question Communist strategy in directing trade-union policy. He had decided to break with the Communists, he explained at the 1949 CIO convention, when they advocated the adoption of a no-strike policy. "I may have been a rugged individualist, but I knew instinctively, as a working staff, as a man who had seen some

[1] CIO Convention Proceedings, 1949, pp. 257–262.

blood spilled—some people don't have a corner on all the blood that has been spilled—I knew as a trade unionist that when the war was over, the same employer who was working with me across the table to win the war was going to go back to the old tactics of fighting us at every turn of the road when we sought an extra dime. So how could I pledge with him that he would deal in good faith after the war was over, how could I pledge no strikes after the war?

"I revolted at that and our union was split wide open over the basic economic question: and whatever relationship I had with these forces up to that point were completely broken, and I would have cracked the skull of anybody that came near me and urged that kind of a program." [2]

The other incident which Joseph Curran held responsible for his breaking with his Party-line associates is also revealing: "There is one more incident I want to relate, because it is important to this issue. Many of you might recall that in 1946, the Maritime Union, the NMU, and ILWU broke over the question of how a strike settlement should be conducted, and we carried a full explanation of it in all our papers. I broke with the gentleman (Harry Bridges) who speaks so highly today of his rank and file and the fact that they vote on everything before it is acted upon. I broke with that gentleman, if you please, because he said that we should have no right to submit any proposition the employers might give us to our rank and file, for a vote, and we broke. I will break with any man who tells me that, and I broke with him." [3]

Rivalry between Bridges and Curran was undoubtedly a factor in the latter's defection, just as a clash of personalities between Lundberg and Bridges at an earlier date led Lundberg to throw in his lot with the AFL.[4] Being forced to operate under remote control must have irritated an independent personality like Curran, stimulating him to revolt. But irreconcilable disagreements over basic issues also played a part. Mounting friction in the NMU came to a head at their 1947 convention. Curran, Hedley Stone, and their associates prepared the ground well. The open break occurred, however, in 1946. A "committee for maritime unity" was formed in 1945 with Bridges and Curran as cochairmen. Curran began to distrust Bridges, suspecting that he was using the CMU to establish himself on the East Coast. "The most serious disagreement arose when Bridges proposed a general strike in the industry in 1946. The collapse of wartime unity between the United States and the Soviet Union led the Communists into a period of labor militancy. Bridges adopted the slogan 'strike time is here.' Curran was not anxious for a strike and felt he could come to a settlement with the industry, but Bridges persuaded the other members of

[2] *Loc. cit.*
[3] *Loc. cit.*
[4] See above, pp. 140–141 and 233.

the NMU that a general strike in the industry was necessary and desirable." [5] The strike did occur in spite of Curran's disagreement and was finally settled. But the rift was widened and the Communist Party became concerned at Curran's belligerent attitude. Bridges attempted to bring about reconciliation but failed. Curran was uncompromising. He centered his attack on the CMU. His contention was based on trade-union lines that the NMU's affairs were being directed by "four craft unions, located 3,000 miles way, together with a fifth union, a shore-side organization, have been dictating all policies of NMU, and have made our great industrial union virtually a stooge for their shotgun unity." He also complained that the NMU was bearing the brunt financially and that its union treasury could be drained by CMU "without a decisive voice on how our money should be spent." [6]

Realizing that a break was imminent, the Communist Party began to lay the ground for discrediting the dissidents. At first, it circulated innuendoes without mentioning names, mostly to the effect that fascists and Trotskyites were in high positions in the NMU. Not only did this attack emanate from the *Daily Worker* and other Communist official media, but it was carried on within the union through Communist control of key NMU officials—including the editor of the official organ. The vice-president in charge of organizers increased his staff with Communist adherents who were sent out to campaign against the Curran group. A membership-recruiting campaign was also launched, with the new members being given a Communist indoctrination course. All these activities were in preparation for the 1946 referendum election of union officials.

Undaunted, and being thoroughly schooled in Communist tactics, the aroused and pugnacious Curran organized a countercampaign. He demanded space in the *Pilot*, which now became the joint campaign organ of both factions. He traveled far and wide to the various ports and campaigned vigorously. He also sent out his associates and henchmen. He made the issue squarely one of Communist domination and meddling. He charged that the Communist Party was spending huge sums of money, placing paid henchmen in the various ports to campaign against him and his associates. He accused the Communist-dominated union officials of incompetence and negligence. He further accused them of espionage against our government for the benefit of the Communist Party. The results of the 1946 elections were inconclusive. Curran was overwhelmingly reelected, but so were most of the Communist-controlled officers. Curran's attempt to expel Communist union officials at a closed meeting also did not succeed.

[5] Max M. Kampelman, *The Communist Party vs. the C.I.O.: A Study in Power Politics*, F. A. Praeger, New York, 1957, p. 67.
[6] *Ibid.*, p. 69.

One thing was certain—Curran's personal popularity with the membership remained unassailable.[7]

But Curran and his group persisted, determined to clean house in the NMU. Controlling several of the newly elected committees, and especially the union appeals committee, the Curran faction lodged charges against the vice-president in charge of the organizing staff. He was charged with "misfeasance in office directly traceable to his Communist membership." He was expelled. In pursuing this course, Curran used the same tactic to oust a Communist that he had used previously to oust his anti-Communist opponents in 1938.[8]

In his report to the 1947 NMU convention, Curran again attacked Communist meddling and Communist control. That the Communists were definitely on the defensive was revealed by the argument of the expelled vice-president who sought reinstatement. He argued that he could work with Curran and would not be a tool of the Communist Party. Curran rejected the overture by declaring that there was not room enough in the union for both of them. He asked the convention delegates to choose and was sustained by a narrow margin, although only one member out of fifteen of the Committee-on-officers report recommended supporting the expulsion.[9] From then on, the anti-Communists wave kept sweeping Communists out of the NMU. In July, 1949, the results of a three-month election among the union's 60,000 showed Curran winning by a margin of nearly 3 to 1. His supporters won every one of the thirty-two posts in the NMU national council, and the Port of New York, key left-wing stronghold, passed into anti-Communist hands.[10]

Considering Curran's role in recapturing the NMU, it seems his bitterest enemies—whom he had ousted from the union in 1938—had been at least somewhat prophetic. No greater tribute to his magnetic hold on the membership could have been paid by his staunchest admirers, nor could his most vehement critics have so drastically impugned his character. "Had Curran wished to line up with the seamen against the Party, the Communists would have been beaten. Though the majority of seamen are not Communists or in sympathy with them, they have faith in Curran. The Communist Party is thus able to mislead them through Curran, whom the seamen have been 'carefully trained' to believe in. The record will prove beyond a doubt that Curran is an unscrupulous liar, who has played ball with the Communist Party 'almost always.'" [11]

[7] Ibid., pp. 65–73.
[8] See above, pp. 141–143.
[9] Kampelman, op. cit., pp. 73–74.
[10] Ibid., p. 75.
[11] We Accuse; A Factual History of the Seamen's Labor Movement, Post Office Box Address, 1st printing March 26, 1940, p. 170.

Quill, another dramatic personality whose ultracontroversial, clownish antics and brusque speech have endeared him to the rank and file, also chose to throw down the gauntlet to his former Communist comrades-in-arms. Quill began to show dissatisfaction with Communist policy as early as 1947. According to his own story, he broke with the Communists because of their political policy which he felt threatened the unity of the CIO and subordinated trade policies to the whims of a political party. Just as the Marshall Plan drew a clear-cut distinction between the Communists and the non-Communists, so did the issue of a third party in the form of the Progressive Party sponsoring Wallace as its presidential candidate. CIO leaders, from Murray down, were convinced that this party was the creature of the Communists. Besides, Truman was the CIO's candidate. In his break with the Communists, Quill was influenced more by this third-party issue than by the Marshall Plan, about which he and his vigorous membership had doubts because it aided Britain. Indeed, he continued to voice opposition to the Marshall Plan while strenuously opposing the Wallace third-party tactic, although in the minds of most non-Communist CIO leaders, the two issues were interdependent. He claimed this procedure would divide the CIO and insisted that trade-union matters should receive prior consideration. He even coined and universally proclaimed the slogan, "Wages before Wallace." In his own words: "I know a little about the Third Party. It is funny, you know, but I have said more than once that I was for Wallace before Wallace was for Wallace himself.... I was told ... that things had changed and that Wallace would lead a political party. Well, I had to make a decision between that kind of politics and saving the Transport Workers and remaining within CIO." [12] Quill's first public break occurred in March, 1948, when he resigned as president of the New York City CIO industrial union council. His action was a protest over the endorsement of the Wallace candidacy.[13] Previously, he had denounced the Communist Party at a union membership meeting of some 2,000. Quill states that he tried desperately to convince the top Communist leaders of the error of their ways and that he even spoke to Wallace. Only after being confronted with their determination to carry out the third-party venture, did he decide that the parting of the ways had arrived.[14]

Actually Quill was being prodded by mounting anti-Communist opposition in his union. The Transport Workers Union membership was mostly Irish Catholic. His popularity as a leader was based on his having served in the Irish Republican Army, his grandiloquent denunciation, in season and out, of the British, and his blunt, crude, but colorful manner, heightened by his melodious Irish brogue. Already, in 1937–1938, a "Progressive

[12] CIO Convention Proceedings, 1948, p. 289.
[13] Kampelman. *op. cit.*, pp. 113–115.
[14] *Ibid.*

opposition" functioned within his union. Their main demand was "the ousting of the 'party line' and the introduction of strict trade-union democracy." [15] This opposition was, however, weak, sporadic, and unorganized. By 1945 and 1946, the opposition began to gain in strength. Catholic clergymen naturally had a part in this development. Priests and others even more influential in the hierarchy began to specialize in labor questions and to become generally interested in the labor movement. Catholic labor schools, as auxiliaries of Catholic higher-education institutions, functioned in important population and industrial centers. Two graduates of one such school in Manhattan, in cooperation with fellow alumni, were leaders of the opposition. "By 1947, the anti-administration forces of the TWU were in a much more cohesive position than they had ever been before. They had representation on the union's executive board and they had defeated the union leadership in a membership referendum concerning the 5-cent fare for New York. While the union leadership defended the 5-cent fare, the membership decided a higher fare would permit wage increases." [16] While it is not possible to evaluate the exact influence of the opposition in Quill's defection from the Communist Party line and in his subsequent vigorous anti-Communist role, it undoubtedly served as an important contributing force. Having declared war, Quill and his group proceeded to eliminate Communist control. His task was not too easy since the vice-president and secretary, two other key officials, were in the Communist fold. One of them, John Santo, secretary, was disarmed by immigration authorities on the grounds that he was an undesirable alien, had entered the country illegally, had obtained citizenship falsely, and was a Communist.[17]

Following a well-directed campaign, Quill gained control of the December, 1948, convention. He was not only reelected, but he succeeded in eliminating all Communist followers from the national executive board. In addition, his man was elected to the other key post of secretary-treasurer.[18] It was indeed a clean sweep. Nevertheless, Quill, according to his own account, wavered about making a clean break. He still carried on negotiations as late as the spring of 1949. "I was so anxious to have a united front with the Communist Party that, as late as April, 1949, I offered the Communist Party at our coming convention to sit down and change the old order in the Executive Board of the TWU." Quill made this offer to the "representative of the Communist Party in TWU," and, when informed that the Party had rejected his "new proposal of a united front" with the statement, "No, we want all or nothing," he replied that

[15] Benjamin Stolberg, *The Story of the CIO*, The Viking Press, Inc., New York, 1938, p. 226; Kampelman, *op. cit.*, pp. 118ff.
[16] Kampelman, *op. cit.*, p. 121.
[17] See below, p. 247.
[18] Kampelman. *op. cit.*, p. 121.

in that event "that is just what they will get, nothing." So, on "the first day of ... convention ... we cleaned them all out from one end to the other, and today there is not a member of the Communist Party in the leadership of the Transport Workers Union in any part of the United States." [19]

Quill was probably a member of the Communist Party. He tells about attending secret caucuses and associating with the highest Communist officials. This kind of experience is not usually granted to non-Party members irrespective of their standing in the esteem of the Party.[20]

The conclusion is simple. Where such an outstanding leader as Curran or Quill undertook to rally the anti-Communist forces and wage battle with Communists, the outcome was bound to be favorable. They knew the tactics of their opponents, they had considerable control of administration machinery in the national office, they had contacts and followers in the organization throughout its jurisdiction, and they were popular with the rank and file. Neither Curran nor Quill were "front men" in the sense that they were picked by the Communists as non-Communists who could be depended upon to follow Communist orders. Curran and Quill were simply on the scene and made their own ways to leadership. "Front men" are usually individuals of limited personality, mediocre intelligence, and average capacity who are not able to pursue an independent course and must, therefore, stay put. Such persons were picked by the Communists to head up MM (Clark) and UE (Fitzgerald). Curran and Quill, on the other hand, are dynamic personalities, resourceful, articulate, even histrionic, and magnetic in personality. The very nature of such persons demands that they be full participants, not merely "front." If such people rebel or dissent, it is not easy to dispose of them. But in the beginning, the Communists had no reason to suspect either Curran or Quill of ever breaking away.

Indeed, front men without any deep ideological conviction or, for that matter, without any convictions, who lacked forceful personality, stayed put more effectively than the dedicated ones with personality. Thus, Phil Murray, in spite of his prestige, his winning and authoritative personality, and his staunch Catholic faith, failed in 1948 to win away Fitzgerald from his Communist cronies and colleagues.[21] They elevated Fitzgerald from obscurity to the prominence of a national figure, despite his mediocrity; without their tutelage and the presidency of the UE he would be but an unknown local official. It is also possible that, in accordance with Communist practice, they might have "the goods" on him. What could Murray offer—a clear conscience in the light of his religious faith and the

[19] CIO Convention Proceedings, 1949, pp. 272–273.
[20] See Kampelman, *op. cit.*, pp. 118ff.
[21] *Ibid.*, p. 100.

uncertain security of a job as organizer? For an indecisive personality and an opportunist, the choice was clear: remain in the secure berth.

An extraordinary instance is that of the Auto Workers. In this case, one high official, as part of the union's administrative machinery, succeeded, with the aid of local officials and militants, in defeating and eliminating those officials who collaborated with the Communists and were strategically in control of the union. This gigantic task was accomplished by Walter Reuther and his associates. In this case, the president, vice-president, secretary-treasurer, and other key officials followed the Communist Party line. They also had control of the official union publication and other media. Nevertheless, Reuther and his group, after waging an aggressive campaign under considerable odds, won out.[22] On the other hand, in contrast to NMU and the Transport Workers where the outstanding leader staunchly adhered to his Communist affiliation, as Bridges did, the opposition remained weak and control was retained by the Communists.

Then there are the cases where the opposition carried on an effective struggle, mustering the support of the rank and file but losing out because the union administrative machinery was controlled by the Communists who cheated the opposition out of its victory. This happened to the rank-and-file group in NMU where they elected practically all the officials but were outmaneuvered and expelled.[23] In MM, the opposition was also outgeneraled following successful support by the rank and file.[24] And in the UE, the opposition—led by the perennially youthful, articulate, and fearless Carey—aroused the membership against an able and ruthless leadership in complete control of the international union's machinery but was cheated at the convention.[25] Thus these oppositions were cheated of their rightful victory through flagrantly dishonest means. Even though they were not in control of part of the organization, however, they succeeded in arousing the membership.

Action on the part of the national CIO office, both in encouraging non-Communist opposition and in taking a direct hand, resulted in eliminating Communist control and domination of municipal and state industrial union councils. The rules placing them under stricter control by the national office and limiting them as to the nature of pronouncements and the support of causes [26] restrained the Communist elements.

Where the Communists resisted, direct action by the national office in reorganizing the councils and in removing dissident organizers accountable to the national office proved effective. A notable case is that pertaining to the California industrial union council. Bridges headed this unit. As a

[22] See above, pp. 145–147.
[23] See above, pp. 141–143.
[24] See above, pp. 133–135.
[25] See above, pp. 147–148.
[26] See above, pp. 151, 156, and 158.

first step, Murray created two councils by dividing the state according to traditional practice and setting up a council for the southern part and one for the northern. In this manner, the southern council was taken out of Communist control. Later, Murray removed Bridges as regional director of northern California, thereby divesting him of all direct power as a direct national CIO official exercising administrative responsibility. He then sent in his trusted organizers from the USWA, who cleaned house.

20

Expulsion Aftermath

Complete house cleaning in mass organizations cannot be expected. It is not surprising, therefore, that Communist influence remained in some unions, especially in the immediate postexpulsion period. Communist influence has even now not been eliminated entirely in the CIO or the AFL, not to mention the trade-union movement as a whole. In a later chapter, the method used by the Communists to work their way back into CIO and AFL unions will be described. Here it is proposed merely to discuss the traces of Communist influence that remained following the wholesale expulsions. The overriding influence of the Communists in the CIO was undoubtedly destroyed by the expulsions, as the CIO leaders claimed,[1] but it is clear that the Communists retained various positions—how strong those positions were is hard to estimate. Communist influence in the United Furniture Workers, for example, remained obscure. A Subcommittee on Labor and Labor-Management Relations for the Senate Committee on Labor and Public Welfare pointed out that at the June, 1950, convention of the UFW, the left-wing majority that had been in control of the UFW's executive board was voted out of office.[2] On the other hand, a prominent staff member of the AFL Upholsterers International Union testified in 1954 to Communist influence in the UFW.[3] But in 1956, as affiliates of the AFL-CIO, these two unions formed "a confederation of the two organizations for common union action." This arrangement is described as "something new . . . to the American labor movement. Both unions

[1] CIO Convention Proceedings, 1950, pp. 20–21 and 238.
[2] *Public Policy and Communist Domination of Certain Unions, Report of the Subcommittee on Labor and Labor-Management Relations to the Committee on Labor and Public Welfare*, 82d Cong. 1st Sess., 1951.
[3] *Hearings by the Subcommittee to Investigate the Administration of the Internal Security Act and Other Internal Security Laws of the Senate Committee on the Judiciary, on S. 23, S. 1254, and S. 1606*, 83d Cong., 2d Sess., 1954, pp. 25–44; see also *Hearings Relating to Communist Activities in the Defense Area of Baltimore, Hearings before the Committee on Un-American Activities Committee*, 82d Cong., 1st Sess., 1951, parts 1 and 2, the latter subtitled, *Maryland Committee for Peace and Baltimore County Committee for Peace.*

will retain their autonomy but will work through a joint board which will pool efforts in organizing, political action, research, and union label work." [4]

Again, the staunchly anti-Communist Reuther administration still finds itself stymied in its efforts to clean out the Communists completely from the UAW. Its chief difficulty has been in the case of Local 600. This Ford local flaunts the International by adopting pro-Communist resolutions and by taking other action of a similar nature. It was placed under receivership, but when it was restored to full self-government, the old officers were immediately reelected. An article in *Political Affairs* in July, 1950, gloats over the failure of the Reuther forces to keep "progressives and Communists" from controlling the elections held in March and April.[5] "Local 600, UAW, CIO is the largest local in the world. Its gigantic size resembles an international union. It has a treasury of $300,000. Local 600 has always been the prime target of the Communist Party. While the actual number of Communist Party members is proportionately small, through their control of the left-wing element within the Ford empire they have always elected a large number of officers," reports the House Committee on Un-American Activities in 1952.[6] Blackwood reports that the Communists were still in control when he was making his study of the UAW.[7]

An even more flagrant case of continuing Communist influence in a strong CIO union is that of the United Packinghouse Workers of America. This union has yet to take any action that is critical of the Soviet Union; its literature does not contain any derogatory references toward communism or Soviet Russia; its anti-Communist leaders have not been able to attain elective leadership. On the other hand, its official publications show that its executive board has adopted resolutions on Korea and other subjects following the Communist Party line. Not infrequently the *Daily Worker* reprinted and featured these pronouncements with approval and praise. For the time being, however, this union has been content to confine its activities to its own organization; it does not attempt to inject itself into the broader area of the general labor movement. For a time the International acted only negatively, not conducting obvious Communist propaganda, but a num-

[4] *IUD Bulletin,* Industrial Union Department, AFL-CIO, Washington, D.C., October 1956, p. 3; see also *CIO News,* Jan. 12, 1957, article entitled, "Two Furniture Unions Open Organizing Drive."

[5] Phil. Schotz, "Some Lessons of the United-Front Victory in the Ford Elections," *Political Affairs,* July, 1950, pp. 79ff.

[6] *Annual Report for the Year 1952,* 82d Cong., 2d Sess., 1952, pp. 10–12; see also *Colonization of Basic Industries by the Communist Party of the United States of America, Hearings before the House Committee on Un-American Activities,* 83rd Cong., 2d Sess., 1954, pp. 7–13.

[7] *Ibid.,* p. 300; for a list of officials of UAW locals seeking Fifth Amendment protection, see also *Public Policy and Communist Domination of Certain Unions, op. cit.,* pp. 7ff.

ber of its districts and locals conducted such propaganda without the International protesting. Indeed, there is evidence that the International supported Communist leadership.[8] During the Korean War, the International began expounding the Communist Party line in its official publications and through its officers. The March, 1953, issue of *The Packinghouse Worker* carried a front-page editorial entitled, "We Speak Up Now," announcing that it would deal with basic issues, such as, "A new type of germ warfare is going on in this nation. It's a creeping disease that strikes at the minds of men and paralyzes their actions. The droppers of this type of bomb are the men who want to drive Americans into subservience to the wishes of the Military and war profiteer." This change of policy was reported at length, with strong approval, in the *Daily Worker*, April 7. Entitled "Packinghouse Union Calls for Defense of Liberties," the article summarizes the editorial. The following quotation reveals the *Daily Worker's* understanding of the new UPW policy: "The statement stressed the link between the new union-busting drive and 'the tragic waste of human life in Korea,' as well as the dangers of bigger war on more fronts. The men and women who work for wages, their unions and union leaders, must speak up now or lose their franchise,' the editorial warned."

President Ralph Helstein recommended the adoption of this policy to the general executive board. Attached to the officers' report was also a proposed statement on public issues. This statement includes a complete denunciation of American foreign policy in the Far East. In the entire discussion of the current and bitter conflict between the Soviet Union and the United States, there is hardly a phrase that gives the benefit of the doubt to United States policy or that could not be subscribed to by an ardent adherent of Soviet Russia.[9]

Top CIO leaders were disturbed by the pro-Communist sentiment within the UPW. In 1953, the CIO investigated the matter with a view to holding expulsion proceedings. In the meantime, Secretary-Treasurer Emil Mazey of the UAW cleared the UPW in a report. Walter Reuther, however, as president of the CIO, ordered the UPW to clean house.[10] From conversations with key people at CIO, it was gathered that the investigation was not carried through, chiefly because the AFL-CIO merger negotiations were in the offing and it was not thought advisable to begin washing CIO linen in public. The lengthy and apparently fruitless merger negotiations

---

[8] *Investigation of Communist Activities in the Chicago, Illinois, Area, Hearings before the House Committee on Un-American Activities*, part 1, 82d Cong., 2d Sess., pp. 3621–3752; and *Annual Report for the Year 1952, op. cit.*, pp. 27–28; *Civil Rights Congress as a Communist Front Organization*, 1947, p. 9.

[9] *The Packinghouse Worker*, April–May, 1953.

[10] *Subversive Influence in Certain Labor Organizations, Hearings before the Subcommittee to Investigate the Administration of the Internal Security Act and Other Internal Security Laws of the Senate Committee on the Judiciary*, 83d Cong., 1st and 2d Sess., 1954, pp. 122–124 and 276–286.

between the UPW and the Amalgamated Meat Cutters and Butcher Workmen, AFL, in which the Communist issue was a factor, are discussed in a subsequent chapter. Communist traces remain in other CIO unions.

In expelling Communist-dominated unions, the CIO did not intend to forsake the jurisdictions covered by these unions or the rank and file, either actual or potential members. In 1949, immediately upon expelling UE, an "International Union Charter" was granted to the non-Communist elements named IUE "for the purpose of assuming jurisdiction over the electrical manufacturing industry." [11] In this instance, plans to contest UE power had already been made and were intensified following its convention in Cleveland. The UE's non-Communist elements, therefore, on the heels of a final, bitter struggle at the convention, proceeded with CIO support to found a committee with headquarters in Washington. They had begun operating and had come into conflict with the UE, including court action initiated by UE, before the CIO convened in November, 1949.[12]

Salvaging IUE was the big boast. At the 1949 convention, CIO officials estimated in one claim that "approximately 48% of the dues paying membership . . . are already represented by the committee of twelve," which would mean approximately 155,000 members.[13] A few pages farther on the estimate was "approximately 50 per cent." [14] The UE was also corrected as to the meaning of this disaffection: "The expelled UE have often times said they have been subject to raids. Never was there a more diabolical lie uttered by any man or group of men. . . . Their organization was undergoing the rigors of internal insurrection. . . . Where those local unions and those local representatives have been free they have exercised the freedoms that they naturally enjoy to rebel against this mob Communistic leadership prevailing in the UE." [15]

At the 1950 convention it was possible to boast that "the development and organizational growth of the IUE-CIO under the chairmanship of James B. Carey during the last year has been phenomenal . . . the IUE-CIO has burgeoned into a great organization that holds official bargaining rights for 276,557 workers in the industry. However, the union membership far exceeds that total because of many thousands of members in plants where the crumbling UE many months ago won representational elections by tiny margins." [16] This number nearly doubles the membership figure given at the 1949 convention. President Carey could gleefully report that, having started "with a staff hurriedly put together on the fourth day of November, 1949 . . . this IUE-CIO is paying per capita tax to the CIO. We no

[11] Ibid., pp. 359, 483.
[12] Ibid., pp. 483–489.
[13] CIO Convention Proceedings, 1949, p. 487.
[14] Ibid., 1949, p. 489.
[15] Ibid.
[16] CIO Convention Proceedings, 1950, pp. 99–100.

longer require financial assistance, we are on our own, and we are proud to say that we are going forward to completely organize the electrical, radio and machine manufacturing industry." Mr. Carey announced trade agreements, gained through NLRB elections, with the leading firms in the industry.[17] Nevertheless, the UE continued functioning as a strong organization for another five years. At present it is rapidly disintegrating.[18]

Plans to salvage subsidiary units and members of other expelled unions were also prepared in advance and implemented immediately following expulsion. These plans do not seem to have been made as meticulously as in the case of UE. Possibly the persons in charge were not as experienced or as competent. Nevertheless, organizational activity was initiated in the spring of 1950 to cover most of the jurisdictions of the other expelled unions. In some instances, new organizations were founded; in others, established CIO affiliates attacked the jurisdictions of the expelled unions. In announcing these salvaging activities, the CIO in most cases exaggerated their extent. Official reports, however, do reveal the manner of CIO procedure in this undertaking.

"As of March 1, 1950, CIO chartered the Government and Civic Employees Organizing Committee, assigning it the jurisdiction of workers employed by governmental bodies or civic agencies. This committee has now passed the 35,000 mark in membership.... In addition the ... Committee has chartered a local union of more than 3,000 members in the Panama Canal Zone and has been recognized as bargaining agent by the government authorities.... Down in the Panama Canal Zone, where the Commies had a strangle hold, our government and civic workers have organized and driven the old Public Workers out of the Zone." [19]

"The Insurance and Allied Workers Organizing Committee was established to cover a portion of the jurisdiction formerly allocated to the United Office and Professional Workers. This Committee, also, has retained within the CIO many of the workers claimed by the ousted organization and has proceeded to expand its membership. Many local industrial unions have also been chartered in the white collar field." [20]

Where the CIO did not found particular organizations, established unions were encouraged to enter as contestants of the expelled unions. "The United Steel Workers of America has had outstanding success in reorganizing membership among workers formerly covered by Mine, Mill & Smelter, particularly in the western areas.

"Part of the jurisdiction formerly covered by the Food, Tobacco & Agricultural Workers has been assumed by the Retail, Wholesale and Depart-

[17] *Ibid.*, 1950, pp. 352–354; see also Murray's comments, pp. 354ff.
[18] See above, pp. 262–263.
[19] CIO Convention Proceedings, 1950, p. 273.
[20] *Ibid.*, 1950, pp. 94–95; see also pp. 109–110.

ment Store Union, with excellent results. Portions are being reorganized by the Brewery Workers and others by the Packinghouse Workers. Remaining locals are being granted local industrial union charters.

"Despite attempts of the ousted groups to pull their crumbling forces together in new alliances, such as the merger of Fishermen and Longshoremen, the high proportion of the workers are remaining with CIO. Among the Fishermen, a number of groups along the West coast and in Alaska have been granted LIU charters.

"In addition to our organizing work in the continental area of the United States, we have extended our drive to Alaska, Hawaii and Puerto Rico." [21]

Another CIO affiliate joined in the salvaging operation. "The RWDSU [Retail, Wholesale and Department Store Union] New England Joint Board defeated the UOPWA in a bitter fight for the Union News Employees in Boston. In New York City one RWDSU local is now engaged with the UOPWA in a contest for the office employees in Lane Bryant and the prospects for the success of this contest is extremely favorable. In Pittsburgh a local of the furriers' union transferred to this international. Locals formerly affiliated with FTA have also contacted this union to canvass the possibility of affiliation with the CIO." [22]

Just as the Transport and Maritime Internationals ousted the key officials who adhered to the Communist Party line, so another affiliate was saved for the CIO by convention action. "At the historic Sixth Constitutional Convention of the United Furniture Workers of America, the membership adopted a resolution by a 4–1 vote supporting the program, policies and principles of the CIO, and firmly placing the Furniture Workers in the ranks of the CIO.... The Communist anti-CIO elements which previously dominated our organization were decisively defeated." [23]

Murray summarized the situation in overly optimistic tones and with exaggerated claims:

"We have brought into being in the last twelve months and conducted successful NLRB elections and also successful collective bargaining negotiations for the people to whom I am about to make reference and the organizations I am here going to enumerate. We have formed a national union of the government and civic employees. We have formed a national organization of the insurance and allied workers. We have formed the IUE, we have absorbed practically all of the Mine, Mill and Smelter workers, either with the Steelworkers' International Union or the Auto Workers. We have brought about comprehensive changes in the makeup of several of our existing national unions that has resulted in the transfer of local unions formerly affiliated with old International unions that belonged to the CIO into international organizations presently affiliated with the parent

[21] *Ibid.*, 1950, p. 95.
[22] *Ibid.*, 1950, p. 103.
[23] *Ibid.*, 1950, p. 104.

206

body." Murray then ended with a cheerful prediction that did not materialize. "I predict that within the next twelve months almost all of those workers who still continue to retain their affiliation with these Communistically dominated unions will leave them and come back into the fold of the Congress of Industrial Organizations." [24]

Vice-President and Director of Organization Haywood summarized the successes of the CIO in salvaging units and members from the Communist-dominated unions in the same hopeful vein as Murray and made the same predictions, albeit in a more colorful and forceful manner. "The CIO, in its organizing activities, has made this great contribution, taking on Communism where it needs to be taken on and driving them out in a real he-man's way.... As has been reported to you in President Murray's opening address, you have more members now than you had a year ago— and I am referring to tax paying members.... I want to assure this delegation that by the time you assemble here a year from now there will be damned little left of these Communist controlled organizations." [25]

But Murray could claim with much justice that "the expulsion of those eleven unions has made our organization stronger today than it has ever been at any time in its history." [26] This controversy with the Communists stimulated the CIO to new activity. It gained in membership, not only recapturing a considerable number from expelled unions but increasing its organizational activity. In addition—and perhaps because of this—its prestige rose. Appraising the outcome of the expulsions, the House Committee on Un-American Activities concluded: "Many results beneficial to the workers resulted from expulsion of the Communist-dominated unions from the CIO." [27]

Most of the salvaging was accomplished by winning over locals or larger units from the expelled unions, but the process was not carried out on a uniform level of success. There were defections of individuals and of groups. Furthermore, when a sufficient number of members were either won away or discontinued affiliation in unions operating in industries that did not lend themselves readily to organization, those unions either collapsed or fused with remnants of other unions. The Food and Tobacco, Office and Professional, and Public Workers unions are instances. The UE and MM, being more substantial, were affected but still retained considerable solidity. The UE suffered more than the MM, although it possessed abler leadership, because it had to contend with a buoyant rival in the creation of the IUE. It is probable that the accomplishment of the IUE could have been duplicated in nonferrous metals had a similar course been pursued.

[24] *Ibid.*, 1950, p. 22.
[25] *Ibid.*, 1950, pp. 272–275.
[26] *Ibid.*, 1950, p. 21.
[27] *Colonization of Basic Industries, op. cit.*, p. 6.

Jensen, who has studied MM and the union situation in nonferrous metals most thoroughly, is also of this opinion: "In facing the problem of replacing Mine, Mill leadership, once expulsion was accomplished, the mistake of the CIO was the decision against establishing a new international, especially for the mining, milling and smelter workers." [28]   Instead, MM was attacked by a number of CIO and AFL unions, each of which succeeded in winning over a small membership.   MM members are, on the whole, accustomed to one particular union operating exclusively in their industry and were not responsive to the appeals of unions most of whose membership belonged to other industries.

The other firmly established union, the ILWU, was least affected, for similar reasons.   It is a closely knit union with a specific jurisdiction. Moreover, the union of the same jurisdiction functioning in the East—the International Longshoremen's Association—was thoroughly discredited, and its lackadaisical leadership was disinterested in undertaking such a gigantic task.   Only in its fringe operations was it possible to secure ILWU defections.   The basic longshore sector was not pierced.   Results were obtained among such appendages as fishermen, inland warehouse and packing workers.   But in a secluded area, such as insular Hawaii, even pineapple, sugar plantation, and related workers persistently adhere to the ILWU, with few exceptions.   The final outcome of efforts to denude these unions is discussed in a later chapter.   The role of employers and others in making it difficult to win away members from Communist-dominated unions is also considered later.

Although the Communists were not unaware of the CIO's determination to expel Communist-dominated unions and win away their membership, they were slow in devising consistent, effective strategy for coping with the problem.   The strongest, best-led Communist-controlled union, the UE, took upon itself the initiation of an offensive against the CIO prior to its 1949 convention.   It was evidently UE's intention to prepare the way for the Communist-dominated unions to withdraw voluntarily, with a view to founding a separate trade-union national center.   Thus, in a statement dated October 7, 1949, the UE demanded that the CIO change its policies under threat of withholding per capita payments.   Not receiving a reply, UE delegates registered at the convention but did not remain to defend themselves against CIO charges.   They were later criticized for this by the labor secretary of the Communist Party.[29]   Then the strategy of con-

[28] Vernon H. Jensen, *Nonferrous Metals Industry Unionism, 1932–1954*, Cornell Studies in Industrial and Labor Relations, vol. 5, Cornell University Press, Ithaca, N.Y., 1954, pp. 393–394.
[29] CIO Convention Proceedings, 1949, pp. 22 and 302–327; *Official Reports on the Expulsion of Communist Dominated Organizations from the CIO*, Publication cf. p. 176, Congress of Industrial Organizations, Washington, D.C., September, 1954, pp. 5–8.

testing the expulsions changed. Defendant unions now remained within the CIO and appeared at the expulsion hearings to defend themselves. Evidently, the tactic was now to make maximum propaganda capital by fighting the expulsions. Thus they resorted to the usual technique of asking for delays, postponements, and additional hearing sessions at which they presented more statements repeating their previous arguments. Although asking for postponements so they could present additional witnesses, none were presented when the hearings were resumed.

Also, the Communists seemed to be undecided concerning the way to conserve their forces after expulsion. For a brief period, they toyed with the idea of founding a third federation. Quill, who was part of the inner circle of the Communist-dominated unions, charged that in 1947, when the Communists sensed mounting opposition within the CIO, they considered such a step. "If anyone tells me a third Federation of Labor was not planned, it is wrong, because I used to travel in very good circles. They never answered my letters but they came to see me personally, and in the month of January, 1947, Bill Foster told me that their National Board of the Communist Party had decided to form a third Federation of Labor, the same as they did the Henry Wallace Third Party....[30] Quill's contention is confirmed by the committee appointed to investigate charges against the ILWU: "Since the conclusion of the hearing there has come to the attention of the committee a 'Statement of Policy on National CIO' adopted by the executive board of ILWU. This statement repeats all of the familiar canards about the CIO invented by the Communist Party and peddled by the unions it controls. In addition the 'statement instructs the national officers of ILWU' to initiate the calling of a national conference of those unions already expelled from CIO or about to be expelled, in order to make appropriate plans and to take all possible constructive steps toward such unions working collectively for their own mutual protection and advantage." [31]

The plan for a third national trade-union center failed to materialize. The weaker unions were consolidated and continued to function with the stronger unions as independent, or unaffiliated organizations. Not having specific instructions from those in higher echelons, it seemed the leaders could not agree on a uniform procedure following the decision to operate as independent unions. Some still wanted to try reconciliation, as they are attempting now. In January, 1951, the labor reporter of the *Daily Worker*, evidently with this idea in mind, criticized "some of the leaders" for calling their opposition "company unions." He counseled a search for opportunities to work with the rank and file, at least of the "right-wing-led

[30] CIO Convention Proceedings, 1949, p. 273.
[31] *Official Reports on the Expulsion of Communist Dominated Organizations from the CIO, op. cit.*, p. 115.

Unions." And the Communist Party labor secretary criticized the "U.E. leaders for 'blind factionalism' " against the IUE, again advising a search for opportunities to work with the rank and file. Of course, this was not a new tactic on the part of the Communists. The Party at its 1951 convention also declared that the "Party rejects the point of view that work in the present progressive-led unions represents the primary base for progressive militant activity." [32]

In the early expulsion period, the Communist-dominated unions and their followers also fought back in various ways. In the case of the NMU, they resorted to strong-arm tactics by taking physical possession of national headquarters following their defeat in open battle at the convention. Taking advantage of the absence of the regularly elected officers, they invaded headquarters and took possession by force. After a few days, the property was regained through a ruse devised by NMU leaders.[33]

The UE relied upon more decorous tactics. They took advantage of the very law designed, in a sense, to eliminate Communist influence in unions, namely, the Taft-Hartley Act. Through this act they secured preliminary injunctions "against the CIO" and the newly created IUE. "That is to be expected, of course. They will use the Taft-Hartley Act, they will use the federal courts, they will use the employers, and they will use the Communist Party to fight the CIO." [34] Similarly, it was reported to the 1950 CIO convention in discussing the opposition efforts of the UE. "The success has not been attained without pain and struggle. The Administrative Committee and the entire membership have been steadily harassed with lawsuits and restrictive injunctions. Litigation has succeeded in keeping tied up in the courts—even today—hundreds of thousands of dollars belonging to IUE locals which have never been certified as IUE affiliates by the NLRB." [35] Most of the litigation revolved around the right of locals to secede and to retain funds and property. On this issue, the courts differed, some favoring the UE version and others the withdrawing locals. A few cases centered around whether locals could be enjoined from seceding; they were decided in favor of the locals. In one case, UE challenged the right of IUE-CIO using a name "similar" to that of UE. The Connecticut Supreme Court ruled that IUE did not infringe on UE rights in the use of its name. All the cases were decided on technical legal issues by the courts. Communist domination was not mentioned in the decisions. On the other hand, the Minnesota Supreme Court ruled that "the Locals had a right to secede after the UE's expulsion from the CIO and to retain the property of the Locals despite a provision in the

[32] Max M. Kampelman, *The Communist Party vs. the C.I.O.; A Study in Power Politics*, F. A. Praeger, New York, 1957, p. 168.
[33] CIO Convention Proceedings, 1950, pp. 457–458.
[34] *Ibid.*, 1949, p. 488.
[35] *Ibid.*, 1950, p. 100.

UE constitution to the contrary. This was on the theory that UE's membership in the CIO, as alleged by the plaintiffs, was an inducing cause for members to join the Locals. Termination of UE's membership in the CIO, therefore excused compliance with provisions of the UE constitution which would have awarded the property to the parent body." [36]

Expulsion of the Communist-dominated unions naturally shook the foundations of the CIO. But both fears and hopes that the CIO could not survive the critical operation proved unfounded, as later events revealed. Because most CIO unions failed to render detailed membership reports, as did the CIO itself, it is not possible accurately to measure the numerical loss sustained by the CIO as a result of the expulsions. Membership figures based on per capita payments, however, were available to the officers of the CIO. Murray, in his report to the 1949 CIO convention, credits the expelled unions with a membership of "less than 10 per cent of our total." [37] Considering that the CIO has credited UE with "nearly half a million members," and accepting the liberal estimate that the CIO had around 5,000,000 members, Murray's figures do not reveal the true strength of the expelled unions. Getting down to absolute figures, Murray stated to the 1950 convention: "The action of the Cleveland Convention in November, 1949, resulted in the removal from membership in our various international unions of a total of about 850,000 to 900,000 members." [38] On the other hand, the report of the organization department contains the declaration that the action of the convention and of the executive board resulted in an immediate loss to the CIO of approximately 675,000 members.[39] Until exact figures are available, it will be possible only to estimate the relative membership of the expelled unions. Murray's figures, however, seem to be the closest approximation to the number of members lost as a result of the expulsions.

The CIO claimed it regained most of its lost membership within a year, at the expense of the expelled unions. Phil Murray reported: "During the past year we have brought back into our organization approximately 70 per cent of all the members of these organizations that were expelled from our union." [40] And the organization department reported in general terms: "We now report that the loss has been made up. Many members of the expelled unions have returned to the CIO and we have added thousands of new members to our organization." [41] The CIO may have regained its former membership, but it is not clear how much of it came back to the

[36] The various cases are summarized in *Digest of the Public Record of Communism in the United States*, Fund for the Republic, New York, 1955, pp. 442–443.
[37] CIO Convention Proceedings, 1949, pp. 54.
[38] *Ibid.*, 1950, p. 21.
[39] *Ibid.*, 1950, p. 94.
[40] *Ibid.*, 1950, p. 21.
[41] *Ibid.*, 1950, p. 94.

CIO from the expelled unions and how much came from other sources. A notable addition this year was "the affiliation of the Communication Workers of America whose 300,000 members make them the third largest CIO union." [42] Most of the affiliated reported some membership gains; the UAW, for example, reported a gain "in dues paying members" of from 958,960 to 1,118,046.[43]

Although the Communist-dominated unions were seemingly intact and stable when they were expelled, dissociation rocked most of them so violently that only a few sturdy ones survived. With the exception of ILWU, even these suffered materially. They had been somewhat affected by the first attack in 1946, while they were still within the CIO, but their numerical losses were not great at that time; their prestige suffered most, and their loss in influence was enormous. Before 1946, their power exceeded their numerical strength, emanating from strategically placed, key followers, union officials under their control, and active union members. Through these pivotal persons, they directed the administrative apparatus, or influenced it considerably, including that of the national office.

Following their expulsion, the unions began to lose strength. They were now open to attack from both the CIO and the AFL unions. At least the predictions of the less reflective CIO leaders that the unions would not survive at all was poor prophecy. The garrulous Quill taunted Harry Bridges: "And you are not leaving CIO because you could not keep your membership for one month. . . . You see, it was a nice, soft business up until now." [44] But Quill predicted more accurately when he said, "We will go to your membership, we will tell them of your double talk, we will tell them we are men who believe in operating like men, and that the CIO will no longer be run by a goulash of punks, pinks, and parasites." [45] This was not exactly the language employed by the other CIO leaders but the thought was there.

Heavy losses began to occur with the Korean War. Now the trend was against them. Now, as many times before, they found themselves suspended on the horns of a familiar dilemma. By being forced to spread the Soviet or Communist point of view, they were labeled automatically. A detailed discussion in a later chapter will delineate their steady losses to AFL and CIO unions. Again, exact figures are not available, but a CIO description of how the expelled unions fared is reasonably accurate: "Five years after the expulsion [1954] process started, the strength of Communist dominated unions in the United States has been tremendously weakened— essentially by the wisdom, fortitude and courage of trade union members

[42] *Ibid.*, 1950, p. 93.
[43] *Ibid.*, 1950, pp. 96–114.
[44] CIO Convention Proceedings, 1949, p. 273.
[45] *Ibid.*, 1949, p. 274.

themselves. A number of these expelled unions have completely disappeared from the American scene: the Food, Tobacco and Agricultural Workers, the United Office and Professional Workers, and the United Public Workers. Some have merged. All have lost membership to democratic labor organizations—most particularly the U.E., which at the time of expulsion, numbered nearly half a million members." [46]

Heavy inroads were made into the membership of some of the expelled unions by both the CIO and the AFL. For instance, the AFL received a substantial windfall by shaking the membership tree of the insurance workers' unions formerly affiliated with the expelled CIO union. Through the new unions and organizing committees, as well as through some of its established unions, the unions of the CIO harvested a good crop of members. The IUE in particular made excellent headway right from the beginning. But the CIO did not make the most of all cases. Metaliferous mining is a good illustration. Jensen states that the Auto, Steel Workers, and District 50 had some success in raiding but not enough.[47]

Lack of concern on the part of employers, even, in some notable instances, their stealthy favor of Communist-dominated unions, hindered the non-Communist unions in their efforts to destroy their rivals. Also, the indifference of NLRB in failing to scrutinize critically the non-Communist affidavits required by the Taft-Hartley Act shielded the Communist-dominated unions. These phases are discussed in a following chapter.

[46] *Official Reports on the Expulsion of Communist Dominated Organizations from the CIO, op. cit.*, p. 3.
[47] Jensen, *op. cit.*, pp. 303–304.

PART IV

Combating Communist Domination

21

Leaders and the Rank and File

The various elements involved in this drama of coping with Communist penetration and domination of the unions played their parts in both a positive and a negative manner.   None pursued a consistent course.   Seemingly, they played by ear instead of by principle.   Their actions seemed, in general, to be motivated by pragmatic considerations.   There were, of course, groups and individuals who were exceptions; these were more sensitive to Communist aims and persistently fought Communist infiltration. The great majority, however, acted when the prodding was continuous and the clamor incessant; otherwise, they were content to let matters drift, even, sometimes, to the point of shielding the Communists.   On the whole, it was easy to induce action on the part of the majority only when vital issues, affecting the welfare of the organization or the nation, arose and could not be met with compromise.   Then public clamor, provoked by indignation and scandal, aroused those under critical fire to take remedial action.

When aroused, the response of the rank and file was favorable.   Glaring instances are, nevertheless, recorded where the members failed to respond to appeals, even in elections by secret ballot conducted by the NLRB. Motivated partly by tactical considerations, labor leaders took every occasion to eulogize the rank and file for its loyalty.   Facts substantiate these constant declarations that the great bulk of membership in Communist-dominated unions was not Communist.   Furthermore, success in winning away locals and individual members bears out this contention.   "Success in this endeavor fully confirms the conviction of our last convention that American workers are anxious for democratic, militant unionism and want nothing to do with any organization dominated by a totalitarian philosophy and subservient to Russia's foreign policy." [1]   The leaders declared that "thousands upon thousands of members of the organizations which were expelled from our ranks have come back to the CIO.   That process con-

---

[1] Vernon H. Jensen, *Nonferrous Metals Industry Unionism, 1932–1954*, Cornell Studies in Industrial and Labor Relations, Cornell University Press, Ithaca, N.Y., 1954, pp. 303–304; CIO Convention Proceedings, 1950, p. 100.

tinues. I am confident that, before long, the influence of the Communist Party in the American labor movement will have been erased once and for all." [2] And a cordial invitation to return was pronounced. "The CIO urges the members of the expelled unions who are loyal to the principles of American democracy and of democratic unionism to return to the CIO and participate in building in CIO powerful industrial unions to protect and promote their trade union and democratic interests. Hundreds of thousands of workers have already done so." [3]

Later, the CIO again found occasion to credit the members with democratic insight and loyalty. "Five years after this expulsion process started, the strength of Communist-dominated unions in the United States has been tremendously weakened—essentially by the wisdom, fortitude and courage of trade union members themselves." [4] Boundless credit in guiding the rank and file should be given to those who are called interchangeably, in the jargon of the labor movement, "active spirits" and "militants." They are the alert, devoted members who possess leadership qualities and are in closest contact with the rank and file. They are, indeed, the leavening in the membership mass. Their role is illustrated in a talk by a rank-and-file president of the Camden, New Jersey, local of the FTA union. He described the "scurrilous" propaganda and "intrigue" hurled against the union by the Communists, how the latter carried the local executive board in favor of a merger of UOPWA, PWA, and FTA. Rank-and-file leaders, however, took the case to the membership and, in two turbulent, well-attended meetings, "the recommendation of the Executive Board to go into the merger" was not concurred in. "And when the vote was taken, there were less than a dozen hands raised for the merger. The whole membership voted almost unanimously against the merger.... The following day in the Executive Board meeting, we passed a resolution to disaffiliate from FTA and to affiliate with the CIO." [5] This testimonial also indicates the reaction of the membership when properly approached.

In presenting members of the administrative committee who undertook to organize the IUE, President Murray paid tribute to rank-and-file leadership. "The committee that this convention has had an opportunity to look

[2] *Ibid.*, 1950, p. 70.
[3] *Ibid.*, 1950, p. 480.
[4] *Official Reports on the Expulsion of Communist Dominated Organizations from the CIO*, Publication no. 254, Congress of Industrial Organizations, Washington, D.C., September, 1954, p. 3; see above, pp. 77–81 and 94–107, for additional discussion of rank and file attitudes.
[5] CIO Convention Proceedings, 1950, pp. 277–279; for other local-union reactions; see CIO Convention Proceedings, 1949, pp. 483–484; and *Investigation of Communist Activities in the Dayton, Ohio, Area, Hearings before the House Committee on Un-American Activities*, part 1, 83d Cong., 2d Sess., 1954, pp. 6852–6857; and *Investigation of Communist Activities in the Newark, New Jersey, Area, Hearings before the House Committee on Un-American Activities*, part 2, 84th Cong., 1st Sess., 1955, pp. 1168–1176.

at here this morning are all rank-and-filers. They came directly from the plants. They hold no office in the organization. They have not served the International Union. They have not received any pay or compensation from the national organization. They are officers of local unions. . . ." [6]

James B. Carey added his testimonial. "But in that eight-year fight [from 1939] in the UE, a group of men and women had solidarity among themselves, brought together through conflict, brought together through opposition to the Communist party doctrines, and they fought vigorously on the floor of the conventions, at the plant gates, against a well-organized machine, extremely well-financed." [7]

The membership in the AFL unions reacted similarly, as described in earlier chapters. And AFL leaders also testified that the overwhelming majority of their members were not Communists.[8]

The passive attitude of the rank and file does not differ from that of the average American. Most people do not concern themselves too seriously about the manner in which the affairs of the organizations to which they belong are conducted so long as the affairs which affect them directly are relatively normal. This is also true of the average citizen where the affairs of his government are concerned. But when problems vitally affecting his particular interests arise, he does become seriously concerned, and he can be roused to drastic action. The same holds true for the rank and file. Quite often, even when the charges are scandalous and the leader and his organization are alleged to be involved in unethical or perhaps unpatriotic practices, it may be difficult to stir the rank and file to action, so long as its special interests are not seriously affected.

This species of human nature explains why the rank and file in Communist-dominated unions have been slow to respond. In part, they are influenced by the smoke screen of the leaders who persist in claiming that the attacks upon them are not only false but are designed to weaken or destroy the organization which has brought favorable results and served its members faithfully. The opposition is accused of ulterior motives and alliances with management. Since the average person possesses some degree of suspicious or skeptical feeling and remembers the struggle of establishing the organization, as well as the constant resistance of management to union efforts, he is bound to be wary of charges against his leaders and will be inclined to give them the benefit of the doubt, fearing that otherwise the fortunes of the organization might be jeopardized.

For similar reasons, the rank and file responded most fervently in supporting union leaders who worked with the Communists in such unions as the NMU, Transport, and Hotel and Restaurant. Also, members sup-

[6] CIO Convention Proceedings, 1950, p. 487.
[7] *Ibid.*, 1950, p. 486.
[8] See above, pp. 77ff. and 94, 112.

ported such non-Communist leaders as the Reuthers in the Auto Workers. In these cases, they supported leaders who had demonstrated their faithfulness and usefulness both to the organization and to the movement. As communism became discredited in this country, it became possible to appeal to the rank and file on that issue. The experience of the IUE and other unions illustrates this. But loyalty to the organization and to the leaders who had demonstrated their ability to obtain tangible results was difficult to overcome. It was necessary to convince the members that their interests would be at least as well cared for by the organizations appealing for their affiliation as they were by the leaders they were urged to abandon. Under these circumstances, members of Communist-dominated unions responded. Similarly, they favored non-Communist leaders over Communist leaders when the former had a record of achievement. Thus, the unions who succeeded in winning away members from Communist leadership were going concerns, successful in their achievements; they could offer adequate protection and service. The motive of the rank and file, like that of most human beings, was therefore mixed: in part it consisted of loyalty to American principles, in part it was a strong attachment to the privileges they enjoyed, in part they were tempted by the prospect of gaining from the change.

The rank-and-filer performed the customary role characteristic of him in all walks of life. Not to be condemned or glorified, he needs mostly to be understood. Not an ardent soul, eager for action, he is content with an unheroic role, placidly believing the union is obtaining satisfactory results and doing as well for him as can be expected under the circumstances. But when he is aroused by exceptional, critical, or scandalous situations affecting his fortunes, he may, given effective leadership, become astonishingly irritable and may even vent his feelings in highly charged emotional orgies, such as wild demonstrations and other reckless acts. Normal routine is supplanted by vitriolic vituperation which, unless leashed by its leaders or others in authority, may lead to irresponsible acts, including violence. Once alerted, the rank-and-filers generally respond with alacrity. Where an appeal is made by competent leaders in whom they have confidence and the issue is presented clearly, they usually respond decisively. Thus, Reuther, Curran, and Quill were handsomely supported by the membership in referenda votes and at conventions. Even in Mine, Mill and UE, the membership supported the non-Communist opposition.

That portion of the rank and file that has remained in Communist-dominated unions either is still indifferent or, if not, is reacting slowly to appeals from non-Communist unions. This attitude is rarely attributed to their belief in or attachment to Communist doctrines. It is, however, influenced by other factors. Some of these people have become frustrated when non-Communist leaders were outmaneuvered because of ineptness or their failure to gain support from higher channels. Others, emotionally aroused, dissipated their energies before results could be achieved. In still other instances, the rank and file did not consider the unions that were attempting to recruit them as the proper ones to cover the jurisdiction to which they had become accustomed. Nevertheless, the fact is that some Communist unions have faded away; others, in order to preserve a few remnants of their membership, have merged, but with little success in holding their ground or in gaining new adherents; that those who have retained their original identity have, with the exception of the ILWU, been declining steadily seems to indicate that the hard-core Communist rank and file was indeed small, even in these unions. Communist strength rested primarily on the strategic placement of its leaders and militants; then, reinforcing their position with clever tactics, the Communists managed to attain and maintain power. In an open campaign, however, they find it more difficult to delude their members, which substantiates the contention of non-Communist union leaders that the rank and file is not, by and large, Communist.

Leaders are generally the key factors in the conduct of affairs in mass organizations. The limited, poorly oriented rank and file is dependent upon its leaders for guidance and enlightenment. Except for rare occasions, leaders in the lower echelons and the more alert members are often hesitant about waging battle without the support of their superiors. Indeed, within the CIO, even officials of international affiliates lacked confidence in coming to grips with the Communists in their respective organizations without the support of the CIO hierarchy. Nevertheless, there were aroused and courageous persons in the CIO who, practically from the CIO's inception, did all in their power to resist Communist encroachment and domination. Even in some of the strongest Communist-dominated unions there were revolts. This sort of reaction also occurred in those AFL unions where the Communists dominated certain sectors.

Most leaders reacted differently, influenced usually by the mixture of organizational and personal angles of the problem facing them. William Green and Matthew Woll represented the type that could discern no benefit in either humoring the Communists or simply tolerating them. They therefore fought them from the outset and continued their forthright opposition at every stage. John L. Lewis and Sidney Hillman, both of whom were very familiar through bitter experience with the way Communists could conduct themselves, overlooked the past because they needed Communist help. Philip Murray and Hugo Ernst found them strongly established within their organizations, performing effectively as trade unionists, although simultaneously serving the Communist cause. Murray and Ernst consequently shielded them and did their utmost to avoid an open conflict that would threaten the stability of the organization. In part, their conciliatory attitude was influenced by their liberal temperaments. William Hutcheson and L. P. Lindelof, both of whom were familiar with Communist designs, were concerned primarily with furthering their jurisdictional claims. This interest led them to overlook the Communist angle by denying its existence. Emil Rieve and Walter Reuther, having a socialist background, were more knowledgeable ideologically and tactically with Communist objectives in trade unions. Rieve kept them out of his union; Reuther ousted them from his union, not merely because he disagreed with them philosophically, but in self-protection. Both Rieve and Reuther grumbled and privately criticized Communist toleration within the CIO. Out of respect for Murray, however, and a desire for solidarity, they refrained from voicing vigorous resentment at public CIO sessions or pressing for definitive action. James Carey, who was at first unaware of undue Communist influence in his union and then found himself engulfed by Communists in his official family, refused to become their puppet and fought them, even though it meant losing the presidency of the UE. As CIO secretary-treasurer, he led the offensive against them within CIO headquarters, encouraging his staff in the conduct of anti-Communist activities and exerting himself in combating and checkmating them. Yet he carried out orders as a CIO delegate to the WFTU by collaborating with them on the international level.

Roy M. Brewer, who spearheaded the eminently successful fight against the Communists in Hollywood, where their domination became a community issue, was sent to the Coast as the international representative of his union in order to protect its jurisdictional interests. Drawing on his socialist background and on people in the know for information, he soon was convinced that underlying the jurisdiction issue was the deeper one of Communist control that capitalized on the narrower issue. By pretending to favor the jurisdictional claims of rival AFL unions, they succeeded in confusing the real attack upon them. Brewer had difficulty even in convincing his superiors in Los Angeles that, to clarify the situation, the Communist issue must first be disposed of. Joseph Curran and Michael Quill, both operating within the Communist setup, turned against the Communists when confronted with the choice of subordinating the trade-union interests of their organizations to that of the Communist Party. They chose to preserve their positions and status within their unions by discarding Communist control.

Thus, those leaders who had no Communist problem within their unions, but appreciated the Communist threat, or those who had a special interest to protect which the Communists, in alliance with others, challenged, were the most ardent in combating them; those who found them influential and useful within their organization, protected them. They made every effort to conciliate their opponents in order to preserve harmony. Only when the

Communists would not be moderate in their conduct, or when overriding issues arose in regard to which the Communists insisted upon championing the interests of Soviet Russia and the Communist Party, did the top leaders respond to pressure by fighting them with decision. Philip Murray begged the Communists to be moderate; so did Hugo Ernst, but the need to carry out Communist policy forced the Communist leaders in the unions to yield to other orders. This situation is well illustrated by what might be considered superficially as a trivial matter. As late as 1947, Murray still seemed to feel that he would be able to reconcile the conflicting elements. With the political pot boiling in anticipation of the 1948 presidential election, the Communists and their allies founded the Progressive Citizens of America, proclaimed by a declaration of principles favoring the foreign policy of Soviet Russia but embellished with pronouncements favoring liberal domestic policy. Simultaneously, the anti-Communist liberals, wanting to have their point of view presented clearly, supported the Americans for Democratic Action. Both groups sought support from CIO leaders and affiliates. By way of avoiding the conflict that threatened and maintaining harmony, Murray induced the vice-presidents to adopt a non-affiliation statement of policy deploring division in the liberal movement. Notwithstanding that, the ADA declaration proclaimed unequivocally the incompatibility of communism and liberalism. Later, because of the determination of the Communist leaders to make a success of the PCA, the Communists in the CIO broke faith by associating themselves with the Progressive Citizens. The non-Communists in the CIO now prevailed upon Murray to acquiesce in their joining ADA.[9] Similarly, the breach was widened over differences about such foreign policies as the Marshall Plan, the Truman Doctrine, and taking sides in the cold war. All efforts of outstanding leaders to mediate and reconcile differences on basic issues affecting the welfare of the labor movement and the country failed.

When the leaders were determined to do so, they were generally successful in eliminating Communist control and influence from the unions. Since the leaders were conversant with Communist objectives and tactics, why did they welcome the Communists at first and then falter and delay before embarking on decisive action? Opposition groups functioned from the very inception of the Communist movement. In example after example, struggles between Communists and non-Communists reached high proportions, involving top leaders; public comment and criticism were rampant; yet the leaders tried to reconcile the groups and to smother the dissension. Like responsible persons in authority in all walks of life, labor

[9] Max M. Kampelman, *The Communist Party vs. the C.I.O.; A Study in Power Politics*, F. A. Praeger, New York, 1957, pp. 81–83; most of the information was gleaned from personal conversations with CIO leaders and staff members at national headquarters.

leaders are slow-moving and loath to resort to drastic action that might weaken the organization irreparably or perhaps destroy it. Like men exercising power in any field, they had certain objectives as their goal and were prone to make allowances in order to pursue their course. The chief, possibly the sole, objective of leaders is to maintain their organization intact, to assure smooth operation and control, irrespective of consequences in the future which can be handled when they arise. Attempting to quiet dissension, leaders will tolerate almost any element, regardless of principle.

Like the rank and file, leaders become engrossed and preoccupied with limited objectives. It is largely a question of building and preserving a strong organization, a movement which has become associated with their personalities. To harm that movement would be like committing violence to their own persons. And as long as their own status is not threatened, or their higher sense of patriotism and devotion to the movement and country is not aroused, they will tolerate such antisocial and even subversive elements as racketeers and disloyal groups. As extroverts with inflated egos, frequently an inflexible type of person, they readily convince themselves that, when the opportune time arrives, they will be able to dispose of these "undesirables." In the meantime, they try to keep them in leash, which they succeed in doing somewhat. With such an attitude, shortcomings or practices of which they would ordinarily disapprove, are overlooked. As men who have battled their way to power against formidable odds, including rising from humble surroundings, they have developed an unbounded confidence in themselves. This characteristic makes for their greatness as well as for their weakness. A feeling that they can overcome any obstacle, any foe when occasion demands it is developed on the basis of their previous, successful experience with oppositions, including Communists. Why should they doubt they can repeat their success if the need arises? In the meantime, they will keep the organization intact, using these elements, even those of potential opposition, to build it into an even greater and more powerful movement.

They did not fail to take a certain measure of precaution, however. Some of these leaders, such as Lewis and Hillman, who had battled with the Communists and defeated them as well as other oppositions in their own unions, insulated their unions against further Communist penetration. But, in building the CIO, they welcomed their aid because there was a scarcity of experienced hands; besides, the Communists were already established in some areas and industries. To have declared war against them in this initial stage in the founding of the CIO would have diverted CIO energies and perhaps have limited its success. CIO leaders were probably wrong in arriving at such a conclusion. We know that in industries such as textile and steel, the Communists were kept out from the beginning, and yet substantial, even strong unions were developed. On the other hand, these unions had adequate, competent leadership. In other areas, as on the Pacific Coast, and in other industries, such as electric manufacturing, maritime, and so forth, this was not the case. Should such industries as these have been neglected, or should they have been organized even though the Communists were in the lead?

The question also arises, Why did the leaders prolong their determination ultimately to eliminate Communist control? Procrastination is a characteristic of successful people as well as of ne'er-do-wells. The latter lack the will to act; the former are either preoccupied with what they consider more pressing problems demanding their attention or they prefer to bide their time for the propitious moment. That the leaders were aware of the problem quite early we know, but they did what men in power always do—unless circumstances force them to act otherwise: they tried reconciliation. When that failed, they—pantherlike—crouched in readiness to spring when the prey was vulnerable to attack.[10] This moment arrived when the domestic and international situations no longer brooked reconciliation. And when the leaders acted, they acted decisively.

Personality factors always are involved in these relationships. To gauge the extent to which they affect situations is rather difficult. Usually, it is not possible to dissociate personal rivalries and ambitions from clashes over issues and policies: these factors are generally too subtly interrelated to permit separate evaluation. Self-assertive individuals are bound to find it more difficult to work harmoniously; frequently, however, they discover a mutually agreeable mode of operation, if necessity requires it. Undoubtedly, there was a clash of personalities between Lundberg and Bridges and Bridges and Curran. There did not seem to be any personality friction between Carey and his colleagues in UE or between Quill and his fellow officers in the Transport Workers. Yet they, too, fought one another. Lundberg, with his "wobbly" background and distrusting temperament, was intuitively suspicious of totalitarian techniques and objectives. Curran and Quill, as personalities in their own right, chafed under strict, remote, and often thoughtless and impractical dictation by outsiders who knew little about the problem of their unions, the CIO, or the American labor movement. Besides, the organizations which they headed, and in the founding of which they played a key role, had now become a part of their personalities. Being men of confidence and of initiative, they dared assert independence. Of course, in doing so, they were not confronted with the unenviable prospect of becoming prophets in the wilderness. A power-

[10] "Perhaps the CIO should have asserted itself more vigorously. Perhaps it would have done so had it been prepared for a showdown fight over the issue of Communism within its own Councils. Not being ready in 1947 to act more decisively on its own problem, perhaps the CIO did as much as was feasible at the time." Jensen, *op. cit.*, p. 194.

ful organization stood ready to embrace and support them, a sympathetic government beamed approvingly, and an appreciative public was prepared to applaud. It was not like walking into a lion's den; rather, it was like entering an arena of admirers. There was undoubtedly some soul-searching before the fateful step was taken, but the risk was not too great for determined, fighting men.

Personality factors, usually a determinant in human relations, happened to accentuate the differences and even to expedite the clash, but, lacking basic issues, open conflict could hardly have resulted. Leadership rivalries were contributory, but had Curran and Quill remained truly dedicated to the Communist program and cause, personality differences could have been bridged. It was when they began to doubt and dissent by placing the interests of their organization above the aims of the Communist movement that the break became inevitable. Naturally, there were some leaders who were not influenced by such complicated considerations and who severed their Communist affiliations for such simple opportunistic reasons as saving their paid positions or because of other immediate monetary considerations. This occurred especially where lower-level leaders took with them locals and district councils in joining non-Communist unions.

While not primarily influenced by selfish considerations, most leaders nevertheless failed to take action against Communist penetration until the situation reached scandalous proportions, or until their status and the future of their organization, or movement, was threatened. Some were more sensitive than others and therefore acted more promptly. AFL leaders, confronted with Communist domination, reacted in a manner similar to that of the CIO leaders.

In the light of these psychological and self-interest factors motivating both rank and file and leaders, an effective opposition, with an aroused public opinion and government and employer participation, becomes indispensable. Only a combination of all these factors will bring satisfactory results in combating subversive or corrupt elements that infiltrate and attach themselves detrimentally to individual organizations and the movement. Indeed, the inertia displayed by leaders as well as by members indicates the need of shock treatment to induce action. Public investigations, pressure from below by local leaders and alerted members, exposure of scandalous situations that arouse public concern and criticism have been the most effective catalysts.

22

Employer Attitude

The behavior of management in its relations with Communist-dominated unions was no different from that of most labor leaders and the majority of the rank and file. On the whole, management gave little heed to warnings against Communist-controlled unions. Employers also showed little interest in cooperating with non-Communist unions or others in opposing Communist-dominated unions in their plants or in dealing with Communists in their business activities. Employers, like labor leaders and others in authority, were influenced primarily in their attitude toward Communists by immediate, practical considerations of plant harmony, advantageous labor relations, and effect on business prospects, rather than by the principle or ethics of having dealings with Communists.

Some catered to the Communists out of fear of hurting their business otherwise. This practice occurred in the motion-picture industry which depends directly upon the patronage of the consumer. Where the Communists exercised powerful influence, management favored those people acceptable to the Communists; those who incurred the enmity of the Communists were informally blacklisted. When public reaction set in, stimulated by the shock of state and congressional investigations and other exposures—making Communist influence in the motion-picture industry a national scandal—management reversed its position. At first it denied the charges and defended its practices on civil rights and ethical grounds. But as criticism and pressure mounted, the financial backers of the industry and management itself adopted a policy of self-policing. The studios unanimously subscribed to what became known as the "Waldorf statement" which pledged them to the following policy: "We will forthwith discharge or suspend without compensation those in our employ and we will not re-employ any of the 10 until such time as he is acquitted or has purged himself of contempt and declares under oath that he is not a Communist.

"On the broader issue of alleged subversive and disloyal elements in Hollywood, our members are likewise prepared to take positive action.

"We will not knowingly employ a Communist or a member of any party or group which advocates the overthrow of the government of the United States by force or by any illegal or unconstitutional methods." Thus far this policy is acknowledged as having proved effective.[1]

In the industries not directly or wholly dependent upon the ultimate consumer, it has been more difficult to arouse management to action. Most employers assumed, or pretended to assume, a neutralist attitude usually favoring the Communist-dominated unions, since they were already established in their plants.

Employers evidently found it advantageous to favor Communist-dominated unions. Jensen describes employer reaction toward Mine, Mill as follows: "Another factor in the situation, paradoxical and of indeterminate importance, is that Mine, Mill has been to a degree preferred by managements which reason that a weak Mine, Mill, even if dominated by the left wing, is to be desired over a more powerful unionism tied to the steel industry and the effect of pattern settlements. . . . The truth is that many managements throughout the industry, when speaking frankly, have said they prefer to bargain with Mine, Mill because it is relatively weak. . . . This of course leaves these managements in a paradoxical position, for by preferring Mine, Mill they are favoring a leadership which many believe is Communist dominated." [2]

Employers in other industries also found it desirable to appease the Communist labor leaders of the unions operating in their establishments. A journalist who made a study of the Communist "fifth column" sarcastically castigates employers: "Certainly it is very naughty for Mr. Murray to appease the Communists, but when one considers those California business leaders who anxiously opposed the deportation of Harry Bridges, and that New York shipping magnate who was honorary chairman of the huge banquet in honor of Communist Ferdinand Smith of the National Maritime Union, one is led to suspect that Mr. Murray's naughtiness has its counterparts in other places than the labor movement." [3]

[1] John Cogley, *Report on Blacklisting*, vol. 1, *Movies*, Fund for the Republic, New York, 1956; this report stirred up considerable controversy so that the House Committee on Un-American Activities initiated an *Investigation of So-called "Blacklisting" in Entertainment Industry; Report of the Fund for the Republic, Inc., Hearings before the House Un-American Activities Committee*, parts 1, 2, and 3, 84th Cong., 2d Sess., 1956. Newspaper comment was profuse; "Editorial Comments on John Cogley's 'Report on Blacklisting' " was reproduced in document form by the Fund for the Republic. For a circumspect review of Cogley's book by a profound student of the subject, see "Wanted, an Ethic of Employment for Our Time," by Sidney Hook in the *New York Times Book Review*, July 22, 1956, pp. 6 and 14.
[2] Vernon H. Jensesn, *Nonferrous Metals Industry Unionism, 1932–1954*, Cornell Studies in Industrial and Labor Relations, Cornell University Press, Ithaca, N.Y., 1954, p. 305.
[3] Andrew Avery, *The Communist Fifth Column: What's the Truth about It, and What Isn't*, reprints of a series of articles appearing between June 24 and July 11 in the *Chicago Journal of Commerce*, 1946, pp. 1, 7, quoted in Max J. Kampelman, *The Communist Party vs. the C.I.O.*, F. A. Praeger, New York, 1957, p. 39.

At least one top executive of a substantial corporation frankly acknowledged in writing that it is advantageous to do business with a Communist-dominated union. The vice-president of the Sonotone Corporation wrote a memorandum on company stationery March 18, 1955, addressed to "all production supervisors, Elmsford and White Plains (strictly confidential)." In it he explained the firm's position:

"My own position and that of the company is that we cannot agree with, nor do we sponsor the UE Union for ideological reasons. Nevertheless, we cannot be unmindful of the economic interest of Sonotone Corporation which must supersede our personal likes and dislikes.

"I believe that in the present weakened position of the UE it is advantageous for the company to continue to deal with them [UE] until such time as the Government takes action now contemplated. In our conference with them recently, we feel we again have a way to lay off and discharge employees with a minimum of risk.

"We have reached certain understandings as to negotiations in the event the UE wins this election and the UE has promised to get behind this incentive system immediately after the election so that we will get 130% production. You can understand that such an arrangement is extremely beneficial to Sonotone Corporation.

"In view of the foregoing, we urge our supervisors NOT to DISCOURAGE *any* employee [caps and italics in original] from voting for the UE in the next election.

"IMPORTANT: This is a very confidential memorandum. Please destroy it immediately after you have read it." (Entire sentence in caps in original.)

The election held March 22, 1955, resulted in a victory for UE. Out of 830 eligible production employees, 676 voted, with the following outcome:

Teamsters	126
UE	392
IUE	144
No union	3
Total	665
Challenged	11
	676

The Teamsters and IUE protested the election. Upon a stipulation by all concerned, including the Sonotone Corporation, the election was nullified. Two documents were presented by the unions as exhibits in their petition for nullification. One was a photostatic copy of the March 18, 1955, Sonotone Corporation memorandum and the other was a copy of the March 23, 1955, column, "Inside Labor," by Victor Riesel. In this column, Riesel writes that Vice-President Christophal "admitted to me that he distributed the memo. I asked why, and he said I had a copy just to read it carefully." NLRB held another election July 12, 1955, in which IUE increased its vote, but the Teamsters and UE suffered slight decreases. UE, however, won this election handsomely, as the returns reveal. Out of 801 employees eligible to vote, 687 voted: [4]

Teamsters	103
UE	358
IUE	218
No union	4
Valid votes	683
Challenged	4
Total cast	687

There is a silver lining behind this black cloud. In May, 1956, this UE local, with others in the area, disaffiliated from UE and joined IUE. Although Sonotone could have demanded an NLRB election to verify the wishes of its employees, it voluntarily recognized the transfer. And in October, 1956, when IUE organized its clerical employees, "which UE had ignored," the corporation again recognized the accomplishment voluntarily.[5]

Extensive available data on the case of the General Electric Company illustrates the dilemma and problems confronting an employer dealing with a strongly established Communist-dominated union in its plants. A serious complicating factor was the estimate of corporation officials that in 1953 "almost a third of our business was in the defense area." [6] Although from its inception in 1949 IUE had made considerable inroads on the UE, the latter, nevertheless, retained a substantial hold on GE. Thus, in elections conducted by the NLRB in 1950 in GE locations, IUE won in "56 units, as against 46 for UE. . . . The IUE, according to this tabulation, will represent some 53,000 employees, while UE will represent approximately 36,000." GE representatives estimated that UE represented in 1950, prior to the NLRB election, "about 100,000 General Electric employees. . . ." [7] But some of the largest plants, like those in Schenectady and Erie, remained under UE control.

[4] NLRB—2RC7147; Sonotone memo reprinted in full in *IUE-CIO News*, March 28, 1955; see also *Fortune*, June, 1955, pp. 62, 66, and *CIO News*, April 1, 1955.

[5] Information supplied by Les Finnegan, Assistant to President James B. Carey, of the IUE, Jan. 7, 1957.

[6] *Subversive Influence in Certain Labor Organizations, Hearings to Investigate the Administration of the Internal Security Act and other Internal Security Laws of the Committee on the Judiciary,* U.S. Senate, 83d Cong., 1st and 2d Sess., 1953–1954, p. 301, hereafter referred to as *Subversive Influence in Certain Labor Organizations.*

[7] *Communist Domination of Unions and National Security, Hearings before a Subcommittee of the Committee on Labor and Public Welfare,* U.S. Senate, 82d Cong., 2d Sess., 1952, pp. 418, 436–437, and 443.

In this struggle between UE and IUE, charges that GE discriminated flew thick and fast. Both sides claimed that GE favored the other. IUE, led by the indomitable James Carey, spearheaded a campaign charging GE with favoring UE for selfish reasons and for reasons contrary to the security interests of the nation. The charges and the controversy attracted the attention of the public, the press, and finally of Congress. The differences between IUE and GE were aired at various congressional committee hearings, with both sides presenting their case in considerable detail. GE officials responsible for public relations and personnel had an opportunity to develop in general the employer point of view and to explore the problems in connection with Communist-dominated unions, in particular those in sensitive areas affecting national security. In testifying before congressional committees, GE spokesmen agreed with labor leaders and others that most American workers are not Communists, that "even in those unions believed to be Communist dominated 99 per cent of the membership is loyal." [8]

These representatives of management also conceded that certain unions were Communist-dominated. They were careful, however, to qualify their statement as being one by "amateurs" in this field,[9] but they agreed that UE was Communist-dominated, although protesting at first "lack of professional information." [10] At a later congressional hearing, they were more positive. After relating specific incidents, Lemuel R. Boulware, vice-president of GE, stated: "In view of these facts and others, we and large portions of the public have long since come to believe the repeated and never disproved charges of UE's Communist leadership." [11]

Smarting from persistent, categorical charges by James Carey and others that GE was deliberately aiding UE because the latter was amenable,[12] the representatives of this corporation lashed out with an emotional defense. They charged that these labor leaders had harbored and sheltered Communist leaders in UE and in other CIO unions and that they had defended and otherwise protected Communist-dominated unions. Some of these charges were documented by GE officials.[13] In their written statement, they concluded that "if responsibility for UE's continued presence with us is to be placed anywhere by this sub-committee, the record requires that it be found to rest in the national office of the CIO, of which Mr. Carey was a part, and where for so long UE was approved, its entrenchment assisted and where it was so well protected from efforts of fellow CIO unions to provide any other kind of a union in the electrical industry; that the much

[8] *Subversive Influence in Certain Organizations*, pp. 291, 306.
[9] *Communist Domination of Unions, op. cit.*, pp. 413–414, 463.
[10] *Ibid.*
[11] *Subversive Influence in Certain Labor Organizations*, p. 288.
[12] *Communist Domination of Unions, op. cit.*, see testimony of Carey and of Benjamin C. Segal, pp. 193–261.
[13] *Ibid.*. pp. 402–432.

publicized effort of the CIO and the 'anti-Communist' unions to clean house have not been sufficiently thorough and consistent, nor have they gone deeply enough into local conditions so as to justify Congress in relying upon such efforts as an excuse for not legislating upon the question of Communism in labor unions." [14]   William J. Barron, labor relations counsel, thus clinched their charge against labor leaders, particularly of the CIO gender: "It should be remembered that from 1935 until about 1950, all of the many employers who dared raise a voice about Communism in the CIO unions were promptly branded 'Red Baiters' and 'union busters.'   But in 1949, the CIO finally got around to expelling unions identified ten years before by Congressional Committees as Communist-dominated.   When that happened, lo and behold, the new party line suddenly became one of charging that some employers prefer Communist unions." [15]   The final employer barrage was an accusation that the labor leaders were guided by "expediency and convenience." [16]

In addition to making this reply to the charges against GE, representatives focused attention on particular problems confronting the company's management.   They were in a dilemma, the blame for which was placed upon Federal government legislation and agencies.   "For almost 20 years the Federal law has compelled employers, as it still does, to recognize and bargain with any labor organization certified to it by the National Labor Relations Board.   And the NLRB continues obliged to certify various unions which have been repeatedly accused of Communist domination before Congressional committees. . . ."   Since "no authoritative legal determination has been made" that UE is Communist-dominated, "consequently the NLRB continues to certify UE as a union with which we and the 300 other employers must deal exclusively as representative of a claimed one-third of a million employees working at locations vital to the economy and national defense." [17]   These management representatives also complained: "It seems incredible that the United States Government should order even defense plant employers to bargain with unions so generally regarded as Communist dominated.   In fact, it is so unbelievable that the average person may be occasionally led to wonder if employers are dealing with Communist unions in defiance of the law, rather than because of a compelling legal obligation." [18]

GE did yield readily when ordered by AEC (Atomic Energy Commission) in 1949 to "withdraw recognition from UE at one of our locations."   Since

[14] *Ibid.*, p. 461.
[15] *Proceedings of Sixth Annual Meeting of Industrial Relations Research Association*, 1953, p. 27.
[16] *Communist Domination of Unions, op. cit.*, p. 415.
[17] *Subversive Influence in Certain Labor Organizations*, p. 288; see also *Communist Domination of Unions, op. cit.*, p. 399.
[18] *Ibid.*, p. 289.

UE was still affiliated with CIO, GE was "attacked bitterly for doing so, both publicly and in the courts, by CIO." [19]   Following expulsion of UE from the CIO, the latter assumed a favorable attitude toward AEC rulings against UE.[20]   (The role of government through legislation, agencies, and the courts is discussed in the following section.)

Evidently concerned by the barrage of criticism, probably also by pressure from government agencies placing defense contracts, and by a realization of the danger in the situation, GE took partial action on its own. "Last year [1953], as an interim measure, pending more adequate Government regulation, we adopted a policy we believed necessary to solve the problem at least in part.   This policy calls for the ultimate discharge of any employee who invokes the Fifth Amendment in refusing to answer questions concerning Communist affiliation before a government authority. . . .   In adopting this policy, we recognized that it was not a complete solution to the problem of possible subversives in our plants.   However, we felt obliged to our employees, share owners and the public to utilize it until the Government adopts measures to adequately cope with the problem." [21]

UE appealed to the courts.   A divided Circuit Court of Appeals, sitting in Washington, in a 2 to 1 decision ruled that a corporation could discharge employees who invoked the Fifth Amendment in refusing to answer congressional inquiries into political affiliations.[22]

On the basis of GE's experience, the company's officials concluded that the responsibility of labeling unions as Communist-dominated and individuals as Communists belonged to the government: "We do not think employers are the proper policemen in a case like this, much as we regard employers highly." [23]   And further, "An employer certainly should not have the right to decide that he will not recognize a union chosen by his employees because he believes that union is Communist dominated." [24]   The opinion of GE representatives was that union or private citizens not be entrusted with this delicate and ultracontroversial task.   "Likewise, we do not believe unions can or should be depended upon to take the place of public police power in this matter." [25]

Organized labor disagreed with this recommendation.   They contended that "there is no need at the present time for additional legislation to deal

[19] *Ibid.*, pp. 398–399, 401.
[20] *Ibid.*, pp. 285–295.
[21] IUE chided GE for this belated action, *Communist Domination of Unions, op. cit.*, p. 294, and GE charged the unions with similar neglect, *op. cit.*, p. 397; *Subversive Influence in Certain Labor Organizations*, p. 290; see also p. 305.
[22] *New York Times*, Dec. 31, 1954; see also "How to Curb Communist Influence in Industrial Relations," discussion by W. J. Barron, labor relations counsel, General Electric Co., IRRA Proceedings, Dec. 28–30, 1953. pp. 26ff.
[23] *Communist Domination of Unions, op. cit.*, p. 396.
[24] *Subversive Influence in Certain Labor Organizations*, p. 289.
[25] *Ibid.*, p. 289; *Communist Domination of Unions, op. cit.*, p. 397.

with the problem of Communist dominated unions. The value judgment which must be made at this point is, as we all know, to balance the security needs of the Nation against the freedom of thought, of speech, and of association on which our democratic system rests." This view was expressed by Allan S. Haywood, vice-president, CIO, who spoke also for Murray; [26] he contended that the unions could do the job.[27] A representative testifying on behalf of the International Association of Machinists, an AFL affiliate, expressed similar views.[28] It is, of course, the traditional position of labor unions, as well as of most social groups and organizations, that they resist government regulation, always insisting they can cope with the problem. Organized labor, like other power groups, is justifiably on guard about various types of legislative and administrative action lest it hamper and weaken their legitimate aspirations and activities. As a result of this fear, they are occasionally illogical. Thus, some of the Communist-dominated unions are still operating, albeit at a great disadvantage. The attacks of the non-Communist unions have taken their toll, but it is the enactment of legislation and action by the government, authorized by legislation, that have thrown Communist-dominated unions into a panic. This is demonstrated in a later chapter.

Like most employers, labor leaders, and government officials, GE groped its way. It only clarified its position and took action within permissible limits, following widespread publicity and severe criticism. In defending its position, it fumbled along in its thinking, clarifying it only after considerable criticism. At first, GE assumed a supposedly neutral position by denouncing different types of unionism indiscriminately. In September, 1948, while the struggle between the Communists and the anti-Communists within GE was raging, GE issued a public statement euphoniously entitled, "A Plague on Both Your Houses." Following a recital of why GE had no preference for either of the contending groups within UE, the statement boldly declares that "we ... still have a special reason for not favoring either of the candidates or groups around them. We disapprove of them both and our disapproval is equal in the case of each. . . .

"While frequently the leader and his associates on one side are termed 'left wingers' and the leader and his associates on the other are wrongly—in our opinion—regarded as 'right wingers' we believe they are in the end the same objectives. . . .

"In our opinion, whether they realize it or not, both are collectivists—

---

[26] *Ibid.,* p. 278.

[27] *Ibid.,* p. 281; see also Segal's testimony, pp. 297ff.

[28] *Ibid.,* p. 325. William Green, AFL president, also expressed doubts that the domination of labor unions by Communists can be dealt with successfully by legislation (see his reply to questionnaire in *Communist Domination of Unions, Subcommittee Report, Replies to Subcommittee Questionnaire,* Committee Print, 82d Cong., 2d Sess., 1952).

believers in Government being big and in people being little." (Italics in original.) [29]

When GE realized that the "message" was "being misinterpreted," it promptly made it clear by another message to its employees that " 'A Plague on Both Your Houses' was directed only at those union leaders who believe in a collectivist society. . . .

"In this latter message which we entitled 'What's the Trouble?' we made it clear that 'there is a third group, of course, which is composed of those American union leaders who wisely reject both of the false economic theories and the freedom destroying measures of the collectivists. . . .' We did not, and do not mean in any way to cast any reflection on this group of Americans soundly seeking the good of their fellow citizens." [30]

When pressed by Senator Hubert Humphrey, chairman of the committee, the GE representative first defended the statement, then qualified his position. Senator Humphrey pointed to "the danger of equating Communists with other radicals who believe in a free society, such as Western European Socialists, particularly the Scandinavian variety. . . . I bring up this point to you because you are an intelligent, responsible person, and you represent a great company in the United States. And I say after having read your article . . . and read this talk about a collectivist state with all the overtones and undertones that those terms have, that it is about time that men of our intelligence and legal understanding come to grips with Communism, on the one hand, or even democratic socialism on the other hand." [31]

GE Vice-President Lemuel R. Boulware stood his ground but was also apologetic. He conceded that "we may have done it imperfectly, Senator, but I argue with you about the difference between Norway and Russia. My view is that we have waited too long until we learned about our system, both our economic and political system, and very late in life, I have been trying to again pick up where I left off back with John R. Commons and Dr. [Arnold B.] Hall in the University of Wisconsin a few years ago." [32] He declared himself "proud" of the "article," however, but again qualified his attitude, "I was only talking about two groups of top leaders within UE, both of whom I thought were far enough down the road to be called collectivists. . . ." But when Jack Barbash, committee staff director, pointed up the issue, "Do you see no difference between a collectivist who is a free agent and a collectivist who represents the interests of a foreign power and is engaged in a systematic conspiracy?" Boulware conceded that "there cannot be any question to your answer there." [33]

[29] *Ibid.*, pp. 202–203.
[30] *Ibid.*, pp. 450–451.
[31] *Ibid.*, p. 453.
[32] *Ibid.*, pp. 453–454; statement and testimony cover pp. 391–467; see also testimony of James B. Carey, especially pp. 223 and 228–229.
[33] *Ibid.*, p. 459.

In its report, the subcommittee was unwilling to express an opinion as to whether the General Electric Company had discriminated between UE and IUE. "The International Union of Electrical Workers (CIO) has charged that the General Electric Corp., has favored the United Electrical Workers (Independent) since expelled from the CIO on grounds of Communist domination. The General Electric Corp., speaking through Mr. Boulware, has vigorously denied this charge. We do not feel that we would be justified in making a definite finding on this issue in controversy, one way or the other."

But the subcommittee was unequivocal and emphatic in reprimanding GE for equating a "Communist union and an anti-Communist union."

"We feel justified, however, in commenting on an attitude reflected in certain statements issued by the General Electric Corp. on the theme of a 'Plague on both your houses'. . . . The essence of the theme is that there is little to choose from between 'left wingers' and 'right wingers.' The reference is to U.E. and IUE respectively.

"We believe—the General Electric Corp. has said—they have in the end the same objectives. We believe that what each side advocates would result, in the long run, in substantially the same thing for our employees, our company and our country (hearings 451).

"This is an amazing statement and shows little comprehension of the forces at work in this world, in the year 1952. It is the attitude on the part of some employers which has made the opposition to the real Communists in the unions very difficult and explains in large part why the Communists have been able to retain as much as they have. If an employer says, in effect, there is no difference between a Communist union and an anti-Communist union, it is understandable why many workers may not pay too much attention to a valid charge that a union is Communist controlled." [34]

[34] *Public Policy and Communist Domination of Certain Unions, Report of the Subcommittee on Labor and Labor-Management Relations to the Senate Committee on Labor and Public Welfare*, 83d Cong., 1st Sess., 1953, pp. 26–27.

23

The Role of Government

Originally the government played a rather negligible role in counteracting and combating Communist infiltration, influence, and domination of unions. Its first action was the investigation by committees of both houses. The public hearings and reports of these committees stimulated discussion and recriminations, created public interest, and roused demands for government action. The earliest specific legislation aimed directly at Communist domination of unions that Congress enacted was section 9(h) of the Labor-Management Relations Act of 1947, popularly referred to as the Taft-Hartley Act. This action took place exactly seventeen years after Congress first manifested interest in the Communist problem.[1]

Section 9(h), effective at first, ultimately proved ambiguous and easy to evade. Lacking specific mandates from Congress, various government branches, confronted with the Communist problem, were indecisive, feeling they lacked necessary authority, and were also concerned about not encroaching on the civil rights of the workers or interfering with their right to organize and bargain collectively through the unions of their choice. They also, in this regard, felt restrained by the NLRB rulings.

The courts, in their customary manner, moved slowly and carefully scrutinized the laws and procedures under which other government branches acted. The Communists aided in slowing the judicial process by resorting to every available technicality to contest any action against them in the courts. In accordance with precedent, the courts, by resorting to the narrow-interpretation principle, restricted other government branches in extending what they considered were their implied powers.

Public concern over the threat of communism in this country induced specific legislation and determined action on the part of the government, just as it roused the rank and file, labor leaders, and employers.

As indicated earlier, the first specific Federal legislative step against Communists in unions was enacted in 1947. This was section 9(h) of

---

[1] *Digest of the Public Record of Communism in the United States,* Fund for the Republic, 1955, part 3, "Public Documents," pp. 489–692, lists the different committees.

the remodeled Labor Relations Act of 1935, transformed into the Labor-Management Relations Act of 1947. Acting on the traditional fear that legislation and administrative acts would be abused to their disadvantage, organized labor opposed the act and took particular exception to section 9(h). President Truman vetoed the act, but it was passed over his veto.[2]

Section 9(h) provides that no labor organization can avail itself of NLRB facilities and benefits unless each officer signs an affidavit that "he is not a member of the Communist Party or affiliated with such Party, and that he does not believe in and is not a member of or supports any organization that believes in or teaches, the overthrow of the United States Government by force or any illegal or unconstitutional methods." [3]

Some outstanding unions, such as Coal Miners, Auto, and Steel, refused to file affidavits as required by the law. They were motivated by their general hostility to the act. In particular, they resented the fact that only labor leaders were required to sign "non-Communist affidavits," whereas employers were not. This action confused the situation and temporarily shielded those Communists who were union officers. Following a Supreme Court decision in May, 1950, sustaining section 9(h), most of the non-Communist unions complied.[4]

At first the Communists did not know how to act. A few unimportant Communist union officers resigned, or refused to sign the affidavits.[5] But such action would not serve Communist objectives, since it meant the voluntary surrender of power in the unions. On the other hand, noncompliance meant placing the unions they controlled at a serious disadvantage. Noncomplying unions "found it increasingly difficult to secure necessary assistance through the National Labor Relations Board, they could not go on the ballot in any Board elections (except pursuant to decertification petitions, where appearance on the ballot normally was disadvantageous), they could not secure authority to execute lawful union-shop agreements, they could obtain no remedy for unfair labor practices. Complying unions thereby secured important competitive advantages, as the Congress intended." [6] Section 9(h) militated against Communist-dominated unions using the facilities of the act, if it did not drive them out of the unions.

The Communists devised techniques for circumventing the provisions of the Taft-Hartley Act. In this undertaking, they were eminently successful. Some leaders announced publicly their resignation from the Com-

---

[2] *Communist Domination of Unions and National Security, Hearings before a Subcommittee of the Committee on Labor and Public Welfare,* U.S. Senate, 82d Cong., 2d Sess., 1952, pp. 98–100 and 295–297.

[3] *Ibid.,* p. 511.

[4] *Ibid.,* decision reprinted on pp. 58–85; ACA v. Douds and United Steelworkers of America v. NLRB, 339 U.S. 382 (1950).

[5] *Communist Domination of Unions, op. cit.,* pp. 53, 112.

[6] *Ibid.,* pp. 92 and 106, Herzog's testimony.

munist Party but brazenly declared they still believed in Communist doctrines. A few Communist-dominated unions amended their constitutions so that most of the leaders remained in their posts and carried out their former duties but were not designated as policy-making officials. A more common practice was merely to sign the affidavits and take a chance that fraud and perjury would have to be proved by the government.[7] Instead of disciplining those who thus evaded the intent of section 9(h), the NLRB single-mindedly contented itself by ruling that it was not the enforcing agency. According to NLRB's understanding of the law, it was required to accept affidavits, and, if it suspected deception, it referred the cases to the Department of Justice.[8] Indeed, Chairman Herzog declared it fortunate that his Board was not required to perform this policing function: "Whatever the difficulties of this arrangement, it has at least spared the Board the intolerable and delaying administrative burden which would have been imposed under an earlier legislative proposal; that of having the Board itself determine, as part of every representation proceeding, whether a particular labor organization had Communists among its officers." [9]

The Senate Subcommittee on Labor and Labor-Management Relations took issue with the Board and concluded categorically that "the National Labor Relations Board has authority under existing law (in its own words) 'to protect its own processes from abuse,'" [10] It called attention to the fact that "in a sense the Board has in one other way gone beyond the concept of being simply a filing cabinet for the 9(h) affidavit. It has taken steps to prevent evasion of the law by union officers who resign from constitutionally designated posts and take so-called administrative positions in the union." [11] At the subcommittee hearings, Senator Humphrey also cited another instance where the Board had gone beyond the concept of being merely a filing agent. He cited a ruling of the Board that it will not recognize a unit on racial lines because it would be against public policy.[12]

At a later period, the Board did follow the suggestion of the subcommittee, but at this time it merely submitted cases of suspected deception to the Department of Justice. Beginning in 1951, over a period of about 14

[7] *Communist Domination of Unions, op. cit.*, pp. 92, 103, 107, 113–117, and 513; *Investigation of Communist Activities in the Pacific Northwest, Hearings before the House Committee on Un-American Activities*, 83d Cong., 2d. Sess., 1954, part 3, section 2, pp. 615ff.; *Investigation of Communist Activities in the Newark, N.J. Area, Hearings before the House Committee on Un-American Activities*, 84th Cong., 1st Sess., 1955, p. 1026; *Investigation of Communist Activities in the Dayton, Ohio, Area, Hearings before the House Committee on Un-American Activities*, 83d Cong., 2d Sess., 1954, part 1, pp. 6183–6186; Benjamin Gitlow, *The Whole of Their Lives*, Charles Scribner's Sons, New York, 1948, p. 316.
[8] *Communist Domination of Unions, op. cit.*, p. 114.
[9] *Ibid.*, pp. 91ff.
[10] *Ibid.*, p. 19.
[11] *Ibid.*, p. 8.
[12] *Ibid.*, p. 43.

months, "68 cases were referred to the United States Attorney General in 19 different judicial districts." By July, 1952, only one indictment was obtained. Justice complained that "it is virtually impossible to develop cases for successful prosecution under the Section as now drawn. . . . Because of [the] requirement that the affidavit be couched in the present tense, a prosecution can be undertaken with some hope of obtaining a conviction only when it is possible to prove that on the very day the affidavit was executed the affiant was a member of the Communist Party or affiliated therewith or was engaged in other proscribed conduct or mental processes. It is a simple matter for an individual to discontinue, formally, the prohibited membership, affiliation, and conduct and execute the prescribed affidavit on the next day and circumvent the law." [13] Then Justice representatives suggested that the NLRB was better equipped to handle such cases. Senator Humphrey did not consider this suggestion a satisfactory solution.[14]

Government operating agencies are primarily responsible for the narrower aspects of security, such as the manufacture of classified products. The two government agencies most affected are the Atomic Energy Commission and the Munitions Board in charge of production for the Defense Department. They, too, found difficulties in forestalling Communist-dominated unions from operating in the areas over which they had responsibility. They complained of the lack of a clear legal mandate which would authorize them to cope with the Communist problem. Those in charge indicated a hesitancy to act on implied power. Fear of encroaching on the civil rights of others also inhibited them. Chairman John Small of the Munitions Board declared: "The problem of how to meet the threat that subversive union leadership may present is one that admits of no easy answer. In adopting a solution we must be careful that the cure is not worse than the disease." [15] They feared they might fail to preserve the basic rights of legal union members; above all, they must operate within the law. In this respect, NLRB officials agreed. Chairman Herzog warned that the danger in proscribing Communists in unions presented a twentieth-century dilemma of "how to combat evil men without doing something bad." [16] And General Counsel George J. Bott indicated that the situation presented "the delicate question of how great is the danger, and how restrictive do you want to make your law with respect to free speech and assembly." [17]

Chairman Small also warned that care must be taken not to interfere with genuine collective bargaining. And he complained that "another factor

[13] Ibid., pp. 54–55.
[14] Ibid., p. 56.
[15] Ibid., p. 19.
[16] Ibid., p. 99.
[17] Ibid., p. 117.

that adds to the complexity of this problem is that no one agency of Government can bear the entire responsibility of solving the problem.... Any attempt to deal with the problem leads inevitably into the field of labor relations into which the Defense Department should not inject itself." [18]

Representatives of these agencies agreed that the vast majority of the workers were loyal but that some of the unions representing the workers were Communist-dominated. Among these they especially singled out for mention UE, ACA, and MM as those consistently following the Party line. "Moreover, we cannot ignore the fact that officials of Communist dominated unions are in a position to obtain valuable information as an incident to their relationship with the workers of their unions who work in defense facilities. Likewise, there is not the least bit of doubt that if the policy of the Soviet Union called for strikes in various industries in the United States then the leadership of those unions would subjugate the membership to strike." [19] Although the threat to industrial security is serious, these dangers should not deter government agencies from exercising superlative caution.[20]

More sensitive to security risks because of its heavy responsibility, the Atomic Energy Commission acted early and rather decisively. Its success was attributed partly to fortuitous circumstances. Several congressional statutes specifically required AEC to take security precautions. Although the law did not mention Communist-dominated unions, AEC acted on its implied powers in proscribing UE and United Public Workers as being Communist-dominated and thus security risks. In securing NLRB support, the Commission was favored by the fact that the plants from which those unions were barred were government-owned. Besides, the officers of these unions had not signed the non-Communist affidavits at this time.

AEC, established in 1946 and having fulfilled statutory requirement to safeguard its classified operations, took action within two years to apply that authority to two Communist-dominated unions, although not specifically mandated to do so. In September, 1948, it took action. General Electric Company, which operated Knolls Atomic Power Laboratory on behalf of AEC, was ordered to disregard UE and have no further negotiations with it that affected the workers employed in Knolls Laboratory. Similarly, the University of Chicago was instructed not to deal with UPW in regard to workers employed at the Argonne National Laboratory. NLRB was notified at the same time.[21] The UPW beat a hasty retreat, announcing in the newspapers that "it had all been a mistake, they had no jurisdiction to organize in private companies anyhow and disappeared."

[18] *Ibid.*, pp. 19–20.
[19] *Ibid.*, pp. 18–19, 21, 26.
[20] *Ibid.*, p. 19.
[21] *Ibid.*, pp. 140–411.

Although it had "a local set-up and had some substantial membership," it had not yet been recognized and evidently did not feel it had sufficient ground for contesting AEC's order.[22]

On the other hand, UE was recognized as the bargaining agency at GE in Schenectady and undertook to fight the directive. Its task was made harder because of a NLRB special ruling to the effect that "any certification resulting from elections herein directed by the employees of the Atomic Energy operation will be conditioned upon compliance by the certified union with the security requirements of the Atomic Energy Commission, a matter exclusively within the jurisdiction of that Commission." [23] These notices were posted in the plant. Evidently the workers took due notice and acted accordingly in the representation election. In "production and maintenance out of 411 eligible votes 248" were cast "for IUE, 30 for UE, and 26 non-union. In the tool and die makers unit—41 eligible, 35 voted for IAM, 2 for UE, none for IUE. In the truck drivers unit—21 eligible, 17 voted for the Teamsters Union, AFL, 1 voted for UE, and 1 for IUE." [24] Thus where the workers were specifically put on notice that their economic interests would suffer if they voted UE, in that they would be without union representation, they rejected that union decisively.

Naturally, UE fought back furiously. Finding itself frustrated, it resorted to abuse in its communications to AEC. It castigated Chairman David E. Lilienthal: "You have yielded to the solicitations of GE, ignored the clear record of facts and joined in an attack against this Union far more cowardly, false and malignant than the one that was made in similar terms against yourself in the U.S. Senate when you were appointed to your present position. You should have no hope that you will be able to appease the ill will of your political enemies by demonstrating your ability to use against others the same smear technique that they have used against you." [25] UE also appealed to the courts, with no success.[26] As UE was still affiliated with CIO, the latter came to its defense. Philip Murray wrote to the AEC chairman on October 1, 1948: "I regret very much that the Atomic Energy Commission saw fit to send these letters blacklisting two international unions affiliated with the CIO without prior consultation, either with the interested parties or with responsible officials of the CIO." [27] Following UE expulsion, the officials of IUE approved AEC action and held it up

[22] *Ibid.*, p. 141.

[23] *Ibid.*, p. 136.

[24] *Loc. cit.*

[25] *Atomic Energy Development, 1947–1948*, U.S. Atomic Energy Commission, 1949, p. 201, hereafter cited as *Atomic Energy Development*. This report reproduced pertinent correspondence with the various interested parties, pp. 191–205.

[26] *Communist Domination of Unions, op. cit.*, pp. 135 and 398.

[27] *Atomic Energy Development*, p. 195; see also *Communist Domination of Unions, op. cit.*, p. 401.

as a model for other government agencies. Benjamin C. Segal, general counsel, stated, "As this committee knows, there is a very persuasive precedent for the procedure we recommend in the action taken by the Atomic Energy Commission with respect to the United Electrical, Radio and Machine Workers and the United Public Workers in 1948." [28]

The Munitions Board, although it was urged to act, contended it lacked authority to pursue a course similar to that of AEC. Whereas the latter owned the plants from which UE and UPW were barred, defense contracts were processed in privately own establishments. Most of those plants also manufacture for the general market. As a result, NLRB rulings on unfair labor practices present the same dilemma about which employers complained. If managements fulfilling defense contracts were required by the Munitions Board not to deal with Communist-dominated unions, the NLRB would intervene on behalf of the proscribed unions since their officers had filed non-Communist affidavits. Thus "any attempt to deal with the problem leads inevitably into the field of labor relations into which the Department of Defense should not inject itself." [29]

Chairman Small further explained how his agency differed from AEC and therefore could not ask NLRB to apply the same ruling it applied in AEC cases. The AEC Act gave it "broad and express authority . . . to deal with potential subversives. Contrast this with the more general authority which the Department of Defense has and which has to be extracted from a reading of three statutes. . . ." [30] Furthermore, because the plants contracting with Defense were privately owned, UE officials had failed to sign the non-Communist affidavits at the time AEC ordered GE not to recognize UE in those particular facilities.[31]

The Munitions Board nevertheless undertook to ascertain whether a course could be charted to cope with the problem. On its initiative, an inter-agency study, including AEC, Justice, NLRB, and Defense, was launched "in attempting to work out a mutual procedure by which private contractors who were directed by the AEC or the Department of Defense, to cease collective bargaining relations with UE or any other Communist dominated unions, were protected from the threat of being adjudged guilty of an unfair labor practice. . . . The only prerequisite which we insisted on was that in such cases our contracts would not be subjected to the hazard of a successful unfair labor practice charge being leveled at them by the NLRB. Unfortunately the NLRB was unable to give such assurance, since it was their opinion that the National Labor Relations Act did not sanction

[28] *Ibid.*, p. 285; for AEC in general, see *Digest of the Public Record, op. cit.*, pp. 95–97, 492, 520, and 626.
[29] *Communist Domination of Unions, op. cit.*, pp. 18–23.
[30] *Ibid.*, p. 23, also pp. 139, 142.
[31] *Ibid.*, p. 23.

it." This attitude on the part of the NLRB "put an end to further efforts on our part to work out an administrative solution to this problem. . . ." [32] Chairman Herzog had explained that the Board had hesitated in the first place to sustain the AEC directive to GE and he felt that the Board would not repeat its decision. He acknowledged, however, that he was not certain "what difference there is between the AEC and Munitions Board problems, and why the Board ruled one way in one instance and another in the other." [33]

In common with others, Chairman Small observed that section 9(h) was ambiguous. It was worded in the present tense, "is not now." And the clause on " 'belief' is likewise unsatisfactory." This terminology presented an additional problem.[34]

The Senate Subcommittee on Labor and Labor-Management-Relations, as was mentioned earlier, differed with the NLRB on its position that it lacked authority in this matter.[35] It recommended that "the NLRB in the exercise of such authority under existing law take judicial notice of . . . circumstances, as reflecting adversely on the good faith of an affiant of a non-Communist affidavit." [36] This urging the Board ignored until a change in its administration resulted in a change of its members.

But the courts had the final voice in the passing on the acts of government agencies. "Taking judicial action" as recommended by the Senate Subcommittee involved action on authority already implied in existing statutes, the diligence of the Department of Justice in prosecuting alleged violations, and finally court interpretation of the meaning of the laws and the power of the particular agency to implement them. As the cases came before them, the courts, like the government agencies, reacted variously.

With the change in the chairman, members, and general council, the Board embarked on a more vigorous application of section 9(h). The courts, however, limited its attempts to "guard against abuse of the processes of the Act resulting from evasions of the non-Communist affidavit requirement." The Board reported that "except in preventing concealment of officers (also known as 'fronting') this effort has been almost uniformly unsuccessful." [37]

The Board was successful in disciplining a Communist-dominated union by applying subsections of section 9(h). This action ultimately led to its dissolution, being the only case on record. On the basis of an administra-

[32] *Ibid.*, pp. 24–25, and 35–36.
[33] *Ibid.*, pp. 99, 101–102, 110, and 118.
[34] *Public Policy and Communist Domination of Certain Unions, Report of the Subcommittee on Labor and Labor-Management Relations to the Senate Committee on Labor and Public Welfare*, 83d Cong., 1st Sess., 1953, p. 14.
[35] *Ibid.*, p. 9; see also *20th Annual Report*, NLRB, 1955, pp. 9–14.
[36] *Ibid.*, p. 28.
[37] *19th Annual Report*, NLRB, 1954, p. 10.

tive investigation, the Board ruled that the National Union of Marine Cooks and Stewards had failed to furnish "to all of its members copies of its financial report." Consequently, the "Union was not in compliance" and it was "ordered that no further benefits of the Act be accorded to any of its affiliates or constituent unions." [38] This lack of compliance disqualified "the union from bringing cases to the Board or from participating in representation elections or making valid union shop agreements." [39]

Specifically, the blow was struck on representation elections. Because the NUMCS had been disqualified on Pacific Coast ships, the Board ordered an election to determine what union, if any, the workers wanted to represent them in collective bargaining. The Sailors Union of the Pacific, a subdivision of the International Seafarers Union, AFL, entered the lists. Feeling it would have a better chance to win the election if the bargaining unit were extended to cover all nonlicensed seafaring personnel, it petitioned the Board accordingly. The Board obliged in accordance with its statutory authority. Bridges' union, the ILWU, joined NUMCS in contesting the ruling but lost in the courts. In the election, the SUP won handsomely and NUMCS was thereby eliminated.[40]

Justice also began an active campaign on prosecuting trade-union leaders for "filing false non-Communist affidavits with the National Labor Relations Board by denying therein their membership in, and affiliation with the Communist Party." [41] A number of convictions were obtained in the lower courts and are now on appeal to the United States Supreme Court.

Among them were included such important and well-known Communist trade-union leaders as Hugh Bryson, president "of the former National Union of Marine Cooks and Stewards (Independent), Maurice Eugene Travis, former President and Secretary-Treasurer, of the International Union of Mine, Mill and Smelter Works, and Ben Gold, former President of Fur and Leather Workers Union." [42] Only the case of Ben Gold has so far reached the United States Supreme Court; because of a technicality, the Court, by a 6 to 3 vote, ordered the case remanded for a new trial.[43] Since then, the government has secured dismissal of the four-year indictment on the ground that certain material evidence is no longer available.[44]

[38] NLRB No. 129, March 1, 1955.
[39] NLRB release of March 1, 1955.
[40] See 218 Fed. 2d. 913, and No. 695; NLRB Brief in opposition, in the Supreme Court of the United States, Oct. term 1954, NUMCS and ILWU, Petitioners v. NLRB, et al.; see also J. C. Record, "The Rise and Fall of a Maritime Union," *Industrial and Labor Relations Review*, October, 1956, pp. 81–92.
[41] Department of Justice advance release, Dec. 27, 1956.
[42] *Ibid.*; see also *New York Times*, Jan. 13 and Dec. 1, 1956, and *Washington Post and Times Herald*, June 4 and Dec. 22, 1955.
[43] *New York Times*, Jan. 29, 1957.
[44] *New York Times*, May 10, 1957, and *Washington Post and Times Herald*, May 10, 1957.

In an effort to extend application of section 9(h), the Board was categorically repulsed by the Supreme Court. In 1954, the Board undertook to declare a union "out of compliance with the non-Communist affidavit requirement . . . because a union officer" falsified his affidavit. Three unions affected by this ruling took their cases to the courts, and in each case the reason for the Board's action was enlarged. In the one involving UE, the issue was simply whether the Board had authority to deprive a union of its compliance status when some of its officers falsified non-Communist affidavits. The Circuit Court of Appeals ruled that "the Board has no authority under the Act to deprive the unions of their compliance status under Sec. 9(h)." [45]

A new angle was introduced in the next case affecting the Fur Workers Union. The Board now claimed that the "membership was aware of the alleged falsity of the affidavit." The Board had rejected Gold's affidavit following his conviction in the lower court, drawing the "conclusion that the Union was aware of the falsity of his . . . affidavit." In a unanimous decision written by Judge David Bazalon, the Circuit Court ruled: "The absence of authority in the Board to deprive the Union of its compliance status under Sec. 9(h) cannot be supplied by membership awareness of the falsity of the affidavit. Congress explicitly provided a criminal penalty for false non-Communist affidavits. It is assumed that this threat of criminal sanctions would be a sufficient deterrent to false swearing by union officers. If these sanctions have proved insufficient, it is for Congress, not the Board, to provide." [46]

The Mine, Mill case was also decided against the Board on similar grounds.[47] During its October, 1956, term, the United States Supreme Court confirmed the rulings of the lower court. Justice Douglas spoke for the Court: "We conclude that the sole sanction of Sec. 9(h) is the criminal penalty imposed on the officer who files a false affidavit, not decompliance of the union nor the withholding of the benefits of the Act that are granted once the complying officers file their Sec. 9(h) affidavits." [48]

At present the Department of Justice is embarking on another approach to enforce section 9(h). In its December 27, 1956, release "concerning the progress made by the Internal Security Division in its fight to combat Communist subversion and treachery against the country," it declares that "the Government struck hard at the attempt of the Communist Party to

[45] New York Times, April 11, 1955; Farmer v. UE, 211 Fed. 2d. 39.
[46] Farmer v. IF&LWU, 22 Fed. 2d. 862.
[47] CIO News, Feb. 7, 1955; AFL News Reporter, Feb. 8 and Nov. 18, 1955; Washington Post and Times Herald, Feb. 10, 1955; for elaboration of the Board's arguments, see Determination and Order re Maurice Travis, et al., 111 NLRB No. 71 and Report of Hearing Officer, Travis, et al., Sept. 10, 1954.
[48] Amalgamated Meat Cutters and Butcher Workmen v. NLRB; see also New York Times, Dec. 11, 1956; and John Herling's Labor Letter, John Herling. Inc., Washington, D.C., Dec. 15, 1956.

infiltrate the labor movement. In November of this year 14 officials and staff members of the International Union of Mine, Mill and Smelter Workers (Ind.), were indicted for conspiracy to defraud the United States. They were specifically charged with having conspired with Arthur Bary, John Williamson, Gil Green and Fred Fine to obtain the services and facilities of the National Labor Relations Board for the benefit of the union, without lawfully and in good faith qualifying the union for those services and facilities. . . . It should be noted that Bary, Williamson, Green and Fine are top Communist Party functionaries who have been convicted of violating the Smith Act." [49]

The Department of Justice's intention to pursue this approach energetically and extensively is illustrated by the action of a Federal grand jury in Cleveland. Eight union leaders were indicted on charges of conspiracy with top Communist officials to file false non-Communist affidavits. The latter were convicted for violating the Smith Act. Some of the labor leaders indicted in Cleveland had been convicted previously in the lower courts for falsifying non-Communist affidavits.[50] Whether Justice will be more successful in the courts through this procedure than the NLRB was in attempting to deny compliance to a union because some of its officers falsified non-Communist affidavits, only the future will tell. Presumably the Justice Department is working on the hypothesis that if a considerable number of key officers and staff personnel are removed simultaneously, the rank and file will bestir itself and replace them with non-Communists. The Communists will certainly contest this new approach most vigorously by sparing no financial outlays.

Several congressional legislative enactments designed to discipline Communists have already indirectly, and may directly, aid the government in combating union domination. Some of the Communists convicted under the Smith Act, which makes it a felony to "conspire to teach or advocate the violent overthrow of the Government," [51] also turned out to be active in trade-union affairs. If they happened to be immigrants, they became subject to deportation. The Immigration and Naturalization Service had in a number of cases, as described above, deported Communist labor leaders and took similar action against those convicted under the Smith Act. Among them were several who had key roles in the labor field. John B. Williamson, former national labor secretary, CPUSA, one of the eleven Communist Party leaders convicted in 1949, was deported in 1955, following the completion of his prison term. Another foreign-born Communist leader, Irving Potash, left the country in 1955 on pain of deportation, after

[49] See also *New York Times*, Nov. 11, 1956.
[50] *New York Times*, Jan. 24, 1957.
[51] Departments of State and Justice, etc. Appropriations for 1956, Subcommittee of the Appropriations Committee, House of Representatives, 84th Cong., 1st Sess., 1955, pp. 281–295.

completing his prison service. Potash was a national committeeman of the Communist Party, and former manager of the New York Furriers' joint council. He entered the country clandestinely in 1957, was apprehended, and is now serving a prison term.[52]

Congressional and state investigations and aroused public concern stimulated additional Federal legislation which could be used to check Communist infiltration of unions. "During the summer of 1954 a comprehensive program of anti-subversion legislation was passed by Congress and signed by the President." One of these is the "witness Immunity Act of 1954," sustained by the Supreme Court. Whether it will be used against Communist trade-union leaders is still uncertain. In recognition of the importance and extent of prosecuting subversive activities, the Department of Justice created an Internal Security Division on July 9, 1954. This division "carries on in all matters relating to subversive activities and to our internal security at the point where the investigative activities of the FBI cease."

Since then the Department has initiated and pursued a more vigorous policy.[53] Recently, the Justice Department has also launched proceedings under the "membership" clause of the Smith Act against Communists. Some Communist labor leaders may be caught in this net.[54]

Congressional and other investigations and a growing public concern with the Communist problem forced Congress to recognize the need for more specific legislation and for a special government agency to cope with the threat. This action on the part of Congress acknowledged that neither the labor movement nor employers could satisfactorily counteract Communist activity in the unions. Congress also recognized that section 9(h) of the Taft-Hartley Act, other statutory legislation giving various government agencies implied power, and administrative action as in the Immigration and Naturalization Service are rather indirect and uncertain procedures, just as some court decisions have revealed. While none of these procedures were abolished or ordered discontinued, it was recognized, nevertheless, that they could not be relied upon to carry a task through thoroughly. In 1950, Congress took the first step toward the control of "Communist action or Communist front organizations." Previous legislation and administrative procedures were directed against individuals. The Subversive Activities Control Act of 1950 introduced a new departure in that it sought to discipline organizations. It was enacted over President Truman's veto.[55]

[52] *New York Times*, Feb. 18, March 5, and May 5, 1955; *Ibid.*, Jan. 5, 6, 12, 1957; see also Department of Justice Release, Dec. 27, 1956.
[53] Department of Justice Release, Dec. 27, 1956; Department of Justice Appropriations, etc. *op. cit.*, 1955, pp. 3, 306–307, and 281.
[54] *Ibid.*, p. 281.
[55] Pub. L. No. 831, 81st Cong., 2d Sess.; for a historical sketch of legislative background and digest of the act, see U.S. Subversive Activities Control Board, *First Annual Report*, 1951, pp. 1–4.

"The Board has no power to initiate proceedings or to conduct investigations. It functions in the field of subversive activities upon petition filed by the Attorney General alleged by him to be Communist Action or Communist front organizations." [56] It soon became clear that by limiting the Board's jurisdiction to "Communist action and Communist front organizations" the act did not make it possible to proceed against Communist-infiltrated and Communist-dominated unions.[57] The 1950 act was, therefore, amended by the Communist Control Act of 1954. This law gives additional power to the Board in that it "includes organizations believed by the Attorney General to be Communist infiltrated," defining such an organization as one "actively engaged in aiding or supporting a Communist-Action organization, a Communist foreign government or the world Communist movement." [58]

Based on the brief experience of SACB, delays in implementing the 1954 act are inevitable. Under the 1950 act, the Attorney General initiated cases against various Communist organizations and fronts. The first case was lodged against the Communist Party and was evidently intended as the test case before the courts. "The hearings took 14 months, the Attorney General presented 22 witnesses, the Party 3. Of the documents received, the Attorney General offered 462, the Party 45." [59] A comprehensive, ably prepared and thoroughly documented finding was issued by the Board April 20, 1953.[60] It found "the Communist Party of the United States is a Communist-action organization and required to register as such with the Attorney General of the United States.[61]

Following publication of the findings, the legal battle began. On June 17, 1953, the Communist Party filed an appeal with the United States Court of Appeals for the District of Columbia. The Party contended that the Act was unconstitutional, that the findings were contrary to the evidence. It also raised other legal questions. The case was argued on April 23, 1954.[62] On December 23, 1954, the Court affirmed the Board's order. The Party then carried its appeal to the Supreme Court, which granted a writ of certiorari on May 13, 1955.[63] It heard the case in 1956.

"In its appeal before the Court of Appeals, the party, in addition to

[56] *Ibid.*, p. 1; each succeeding report contains an analysis of the act, its functions, and a description of its yearly accomplishments.

[57] See particularly *Subversive Influence in Certain Labor Organizations, Hearings before the Subcommittee to Investigate the Administration of the Internal Security Act and Other Internal Security Laws of the Committee on the Judiciary,* U.S. Senate, 83d Cong., 2d Sess., 1954, testimony of Senator Barry Goldwater, pp. 45–73.

[58] U.S. Subversive Activities Control Board, *Fifth Annual Report,* 1955, pp. 5–6; *Sixth Annual Report,* 1956, pp. 5–6.

[59] *Ibid., First Annual Report,* pp. 7–9; *ibid., Second Annual Report,* pp. 7–8.

[60] Reprinted as Senate Document no. 41, 83d Cong., 1st Sess., 1953.

[61] Digest of findings in the *Fourth Annual Report,* 1954, of the U.S. Subversive Activities Control Board, pp. 9–10.

[62] *Ibid.,* p. 10.

[63] U.S. Subversive Activities Control Board, *Fifth Annual Report,* 1955, p. 12.

raising issues of fact as to the findings of the Board and to challenging the constitutionality of the Act, had moved the court to remand the case to the Board for the taking of evidence as to the credibility of three witnesses. . . . The Court of Appeals after consideration of the entire case overruled the Party's motion to remand and rendered judgment sustaining the Board's findings and the Act's constitutionality.

"Reversing the Appellate Court ruling on the motion with respect to the three witnesses, the Supreme Court on April 30, 1956, remanded the case with instructions to hold a hearing . . . to ascertain the credibility of the witnesses. . . . Other questions which the Party raised, including those of the Act's constitutionality, were left undecided. . . . As of June 30, 1956, the case was again pending before the Board." [64]

"After expunging the testimony of the questioned witnesses [December 18, 1956] the Board again found that the Communist Party was controlled and dominated by a foreign government and again ordered it to register as a Communist-Action organization as defined by the Act. The Party's attorneys have stated they will appeal." [65]

Of the cases thus far handled by SACB, one in particular may affect a number of Communist leaders in the way the Smith Act did. This is the case against the United May Day Committee, which, as the name implies, promoted, organized, and conducted annual May Day demonstrations in New York City. Its activities featured Communist propaganda. The case was lodged with the Board in 1953, it was heard in 1956, and the Board issued its findings and order on March 15, 1956, declaring that this committee "is a Communist front" organization.[66] Because it acted primarily through unions with prominent union leaders on its board, the committee has been in a position to exercise considerable influence in certain sectors of the labor movement. Labeling it as a "front organization" will undoubtedly affect its influence. Indeed, its effectiveness has already waned, not only because of the findings of the Board, but because of the general exposure of Communist tactics in the unions, thus alerting the non-Communist union membership and leaders. General reaction against Soviet Russia and the Communists because of recent developments in international affairs has also accounted for the loss of Communist influence. Simultaneously, various trade-union leaders who denied Communist connections were unmasked in the hearings of this case. Undoubtedly others will be exposed in other cases brought before SACB.[67]

[64] U.S. Subversive Activities Control Board, *Sixth Annual Report*, 1956, p. 11.

[65] U.S. Subversive Activities Control Board, Modified Report, Herbert Brownell, Jr., Attorney General of the United States v. The Communist Party of the United States of America, Docket No. 51–101, 1956; *New York Times*, Dec. 19, 1956.

[66] Brownell v. United May Day Committee, Docket No. 111–53, March 15, 1956; U.S. Subversive Activities Control Board, *Sixth Annual Report*, 1956, p. 9.

[67] For a list of cases, see *ibid.*, pp. 8–9.

Under the mandate of the 1954 act, the Attorney General announced and initiated a vigorous program against all allegedly Communist-dominated unions. Now, in addition to proceeding against Communist trade-union leaders, it was possible to act against unions directly.[68] Charges were lodged, up to this point, against two international unions notoriously regarded as Communist-dominated. On July 28, 1955, the Attorney General petitioned the Board to declare the independent International Union of Mine, Mill and Smelter Workers a Communist-infiltrated organization. It was charged that Mine, Mill "is and has been under domination and control of members of Communist organizations and has been made into an instrument for the promotion and advancement of the aims and objectives of Communist organizations, foreign Communist governments and the world Communist movement." It was further alleged that "without the knowledge of a great majority of the membership the union leaders had used its resources to support Communist organizations, Communist governments and the World Communist movement." [69]

On December 20, 1955, the Attorney General followed up his new procedure by petitioning SACB to declare the independent union, United Electrical, Radio and Machine Workers, a Communist-infiltrated union on charges similar to those made against MM.[70]

MM has thus far reacted by merely attacking the charges as a "Communist smear." But the superlatively combative and financially better off UE immediately took the case to the courts, aiming to block government proceedings. It claimed that the Communist Control Act of 1954 was invalid and demanded an injunction against the Attorney General and SCAB. The United States Court of Appeals of the District of Columbia, having previously pronounced the 1950 act as constitutional, dismissed the suit.[71] Thus far this case has not been heard by SACB.[72]

A *New York Times* correspondent waxed eloquent in reporting the new policy. "This government brandished a new weapon against a new adversary today in its warfare on subversion.... The Department of Justice used it for the first time" against an important union. "It also was the first action in the field of alleged subversion against a labor group. Justice Department officials indicated that they might brandish the weapon against other unions that may become captives of an allegedly disloyal leadership." [73]

But the judicial process is slow, as is commonly known. The highest

[68] Department of Justice Appropriations for 1956, *op. cit.*, pp. 3 and 6; *New York Times*, July 8, 1955.
[69] Release by the Department of Justice, July 28, 1955, and Petition, Brownell v. Mine, Mill to SACB, mimeographed, n.d.; *New York Times*, July 29, 1955.
[70] *New York Times*, Dec. 21, 1955; *John Herling's Labor Letter*, Dec. 24, 1955.
[71] *New York Times*, April 6, 1956.
[72] U.S. Subversive Activities Control Board, *Sixth Annual Report*, 1956, p. 8.
[73] Luther A. Huston, *New York Times*, July 29, 1955.

court has not yet passed on the constitutionality of the 1950 act. And SACB has only begun hearings on the MM case brought under the 1954 act. It will take several years before these acts can be enforced, if at all.

Nevertheless, the Communist leaders foresee a serious threat in the 1954 Communist Control Act. By way of penalty, it provides that unions found to be Communist-infiltrated be denied the facilities of the NLRB. This action would make the union ineligible "as representative or bargaining agent" for its members. Moreover, if such union had "heretofore been certified by the National Labor Relations Board . . . [it] shall on petition of no less than 20 percent of the membership, conduct new elections to determine whether the employees desire different representation." [74] With the Communist-infiltrated union excluded from the ballot, the affected employees would have no choice but to vote for a rival union, should they desire to continue having a labor organization to look after their interests. Judging by results in the Schenectady case and others, the Communist-infiltrated unions would find themselves repudiated by their members and by other employees. This dismal prospect threw the Communist union leaders into a frenzied panic. They could not circumvent this act as they did NLRA section 9(h) when they boldly signed non-Communist affidavits. Nor, if the act were declared constitutional, could they expect exemption of the union even though the members were aware that the leaders had Communist sympathies. Under the 1954 act, these unions would lose their collective-bargaining rights and status with the NLRB. They would, therefore, become easy prey of rival unions. Such a penalty is indeed stringent.

Always on the alert for escape provisions, Communist leaders believe they have found a clause in the act that might save them from complete dissolution. In order not to discommode non-Communist unions, the leaders of which opposed this measure,[75] the act declares that "affiliates in good standing with labor organizations whose policies and activities have been directed to opposing Communism are presumed, *prima facie*, not to be infiltrated" [italics in original].[76] There is some difference of opinion whether Communist-infiltrated unions could find complete protection under this clause by amalgamating with AFL and CIO unions, or with other labor organizations. At any rate, the Communist trade-union leaders began frantically to seek cover in established AFL and CIO unions. The manner and success of their shopping around is discussed in the next chapter. In the meantime, the new tactic was aired publicly. Senator John Marshall Butler, author of the 1954 act, aroused and disturbed, declared: "I suggest that the Department of Justice immediately look into the obvious attempt of communist-tainted unions to don the cloak of respectability by seeking

[74] U.S. Subversive Activities Control Board, *Fifth Annual Report*, 1955, pp. 5–6.
[75] Subversive Influence in Certain Labor Unions, *op. cit.*, pp. 442–453.
[76] U.S. Subversive Activities Control Board, *Fifth Annual Report*, 1955, p. 5.

to affiliate themselves with respectable and responsible unions of the American Federation of Labor and the Congress of Industrial Organizations.

"I am certain that the AFL and CIO are aware of this effort to infiltrate patriotic unions and that they will move vigorously to resist it. But the Attorney General, who is charged with the enforcement of the antisubversive statutes, could give valuable assistance to them by moving vigorously against this typically Communist scheme." [77]

The AFL and CIO leaders reacted in a similar way. At its 1955 Miami Beach, Florida, winter session, President George Meany reported to the AFL executive council, warning against a mass effort of Communist-led unions to enter the federation. He served notice that the AFL would not permit itself to be used as "an umbrella for the Communists to come in under until the rain stops." He declared further that "the new Communist line is to try to look respectable, but we will be careful not to take in any Communist unions. We are certainly not providing a haven for reds kicked out of the CIO." [78]

The CIO also acted. At the top of page 2 in its official paper, a "Note to All" appeared, running the entire width of the page. It was entitled, "CIO Warns Unions on New Red Infiltration Tactics." Its first paragraph read: "A warning that the Communist Party apparently has a program of 'infiltrating its remaining organizations into the AFL and the CIO' in order to evade the Communist Control Act was sent all CIO affiliates last week by CIO General Counsel Arthur J. Goldberg." CIO unions were cautioned that "they must be careful to distinguish between genuine rank-and-file rebellions against the Communist leadership of such unions and the camouflaged attempts of the red leadership itself to seek shelter within the covering cloak of CIO affiliates." [79]

The extent to which AFL and CIO unions observed this warning will be discussed in the succeeding chapter. It would also seem that what was considered a body blow to the Communist-dominated unions administered by the government through this legislation has not yet materialized. It did, however, contribute to increasing the successful raiding operations already begun by the non-Communist unions. With the exception of the ILWU, Communist-dominated unions seem to be slowly disintegrating. If they survive, it will be as mere shadows of their former selves. Perhaps the prosecutions under the Communist Control Act will eventually eliminate them entirely. But the Communists are not surrendering. They are already beginning to infiltrate the unions again through new tactics discussed in the following chapter.

[77] Release, March 17, 1955; *New York Times*, March 18, 1955.
[78] *AFL News Reporter*, Feb. 4, 1955; see also *New York Times*, Feb. 3, 1955.
[79] *CIO News*, Feb. 21, 1955.

24

Running for Cover—
Current Developments

Despite the fact the Communists were unnerved by the new legislation and by their reverses in the labor movement, they set about devising strategy that would enable them to maintain their position within the unions where they had a foothold. Part of this strategy consisted of trying to affiliate the unions they controlled with non-Communist unions. The explanation of this new tactic—as well as of their failures in the labor movement—took the form of their customary self-criticism: an official Communist declaration claimed that errors in judgment had been made because the Communists, in adhering strictly to doctrinaire preconceptions, had misread conditions.

Pursuing their habitual and extremely didactic approach, accompanied by violent verbal flagellations, the Communists readily admit the failure of their former trade-union policy. Their customary self-criticism almost takes the form of psychoanalysis as they publicly reveal their innermost thoughts. Because their permanent accomplishments are few and they therefore have few genuine boasts, they tend to overmagnify, for dramatic emphasis, their errors, which are many. Thus, they offer a lengthy explanation of their rout in the labor movement. "Our policies and tactics in regard to the most important aspect of our work, our relations with the labor movement, did not escape the influence of sectarianism. We did not view the labor movement realistically in the light of its actual level of development. Rather, our point of departure was our own concept of what the labor movement should be. We, therefore, projected standards of achievement for Communists and Progressives in the labor movement, as well as for the labor movement as a whole, based on our estimate of what was urgently needed, rather than on what was possible under existing conditions.

"This led to cumulative strains in the relations between the Party and the most friendly sections of the labor movement. It was in great part responsible for isolating us from the membership and the leadership of the unions toward whom we often adopted not only a sectarian, but even a factional, attitude. This was demonstrated not only in the failure to wage a skillfull and consistent fight to prevent an irreconcilable rupture with the progressive and center forces in several CIO unions, but also in the development of a policy of waging the sharpest struggle against those we characterized as the 'center forces' in the CIO, and as 'Social Democrats.'

"Within the conservative led unions, this sectarian approach also proved to be very costly. Communists and Progressives were often faced with the alternative of either pursuing policies which led to their isolation, to loss of positions of leadership, and often to loss of job in the shop as well; or taking a more flexible position and being branded as opportunists by the Party. The history of the past period is replete with examples of both consequences. In the vast majority of cases it led to the isolation of the most militant trade unionists from the masses of the workers. In many cases, it caused militant and progressive workers and union leaders to break relations of long standing with our party. These mistakes are, in large part, responsible for our failure to build the strength of the left in the A.F.L. and the conservative led unions of the C.I.O." Consequently, it is necessary to make a "serious effort to influence the left-led unions to reenter the mainstream of the labor movement." [1]

Their various efforts to seek haven by merging with non-Communist unions do not lend themselves readily to thorough documentation. Sufficient information has been gathered, nevertheless—primarily in informal conversations with labor men and others who, on the whole, prefer to remain anonymous—and supported by limited documentary data to construct an authentic account.

The first—and still—prime effort of the Communists and of left-led unions to enter the "mainstream of the labor movement" was to preserve their organizations intact, preferably as autonomous affiliates of other unions. Jurisdictional considerations, similarity in occupations, or work performed by members, were disregarded. The object was to get under cover by joining a legally accepted union. Thus, the three outstanding Communist-dominated unions, NMU, UE, and ILWU, made overtures to the International Brotherhood of Teamsters. President Dave Beck suggested that they contact other unions with related or overlapping jurisdictions.[2] In other instances, the Communist trade-union leaders did approach unions having either parallel or allied jurisdiction. MM fervently solicited the AFL Metal Trades Department. It also tried the Molders, Operating Engineers, and Building Laborers. UE contacted the International Asso-

---

[1] Draft of a political resolution to be submitted by the national committee of the Communist Party of the U.S.A. for the national convention, *New York Times*, Sept. 23, 1956.

[2] *New York Times*, March 9 and 18, 1955.

ciation of Machinists and the IUE. While making public denials, Bridges has been attempting to insinuate his union into a merger with the International Longshoremen's Association, Independent, expelled by the AFL as dominated by racketeers.[3]

Only two Communist-dominated unions succeeded in their efforts to amalgamate with other unions. Technically, it was only one. The Fur Workers were taken in by the Amalgamated Meat Cutters and Butcher Workmen, following long, disturbing negotiations over the AFL's original objections. The other union, FE, had merged with UE following the expulsion of both of them from the CIO. Later, most of FE withdrew from UE and amalgamated with the UAW. The admonition of the CIO and AFL to insist on a complete house cleaning was not demanded of these unions when they were taken over. It is doubtful whether all the Communists and fellow-traveler leaders have yet been eliminated. Furthermore, when the regular unions accepted subdivisions of the Communist-dominated unions, they rarely took the necessary precaution of making certain that tainted leaders were not included.

The path toward the amalgamation of the Fur Workers and the Meat Cutters was indeed a rough one. Negotiations were extended, postponed, and renewed. During the procedure, the movement—AFL and CIO leaders as well as outsiders—expressed concern and, in some cases, strong opposition. There was also dissension within the Fur Workers themselves. Finally, a non-Communist element consisting mostly of leather workers in the New England states spearheaded the opposition and affiliated with the CIO.[4]

Negotiations between the Meat Cutters and Fur Workers were conducted for well over a year. As criticism and general comment increased, the AFL executive council acted. In January, 1954, it was reported that "high officials would not approve a proposed merger of the Fur Union with the . . . Butcher Workmen."[5] By the end of that year, the AFL executive council, after hearing the president and secretary-treasurer in a "special session held in Washington, unanimously disapproved of [the] proposed merger."[6] Joining in the opposition, "the CIO Executive Board sharply criticized the leadership of the AFL Meat Cutters . . . for the unscrupulous

[3] *New York Times*, April 5, 16, and 22; July 20; Sept. 26; Nov. 11, 17, 1955; Oct. 28 and Nov. 11, 1956; *John Herling's Labor Letter*, John Herling, Inc., Washington, D.C., Oct. 29, 1955; *AFL-CIO News*, May 12, 1956; *Fortune*, June, 1956, p. 61; see also Philip Taft, "Independent Unions and Merger," *Industrial and Labor Relations Review*, Cornell University, Ithaca, N.Y., April, 1956, pp. 438–440; *Proceedings of the 45th Annual Convention*, Metal Trades Department, AFL, Sept. 13, 1954, p. 31.

[4] For a summary of the general reaction toward taking these two unions into the mainstream of organized labor, see *John Herling's Labor Letter*, Aug. 6, 1955.

[5] *New York Times*, Jan. 4, 1954.

[6] *AFL News Reporter*, Dec. 17, 1954.

opportunism with which it is pushing a merger with the Communist-dominated Fur and Leather Workers." [7]

Despite opposition, negotiations proceeded between these two unions. The Fur Workers Union made various changes by way of "decommunization." As the chief concession, the merger agreement provided that Ben Gold and Irving Potash, former key officers, were to be eliminated. On the other hand, the Fur Workers' interests were to be safeguarded by that union's being made a department of the Meat Cutters with autonomy to "set its own economic policies and elect its own officers." Evidently to demonstrate that the procedure was democratic, it was agreed that the merger conditions would be acted upon at a special convention of the Fur Workers so as to give the arrangement validity; the convention overwhelmingly approved, and so did the local unions when the matter was submitted to them. At stake were about 9 million dollars in the treasuries of the International and its locals.[8] Apparently because of continued criticism, the Meat Cutters emphasized that the new department would be subject to their union constitution. The leaders stressed particularly the provisions which bar subversives from membership and authorize confiscation of the treasury and property of any local that bolts the merged union.[9] When an objection still existed on the part of AFL leaders, the two unions delayed merger action, but negotiations were continued. Aware of the determination to consummate the merger, "the AFL Executive Council, for the second time, warned the Meat Cutters and Butcher Workmen that if it persisted in a proposed merger with the Fur Workers Union, it may face possible ouster at the 1955 September convention." [10] Within two weeks following this warning of possible expulsion by the executive council, the Meat Cutters International executive board, defying the AFL executive council, approved the merger. Shortly thereafter, the Fur Workers announced that a referendum vote of its members resulted in "an overwhelming approval of [the] merger." Simultaneously, Patrick E. Gorman, secretary-treasurer and dominating figure in the Meat Cutters, declared that his union did not regard the completion of the merger as defiance of the AFL. He repeated that the necessary safeguards had been taken to discipline the Communists in compelling officers and staff members of the Fur Union to file non-Communist oaths in order to hold their jobs in the new department.[11] Considering that some of these persons had previously signed non-Communist affidavits and that the Communists had devised means of evading the provisions, this was indeed a gratuitous gesture.

[7] *CIO News*, Feb. 7, 1955.
[8] *New York Times*, Jan. 3 and 23, 1955; *Labor Fact Book*, International Publishers Co., Inc., New York, 1955, pp. 98–99.
[9] *New York Times*, Jan. 30, 1955.
[10] *AFL News Reporter*, Feb. 11, 1955; *New York Times*, Feb. 1 and 5, 1955.
[11] *New York Times*, Feb. 18 and 23, 1955.

The Meat Cutters, however, proceeded to demonstrate their good faith in tangible form. In the New Jersey–New York area, where the Communists were strongest, the Meat Cutters' district council initiated a cleansing program. It took a spectacular step related not directly to dispelling Communist influence in the union but to making an impression by closing a camp in New York State, adjacent to New York City and the New Jersey area, described as a "Communist indoctrination center in which swimming and tennis were incidental to Marxist education courses." The value of this resort was estimated at 3 million dollars. More directly, delegates to the district council were to take a non-Communist oath as provided in the overhauled bylaws. The revised rules also prohibited any officer's or delegate's allowing his union connections to be used in political campaigns or in petitions for fund-raising appeals, except where such political activity had been endorsed by the parent union or the district council. Trial machinery was also instituted for disciplining any local that insists upon sending delegates who violate these rules to the district council.[12]

At the spring session of the executive council, the Meat Cutters' leaders appeared in order to defend their position in admitting the Fur Workers. Confronted with a changed situation, AFL leaders proceeded along a different course. Although still threatening expulsion, they began to prod the Meat Cutters into cleaning house by extending the AFL's time of decision so that the Meat Cutters could purge themselves of Communists. Through President George Meany, AFL leaders indicated that, while they were satisfied the union was making progress, they did not consider that the task was completed; they decided to consider the affair again at their summer meeting.[13]

Communist purging continued simultaneously with tilting with the executive council. The "decommunizing" program in the strategic New Jersey–New York area encountered difficulties. It became necessary to postpone indefinitely the election of union officers by the 15,000 furriers in this region's New Furriers' joint council. Apparently, some of the candidates for office were on the list of those intended for purging by the parent union. Ultimately, eleven officers were expelled from this fur unit, and expulsion of officers was also carried out in Canada.[14] The joint fur council was placed in trusteeship.

These achievements were reported to the summer 1955 meeting of the executive council in session in Chicago. It had before it a staff report "made just before the Chicago meeting, which said that the Fur Workers seemed just as infiltrated as previously ... with some exceptions." According to Meany, "the AFL was not convinced that sufficient progress had been

[12] *New York Times*, March 27, 1955.
[13] *Ibid.*, May 4, 1955.
[14] *New York Times*, June 20 and Aug. 10, 1955.

made in ridding the Fur Workers of Communists." Still skeptical of whether a thorough job had been done, the AFL executive council postponed its decision until fall. With the threat of expulsion still dangling over the Meat Cutters' heads, their secretary-treasurer announced that, unless he was sure the Fur Workers had been cleansed of Communists to the satisfaction of the AFL, he would exercise the option to end the merger. He further declared that he did not want to put the prestige of either the AFL or the Meat Cutters in jeopardy.[15]

Shortly before the 1955 fall executive council meeting, the Meat Cutters announced that "more than 100 Communists" had been removed from its fur and leather division.[16] And a week later, the AFL News Reporter, official organ, printed the following account in its October 28, 1955, issue:

"AFL WITHDRAWS OBJECTION TO BUTCHERS, FUR MERGER

"New York City.—The American Federation of Labor objections to absorption of the Fur and Leather Workers by the Amalgamated Meat Cutters and Butcher Workmen were withdrawn by the AFL Executive Council in meeting here.

"George Meany, president, said that the Meat Cutters had done a good job in eliminating Communist control from the Fur Workers. All known Communists have been forced to resign or have been barred from running for re-election for top leadership posts in the Fur Workers, and from offices in locals in New York City, Chicago, Los Angeles and Canada.

"The Meat Cutters also have closed the doors of a summer camp run by the Fur Workers in New York state, which had been reportedly used to train Communists.

"Archie McVickars, AFL organizer, has been assigned to work with the Meat Cutters for the next six months to aid in further cleaning Communists from the union. He will report back to Meany."

In knowledgeable labor circles there is still skepticism as to whether Communist influence in the fur branch of the Meat Cutters has been effectively eliminated. Many of the well-informed hold serious reservations.[17]

The cleansing treatment of the fur unit and the not too happy experience of the FE as a part of the UAW, while not resulting in a complete purge,

[15] AFL News Reporter, Aug. 12, 1955; New York Times, Aug. 10, 1955 and Aug. 25, 1955; Washington Post and Times Herald, Aug. 10, 1955.

[16] Washington Post and Times Herald, Oct. 22, 1955.

[17] Fortune, February, 1955, pp. 66 and 68; for the Communist record of the IF and LWU, see Digest of the Public Record of Communism in the United States, Fund for the Republic, New York, 1955, pp. 93, 94, 158, 519, 554, 555, 574, 587; and for a study of its activities in Massachusetts and the surrounding area, see Massachusetts, Special Commission on Communism, Subversive Activities and Related Matters within the Commonwealth, House Document no. 3080, Fourth Interim Report, July 25, 1955.

lessened the ardor of the Communist-dominated unions for merging. More cautious now in their overtures, their original frantic stampede has slowed down to a devious crawl. Their leaders are still shopping around, but much more carefully. In the meantime, the mergers that are being consummated are on a regional and local basis.

Although the national trade-union centers and their affiliates rebuffed overtures of the Communist-infiltrated national unions to affiliate as solid entities, they have taken advantage of their panicky attitude to wean away subordinate units as district councils and locals. Some of these, genuinely disturbed by the Communist complexion of their international, broke away as soon as the issue became acute. Others, and particularly their leaders, were merely seeking a safe haven for themselves in imitation of their superiors at national headquarters. It also appears that, in some instances, these "defections" were encouraged by Communist sources as a means of salvaging as much as possible in order to obtain a foothold through "plants" in non-Communist unions. This new tactic seems to increase in proportion to the diminution of merger prospects on the national level.

The non-Communist unions, on the other hand, in their competitive eagerness to profit as much as possible, embarked on energetic campaigns, thereby uncritically accepting the defecting units. Stimulated by jurisdictional rivalries, they disregarded their own previous experience with Communist infiltration, as most leaders did in the thirties and forties. In practice, they also paid no heed to the warnings of their parent trade-union centers, although they voiced the latter's sentiments.

In some situations, these jurisdictional rivalries resulted in bitter controversies among non-Communist unions. Indeed, the rivalry has led some non-Communist unions to collaborate with Communist unions in conducting collective-bargaining negotiations. In attacking MM, the United Steelworkers of America–CIO undertook to include all the workers in and around nonferrous mines; that is, they tried to organize on an industrial-union basis, including the surface and subsurface workers, as they did with iron mines at the beginning of their existence. But unions affiliated with the AFL Metal Trades Department took exception. They claimed the "workers properly coming under the jurisdiction of the crafts or the maintenance work and operation of the mills and smelters." A strong precedent existed in the Butte, Montana, mining region that MM honored. In order to counteract the Steel Workers' union, the Metal Trades suggested that the AFL issue a charter to either the MM or its locals operating under the surface, thereby leaving other workers to the jurisdiction of the "crafts." Thus far, the parent body has failed to act on this recommendation.[18]

Since MM has not challenged the jurisdiction of the crafts, they have collaborated with it in collective-bargaining negotiations. "In the summer

[18] Proceedings, 45th convention, Metal Trades Department, AFL, Sept. 13, 1954, pp. 31, 86, 125; *ibid.*, 47th convention, 1956, pp. 35–36 and 106–107.

of 1955, over a dozen unions battled together ... in a joint strike for a fair wage increase and other improvements from major mining and smelting companies ... (Rocky Mountain and adjacent areas). Newspapers generally, in reporting the strike, had mentioned only Mine, Mill and Smelter Workers, which is the bargaining agency for production workers. Actually, the walkout is sponsored by a 'joint council,' embracing also the rail labor organizations and other AFL craft unions. Participating in this joint council were "MM, Machinists, Electrical Workers and other rail shop craft unions." [19] Employers seem to prefer the present arrangement to one industrial union and have indirectly encouraged the antagonism of the other unions toward the Steel Workers.

As a result of union rivalry and their employers' favorable attitude, MM has been reasonably successful in staving off serious union attacks. James A. Brownlow, president of the Metal Trades Department, concedes that MM has "the vast majority of employees in the industry." [20] It is questionable whether with the present union setup other unions can win away the workers from MM. A resolution of the Metal Trades Department describes the reasons: "It is generally believed that the metal miner is desirous of having a union of his own. He does not want to be included in a union of steel workers or of any other group. He definitely wants the word 'mining' to be associated with any organization of which he is a member." [21] It is not only in metal mining proper that MM has retained its position; it has also retained most of its followers in allied fields. Still the dominant union in the copper-fabrication region of the Connecticut River Valley and in other areas such as Rome, New York, its relations with management are as amicable as that of any other union.[22]

Although other unions have succeeded in winning away units from MM, they were chiefly on the periphery or in new organizing areas like uranium mining and processing. In a previous chapter, it was mentioned that the Steel Workers have made a slight dent in MM membership; other unions have also made limited gains. The AFL Operating Engineers defeated Mine, Mill and Smelter Workers in a National Labor Relations Board election at the Duvall Potash plant in Carlsbad, New Mexico.[23] And the Stone and Allied Workers, CIO, won over "the hardrock miners of the Potash Company of America from the Mine, Mill Union" at Carlsbad, New Mexico.[24]

The Communist unions' most successful efforts in thwarting MM are

[19] *Labor*, July 16 and Aug. 27, 1955; *New York Times*, Aug. 13 and 16, 1955.
[20] Proceedings, 47th convention, Metal Trades Department, 1956, p. 281.
[21] *Ibid.*, 1956, pp. 135–136.
[22] *New York Times*, Feb. 9, July 12 and 26, 1955; *Washington Post and Times Herald*, July 9, 1955.
[23] *AFL News Reporter*, July 1, 1955.
[24] *CIO News*, Sept. 12, 1955; *Labor Fact Book, op. cit.*, 1955, pp. 94–96, for description of MM efforts to resist raiding.

in unorganized areas. With uranium discoveries, the Metal Trades Department, through its nonferrous metals councils, has made considerable progress in extending its organization against MM. Nevertheless, Brownlow estimates that the Metal Trades Department unions have only about 14,000 or 15,000 members in nonferrous mining. On the other hand, MM has some 40,000, and other unions have between 2,000 and 3,000 members.[25] In the meantime, sentiment in the merged movement is developing against collaboration with MM or any other Communist-dominated union. The Steel Workers have succeeded in inducing one rival AFL union to cancel its alliance with MM. The leaders of the International Teamsters Union let it be known, after the AFL-CIO merger, that the mutual assistance pact entered into between its western conference of Teamsters and MM in December, 1955, was "dormant." [26] Similarly, the nonferrous metals council of the Metal Trades Department, in convention in April, 1956, "requested that Council affiliates cease unity meetings with metal unions outside the AFL-CIO." [27]

More effective inroads on UE have been made by both CIO and AFL unions. IUE-CIO made the greatest headway, but the Machinists, International Brotherhood of Electrical Workers, UAW, Steel Workers, and others are also cutting in on UE. There is a difference of opinion among top UE officials concerning policy in saving remnants of their following in unions where their hold is being dislodged. A factor which weakens their position is the imminent deportation of their director of organization, James G. Matles, to his native Rumania; Matles is one of their key people.[28] UE lacks the advantage of tradition that MM enjoys in operating as the sole union in its particular industry. Unions seeking UE affiliates also operate on an industrial union basis and do not seek to split the workers into their respective crafts or occupations. Moreover, IUE and IBEW indicate by their names that they are unions operating in the electric equipment industry. But even such unions as the Machinists and UAW have been organizing electrical workers for some time. As comparatively newly organized workers, however, they lack the mantle of tradition worn by MM.

UE seems to be slowly disintegrating. At its peak, it was credited with having more than 500,000 members. At present it claims 175,000, but authoritative sources give it less than 100,000.[29] UE is still seeking, by

[25] Proceedings, Metal Trades Department, *op. cit.*, 1956, pp. 27–28, 106–107, 135–136.
[26] *New York Times*, March 9, 1956.
[27] *AFL-CIO News*, April 21, 1956.
[28] *John Herling's Labor Letter*, Oct. 29, 1955; *New York Times*, Feb. 26, 1957.
[29] *John Herling's Labor Letter*, Oct. 29, 1955; *Fortune*, June, 1955, p. 61; *New York Times*, July 11 and 19, 1955, and May 15, 1956; *Labor Fact Book, op. cit.*, 1955, pp. 97–98.

various means, to become part of the mainstream of organized labor. It still desires amalgamation as an autonomous unit with either IUE or some other non-Communist union. But this arrangement is out of the question since article IV, section 6 of the AFL-CIO constitution forbids, under penalty of suspension, accepting into the fold any organization that "has seceded or has been expelled" by the federation or its component units. Because of UE persistence, the IUE executive board recently repeated its position that "there will be no merger of the Electric, Radio and Machine Workers and the unaffiliated United Electric Workers." The executive board also made clear that "there cannot be a no-raid agreement between UE and IUE" nor "joint collective bargaining by the two unions." [30] In the meantime, subordinate UE units are being welcomed and absorbed by rival unions. The bulk of these units are choosing to affiliate with IUE.

As previously indicated, ILWU has not been affected in its main operations on the Pacific Coast docks and on the docks, plantations, and in other sectors of Hawaii. Indeed, a subcommittee on internal security reported to the Senate that ILWU has succeeded in penetrating the Port of New Orleans. This is the first instance of ILWU's getting a foothold in an Atlantic or Gulf port.[31] On the fringe of its operations, ILWU has met with some opposition, mostly from the Teamsters. This union also claims jurisdiction over inland warehouses and related services. To illustrate, ILWU Local 208 had a contract with Walgreen's drug warehouse in Chicago for sixteen years. In 1950, the Teamsters Union challenged its representation in an NLRB election. The first test resulted in no majority for either contestant. The Teamsters lost in the runoff election. Undaunted, the Teamsters pursued an energetic campaign in which communism was an important issue. Bread-and-butter issues were also raised. In another NLRB election which was held in 1957, the Teamsters Miscellaneous Warehousemen's Local 781 won by a decisive majority of 138 to 110.[32]

Of the eleven unions expelled by CIO, two have succeeded in retaining their individual identities by managing to carve out sanctuaries in which they function very effectively. Although the *Directory of National and International Labor Unions in the United States*, prepared by the competent and professionally objective Bureau of Labor Statistics, lists the United

[30] *AFL-CIO News*, May 12, 1956.
[31] *New York Times*, March 1 and 17, 1957; see also *Communism on the Water Front, Hearings before the Subcommittee to Investigate the Administration of the Internal Security Act and Other Internal Security Laws of the Senate Committee on the Judiciary*, U.S. Senate, 84th Cong., 2d Sess., 1956, part 30; *Ibid., Report for year 1956*, Section III, pp. 33–40 and 48.
[32] *The Teamster*, January–February, 1957, pp. 16, 25.

Public Workers under "unions which are inactive or have gone out of existence," the Senate's subcommittee on internal security found it most active, both physically and vocally, in Hawaii. Under the patronage of the ILWU, the UPW has proved an effective ally in dominating the union situation in that island territory.[33]

Similarly, the American Communication Association is operating with considerable success in its particular enclave. Its chief stronghold is in the New York metropolitan area's Western Union office and in RCA Cables, where it is certified as the bargaining agent by NLRB. These offices handle international communications as well as domestic business. In this connection, they service the various branches of the armed services and other government departments. In addition, ACA has a membership of some proportions among maritime radio operators. Public hearings of government investigation bodies reveal that it is still completely Communist-dominated. In spite of these exposures and the challenge of the Commercial Telegraphers Union, AFL-CIO, it is retaining its hold on a strategic and sensitive sector of the communications industry.[34]

But perhaps even their present favorable position can be shaken if the Subversive Activities Control Board rules that these unions are Communist-dominated, providing the Board's findings are upheld by the courts. By losing their NLRB status and being officially designated, through judicial process, as Communist-tainted, they will undoubtedly become more vulnerable. It is true that the United Mine Workers Union is thriving in spite of its losing its NLRB status because its officers refused to sign non-Communist affidavits. But its privileged position is not comparable to that of the Communist-controlled unions. No union has contested its jurisdiction in the coal mining areas in which it operates. Besides, the issue of communism is absent.

By taking over whole units, including their officers, without screening, non-Communist unions are undoubtedly giving refuge to Communists and their allies in important union positions. This procedure is being justified chiefly on the ground that it is the best course to follow to avoid friction that might prove very costly and might even destroy the organization involved. Assurances are offered that the suspected Communists are being

[33] *Subcommittee to Investigate the Administration of the Internal Security Act and Other Internal Security Laws of the Committee on the Judiciary,* U.S. Senate, *Report for 1956,* sec. 3, pp. 35–39, 48; H. S. Roberts, "Hawaii, Labor Relations," *Labor Review,* U.S. Department of Labor, December, 1955, pp. 1431–1439.

[34] *Subcommittee to Investigate the Administration of the Internal Security Act and Other Internal Security Laws of the Committee on the Judiciary,* U.S. Senate, *Report for 1956,* sec. 3, pp. 47–48; see also subcommittee releases, May 8 and 9, June 27, 1957, mimeographed; committee hearings of Nov. 21, 1956, part 44 of *Scope of Soviet Activity in the United States; Investigation of Communist Penetration of Communication Facilities,* part 1, House Committee on Un-American Activities, 85th Cong., 1st Sess., 1957; and *Labor Fact Book, op. cit.,* 1955, pp. 96–97, describing trade agreements with RCA Communications, Inc. and Western Union Cables.

watched and can be managed. This reasoning resembles that of the labor leaders in the thirties and forties. By way of further assurance, present labor leaders—like their confreres earlier—point to their past experience with the Communists to indicate they can cope with the present threat.

Two internationals have already initiated formal procedures for eliminating Communists from leadership units taken over from Communist-dominated unions. These two instances are in addition to the one of the Meat Cutters when they attempted to purge their Fur Workers Division.

A novel procedure was announced by the Teamsters Union. Two business agents of a local consisting of New York City employees had formerly been officials of the Communist-dominated United Public Workers. They had appeared before some of the government investigation committees and had pursued the usual course of others suspected of being Communists. A rival union publicized the facts. International President Dave Beck cautioned his New York regional office in charge of this local that it must conduct itself in a manner beyond reproach. Regional officials then decided on an unprecedented course: they announced they would form a committee of prominent citizens to hold hearings in order to decide whether or not the two accused business agents were still pro-Communist. Names of eminent specialists in the field of labor relations and civil liberties were mentioned as possible persons to serve on such a fact-finding committee; the fact-finding session was to be public and would be conducted in a dignified manner. In the meantime, the two accused business agents were transferred to inactive status.[35]

About two months later, a news item appeared in the *New York Times* headed: "Union Ends Plan for Unit to Shift Charges against Aids."

"The International Brotherhood of Teamsters yesterday dropped its plans to have an independent citizens' committee investigate charges of Communist affiliation against two union organizers.

"The Official explanation was that the refusal of the Federal Bureau of Investigation and other Government agencies to make their files available to private groups killed the committee's potential usefulness.

"However, observers familiar with the union's operations suggested that an outside inquiry might have turned up embarrassing links between higher-ups in the union and prominent city officials."

This decision was made at the beginning of an interim investigation of the Teamsters Union by the Select Senate Committee on Improper Activities in the Labor or Management Field. If seriously pursued, the procedure, initiated and then discontinued by the Teamsters, might have held promise.

A more determined approach to eliminating Communists from units taken over from Communist-dominated unions is being carried through by the International Association of Machinists. Aroused in part by the careless-

[35] Victor Riesel's column, *New York Daily Mirror*, Dec. 22, 1956.

ness of some regional officials and in part by the charges of its IUE rival that it was harboring Communists in important positions taken over from UE,[36] the IAM undertook to enforce its constitutional ban on admission to membership of "persons who advocate or encourage Communism, Fascism or Nazism, or any other totalitarian philosophy." A fact-finding committee was appointed in September, 1956, consisting of top International officials. It held hearings in several cities, but it also relied in its findings on "available public records." On the basis of the findings, the Machinists "dropped from its staff ten union representatives inherited from the dying United Electrical and Radio Workers Union in the transfer earlier this year of forty-one locals to the IAM. . . . Acting on the committee's report, the IAM has rejected applications for membership of nine individuals. . . . In addition, eight others who were members of the IAM at the time the investigation began will be brought to trial under the laws and procedures of the IAM. . . . No action has been taken against seven others about whom questions had been raised." [37]

Once again, exposé procedures of a government agency have proved helpful to a union desiring to eliminate Communists. Since it has become the practice of some union officials and members, when appearing before legislative investigating bodies concerned with either subversive or racketeering activities, to seek refuge in the Fifth Amendment, the AFL-CIO, in its recently adopted *Codes of Ethical Practices*, has incorporated a categorical statement on the use of that amendment by union officers and members. In accordance with its "efforts to carry out and put into practice the constitutional mandate to keep our organization free from any taint of corruption or Communism," [38] the executive council, on January 28, 1957, adopted a statement "regarding cooperation with all appropriate Public Agencies investigating racketeering." This statement concludes:

"We recognize that any person is entitled, in the exercise of his individual conscience, to the protection afforded by the Fifth Amendment and we reaffirm our conviction that this historical right must not be abridged. It is the policy of the AFL-CIO, however, that if a trade-union official decides to invoke the Fifth Amendment for his personal protection and to avoid scrutiny by proper legislative committees, law enforcement agencies or other public bodies into alleged corruption on his part, he has no right to continue to hold office in his union. Otherwise, it becomes possible for a union

[36] This difference between the IAM and the IUE, which threatened to break into a bitter feud, has since then been adjusted by the signing of an agreement "to avoid costly jurisdictional disputes and interunion friction," Joint press release, Nov. 4, 1957, mimeographed; *IUE News*, Nov. 11, 1957; *AFL-CIO News*, Nov. 9, 1957; for IUE charges, see *IUE News*, Dec. 24, 1956, entitled "IAM Embarrassed by Reds"; these charges were made to President George Meany, AFL-CIO; IAM retaliated by instituting a libel suit.

[37] IAM release, Dec. 16, 1956; *Labor*, Dec. 22, 1956.

[38] *AFL-CIO Codes of Ethical Practices*, Washington, D.C., 1957, p. 8.

official who may be guilty of corruption to create the impression that the trade union movement sanctions the use of the Fifth Amendment, not as a matter of individual conscience, but as a shield against proper scrutiny into corrupt influences in the labor movement." [39]

While this policy statement refers only to corruption, some of the affiliated unions, in adopting it, enlarged its meaning to apply to those who resorted to the Fifth Amendment when investigated on grounds of communism. On March 19, 1957, the IAM, in a resolution adopted by its executive council, broadened the application by providing for the removal "from office of any officer and to terminate the representative status of any member of the International Association of Machinists who invokes the Fifth Amendment of the Constitution of the United States or who uses any other means or strategy to avoid the scrutiny of his conduct in union office or position of union trust by any properly constituted inquiry conducted by a legislative committee, law enforcement agency or other public body into crime, corruption, communism, fascism, or any other totalitarian philosophy within the trade union movement." And since "the IAM Constitution provides that no person who advocates or encourages Communism, Fascism, Nazism, or any other totalitarian philosophy or who, by other actions, gives support to these philosophies is eligible for membership in the union . . . the IAM executive council will make a thorough study of all evidence concerning these men to determine what action shall be taken concerning their continued membership. . . .

"All three were former representatives of the dying United Electrical and Radio Workers Union. They were inherited by the IAM during the past year following the transfer of more than forty-five (45) UE locals to the IAM." [40]

Should this combination of exposure by government investigating agencies and subsequent action by unions prove effective, another course will have been made available for detecting and disposing of disguised Communists and fellow travelers. Not only could they then be removed from positions of influence in the unions, but they could also be completely eliminated from union participation and membership. The courts have already recognized the right of employers to apply sanctions where employees have invoked the Fifth Amendment.

At present, the Communists are embarking on another program of trade-union penetration. Operating under cover, Communists are "planted" in labor organizations, mostly on the lower levels. These individuals completely conceal their Communist affiliation and sentiments. Most of the

[39] *Ibid.*, p. 12; see also statement, "Racketeers, Crooks, Communists and Fascists," pp. 23–26.
[40] IAM release, mimeographed, June 11, 1957; see also *AFL-CIO News*, June 15, 1957; and Senate Internal Security Subcommittee summary of hearings, June 6, 1957, mimeographed.

new crop are well educated and many have had technical training in higher educational institutions. Few possess any important previous public record of Communist affiliation and activity; most of them have none. In order to conceal their identity more effectively, they falsify such information as that pertaining to their place of birth, formal education, and references of previous employment by giving names of persons and firms with concealed Communist connections. This tactic, used previously in the "colonization" of followers in unions, vital industries, and various civic and political organizations, is now being expanded. These concealed Communists studiously avoid participating in the consideration of broad social issues or in maintaining contact with overt Communist activities and agencies. They concentrate on siding with dissident elements in the unions, instigating discontent, subtly planting and circulating rumors, and even resorting to other means of discrediting the current leadership. In this manner they hope to rise to leadership and power. Some of them have already achieved that aim.[41]

Their present objective is limited to reestablishing and rebuilding their forces. Simultaneously, an effort is being made to restore respectability to the Communist movement in this country and the inclination to cooperate with other groups. The new party line, in accordance with ideas of its international mentor, features the "possibility of achieving under existing conditions a protracted period of peaceful coexistence." [42] In the trade-union orbit, assurances are offered that the Communist Party intends to function only as an open educational element: "The Communist Party recognizes and respects the complete political and organizational independence of the trade unions and other organizations of the working class and people. It rejects any policy of interference in their internal affairs. It repudiates any allegation that it seeks to capture or control these organizations or to 'bore from within.' Its attitude to them is the same as to the working class and the people generally whom it tries to influence publicly by political discussion, persuasion and example." [43]

Such procrastination has been made before and now, as previously, it does not conform to actual practice. The Communist Party has already launched a new policy of covertly penetrating industry and the labor movement through a form of "colonization."

[41] See 1956 *Report*, Committee on Un-American Activities, 85th Cong., 1st Sess., U.S. House of Representatives, January, 1957, pp. 41–52; see also *Senate Subcommittee to Investigate the Administration of the Internal Security Act, etc.*, 1956 *Report*, sec. 3, pp. 40–47; and *Investigation of Communist Activities in the New Orleans, Louisiana, Area*, Hearings before the House Committee on Un-American Activities, 85th Cong., 1st Sess., Feb. 15, 1957.
[42] *New York Times*, Sept. 16, 1956.
[43] Draft resolution, reprinted in the *New York Times*, Sept. 16, 1956; see also "Main Political Resolution," Proceedings, 16th Convention, CPUSA, 1957, New York, p. 289.

It is still uncertain whether in the pursuit of their new strategy of informal infiltration, the Communists and their allies can be readily detected. Detecting the "colonials" and "colonizers" is primarily a security function, fraught with more than the usual difficulties. Where the ordinary sanctions for eliminating them are not feasible, exposure through government investigation might serve the purpose. Non-Communist labor leaders, active rank-and-filers, and others knowledgeable in this subtle area could be of inestimable assistance. With the abatement of the favorable intellectual climate that proved so useful to the Communists, the task of counteracting their activities might be lighter. It should be borne in mind, nevertheless, that if the Communists are at present weak in comparison with their earlier strength, they were also then a relatively minor factor.

Fortunately, certain factors inherent in the Communist movement force it automatically to expose itself; it then unabashedly confirms by uninhibited self-criticism the charges of deception made against it by its severest critics. Periodically, in the nature of the movement, the undercover activities must be brought to the surface. In order to obtain "mass support" for the cause, and especially for the particular current issues being featured, they must arouse mass sympathy. To an aggressive and aggrandizing world movement, the need to bring issues out into the open is imperative. But this urge also creates an unconquerable dilemma. Benjamin Gitlow, formerly one of the highest Communist functionaries in the United States, describes this predicament which has in the past induced self-exposure, thereby aiding in combating Communist penetration and domination of unions. "To maintain its trade union machine in such a way as not to expose the connection between the Party and its trade union people was not an easy matter. Domestic Communist trade union policies had to coincide with Moscow's interests. The Party was bodily tied up with a world wide Communist trade union machine. What the American Communists did had to jibe with the objectives of the world wide machine. This position of the American Communist Party makes the development of the trade union policies and the control of the trade union machinery by the Party an exceedingly difficult task, especially when directives from Moscow run counter to the patriotic instincts of American workers." [44]

Gitlow's penetrating observation is officially, albeit circuitously, confirmed by the sixteenth convention of the Communist Party of the United States of America, held in 1957. In analyzing the failure of the Communists in trade unions, the Communists chastise themselves: "We did not realize that a union might elect some left forces to leadership without being a left union.... With our somewhat inflated estimates of our base, we proved inflexible when the time called for flexibility in tactics. On too

[44] Benjamin Gitlow, *The Whole of Their Lives*, Charles Scribner's Sons, New York, 1948, p. 286.

many occasions when ruptures had become probable, we helped to make them inevitable. . . . This split took its deadly toll. . . ." [45]

And the Communists are again stressing that the labor movement is the vital channel through which to enlist mass followers, disseminate their propaganda, and promote their objectives. In order to attain this pressing goal, the Communist adherents, operating covertly in the unions and in related organizations, are impelled ultimately to reveal themselves, as they have in the past, as champions of Communist and Soviet policy. Unless they do so, they will not be serving the cause to maximum need. It is this compulsion that germinates their own seed of periodic self-exposure. But it is not safe to wait complacently for the opportune moment. Lest they do considerable harm in the interim, it behooves all concerned to be guided by the old and tried adage that "eternal vigilance is the price of liberty."

[45] "Main Political Resolution," *op. cit.*, p. 282.

Name Index

Subject Index

Communist Party (USA), policies toward unions, 10, 11, 124, 181
postwar, 157, 158, 161, 163, 164, 168, 171, 182
Conference of AFL Studio Unions, 42
Conference of Motion Picture Arts and Crafts, 38
Conference of Studio Unions, 26, 29, 35, 40–47, 54, 55, 57, 59, 67, 75, 77
membership, 42, 43
organizations supported by, 44–47
strike, 1945, 58, 59, 70, 72
supporters, 69, 70
Congress of American-Soviet Friendship, 56
CSU News, 44

Daily Worker, 19, 21, 105, 108, 147, 160, 161, 180, 194, 202, 203, 209
Dual unionism, 3, 4, 9–11, 40, 125

Electrical, Radio and Machine Workers, International Union of, 210, 220, 229–231, 236, 242, 256
formation of, 191, 204, 206, 207
gains in membership, 213, 262, 263, 266
Electrical, Radio and Machine Workers, United, 122, 134, 147, 210, 222, 225, 251, 255, 256, 267
expulsion of, 172, 173, 180, 182, 190, 191, 204, 208
Atomic Energy Commission reaction to, 241–243
employer reaction to, 229–236
falsification of non-Communist affidavits by officers of, 246
loss of membership, 205, 207, 210, 211, 262, 263, 266
Members for Democratic Action, 155
non-Communist membership, 184, 185
opposition to control in, 151, 155, 167, 168, 198, 199, 220
Electrical Workers, International Brotherhood of, 70, 72
Engineers, International Union of Operating, 255, 261
European Recovery Program, 163, 164

Farm Equipment and Metal Workers, United, 127, 146, 166
expulsion of, 173, 180, 190, 191
jurisdictional dispute with United Automobile, Aircraft and Agricultural Workers of America, 167, 173, 256, 259

Federation of Labor, plans for third, 208, 209
Fishermen and Allied Workers of America, International Union of, 30n.
expulsion of, 190
merger with International Longshoremen's and Warehousemen's Union, 206
Food, Tobacco, Agricultural and Allied Workers Union, disappearance of, 213
expulsion of, 179, 185, 189, 218
loss of membership, 183, 184, 205–207
Food Workers, Amalgamated, 83
Food Workers Industrial Union, 82–85
merger with International Alliance of Hotel and Restaurant Employees and Bartenders, 83, 84
Fur and Leather Workers Union, International, expulsion of, 179, 180, 182, 183, 189, 245
falsification of non-Communist affidavits by officers of, 246
merger with Amalgamated Meat Cutters and Butchers, 256–259, 265
non-Communist membership, 184, 185
Furniture Workers of America, United, 190, 201
elimination of Communist influence, 206

Garment Workers' Union, International Ladies', 148
General Electric Company Union, Schenectady, 123
General Electric Corporation, 155, 244
attitude toward expelled unions, 230–236, 241–243
Government and Civic Employee Organizing Committee, formation of, 205
Government Employees General Council, 42
Growth of a Union: The Life and Times of Edward Flore, 87

"Hollywood Ten," 65, 75, 79, 227
Hosiery Workers Union, Full Fashioned, 122
Hotel and Restaurant Employees and Bartenders, International Alliance of, 82–89, 91, 100, 109, 110, 113, 115
Convention, 1947, 94–96
defense of Communists in, 96–98

276

Hotel and Restaurant Employees and Bartenders, International Alliance of, investigation commission findings, 92, 93
Local 6, 103–106, 110, 114
merger with Food Workers Industrial Union, 82–84
House Committee on Education and Labor, 27
House Un-American Activities Committee, 106, 156, 202, 207

"IATSE Progressives," 31, 32
Illinois Miner, 131
Industrial Workers of the World (*see* IWW)
Insurance and Allied Workers Organizing Committee, 205
International Confederation of Free Trade Unions, 182
International Labor Defense, 44, 141
IWW, 3, 5–7, 132

Jurisdiction struggles, 21, 27–29, 70, 77, 166, 173, 222, 255, 260–262

Kibre documents, 30, 35, 40, 55
Knights of Labor, 3
Knolls Atomic Power Laboratory, 241

Labor Fact Book, 166
Labor Herald, 10n.
Labor-Management Relations Act of 1947 (*see* Taft-Hartley Act)
Labor Research Association, 166
Labor's Non-Partisan League, 47, 56
Lawyers Guild, National, 155
Longshoremen's Association, International, 132, 208, 256
Longshoremen's and Warehousemen's Union, International, 30n., 31n., 38, 126, 132, 152, 208, 209, 221, 245, 253, 255, 256, 263, 264
expulsion of, 178, 184, 189
merger with International Union of Fishermen and Allied Workers of America, 206
non-Communist membership, 184, 185
Los Angeles Central Labor Union, 30n., 39, 68, 70, 77
Los Angeles Citizen, 30n.
Los Angeles Industrial Union Council, 46, 148, 206

Machinists, International Association of, 234, 242, 255, 256, 261, 262, 265–267
March of Labor, 107

Marine Cooks and Stewards, International Union of, 133, 141
disciplined by NLRB, 245
expulsion of, 186, 189
Marine Firemen, Oilers, Water Tenders and Wipers Association, Pacific Coast, 133, 141, 149
Marine Workers Industrial League, 132
Maritime Union, National, 126, 127, 155, 168, 176, 177, 190, 255
Communist control of, 132, 133, 219
elimination of Communist influences in, 158, 192–195, 199
employer reaction to Communist control, 228
opposition to control of, 141–143, 150, 199
Marshall Plan, 157, 158, 161, 163, 164, 182, 196, 223
Meat Cutters and Butcher Workmen, Amalgamated, Communist influence in, 204
merger with International Fur and Leather Workers Union, 256–259, 265
Merger, AFL-CIO, 201, 203
Metal Trades Department, AFL, jurisdictional disputes with Mine, Mill and Smelter Workers, International Union of, 255, 260–262
Mine, Mill and Smelter Workers, International Union of, 126, 128, 129, 150, 205, 241, 245, 251, 252
Communist control of, 133–135, 149, 176, 177, 198
expulsion of, 176–178, 189, 228
falsification of non-Communist affidavits by officers of, 246, 247
jurisdictional disputes with Metal Trades Department, AFL, 255, 260–262
loss of membership, 206–208, 262
opposition to control of, 140, 149, 155, 220
Mine Workers of America, United, 120, 122, 136, 238, 264
Minnesota Industrial Union Council, 158
Molders and Foundry Workers Union of North America, International, 255
Montgomery Ward strike, 152
Motion Picture Alliance for the Preservation of American Ideals, 69, 78, 81
Motion Picture Association of America, 68, 75
Motion Picture Crafts, Federated, 28, 37n.

Seamen's Union, International, 132
Senate Committee on Labor and Public Welfare, 201
Senate Subcommittee on Labor and Labor-Management Relations, 201, 239, 244
Shoe Workers of America, United, 148
Smith Act, 247, 248
Socialist Labor Party, 4, 5
Socialist Trade and Labor Alliance, 4, 5
Sonotone Corporation, attitude toward expelled unions, 229, 230
Steelworkers of America, United, 122, 169, 178, 200, 205, 206, 238, 260–262
Stone and Allied Products Workers of America, United, 261
Studio Basic Agreement, 1926, 27–29
Studio Unemployment Conference, 36, 37, 47, 55
Subversive Activities Control Act of 1950, 248, 252
Subversive Activities Control Board, 249–252, 264
Syndicalists, 3

Taft-Hartley Act, 162, 167, 177, 213, 237
section 9(h), 237–239, 244–246, 248, 252
Teamsters, Chauffeurs, Stablemen and Helpers of America, International Brotherhood of, 68, 74, 229, 230, 242, 255, 262, 263, 265
Textile Workers Union of America, 148
Theatrical and Stage Employees and Motion Picture Machine Operators of the United States and Canada, International Alliance of, 20, 21, 25, 26, 28–41, 43–46, 52, 54, 58, 62, 73, 74

aid to Motion Picture Painters and Scenic Artists, 29, 46, 47
early history, 27, 28
jurisdictional disputes, 43, 53, 67
supporters of, 68, 69
Third Party (*see* Progressive Party)
Trade autonomy, 185, 186
Trade Union Congress, British, 164
Trade Union Unity League, 11, 15–18, 82, 101, 121, 123*n*., 124, 132, 135
Transport Workers Union of America, 127, 131, 147, 176, 190, 225
Communist control, 147, 219
elimination of Communist influences in, 196–199
opposition to control of, 158
Truman Doctrine, 157, 164, 182, 223

United American Spanish Aid Committee, 47
United May Day Committee, 250
University of Chicago, 241
Upholsterers International Union of North America, 201

Variety, 26, 33, 41, 69, 70

Wage Earner, 138
Wage Stabilization Board, 114
Wagner Act, 162
"Waldorf Statement," 227, 228
William Schneiderman Committee, 47, 56
Witness Immunity Act of 1954, 248
World Federation of Trade Unions, 44, 45, 47, 72, 101, 161, 163, 164, 168, 182, 222
CIO withdrawal, 169
Writers, League of American, 44